ENDANGERED RIVERS
AND THE
CONSERVATION
MOVEMENT

ENDANGERED RIVERS AND THE CONSERVATION MOVEMENT

SECOND EDITION

Tim Palmer

ROWMAN & LITTLEFIELD PUBLISHERS, INC.
Lanham • Boulder • New York • Toronto • Oxford

ROWMAN & LITTLEFIELD PUBLISHERS, INC.

Published in the United States of America
by Rowman & Littlefield Publishers, Inc.
A wholly owned subsidary of The Rowman & Littlefield Publishing Group, Inc.
4501 Forbes Boulevard, Suite 200, Lanham, Maryland 20706
www.rowmanlittlefield.com

PO Box 317
Oxford
OX2 9RU, UK

Front cover photograph: Stanislaus River above Parrotts Ferry, California, flooded
by New Melones Dam in 1982

British Library Cataloguing in Publication Information Available

Library of Congress Cataloging-in-Publication Data

Palmer, Tim, 1948–
    Endangered rivers and the conservation movement / Tim Palmer.—
2nd ed.
        p.   cm.
    Includes bibliographical references (p.) and index.
    ISBN 0-7425-3140-6 (hardcover : alk. paper)—ISBN 0-7425-3141-4
(pbk. : alk. paper)
    1. Stream conservation—United States.   I. Title.
QH76.P35   2004
333.91′6216′0973—dc22   2003020112

Printed in the United States of America

♾ ™ The paper used in this publication meets the minimum requirements of American
National Standard for Information Sciences—Permanence of Paper for Printed Library
Materials, ANSI/NISO Z39.48-1992.

To Bob McCullough,
working to save his rivers,
and helping me at the start

CONTENTS

PREFACE

Walk the easy way, downhill, and sooner or later you will probably come to a river. Then look around at the high country. All of it drains to that low, wet divider of the valley. The river is the center of the land, the place where the waters, and much more, come together. Here is the home of wildlife, the route of explorers, and a recreation paradise. The word river is so symbolic that it is used in the titles of scores of novels having nothing to do with water flowing toward the sea.

To many people, rivers are the most extraordinary part of the land. Only fragments of our inheritance remain unexploited, but these streams are more valuable than ever.

People have worked to protect the rivers—to leave some of them the way they are—and this book is the story of those efforts.

PREFACE TO THE
SECOND EDITION

Endangered Rivers chronicles the history of people's efforts to protect free-flowing rivers.

The battles against large dams were central to river conservation up through 1980, and, as luck would have it, I wrote the first edition of this book in 1984, during the final gasps of the big-dam-building era in the United States. No doubt, more projects of some kinds will be built, and the threats of unnecessary river destruction will never end completely, but nonetheless, the times had changed as the first edition of *Endangered Rivers* went to press. Today, twenty years later, the original edition still offers a fairly complete account of a vital chapter in the history of conservation and public policy.

The dedication of many people covered here represents what might be called a golden age of river conservation. Most dramatically, this spanned the decades of the 1960s, 1970s, and 1980s, though action began as early as 1900 and continues with far more people involved today. But at the heart of this era, many people acted with an unprecedented and unrepeated sense of urgency for our rivers and streams. In fighting dams, they opposed Goliathan forces that would not only damage the environment but completely eliminate whole segments of rivers by flooding them deep under the flatwater of reservoirs. These were all-or-nothing battles, and they brought out intense feelings and responses—from poetry to economic analysis, from the subtle politics of persuasion to lying down in front of bulldozers. Starting with almost nothing, the activists of that era created a movement of vast public importance in the United States. For the first time ever, citizens expressed broad-based concern for the fate of our waterways. They articulated the values at stake when faced with the prospects of losing a section of river completely. They organized support in ways that became classic models for citizen action.

For these and other reasons explained throughout the book, I believe that the *Endangered Rivers* story is one of timeless importance. The role of river conservationists who brought the era of big-dam building in America to a halt is, in fact, one of the greatest success stories in the environmental history of our country. We might do well to remember this story while efforts to safeguard the environment expand in other directions and as new threats arise from modern forces no less troubling—and often worse—than those of the past.

The book was written at a time when the greater movement to protect rivers was young. But now, in the year 2004, a tremendous maturing has taken place. Most people today accept that rivers have intrinsic natural value, and many people recognize an obligation to be responsible for the welfare of their river-place on earth.

Perhaps most important in my reflections about the intervening twenty years spanning the first and second editions of *Endangered Rivers*, peoples' successful efforts to halt unnecessary large dam construction have opened the way for a second generation of river conservation. This includes tackling the problems of depleted flows below diversions that dry-up riverbeds, floodplain development that ruins shorelines critical to the health of streams, polluted runoff from farms and cities, and habitat destruction that eliminates the diversity of life and keystone species such as salmon. Finally, the new approach includes watershed health reaching far beyond the riverbanks.

In this second edition of *Endangered Rivers*, I have converted events of the 1980s to past tense and updated some of the facts but otherwise left the original book intact. I have, however, added two significant chapters. These update ongoing controversies from the original text. I've discussed the second generation of river conservation, which involves a myriad of threats—less dramatic than the old specter of dams but even more ubiquitous. I've added coverage of the Great Mississippi Flood of 1993 and the floodplain management reforms that came in its wake. I've covered the intensified efforts to protect salmon, additions to the national wild and scenic rivers system along with changing attitudes about that pantheon of protected rivers, and the growing momentum for dam removal—a phenomenon I predicted in the first edition. Finally, with the guidance of key players from the past and present, I discuss the defining forces that will shape the work of river conservationists in the twenty-first century.

Readers wanting to know more about modern-day issues should be aware that my subsequent book, *Lifelines: The Case for River Conservation* (initially published in 1994), is also being updated and reissued in 2004 by Rowman & Littlefield. While *Endangered Rivers* is primarily a history, *Lifelines* focuses on the contemporary aspects of river conservation in the United States. Filling other gaps in the meta-story of rivers in America, my book, *The Wild and Scenic Rivers of America*, published in 1993, details all aspects of the national wild and scenic rivers system. *America by Rivers*, published in 1996, tours the nation from east to west in order to lend an informed geographic understanding of our total rivers estate. Other books I have written add to a riverine perspective on America by featuring the Columbia River, the Snake River, and the Youghiogheny River.

Perhaps in another twenty years, a third edition of *Endangered Rivers* will tell how we cut wasteful subsidies for development on the floodplain, how our nation finally addressed the requirements of the 1972 Clean Water Act along with the difficult promise of protecting wild and scenic rivers, and how the Pacific salmon were rescued from the brink of extinction. Or perhaps the losses coming with unlimited population growth and the politics of greed will be unconscionable by today's and yesterday's standards of justice and livability. In any event, it is only by knowing the past that we might grapple effectively with our own future and thereby influence the fate of our rivers and of all life on earth.

ACKNOWLEDGMENTS

All across the country there are people who enjoy rivers and work to protect their special streamside places. I want to thank these people for what they have done, and for sharing their experiences, their homes, their boats, and their scrapbooks with me.

Sometimes friends give encouragement that makes a difference a decade or two later, and for this I want to thank Peter Fletcher, Jim McClure, and Bob Butler. Without their enthusiasm for the Appalachian streams of Pennsylvania, I may never have looked so closely at rivers. Ernest Callenbach of the University of California Press supported the book originally, and editor Brian Romer of Rowman & Littlefield had the vision to see it through its second edition.

The original manuscript was reviewed by Samuel Hays, Jerry Meral, Jeffrey Stine, and Brent Blackwelder, each drawing on a wealth of experience in conservation history, water development, and river protection.

The staff of American Rivers contributed much information, and also their files, newsletters, address books, and telephones. Special thanks go to Howard Brown, one of the first people who agreed that I should write the book in 1976. He offered valuable knowledge and sound advice on people to see. Pat Munoz, Christopher Brown, Ron Vlaskamp, and Bill Painter (the first director) of the council all shared their experience. Jeffrey Stine, at that time a historian under contract to the Army Corps of Engineers, offered information, fine perspectives, and a valuable list of sources. Barbara Lekisch, the Sierra Club's librarian in San Francisco, was very helpful. Martin Reuss, a historian at the chief of the Army Corps of Engineers' office, provided reports found nowhere else and agreed to let me use draft manuscripts from an informative series of publications that he was editing.

Endangered Rivers leans heavily on more than a hundred people who
took the time to talk to me. Most of these are listed as sources, and I want
to thank each individual. For various reasons, some people asked that their
names not be printed, and I have respected this request. I appreciated
important meetings and talks with former secretary of the interior Stewart
Udall, Congressman Robert Edgar, and wildlife biologist John Craighead.
Also Brent Blackwelder of the Environmental Policy Center; Chuck Hoffman of the River Conservation Fund; Ted Schad, who held several important jobs; John Kauffmann and Ted Swem, formerly of the National Park
Service; Richard Leonard of the Sierra Club; Robert Herbst and Guy Martin, formerly of the Carter administration; Gaylord Nelson of the Senate and
the Wilderness Society; Bob Teeters of the Army Corps of Engineers; and
Robert Broadbent, commissioner of the Bureau of Reclamation. Before I
started the book, it was a privilege to discuss river protection with Governor
Tom McCall of Oregon and Congressman John Saylor of Pennsylvania.

Don Elder of River Network and Kevin Coyle, formerly of American
Rivers, were helpful as I wrote the final two chapters of the second edition.
Along with Rebecca Wodder of American Rivers and Chris Brown of the
National Park Service, they reviewed Chapters 11 and 12.

The book draws from articles in magazines and newspapers, from government reports, and from books about conservation and water develop-
ment. The major works are listed at the end of the book under Sources.
Excellent accounts of certain aspects of river conservation have been written
by William Amos, Paul Brooks, David Brower, Bruce Brown, John Cassidy,
John Graves, Mark Harvey, Norris Hundley, Verne Huser, John Kauffmann,
George Laycock, Luna Leopold, James Nathan Miller, Roderick Nash,
Anthony Netboy, Fred Powledge, Marc Reisner, Elmo Richardson, Rich-
ard Roos-Collins, Wallace Stegner, T. H. Watkins, Gilbert White, and
Donald Worster.

I'd like to thank Yvon Chouinard and Patagonia for financial support
to cover some of my writing time on this second edition. Finally, the most
thanks go to my wife, Ann Vileisis, for helping me in every way imaginable.

1

RIVERS AND DAMS

Settlers drained swamps at Jamestown, Virginia, and ever since, the waters of America have been changed for people's use and economic gain. Projects grew from small reservoirs and ditches to dams taller than seventy-story skyscrapers and canals hundreds of miles long delivering water to desert cities. Seventy-five thousand dams six feet or greater in height in the United States affect every major river outside Alaska but one—the Salmon in Idaho.

Reservoirs have flooded the oldest known settlement in North America, the second-deepest canyon, the second most popular whitewater, the habitat of endangered species, one of the first national parks, tens of thousands of homes, rich farmland, desert canyons, and virgin forests. In building dams we have blocked the best runs of salmon and broken the oldest Indian treaty—one that George Washington signed.

For generations, the manipulation of flowing water seemed useful and good. Through water development, the West was settled. California farmland is irrigated to grow nearly one-quarter of the nation's food on what used to be drylands. The Ohio River is fitted with locks to serve more commerce than the Panama Canal. Twenty-six thousand miles of waterways are channeled for shipping, fifty-eight million acres are irrigated, thirty million kilowatts of hydroelectricity can be generated, and four hundred large dams lower the levels of floods. Our society, as we know it, cannot function without some of these water projects. People say that the places buried by reservoirs are simply one of the costs to be paid.

For other people, the damming of a river means landscape consumption worse than paved-over farms or strip-mined mountains. Flooding by a reservoir is seen as complete and permanent, the ultimate in change, leaving

1

nothing of the past. When a dam is proposed, some people may gain but others will lose: landowners, the homes; farmers, the fields; fishermen, the pools and riffles hiding trout; canoeists, the rapids and water trails; wildlife watchers and hunters, the animals; historians, the sites and reminders of old importance. And the dams cause secondary effects that nobody wants: they block the migration of fish to spawning beds; they trap nutrients in a way that damages the streams, the estuaries, and even the commercial fisheries at sea; they pose safety risks. Dams are usually paid for by the taxpayers but sometimes benefit few people. So rivers have become a battleground for those who want to keep certain parts of the land the way they are, against those who want more water development.

River protection began in the first decade of this century and gained momentum, and important places were spared. In the 1960s, full-page advertisements in the *New York Times* warned the nation that the Grand Canyon needed saving from dams. The Oklawaha River and its swamps were partly dammed and dredged for a canal, but the project was halted to prevent the loss of Florida's groundwater. At the Delaware, conservationists and landowners stopped Tocks Island Dam, and Congress designated a national wild and scenic river instead. Dozens of waterways still flow free because thousands of people worked to save special places.

Through the 1980s, new proposals threatened other sites—hundreds of them—but developers faced high costs and dubious gains in blocking the remaining sections of rivers. In Oklahoma, 70 percent of the benefits of a proposed federal project would go to one catfish farmer. Auburn Dam would cost $2.5 billion and flood forty-three miles of canyons to deliver subsidized water to farmers who are not yet using existing supplies. The most expensive project of all was the Tennessee–Tombigbee Waterway, requiring $4 billion to serve barges already floating on other rivers and to move goods already moved by railroads. The Garrison Diversion in North Dakota would take 220,000 acres out of agricultural production to irrigate 250,000.

Government water projects were originally meant to entice family farmers to the unsettled West, but many of the benefits now go to absentee agribusinesses and urban developers. Through taxes, easterners from economically depressed areas help to pay for federal projects that lure settlers to the booming Sun Belt. Billions were spent on the Central Arizona Project serving Phoenix, and corporate farmers, including oil companies, enjoy subsidies of millions every year.

Dams become unsafe without maintenance, and even with it, reservoirs fill with silt that settles to the bottom of the lakes. Some have become brown quagmires after thirty years. Most reservoirs are designed for only a hundred years. What will become of the dams when they are white elephants? Who will pay the costs or live with the safety risks then?

Underlying many aspects of water development is a myth: the myth that we must always have more. Meeting needs is one thing, but recklessly subsidizing waste is another. For generations we have used water as though it were free: we wash sidewalks with it, grow rice in the desert, spend millions so that ocean-going vessels can reach Idaho, Oklahoma, and Minnesota. A toilet (invented in Shakespeare's time) uses four gallons per flush when one gallon would do. Up to four thousand gallons of water is used to put one pound of beef on the table. The nation's tallest fountain, three hundred feet high, decorates an Arizona subdivision within view of Yavapai Indians who were asked and pushed to give up the Verde River so that Phoenix could sprawl farther (the Indians did not yield).

Back when we were getting by on less Will Rogers said, "Everybody can get along on half of what they think they can." Vast amounts of water can be saved, and today's supplies can be stretched far into the future. Eighty-one percent of the water consumed in America is for irrigation, and the General Accounting Office reported that 50 percent of irrigation supplies were wasted. New York City reduced its water use by 150 million gallons a day in 1980 through public information only. Marin County, California, cut its use by 75 percent. Ten-cent flow-reducers curb shower consumption—one of the big water spenders in the home—by one-third.

Other approaches that do not depend on costly dams have been mostly ignored. Floodplain management—reserving lowlands for uses, such as farming and parks, that do not incur heavy damage—can be cheaper than building dams to catch floodwater. The Army Corps of Engineers recommended an economic nonstructural approach—buying the floodplain—for the South Fork of the Platte River in Colorado. Billions are spent on barge canals without consideration for total transportation planning, and expanded locks and channelization in the Mississippi may lead to bankrupt railroads that could require subsidies from the same government that built the competing barge route. Free river recreation is eliminated at great cost by dams that are justified in the name of flatwater recreation.

Changes in water policies have been proposed to embrace traditional values: cut waste, build only economic projects, require people who benefit to pay the costs, recognize the value of natural rivers as homelands and as places for escape and recreation.

While budgets for other domestic agencies were cut to the bone, a 25 percent increase was handed to the Bureau of Reclamation—the largest dam builder in the West. More than 450 new projects were authorized for construction by the Army Corps of Engineers. Private hydroelectric developers were encouraged by the Public Utility Regulatory Policies Act of 1978, causing permit applications for new hydropower facilities to jump from 18 in 1978 to 1,859 in 1981. By 1983, more than six thousand applications for dams were on file. In California alone, six hundred applications were filed between 1978 and 1983, including a proposal to dam the Tuolumne—the river where protection efforts began eighty years ago when John Muir tried to save Hetch Hetchy Valley.

Except for Chapter 3, *Endangered Rivers* is about people protecting rivers. Readers who want to learn more about water development face no difficult search. Dozens of books accept the wisdom of "harnessing the rivers" and tell about the Tennessee Valley Authority "working wonders" in Appalachia, the Bureau of Reclamation creating "gardens in the desert," and the Army Corps of Engineers "taming the raging floods." Other books acclaim the wildlife, beauty, and recreation along rivers but do not cover the threats from development. Whereas many excellent articles and a few books relate the stories of certain streams, the larger story of river protection has not been told. Much of *Endangered Rivers* focuses on the fights against dams, because they completely destroy their sections of rivers and valleys. I have stressed the changing attitudes about rivers. The control of water pollution and the management of riverfront land are discussed in Chapter 11 but also deserve entire volumes of their own.

2

A DELICATE BALANCE

Three and a half million miles of rivers and streams have penetrated every part of the country, and they affect the lives of people in countless ways. The water shapes the land. The topography in a place like West Virginia seems chaotic but is the result of a simple rule—water runs downhill and carries soil with it. Because of this, the landscape drops an average of one foot in ten thousand years, and some places erode much faster.

The rivers and land share a partnership: mountains and landforms determine the routes of rivers, then the rivers further mold the land. Flooding shows this give-and-take. With rain and runoff, streams swell until the banks are full. In canyons, rivers carve deeper because they cannot spread out, but most valleys have floodplains—flat areas just above the banks. Here the river overflows, and silt in the muddy water settles to the ground to build terraces that grow higher—sometimes two inches—during each flood. In this way rivers fertilize the fields by bringing rich soil from many square miles and concentrating it at one workable place. Floodplains are temporary storage reservoirs, lowering downstream floods. While ponded, water soaks through the soil to underground reservoirs that can be pumped out later or that seep slowly back to the river and add to its flow during dry seasons.

Wet, fertile, and next to the water, floodplains are ideal for wildlife, for trees, and for some kinds of farming. In most ways, the plains are ideal for towns, roads, and railroads—the land is flat and next to the river, which was often a transportation artery. But when people build along the river, they compete directly with it, and sooner or later they are hit with high water.

The soil that is added to the floodplain comes from up above. It washes loose with sheet erosion from places without plants, such as strip mines or plowed fields. Other soil comes from riverbanks where the current cuts on the outside of bends. Forty-foot widths of floodplain have vanished in one night, sliced like butter by the Mississippi or the Yukon.

Water is always working, reorganizing the land. Rivers follow paths of least resistance, cutting first through soft rock. The water carves slowly like a sculptor, creating smooth, rounded forms. Even in flat valleys without hills or bedrock to guide the flow, the river veers back and forth, rarely flowing straight for more than ten times its width.[1] Abandoned channels where the current used to run can be seen in swales behind banks, in swamps, and in oxbow lakes along flatland streams. If left alone, the river will someday return to these old channels, each time wearing a deeper path. Eroded soil eventually reaches the ocean and forms a delta. Forty tons of soil per hour are delivered to the delta of the Mississippi.

Three kinds of rapids form in the river: Outcrops of bedrock block the flow, holding back water before it drops over the ledges. At landslides, boulders clog the channel and make whitewater. But the most common rapid is where water runs over gravel bars, often at the mouths of streams. Where tributaries meet the river, their speed is checked, and rocks that had been washed down from the mountains pile up and form bars. Young rivers are full of these ledges, boulders, and bars that cause steep drops, then pools, then steep drops again. The rocks causing the rapids eventually wear away, leaving the steady gradient of ancient streams.

Steep pitches of a river are rocky because the fast water rolls smaller and lighter stones away. As the current slows down it sorts the rocks by dropping the largest first and smallest last. Rocks as big as watermelons might lie in a riffle at the upstream end of an island. Farther down, the river drops cobbles, gravel, pebbles, sand, and fine silt at the lowest point, where channels from either side of the island meet and eddy into a quiet pool.

Gradient causes the river to churn, to hiss onto sandy beaches, to boil into holes, and to pile up in haystack waves. During floods the river clatters, rolling stones down its bed, and it rattles the brush. The river pounds over falls, then as a gentle force it is almost unheard.

LIVING WITH THE RIVER

Entire communities of plants and animals depend on the streams. Floodplain forests need water and alluvial soil that is washed in. Stands of silver maple in the East, cypress in the South, cottonwood on the Plains, and cedar in the Northwest grow at the water's edge. Hemlocks throw shade over Appalachian trout pools, blocking summer heat.

The sycamore is tailored to the riverfront. Roots of most other trees die if soaked in water for more than a few days, but the sycamore thrives, shading the stream while miles of roots tie the loose-knit soil together and hold it. Other trees suffocate if dirt is piled around their trunks, but the sycamore keeps growing even with three feet of fresh flood-deposited gravel. After a century, when a sycamore finally dies, its usefulness is not over. The wood resists rot and lies as a "sweeper"—shelter that lasts for many generations of fish. Wild rice, cattails, arrowhead, and hundreds of plants grow as forage. Royal ferns in the Appalachians have a special adaptation: their fronds are on foot-long stalks reaching above the high-water surges of summertime.

The water's edge is the most important place for wildlife. Raccoons eat crayfish, and grizzly bears eat salmon. The river is the only home for many animals. Otters are fast swimmers and are playful, sliding down mud banks, wrestling, and balancing stones on their noses. Some fishermen shoot the furbearers, thinking that they kill trout, but research shows them eating suckers, mudminnows, sticklebacks, and other slow forage fish. Before 1800, otters lived in rivers all over the country except in the Southwest, but because of shooting, trapping, pollution, habitat loss, channelization, and dams they survive only in wild pockets of their old range.

More than half of the American bird species nest near waterways. Sandpipers and yellowlegs eat insects just above the waterline. The water ouzel or dipper walks underwater to catch insects at rapids. Flaps seal each nostril from the water, a nictitating membrane or specialized eyelid works like a windshield wiper, and a preen gland secreting waterproof oil is ten times the size found in other perching birds. The heron has stilt legs so that it can wade in the shallows and spear minnows, frogs, salamanders, and snakes. The kingfisher snatches minnows and rattles its call as it flies to another limb over the water. With sticks, the osprey builds a nest that grows larger each year in the top of a dead tree. This hawk dives from a hundred feet to catch fish with its inch-long talons. Thirty-four kinds of American ducks live on freshwater. Mallards, wood ducks, pintails, and teals are dabblers, usually swimming near shore and poking their heads underwater to snap up food. Some other ducks are divers: the sleek merganser swims underwater for fish, frogs, insects, and crayfish. Mergansers are so bad tasting that hunters ignore them.

The streams teem with life, including thousands of species of insects. Five hundred kinds of mayflies are a favorite feed of trout. Riffles are high in oxygen needed by the caddisfly, whose larva covers itself with sand, glued together as armor against the current. The water scorpion breathes through snorkels, the water boatman rows with legs like oars, the water strider walks on water, its legs covered with waxy hairs. Warm shallows house minnows, frogs, and turtles. Deep pools hide trout and large fish.[2]

Algae are basic to the chain of life. Brown and slimy on rocks or green like seaweed, these plants collect nutrients and are later broken down by bacteria and fungi. Insects and clams are primary consumers that sift out algae and organic particles and convert plants to animal tissue. Secondary consumers are dragonflies, hellgrammites, and minnows. They eat smaller creatures, then are eaten by larger ones. Mature fish hunt higher on the food chain, and on top are the animals eaten by no one: the kingfisher, merganser, osprey, otter, and people.

Fish are divided into warm-water and cold-water species. Trout, salmon, pike, and muskellunge live in the cold water of the north and the mountains. If water temperatures climb above seventy-seven degrees Fahrenheit for more than a few days, trout die. Bass, sunfish, and perch live in the warm water of southern streams. Some warm-water fish can flourish where nutrients are high from silt, farm waste, or sewage.[3] These are suckers, catfish, and carp, sometimes called trash fish. Carp can live with hundred-degree temperatures and are found even at the hot-water outlets of power plants.

It is a delicate balance that keeps the river creatures alive. Pesticides from farms flow into streams, where they are absorbed by insects, which are eaten by minnows. The eggs of many eagles and osprey were too weak for their young's survival because of DDT. Since DDT was banned from everyday use the osprey have begun to recover. Toxic wastes such as mercury contaminate fish that people eat. By volume, sediment is the largest pollutant; logging, plowing, and earth moving speed erosion far past the natural amount. The average cultivated acre in Pennsylvania loses twelve tons of soil a year. Raw sewage with coliform bacteria is consumed by microorganisms that use oxygen, leaving little for fish. Acid drainage from coal mines has killed the fish in eleven thousand miles of streams, and the poison discharges—often incorrectable—may last for hundreds of years. Acid rain from air pollution threatens streams and lakes of entire regions, especially in the Northeast.

When a stream is channelized it is straightened and dug to a uniform depth, causing water to run faster but destroying the habitat, increasing erosion, and aggravating downstream flooding. Levees protect local areas but cause worse floods downstream by speeding the flow and by eliminating the temporary reservoir of the floodplain.

But the most complete and permanent destruction of a river is by a dam. The rapids, streamside plants, and valley landscape are flooded. The current stops and the chemistry and temperature of the water change. Deep water blocks sunlight and stops the growth of bacteria and other building blocks in the food chain. Creatures needing the current to deliver food have nothing to eat.

Many fish need spawning beds of gravel that are washed and cleaned only by the current. Riffles are needed to bring fresh oxygen to fish eggs and to the larvae of mayflies, stoneflies, and other fish-feed, so all of these disappear. Nutrients may not hurt the river, but when the flow is stopped and the sun warms the reservoir's surface, eutrophication begins—an over-fertilization when algae, including toxic blue-green species, bloom and stifle other life. Then the algae die and their rotting consumes oxygen and allows fungi, bacteria, sludge worms, and other anaerobic life to thrive. At reservoirs, cold-water and game fish are often replaced with warm-water species and carp. Eventually silt accumulates on the floor of the reservoir, suffocating life that might have survived until then. Few plants grow at the edge of the reservoir because the water level is constantly raised and lowered.[4]

As the buffalo were to the plains, salmon were to the Northwest. Indians, settlers, and wildlife lived on them. They made a cash economy unnecessary. To spawn, seven species of salmon plus steelhead trout, shad, blueback herring, and other anadromous fishes migrate from the seas up the rivers, sometimes twelve hundred miles. Now dams block their paths. Salmon are eliminated from almost every river in the Northeast, and two-thirds of the spawning grounds in the Columbia basin are plugged. Fish ladders allow some salmon and steelhead to climb over some dams, but many fish die. Those that survive the hazards reach the headwaters and spawn, but when the young run back to sea, up to 80 percent are lost in fields—dead ends of unscreened irrigation ditches. Nitrogen gas, concentrated from the air as water falls over the spillways of dams, dissolves into a supersaturation and blinds, cripples, or kills fish by the millions on the Columbia and Snake Rivers.[5] Spillway deflectors that change the way the water flows over the dams have reduced the nitrogen problem at some sites.[6] As they descend the river, 15 percent of the fish may be killed at each large dam.[7]

Today's salmon are only a token from past runs. On hundreds of streams above dams without ladders, no anadromous fish can return, and on other rivers, including the Salmon in Idaho, fish and game officials had to outlaw sport fishing for salmon because the runs shrank dangerously toward extinction. Now we are dependent on the costly plumbing of hatcheries, which often hurt the surviving wild salmon. In 1979 the Department of the Interior began studies to determine if the Columbia River salmon—once the world's most plentiful—should be added to the threatened or endangered species list. The Reagan administration dropped the effort, a spokesman saying that "enough conservation programs already exist."[8] Many runs were later listed as endangered or threatened.

Estuaries depend on rivers. Chesapeake Bay, fed mainly by the Susquehanna River, once teemed with oysters, crabs, fish, and waterfowl. In the early 1900s hydroelectric dams on the lower river blocked the force of high water and the flow of spring ice that had scoured out the upper bay. Biologists think that this allowed an accumulation of silt that chokes water plants needed by ducks and geese, which survive only in a fraction of their earlier numbers.

Even the oceans are fed and fertilized by rivers. Silt and organic detritus carried to the sea by streams are the food of plankton, which produce up to 80 percent of the earth's oxygen. Commercial fisheries thrive on nutrients entering the ocean's Japanese Current from the rivers of the West Coast. When these are dammed, the silt and nutrients settle to the bottom of the reservoirs instead of flowing out to sea.[9]

MORE THAN RECREATION

Waterfronts are used for recreation more than any other part of the land. People find relief from urban pressures along the Chattahoochee in Atlanta, the Susquehanna in Harrisburg, and the American in Sacramento. Nature refreshes and replenishes, and nowhere can this be seen better than along a river, where rain and snow are always sending new water. To float in a canoe or raft is to be part of the river. The rivers are an alternative way to travel—a way to see a different part of the land.

Whitewater paddlers on the Youghiogheny in Pennsylvania increased from 5,000 in 1968 to 110,000 in 2002.[10] The rapids of California's South Fork American drew almost as many people. In Missouri 250,000 canoeists travel the Jacks Fork and Current rivers each year. Ohio's Mohican and California's Russian are jammed with canoes on weekends. The upper Delaware lures New Yorkers and Philadelphians to clear water and green shores. People look for escape and excitement; they want to be participants instead of spectators, and to return to nature. They find all of these things in river travel: in the challenge of paddling whitewater or in the peace of drifting on a quiet stream and camping on its shore.

People spend five hundred million days a year swimming in rivers, lakes, and oceans. Forty million people fish for sport,[11] spending three hundred million days a year. In a five-year period, canoe manufacturing increased fivefold. More than a million are in use. And much of the river activity goes beyond the idea of recreation as sport. To some people, rivers are a way of life, a source of food, a place to live. The two-car garage is one American dream, and Huck Finn is another. Fishing poles, campfires, and leaky rowboats have been replaced by television and video games for many, but who does not regret the loss of youth and wilderness on islands and riverbanks?

A CULTURE OF RIVERS

Rivers were highways and gardens for whole Indian nations. In 1854 Suquamish Chief Seattle said: "The rivers are our brothers. They quench our thirst. The rivers carry our canoes, and feed our children. If we sell you our land, you must remember, and teach your children, that the rivers are our brothers, and yours, and you must henceforth give the rivers the kindness you would give any brother."

The explorers followed river routes: Cartier up the St. Lawrence; La Salle, Marquette, and Joliet down the Mississippi; Brulé on the Susquehanna; John Wesley Powell through the Colorado's canyons. We can read books or visit museums, but by traveling the water routes we can see and do the same things that the explorers did. One hundred and fifty miles of Montana's upper Missouri River remain mostly untouched since the journey of Lewis and Clark.

River stories are as old as the nation: Thoreau's Merrimack, James Fenimore Cooper's Hudson, Mark Twain's Mississippi, Hemingway's Big Two Hearted, Steinbeck's Salinas, and Wendell Berry's Kentucky. The Platte is the setting of Michener's *Centennial*, the Kennebec of Kenneth Roberts's *Arundel*, the Missouri of A. B. Guthrie's *Big Sky*, the Skagit of Tom Robbins's *Another Roadside Attraction*, and the Yukon of John McPhee's *Coming into the Country*.

Since Cro-Magnon Man, people have loved riverfronts as places to live. Here they found food, drinking water, transportation, and fields for crops. Farmers still plow fertile plains along Virginia's Jackson and James, and along hundreds of other rivers. Ranchland along the upper Yellowstone deserves its name: Paradise Valley. The waterfront is still a community center at Millersburg, Pennsylvania, where the Susquehanna ferryboat docks. People celebrate river festivals in dozens of towns.

Lacking Europe's centuries of cities, generations of artists, and landmarks of architecture, much of the American culture was shaped by the powerful presence of nature. But when the land and the rivers are changed or disappear, what happens to the national character? When children need tickets to swim and when older people have no place to fish, has something of value been lost?

3

CHANGING THE FLOW OF WATER

The story of water development is not only an important volume in the environmental journal of America, but also a small-scale version of the history of the United States itself. Take away the manipulation of rivers, and someone would have to rewrite the books about this nation. Take away the canals, dams, and ditches, and the westward movement—that bustling, bloody, promising pilgrimage that continues even today—would be more like the rush to Siberia. The story of what we did to rivers is the story of migration, of meeting a growing nation's needs, of ingenuity in squeezing wealth from the land, of technology, of politics, of governmental growth, of disregard for the natural world, and of homogenization on the land—giving everyplace the promises and the looks of anyplace else.

At first clinging to the lush Atlantic Coast, settlers did not need much development of water, but the farther west they went, the greater the call for canals or dams. Routes to the frontier were by water, and the Army Corps of Engineers' first job on rivers was to clear trees and sandbars from the paths of the Ohio River steamboats in 1824. The Bureau of Reclamation was created to populate the West by selling subsidized water for whatever price farmers could afford. The frontier outlook was that the land should be settled and subdued at all costs, and this dictum applied equally to rivers. The waterways were thought to exist for people—for turning the desert green and establishing a civilization like that of the rainy East.

Water projects served growth of many kinds. Hydropower by Yankee go-getters brought the Industrial Revolution to New England. Dams reduced floods in low-lying towns after 1936. Without diversions from distant basins, Los Angeles, Denver, and other cities could not have sprawled across so much land. With irrigation water, property values in parts of Cali-

SELECTED EVENTS IN CHAPTER 3

300 B.C. Hohokam Indians dug irrigation canals.

1623 Piscataqua River dammed.

1717 Levees built at New Orleans.

1718 Missionaries dug irrigation canals at San Antonio, Texas.

1750 First municipal water system built in Philadelphia.

1776 Vineyards irrigated at Mission San Diego de Alcala.

1789 Hadley Falls Dam built on Connecticut River.

1799 Army Corps of Engineers organized.

1823 Corps authorized to study Presque Isle Harbor.

1824 Congress appropriated money for the corps to work on Ohio River.

1829 Erie Canal built.

1832 Arkansas River used for irrigation in Colorado.

1834 Pennsylvania Canal built.

1837 Columbia River used for irrigation.

1838 Kennebec River dammed, salmon eliminated.

1842 Croton River dammed, water delivered to New York City.

1847 City Creek diverted for irrigation at Salt Lake City.

1850 Corps of Engineers authorized to study Mississippi flood control.

1862 Homestead Act passed.

1869 John Wesley Powell led first trip down Colorado River.

1878 Powell published *Report on the Lands of the Arid Region of the United States.*

1879 Mississippi River Commission formed.

1882 First hydroelectric plant built, on Fox River.

1884 Big Bear Valley dammed for water supply in southern California.

1893 California Debris Commission formed.

1896 First major hydroelectric plant built, at Niagara Falls.

1902 Newlands Reclamation Act passed.

1903 Reclamation Service built Theodore Roosevelt Dam.

1904 Imperial Valley flooded by faulty irrigation system.

1907 Los Angeles passed bond issue to build Owens Valley Aqueduct.

1908 Pittsburgh completed flood control plan.
Inland Waterways Commission called for integrated water development.

1911 Reclamation Service built Jackson Lake Dam.

1912 Elwah River dammed.

1915 Miami Conservancy District formed.

1917 Flood Control Act authorized Corps of Engineers to study flood control and hydropower.

1922 Colorado River Basin Compact established.

1923 Reclamation Service changed to Bureau of Reclamation.

1925 Senate Document 308 authorized Corps of Engineers to study most large rivers.

1928 Boulder Canyon Project Act passed.
Metropolitan Water District created for southern California.

1929 First Ohio River navigation system completed.

1932 Rock Island Dam was built on Columbia River.

1933 Tennessee Valley Authority created.

1935 Corps's first large dam authorized, for Tygart River.

1936 First major flood control act passed.

1938 Bonneville Dam built.

1939 Reclamation Project Act expanded Bureau of Reclamation responsibilities.

1941 Hoover (Boulder) Dam built. Colorado River Aqueduct built.
Grand Coulee Dam built.

1944 Shasta Dam built by Bureau of Reclamation.

1956 Recreation authorized as reason to build dams.

1958 Corps's Southeast Basins Study expanded dam purposes.

1964 Glen Canyon Dam built.

1965 Water Resources Planning Act strengthened state roles and created Water Resources Council.

1966 Corps's international program announced.

1978 Public Utility Regulatory Policies Act encouraged small hydroelectric projects.

1983 Interior Secretary James Watt disbanded Water Resources Council.

fornia soared 1,400 percent, and statewide, dams and ditches nurtured more than $12 billion worth of farm products in 1982.

Engineers achieved impressive feats of technology. Three times the yearly runoff of the Colorado River is trapped in two dams, each higher than seven hundred feet. Through dark tunnels bored beneath the Continental Divide, water streams to Denver. For southern California, the Feather River is dammed six hundred miles away and pumped over a mountain range three thousand feet high.

The government paid for much of the water development, and the costs were great. By 1971, $200 billion in 1958 dollars had been spent.[1] In the early 1980s the Army Corps of Engineers and the Bureau of Reclamation spent about $4 billion yearly. In 1983, a single dam in California was proposed at a cost of $2.2 billion.

The rearrangement of waterways grew in dimensions that are still expanding. More than twenty-six thousand miles of streams were dredged or dammed for barges. Thousands more miles were channelized to speed runoff, while four hundred large dams and thousands of small ones were built to slow runoff and control floods. Tens of thousands of miles of streams are flooded to make twelve million acres of reservoirs—about the size of New Hampshire and Vermont. Fifty interstate compacts or international treaties allocate water to competing users, sometimes leaving dry riverbeds and nothing for fish, wildlife, recreation, and Mexico.

The development of water broke down differences between places. It reduced high water from valleys infamous for floods, it opened access to wilderness, it allowed cities and farms to grow in the lands of roadrunners and rattlesnakes. Drylands in California were flooded for rice paddies as in Louisiana. Semiarid valleys were dotted with Holsteins as in Wisconsin. Instead of adapting to the environment, people bent the environment to meet the needs of a society in which one of the few absolutely understood goals was to make money. The Southwest that housed Indians, miners, and scattered cattlemen boomed with homes and industries in developments that could be carbon copies of suburban Atlanta. Golf courses, swimming pools, and sprawling subdivisions were fed by dams. Water—once an unequalizer between regions—was imported, allowing for a future that many people thought was unlimited.

THE FIRST CHANGES

Hohokam Indians along Arizona's Salt and Gila Rivers dug canals to irrigate thousands of acres around 300 B.C.[2] Small dams were also built in New

Mexico's Rio Grande basin, but by the year 1400 the Hohokam were gone. Maybe salt accumulated in the irrigated soil, or maybe a thirty-year-long drought drove people away.[3] Through the rest of North America, Indians accepted the rivers for what they were—rich providers of life. They were not to be changed, and to the extent that rivers were problems, people adjusted their lives to fit: they got off the floodplain when the water came up.

For European emigrants, tampering with the flow of water became a cultural obsession, essential to what was planned. They started soon after landing. At Jamestown men dug ditches to drain runoff from their swampy, mosquito-infested site—one of the first places where the European conquest of America began. Wanting lumber for houses, pioneers built a log dam in 1623 on Maine's Piscataqua River to power a sawmill,[4] and in 1717 the first levee was built to save New Orleans from the Mississippi. A year later, Spanish missionaries at San Antonio, Texas, dug irrigation canals to water crops, and in 1776 they used Indian labor to lay ditches through San Diego vineyards.[5] A dam built by the Spanish at Santa Barbara, California, is the oldest standing dam in the country. In 1789, Hadley Falls Dam on the Connecticut River blocked three hundred miles of waterway from the spawning of salmon and shad.[6] In defiance of state law, developers built a dam in 1838 at Augusta, Maine, eliminating salmon from the entire Kennebec River basin.[7]

Most people were oblivious to the values of a free-flowing stream. Rivers were to be used. Around 1850 a writer praised the Hudson, but only for its commerce: "It would outrage one's sense of justice if that broad stream were to roll down to the ocean in mere idle majesty and beauty."[8]

TO TURN THE TAP

In 1750 America's first municipal water system delivered Schuylkill River supplies to Philadelphia, then the nation's largest city. Some of those wooden pipes are still used. Street washing was intended to curb yellow fever epidemics that had sent thousands fleeing to the country. People had taken water freely from wells or the river, and a Philadelphian predicted, "It will be some time before the citizens will be reconciled to buy their water." The first year's receipts were only $537, but in thirty years, New Orleans, Richmond, and St. Louis also had public supplies.[9] When Pittsburgh's system was built in 1827, homeowners dumped trash in wells, now the targets of urban archaeologists.

New Yorkers bought water by the pail from vendors pushing carts, but after cholera epidemics in 1832 and 1834, and after firemen had to battle uncontrolled blazes with dynamite because water was so short, the city built a fifty-foot-high dam on the Croton River thirty miles away and in 1842 imported water through America's first large city aqueduct. Tadpoles were swept through the pipes, and New Yorkers had "dreadful apprehensions of breeding bullfrogs inwardly."[10]

Setting a pattern that lasts to this day, public water was wasted even when it was a novel luxury. In 1853 the Boston Water Board estimated that people squandered two-thirds of their supply in livery stables and in urinals and commodes that never quit flushing. People opened taps wide to prevent freezing in winter. Only seven years old, city reservoirs were almost dry, and inspectors sneaked around houses at night listening for running water, then warned people that their supplies would be cut off. But the main solution was to develop new sources that seemed unlimited.

Some of the Catskill Mountain streams ran to the Delaware River and on to Philadelphia, but New York officials dug new routes, diverting the water to their Hudson. They reduced the Neversink River to a trickle.[11] Called by author Marc Reisner "the most magnificent water system the world has ever seen," the New York City network included eighteen dams, three aqueducts, and a siphon tunnel built in 1912 deep beneath the Hudson River.

In the West, one of the first dams for city water was built in 1884 at Big Bear Valley to serve Redlands in southern California. Los Angeles developed local streams and groundwater sources that were adequate only through the 1800s.

FLOATING TO THE HEARTLAND

Canals may be the best known and most romanticized of early water developments.[12] From 1829 to 1889 the Erie Canal lay as a thoroughfare from New York to the Great Lakes and the Midwest, the only east–west water route south of the St. Lawrence. Freight costs from the lakes to the coast plummeted from $100 to $5 a ton, and the canal helped transform New York City from a second-class seaport to the dominant American city. In 1834 the Pennsylvania Canal was the first to cross the Appalachians, boats being portaged by railroad locomotives from the Juniata River and over the eastern continental divide. The Illinois Canal launched Chicago's growth in the mid-1800s. Four thousand miles of canals were built between 1815 and

1860. Eighty percent of the investments were paid off, but some routes were dismal failures. Before the Chesapeake and Ohio Canal was finished along the Potomac River from Washington to Cumberland, Maryland, the Baltimore and Ohio Railroad carried freight cheaper and faster. Today the canal's greatest use is by hikers, runners, and bicyclists.

On larger rivers with gentle gradients, flatboats and keelboats floated people and everything they owned. Pioneers trekked on the National Road across Pennsylvania's Appalachians, then drifted down the Monongahela River to the Ohio at Pittsburgh, then to the Mississippi. Steam power revolutionized river travel through the interior; Morgan Neville wrote with considerable hype about the steamboat in 1829: "The art of printing scarcely surpassed it in its beneficial consequences."[13] Private companies developed some rivers, such as the Monongahela where eight-foot-high dams were built in 1844. These were uneconomic and were destroyed during floods. By 1860 steamboats cruised the Ohio, Mississippi, Missouri, Arkansas, Red, Rio Grande, and Columbia Rivers. Gold miners were later hauled up the Yukon on boats powered by cordwood.

GRINDSTONES AND TURBINES

While cities diverted streams for drinking water and navigation companies dug canals, easterners built dams to tap rivers that powered the Industrial Revolution. Through the use of falling water, Lowell, Massachusetts, and Patterson, New Jersey, became two of the first manufacturing towns in the early 1800s.

Most of the work involved in hydropower is done by the sun as it evaporates ocean water into water vapor that is then carried by wind to mountains where the air cools and drops rain or snow. All the power broker needed to do was to catch the water as it came falling home toward the sea, and divert the flow through a channel where waterwheels were geared to grindstones, sawblades, or other hardware. Storage dams were needed to yield a regular flow so that power could be delivered at people's whims, not nature's, and to create a "head" with a sudden drop where water fell with force.

In 1882 Thomas Edison built the world's first electric generating station in the heart of Manhattan, and only twenty-six days later, on the Fox River in Appleton, Wisconsin, the first hydroelectric plant was built to power 250 lightbulbs. At Niagara Falls, Westinghouse constructed the first major hydroelectric plant in 1896.

The basic hydroelectric system involves a reservoir for storage and a pipe to carry water from the top of the dam to its bottom, where it turns turbine blades. These turn a rotor—the moving part of an electric generator—where coils of wire sweep past a stationary coil and make electricity. In large projects, engineers embellished the formula: they dug tunnels through mountains to dump one river into another, and they arranged whole groups of reservoirs to store and release water to canals, pipes, and turbines. In a sense, rivers were dismantled and then reassembled by pipe fitters. By 1900, 57 percent of the nation's electricity came from hydroelectric power, dropping to one-third through most of the first half of the twentieth century, when fossil fuels were used. Many of New England's eleven thousand existing dams are relics of the hydropower era at the turn of the century.

Hydroelectric dams on the lower Susquehanna, the Connecticut, and New England streams generated power for eastern cities but destroyed salmon, shad, and eels having high commercial value. When the salmon disappeared from the rivers of Maine, 433 laws about fisheries were on the books, but few were enforced. Having learned from the East, where salmon were almost extinct, the first legislature of the state of Washington required fish ladders with any dam, but in 1912 on the Elwha River, a power company illegally constructed an eighty-foot-high dam without ladders, and the law was changed to allow the building of hatcheries—many of them ineffective—instead of ladders. Seven more dams in Washington followed shortly after. The Columbia River, larger than all United States rivers except the Mississippi, St. Lawrence, and Ohio, was blocked in 1932 when the Puget Sound Power and Light Company built Rock Island Dam.[14] Devastating impacts on the salmon came later with huge Columbia dams built in the 1940s.

RELIGIOUS COLONIES AND
BROKEN DREAMS

Spanish priests watered grapes at the Mission San Diego de Alcalá in 1776, and other Spaniards diverted the streams of the Sierra Madre in southern California. In 1832 ditches carried water from Colorado's Arkansas River, and in 1837 Marcus Whitman took water from creeks to irrigate mission gardens near the Columbia. Mormons herded mules carrying barrels of irrigation water across the Utah desert,[15] and these industrious settlers wasted no time in pioneering irrigation on a large scale by diverting City Creek in

1847 to grow potatoes at Salt Lake City. By 1865 they had built a thousand miles of canals to water 1.5 million acres.[16]

The Homestead Act of 1862 lured droves of easterners to the West. Myth and fantasy were mustered against the great American desert beyond Kansas. Speculators and real estate sharks promised that rain would follow the farmers because of evaporation from plowed soil. Rain would follow the train because smoke particles would give water vapor something to cling to. Even Ferdinand V. Hayden, director of the federal government's Geological and Geographical Survey of the Territories, in 1867 stated, "The planting of ten or fifteen acres of forest-trees on each quarter-section will have a most important effect on the climate, equalizing and increasing the moisture and adding greatly to the fertility of the soil."[17] If only because God was on the settlers' side, rain would fall. Those who were lucky enough to claim stream frontage dug ditches and sometimes controlled the flow of water and the lives of later settlers in a system more like vassalage than rugged independence. Homesteaders plowed the plains and destroyed a wealth of rangeland, described by Conrad Richter in *The Sea of Grass*. In dry seasons the exposed soil blew away. Two out of three homesteaders failed for the simple reason that they were trying to settle a desert and a semiarid steppe. A hostile environment was blamed for the suffering and disappointment of the miserable program, despite the warnings of John Wesley Powell.

A legendary figure of the West, the one-armed Powell had led the first river trip down the Colorado River in 1869. His scientific expedition—the last great exploration within the continental United States—started with four boats and nine men and ended a thousand miles and three months later with two boats and five men.[18] Powell was the second director of the U.S. Geological Survey, and warned against indiscriminate settling of the drylands: "I think it would be almost a criminal act to go on as we are doing now, and allow thousands and hundreds of thousands of people to establish homes where they cannot maintain themselves."

In 1878 Powell published his Report on the Lands of the Arid Region of the United States, proposing that the government reserve dam sites from settlement and that irrigation districts be organized by people who would draw up a plan and apply for a federal survey. His gospel was simply that settlement should be planned. Otherwise, lack of water, homestead failures, and water monopolies would cripple the growth of the West. At an irrigation convention in 1893 Powell angrily said, "I wish to make it clear to you, there is not sufficient water to irrigate all the lands which could be irrigated, and only a small portion can be irrigated. . . . I tell you, gentlemen, you are piling up a heritage of conflict!"

Under Powell's direction, federal surveyors located sites for water projects, but speculators trailed the surveyors and filed for lands before they could be reserved. To save the program, the General Land Office temporarily closed public lands from claiming, but western congressmen fought any curb in the federal giveaway and killed the irrigation survey in 1890.[19] Powell quit four years later, but in 1902 many of his recommendations became law in the Newlands Reclamation Act.

Powell is curiously a hero of both dam builders and river runners. The Bureau of Reclamation credits him for their dam-building heritage; the reservoir behind Glen Canyon Dam is named Lake Powell. Whitewater boaters who hate Lake Powell regard the man with awe because he was the first to run the Colorado River. Yet Powell was set on damming and irrigating the West. He wrote that the flooding rivers were "wasting into the sea."[20] He championed federal involvement, but in a limited way. Regarding the building of projects, he cautioned, "I say to the Government: Hands off: Furnish the people with institutions of justice, and let them do the work for themselves."

The California Gold Rush spurred irrigation as farmers supplied mining camps with food. By 1890, 3.7 million acres in the West were watered,[21] but at the turn of the century 90 percent of private irrigation companies were in or near bankruptcy because their projects were uneconomic.[22] William F. Cody, alias Buffalo Bill, invested in one of these doomed schemes, later completed as the Shoshone Project by the federal government, which did not have to worry whether irrigation was economic or not.

In the bungling of private irrigation, the California Development Company stands in a class by itself. The company intended to profit from a rare geographical twist: the Colorado River, through silt deposited during floods, had formed a forty-foot-high dike between it and southern California's Imperial Valley, which lay below sea level. Gravity flow from the Colorado could water new farms in the valley if a canal were sliced through the natural dike, though, like an inland Holland, the valley sat precariously below the level of the river. The canal was dug, and when an intake channel silted up in 1904, the directors waited for more cash before fixing it. The Colorado burst through a malfunctioning gate, washed out the new farms, and created the Salton Sea, which is still there. The investors' solution was to declare bankruptcy. This fiasco and others fueled the support for federal water development.

In 1887 California had passed the Wright Act, allowing county groups to form water districts with governmental power to dam rivers. Plagued with corruption, most districts failed until the 1920s, when many small- and medium-sized projects were built.[23]

The same year that Powell resigned, the Carey Act offered one million acres of federal land to any state that would irrigate it, but eight years later only 7,640 acres were patented. The states did not want to pay for water development. Western cities, however, were different. They needed water and reached far from home to dam and divert the rivers.

INFANT EMPIRES

In the 1890s Los Angeles had already tapped its local supplies, which were dependent on fifteen inches of yearly rain (Boston has forty-three and Jacksonville fifty-three). After the 1903 and 1904 droughts, the city water chief, William Mulholland, saw that new sources must be captured if the city was to grow. He took a buckboard ride to the distant Owens Valley in 1904 and devised a plan to drain the eastern Sierra runoff to the city. Los Angeles agents secretly bought land and water rights, and a bond issue was passed in 1907 to fund a 238-mile-long aqueduct to divert the water south.[24]

This marked one of the largest municipal water projects, the introduction of complex schemes to bring water to western cities, and one of the most intense conflicts between local people and distant water users. During the same years, San Francisco planned to import water 150 miles from Yosemite National Park, sparking America's first great environmental debate.

The development of water had grown and accelerated since the pioneering settlers, but all of this was only preparatory; private developers lacked the capital, the authority, and the political solidarity to accomplish truly enormous changes on the land. The massive changes in the flow of rivers were caused by federal agencies, beginning with the army.

THE CORPS

With no visions of dams or canals, the Continental Congress, on June 16, 1775, authorized the hiring of a chief engineer and two assistants for General Washington's army of revolutionaries. Washington appointed Colonel Richard Gridley, who directed the building of fortifications at Bunker Hill, where he was wounded on his first day at work. This was the beginning of the Army Corps of Engineers, formally organized in 1799, reconstituted in 1802 to start West Point, and now the world's largest engineering organization.

The primary mission of the corps was to support the military, but its civil responsibilities shaped American life and landscapes. The corps administered Yellowstone Park before the National Park Service was formed, built the Alaskan Highway, and helped to develop the atomic bomb.[25] The maintenance and improvement of waterways for navigation became a corps job with an 1823 survey of Lake Erie's Presque Isle Harbor and with studies the next year to determine "the routes of such roads and canals . . . of national importance, in a commercial or military point of view." A role with rivers began in 1824, when Congress appropriated $74,000 for the corps to dig up sandbars in the Ohio River and tow dead trees away so steamboats would not crash as often.

The maintenance job soon included the Mississippi, and construction work began in 1830 with locks to bypass the Falls of the Ohio (a rapid) at Louisville. Between 1910 and 1929, forty-six dams and locks blocked every inch of the 981-mile-long Ohio, and ninety-one dams were built on tributaries. To store water for higher flows needed by barges during dry months, the corps's first large dam was authorized in 1935 for West Virginia's Tygart River.[26] After World War II, the Ohio and Mississippi channels were deepened, and locks and dams were enlarged in a process that still continues. By 1973 the Ohio River Project was consolidated to twenty-six dams. Strings of barges a thousand feet long can fit through many of the locks and travel the Ohio's length in less than a week.

Twenty-six thousand miles of commercially navigable waterways and locks at 265 sites (not counting the Great Lakes) have been developed, most of them by the corps, at a federal cost of over $10 billion. Main routes are the Mississippi, Ohio, Illinois, Missouri, Arkansas, Tennessee, Hudson, St. Lawrence, and Columbia. Navigation improvements dominated corps activities until the late 1930s, when flood control reservoirs became the main program, but in 1965 navigation again received the largest share of the budget.[27] Nine percent of domestic freight travels on inland waterways, including the Great Lakes' St. Lawrence Seaway. Oil and coal products account for 61.4 percent of goods; grains are the second-largest group.

IMPROVING THE ODDS AGAINST FLOODS

The corps's work in flood control began in 1850, when Congress authorized a survey of the Mississippi. Recognizing that some flood problems were too complex for single states, the federal government formed the Mississippi River Commission in 1879. For two decades, federal funds, often matched by local communities, were spent for levees. With the California Debris Commission in 1893 the corps developed plans to control silt that had resulted from hydraulic gold mining and that aggravated flooding. In 1917 a flood control act was passed authorizing further work on the Sacramento and Mississippi, but these jobs were not large, and they diverted little of the corps's attention from navigation.

The first plans for flood control dams were drawn by local groups. In 1908 the city of Pittsburgh wrote the pioneering American plan for trapping high water, then releasing it slowly to reduce downstream flooding. But the city's Flood Commission and its president, H. J. Heinz, sought federal help without success, and none of the dams was built.[28]

In 1913 the Miami River in Ohio flooded, killing 360 people, and two years later the Miami Conservancy District was formed to help in rebuilding the damaged towns. This led to a second group, the Miami Valley Flood Prevention Association, and it did not wait for federal aid. The association collected $2 million from twenty-three thousand subscribers to build five dams and to clear the river's channel through the cities. Landowners were assessed, bonds were sold, and the dams were built. As proof of the project's success, the association later refunded many of the contributions.

The Miami program is significant because it was privately organized and financed by direct beneficiaries, not taxpayers. It was also a milestone in hydrologic planning. Similar plans were followed on Colorado's Arkansas River at Pueblo and on New Mexico's Rio Grande near Albuquerque. But along the Muskingum in Ohio, local initiative and funding evaporated in the 1930s after the federal government stepped in. This, rather than the Miami experience, became the model for the future. In *The Flood Control Controversy*, Luna Leopold and Thomas Maddock concluded, "Where the damage is great and the benefits are real and recognizable, as in the case of the Miami Conservancy District, local communities can and will contribute a large portion of the cost of flood control facilities for their protection. If there is a federal subsidy, as shown in the Muskingum example, they will not."

Following a large flood on the Mississippi, the first major federal role in flood control began in 1928 when the corps expanded its program of levee construction. The corps argued against reservoirs, believing them to be too costly and of dubious value, but when levees failed and were overtopped, dam building began to gain acceptance anyway. During the Depression, work relief projects by the corps included Fort Peck Dam on the

Missouri River, Conchas Dam in New Mexico, Winooski River dams in Vermont, and Muskingum River dams in Ohio, all for flood control, and all establishing a growing federal role.

In 1936, severe floods in the Ohio basin and the East moved Congress to pass the first major flood control act. Comparable in importance to the reclamation law of 1902, the Flood Control Act of 1936 set a policy of dam building that clinched the fate of hundreds of rivers. Declaring flood control to be a nationwide responsibility of the corps, the law stated, "It is hereby recognized that destructive floods upon the rivers of the United States, upsetting orderly processes and causing loss of life and property . . . constitute a menace to national welfare; that it is the sense of Congress that flood control on navigable waters or their tributaries is a proper activity of the Federal Government." With the hardships of the Depression outdone only by those of high water, nothing could have been more popular than the corps spending millions to hire men, move earth, and stop floods. The corps was regarded as a savior, and riding this wave of popularity, the agency built dams not even authorized by Congress. One unauthorized "project modification" relocated a dam a hundred miles to another river and another state—from the West Fork in West Virginia to the Youghiogheny in Pennsylvania.[29] Now that advanced technology made huge dams possible, the flood control act and the hydroelectric dam authorizations during the Depression started the big-dam era.

About four hundred large flood control dams have been built by the corps. The Tennessee Valley Authority and the Bureau of Reclamation also built dams, and the Soil Conservation Service constructed hundreds of small flood control dams. Including private power dams managed partly for flood control, eight thousand dams help to reduce downstream floods, though the corps inspected half of these and in 1979 reported that one-third—mostly in private ownership—were unsafe with the potential of causing more harm than good. The corps built more than 9,000 miles of levees and 7,500 miles of channels intended to contain floods, and about a thousand flood control projects all together.

The corps has estimated that its flood control investments have returned $3.50 per dollar spent. Construction peaked in the 1950s and 1960s and has used 28 percent of all the corps's funds, compared to 23 percent for navigation.[30]

By 1999 flood control expenses by all federal agencies exceeded $25 billion, yet destruction grew worse, both because flood control did not keep up with new floodplain development[31] and because projects enticed people to build on lowlands that were not protected from the worst floods. Support for flood control waned in the 1970s owing to the completion of important projects, citizen opposition, and federal policies encouraging floodplain management, but it seemed that damming for hydroelectricity would grow.

WIRING THE RIVERS

The corps bought a dam with a hydroelectric plant on Michigan's St. Mary's River in 1909, and in 1918 it built a small dam with generators on the Tennessee River, but the agency's first large hydroelectric project was on the Columbia, which carries ten times the flow of the Colorado. Bonneville Dam was a New Deal jobs project employing five thousand workers. When a 518-megawatt power plant was installed in 1938, *U.S. News and World Report* wrote that with hydropower industrialists believed that the Northwest "could rival the productive abilities of the North Atlantic and Great Lakes regions." Fishermen saw that the country's richest runs of salmon would be destroyed and wondered why anyone would want to turn the Cascades into another Appalachia, but they had no influence. More Columbia dams built by the corps and by the Bureau of Reclamation brought cheap electricity, and the region captured one-third of the nation's aluminum production. The corps generated power at Grand Coulee Dam, built by the Bureau of Reclamation on the Columbia in 1941. Producing 3,492 megawatts, this has been the world's largest single source of electricity.[32] With a height of 550 feet and a reservoir 150 miles long, Grand Coulee was the first structure in the world with more volume than the Great Pyramid of Cheops.[33] It also eliminated a thousand miles of salmon-spawning streams, but this was overlooked in the hype of dam building. Even youth got the message: *Scholastic* magazine, a high school weekly, reported, "A giant river is being harnessed to make the life of our people more secure."[34] John Day Dam, also on the Columbia, is the country's second largest for hydropower. It and The Dalles Dam each produces two times the electricity of the largest nuclear plant. In the late 1960s, 78 percent of the Northwest's electricity came from dams.[35] This percentage decreased in later years.

The corps generates more hydropower than any other producer. Sixty-five projects are capable of 15,600 megawatts, or 4.4 percent of United States electricity and 27 percent of its hydroelectricity in 1980. About two-thirds of corps-generated power comes from the Columbia.

All hydroelectricity in the United States accounted for 12 percent of the electrical supply, having grown from 7,800 megawatts in 1930 to 69,000 megawatts at 1,400 plants in 1978.[36] Dams in the Columbia and Tennessee basins produced half of the nation's hydropower. By 2002, the hydroelectric share had dropped to less than 9.7 percent.

THE CORPS'S ACCOMPLISHMENTS

The corps lists its responsibilities as constructing and operating navigation projects, flood control, major drainage, shore and beach restoration and protection, hurricane flood protection, hydroelectric power production, water supply, water quality control, fish and wildlife conservation and enhancement, outdoor recreation, emergency relief, protection and preservation of navigable water, emergency flood control and shore protection, and other jobs.

The agency was running out of economic projects in the United States when worldwide markets for dams opened up. President Johnson introduced a "Water for Peace" program calling for corps dams in undeveloped countries. Announcing the program at the corps's Summersville Dam dedication at West Virginia's Gauley River in 1966, the president said, "We are in a race with disaster. Either the world's water needs will be met, or the inevitable result will be mass starvation. . . . If we fail, I can assure you today that not even America's unprecedented military might will be able to preserve the peace for very long."[37] The president reasoned that sending the army corps to Third World countries was better than sending the army itself.

In 1981 the corps's civil works division employed thirty-two thousand civilians and three hundred officers working out of thirty-eight district offices. More than four thousand civil works projects of all types were built. Most required continuing maintenance. The corps was responsible for 538 dams, not counting ones built by other agencies but managed by the corps. At four hundred large reservoirs the corps counted 350 million recreation visits a year—more than the national parks. One hundred and fifty corps projects supplied water to towns or industries.[38]

Excluding the Mississippi River, 284 projects were under construction by the corps in 1982. More than 450 others were authorized, though 271 of these were approved long ago and are now inactive. Another 323 studies were under way. The 1983 corps budget was $3.3 billion, but in 1984 the budget was cut to $2.7 billion.

THE BUREAU AND THE WEST

Homesteaders had tried to settle the West, but, as John Wesley Powell warned, they found that land was worthless without water. The Riparian

Doctrine was used in the East: people owning stream frontage held the rights to the water. No one needed to irrigate, so conflicts were rare compared to the West. There, many farmers and ranchers without stream frontage needed water, so after a period of gunfighting and dynamited dams, the Wyoming Doctrine was devised, granting water rights based on applications, preference going to the first person who applied. A continuing right was dependent on the person's using the water for a "beneficial" purpose. That usually meant raising cattle or crops. A few private dams were built, but most of the people with water were ranchers who simply dug ditches from streams. The success of further settlement depended on dams to store the water.

The land and the rivers would change with President Theodore Roosevelt, who had been a cowboy in the Dakotas and had traveled through the West. In his autobiography he wrote that the "first work I took up when I became President was the work of reclamation." This did not mean the reclaiming of anything, but the damming of rivers to irrigate and cultivate arid lands for the first time. Roosevelt's objective was not to cash in on crops but to lure families west. He said, "Successful homemaking is but another name for the upbuilding of the nation." Asking for passage of the reclamation act, he stated, "If we could save the waters running now to waste, the western part of the country could sustain a population greater than even the legendary Major Powell dreamed."[39]

The Army Corps of Engineers, already active for more than a hundred years, fought the creation of a competing agency, but the Newlands Reclamation Act was passed in 1902 and created the Reclamation Service to dam rivers in the seventeen western states. (In 1923 the agency's name was changed to the Bureau of Reclamation. In 1976 it was changed to the Water and Power Resources Service, but in 1980 it was changed back to the Bureau of Reclamation.) The government's costs were to be recovered through water sales. According to the bureau, these "reimbursable" costs constitute more than 86 percent of total investments,[40] but repayment rates are based on the farmers' abilities to pay, and no interest on the investments is charged, resulting in a substantial subsidy. Roosevelt and lawmakers saw how this could yield enormous profits to businessmen instead of benefiting family farmers, so a provision prohibited the sale of water to farmers owning more than 160 acres. This was later interpreted to mean 320 acres for a farmer and his wife, but the limit was often overlooked and argued about, and new, generous limits were set in 1982.

Starting in 1903, the Salt River Project's 280-foot-high Theodore Roosevelt Dam formed the largest of the early reservoirs. This was the government's first combined irrigation and hydroelectric effort, serving farms and eventually real estate development near Phoenix.[41]

In 1904 the bureau began the Lower Yellowstone Project in Montana, digging 75 miles of canals and 250 miles of ditches with manual labor and horses, and building a small 9$^{1}/_{2}$-foot-high diversion dam. Without this and five other small diversion dams, the Yellowstone would be the longest undammed river in the forty-eight contiguous states. Other early projects were on the Snake River, where Jackson Lake Dam flooded a spectacular valley at the foot of the Grand Teton in 1911. Lake Tahoe Dam in 1913 raised the level of that natural lake; Elephant Butte Dam was built in 1916 on New Mexico's Rio Grande; and nineteen other projects were authorized in 1907.[42] Some of these were large dams, but it was the bureau's work on the Colorado River that really brought multiple-use reservoirs to the forefront of western development.

DAMMING THE COLORADO

The Colorado begins as free as a river can flow in alpine meadows of Rocky Mountain National Park, but only 7.6 miles from its source the North Fork is diverted into the Red Top Ditch, dug for ranchers in 1910. Other parts of the river are diverted through tunnels beneath the Continental Divide to irrigate east-slope farms, though most of the river plunges down the western side of the Rockies, through red-wall canyons of Utah, and through the Grand Canyon, which the river created. After 1,440 miles the Colorado meets the Pacific Ocean at Mexico's Gulf of California. The basin averages only fifteen inches of precipitation a year, and the river's volume annually varies as much as 600 percent. Though it has only the flow of the Delaware River and less than Indiana's Wabash or Florida's Apalachicola, the Colorado drains one-twelfth of the nation and is the Southwest's only major river.

The desolate beauty of the river is unbroken by large cities. Urban Colorado is east of the Rockies; in Utah the river runs safely southeast of Salt Lake City; in Arizona its canyons lie hundreds of miles from Phoenix; and, bordering California, the river flows no closer than 250 miles from Los Angeles. So Denver tapped the South Platte, which runs through town; Salt Lake City drained local streams; Phoenix pumped groundwater; and Los Angeles captured the Owens Valley. These supplies, however, were not enough for those four promising empires, so the cities each turned to the Colorado, eventually diverting it to serve half of the population of the West, in the process calling in presidents, the Supreme Court, and the National Guard. The question of dividing the waters of this river became one of extensive legal debate, moral conscience, and political muscle.

The Colorado River Basin Compact of 1922 cut the river in two, and because of this division one of the finest desert canyons would be dammed. The compact allocated the water equally to an upper basin of Colorado, Wyoming, Utah, and New Mexico and a lower basin of Arizona, Nevada, and California. Upper states held nearly all of the river's source, but they guaranteed 7.5 million acre-feet a year to the lower basin. The upper states expected to receive the same amount plus surplus flows.

All of this was based on a mistake that may become one of the most consequential errors in American hydrologic planning. In 1922 engineers estimated that the river carried 16.8 million acre-feet (maf) of water per year. With 1.5 maf guaranteed to Mexico in 1944, a total of 16.5 maf was allocated.[43] But a dry cycle began in 1924, and the flows from 1922 to 1976 averaged only 13.9 maf. There is not enough water in the river to give all states and Mexico their legal shares. In 1980 85 percent of the river was used. No plan exists to solve the problem.

In the 1920s, southern California developers predicted one of their many growth booms and were not about to let a shortage of water interfere. They needed the Colorado, and they found an unlikely ally in Herbert Hoover. He had normally championed private utilities and opposed government dams, but he was also an engineer who could not resist the challenge of the Colorado, and he pursued its damming with an enthusiasm not shared for other pressing social and economic problems.

Congress passed the Boulder Canyon Project Act in 1928, authorizing the Bureau of Reclamation to build a 726-foot-high dam, the world's tallest at the time and America's largest single-site public works project ever. Contractors poured enough concrete for a sixteen-foot-wide highway from San Francisco to New York. Boulder Dam, later renamed Hoover Dam, was the prototype of a large multiple-use project,[44] incorporating irrigation, hydropower (nearly one-third of it for pumping water to California), flood control, cities, and industry. The reservoir—Lake Mead—could hold the entire flow of the river for two years and was large enough to flood Pennsylvania one foot deep.

Also in 1928, the California legislature created the Metropolitan Water District, an agency that became the largest water agency in the country, supplying one-half of all water to southern California cities and suburbs.[45] To move the water from Hoover Dam to the customers, the district built the Colorado River Aqueduct, stretching 242 miles from the river to Riverside, including a 1,617-foot pumped lift carrying one billion gallons a day. Arizona did not agree that California should take so much water, and when work began in 1934 on Parker Dam to divert water into the aqueduct, the governor of Arizona dispatched the National Guard to prevent contractors funded by the Metropolitan Water District from landing on the Arizona shore. Just before the militia reached the site, the secretary of the interior ordered a temporary halt to the work. In 1941 the aqueduct was finished, but court battles between the two states continued until 1963, and animosity persists to this day.

Though California had only 1.6 percent of the 243,000-square-mile Colorado basin, state negotiators secured more than one-fourth of the water—4.4 million acre-feet a year. California had a tight grip on the other states, and agribusiness had the grip on California: whereas 3.85 million acre-feet went to big farms, only 0.55 million acre-feet went for urban use. Although this was a large addition to Los Angeles's Owens River supply, it was not enough. The other six states were not ready to use their full shares of the Colorado, so the Bureau of Reclamation agreed to a California plan to divert one million acre-feet of surplus water until Arizona could use it. Many cities grew on borrowed money, but southern California grew on borrowed water. Alternate supplies could be considered later. California hoped to gain permanent title to the water simply by using it, but this plan failed.

Hoover Dam was planned in the ambitious years of the 1920s, built during the Depression, and finished in 1941, when people saw it as a marvel of technology meeting real needs. Tourists stand awestruck at the face of the dam as at an Egyptian pyramid. The next big Colorado River project—Glen Canyon Dam—was different. It created Lake Powell, drowning one of the most sublime of all desert canyons. Completed by the Bureau of Reclamation in 1964, the dam became a symbol of wild river and wilderness destruction. Lakes Powell and Mead are the two largest reservoirs in the country, and with its total of fourteen major dams, the Colorado River has more consumptive use and more interbasin transfers of water than any other river.[46]

Another part of the bureau's work on the Colorado is the Central Arizona Project, with a three-hundred-mile-long canal and a two-thousand-foot lift from Parker Dam to the Phoenix–Tucson area, where groundwater is overdrawn while urban growth booms—Phoenix expanding from one hundred thousand to eight hundred thousand people in thirty years.[47] The project was authorized in 1968 only after resolution of the forty-year-long feud between California and Arizona over allocations. The new supply will initially be 1.2 million acre-feet, but whereas the urban area is expected to double during the next fifty years, Colorado River supplies will sharply decrease when upper-basin states finally take their share of the river. This bleak future does not even consider reductions that will be needed because of the overestimated volume of the river. People may someday regard Phoenix as a geographical blunder the likes of which built San Francisco on the fault and New Orleans on the floodplain, but none of these problems is taken seriously as long as the engineering fix is available. The Bureau of Reclamation describes Arizona's problem as the "relative inefficiency of nature in producing precipitation at the times and places where it can be better utilized for man's benefit,"[48] and in an effort to improve the situation, the agency seeds clouds over the Colorado mountains to increase snowfall and runoff. With the bureau "stealing" the moisture from downwind regions, a quagmire of court cases will probably be heard over the ownership of no less than the clouds in the sky. Another way Arizona could meet its urban demands is simple but expensive: cities could acquire agricultural land now using 89 percent of the water.

Indian water rights could supersede many others in the allocation of the Colorado and water throughout the West. Under the Winters Doctrine, the Supreme Court ruled that Indians on reservations may claim all the water that they can use. But in 1973 the National Water Commission stated that developments were built "with little or no regard for Indian water rights." On the Gila and Papago reservations in Arizona, upstream diversions and wells outside the reservations depleted Indian supplies without compensation.[49] Sprawling 25,000 square miles, the Navaho reservation has enough irrigable land to use most of the Colorado River, and claims are unresolved. Indians are girding themselves with legal and scientific expertise to gain title to many water sources.

Demands for water in the Southwest seem to be increasing so irreversibly that the pressure to import water from rivers in Oregon and Washington could overcome the opposing votes of the sparsely populated north. At the insistence of Senator Henry Jackson from Washington, Congress agreed to a temporary moratorium outlawing the discussion of northwestern water transfers.

WATERBOY OF THE WEST

The Central Valley Project (CVP) in California is the Bureau of Reclamation's largest piece of work, comparable to what the Tennessee Valley

Authority did in size and complexity. Beginning with Shasta, Friant, and Keswick dams in the late 1930s and early 1940s, the project grew to include seventeen other dams. Investments costing $6 billion were designed to deliver 6.5 million acre-feet of water a year from the north and the Sierra Nevada to Central Valley farmers and to cities. The 560-foot-high Shasta Dam stores water that is released to the Sacramento River and then to the dry but fertile south. The Interior Department's Office of Audit found that in spite of repayments required under the reclamation law, the CVP is operating at a deficit projected at $10 billion by the year 2038 if water prices do not radically change.[50]

Another important part of most bureau dams is hydroelectricity—the strong leg that the agency leans on to subsidize uneconomic irrigation. The original agricultural emphasis of bureau projects was broadened with the Reclamation Project Act of 1939 to include flood control, navigation, and municipal and industrial supplies. The bureau now describes its goals as "multipurpose water development to meet the diverse water needs of a maturing economy and an expanding population." Project purposes are municipal and industrial water service; hydroelectric power generation, transmission, and marketing; irrigation water service; water quality improvement; fish and wildlife enhancement; outdoor recreation; flood control; navigation; river regulation and control; and related uses.

Dams proposed by the bureau at Echo Park, Glen Canyon, the Grand Canyon, the Stanislaus River, and elsewhere led to intense environmental struggles. Even more than the corps, the bureau would be criticized for the flooding of irreplaceable resources, for faulty benefit–cost analysis, and for misuse of government subsidies. In 1982 when the corps dropped consideration of construction of Big Sandy Lake in Texas because of its poor economics, the bureau adopted the study. Whereas the corps used reformed rules for project evaluation, the bureau pushed for elimination of the criteria, and in 1983 Interior Secretary James Watt—in charge of the bureau—rescinded the rules.

By 1980 the Bureau of Reclamation built 329 storage reservoirs, with enough water to flood New England three feet deep and 346 diversion dams. Distributing the water were 15,545 miles of canals, 239 miles of tunnels, and 196 pumping plants of more than one thousand horsepower each. More than 16,000 miles of drains channeled wastewater, and fifty power plants made electricity (this increased to 58 by 2003). In 1980, twenty-seven million acre-feet of reclamation water irrigated all or part of 148,000 farms and 10.2 million acres growing $7.4 billion worth of crops, enough to feed thirty-nine million people (by 2003 the acreage had been reduced to 9.2

million acres with a value of $8.7 billion per year).[51] Each year 620 billion gallons of bureau water were delivered to sixteen million people in cities and towns. Flood control savings were listed at $1.2 billion, and annual hydropower output at forty billion kilowatt hours—enough to supply New York City, Washington, D.C., Dallas, Chicago, and San Francisco. The bureau counted sixty million annual visitor days at 251 recreation sites. More than $11 billion had been spent, and construction continued at about seventy-five projects;[52] some of them, such as the Central Valley Project and the Central Arizona Project, embraced many dams. Ninety projects were in planning but not authorized in 1981, when the bureau employed 9,075 people with a budget of nearly $800 million. Under President Reagan the bureau saw budget increases of a larger percentage than those of the defense department. By 2002, bureau staffing had been cut to 5,954. One project was under construction and no others were planned. The bureau's budget in 2001 was still $748 million. In the last quarter century, bureau engineers exported dam-building technology to sixty-two countries by working through the Agency for International Development, the Department of State, the World Bank, and the United Nations.

Total irrigation by all groups and agencies in the United States covered fifty-eight million acres, one-fourth of it in California, one-eighth in Texas, and one-fifteenth in the East, where Florida irrigated more than all other eastern states combined. Nationwide, irrigation took 47 percent of all water withdrawn and 81 percent of all water withdrawn and not returned to a stream.[53]

A CORPORATION WITHIN
THE GOVERNMENT

Theodore Roosevelt vetoed a bill to license a private hydroelectric dam at Muscle Shoals on the Tennessee River, opening the door to government development of this site. Bills for a federal dam were passed in 1928 and 1931 but vetoed by President Coolidge, who did not believe that the government should act as an electric utility company, and by Hoover, who was called "the great engineer" but said that the Muscle Shoals Project would "break down the initiative and enterprise of the American people" and was "the negation of the ideal upon which our civilization has been based." Henry Ford proposed to build the power plant, but he wanted the government to build the dam.[54]

Franklin D. Roosevelt endorsed the Muscle Shoals site in his 1932 campaign. During his famous One Hundred Days, when fifteen major laws were passed in 1933, the Tennessee Valley Authority (TVA) was created. The Muscle Shoals proposal was the start of the nation's largest plan for regional development. The president called the TVA "a corporation clothed with the power of government, but possessed with the flexibility and initiative of a private enterprise."

Few regions of the country had more people on relief or earning less money than along the Tennessee, 650 miles long and draining parts of seven states. The TVA's first chairman, Arthur E. Morgan, wrote, "Three fortunes had been taken off that country—forests, oil and gas. . . . The wreckage of the rugged individualism has been handed to us with a request that we try to do something about it." The agency, promoting navigation, flood control, reforestation, agricultural and industrial development, and defense, became America's largest electric utility.

New dams were at the cutting edge of the TVA, and the national attitude about rivers was reflected and shaped by the agency. Senator George W. Norris, who sponsored TVA legislation, spoke of "the dawning of that day when every rippling stream that flows down the mountain side and winds its way through the meadows to the sea shall be harnessed and made to work for the welfare and comfort of man."[55] Even in 1963, when Stewart Udall wrote *The Quiet Crisis*—a history of conservation—the free-flowing Tennessee was not called a great river of the East, but "a final piece of mockery," because it "had a score of superior hydro-power sites and yet its silt-swollen waters rushed unharnessed and unchecked through counties and states where very few farmers had electricity."

The damming began and continued with speed and painstaking thoroughness unmatched in the history of water development. Wilson Dam at Muscle Shoals was completed, and Cove Creek Dam on the Clinch River was built and renamed Norris Dam. In ten years, more than seven hundred miles of streams were channeled or dammed for barges. In twelve years, sixteen of the TVA's twenty-three major dams were built. Programs for soil conservation, tree planting, recreation, and fertilizer production were begun. Critics complained of socialism, but others called the TVA "the greatest peace-time achievement of Twentieth Century America." It became the "exemplar" of multiple use of resources for social change and the "resource conservancy project" most visited by leaders from other countries. Although President Truman asked that similar authorities for the Missouri and Columbia Rivers be created, Congress did not approve.[56] Nine major dams were eventually built on the Tennessee River and forty-two on tributaries, costing $1.47 billion and flooding 635,400 acres of river channels and land. More flatwater shoreline was created than encircles the Great Lakes. Forty-nine TVA hydroelectric plants with one corps plant can produce 4,600 megawatts of electricity.

Not all the analysis is so flattering. In *The Myth of TVA*, William Chandler of the Environmental Policy Institute reported in 1984 that the agency used 1930 costs against 1980 benefits to make investments appear sound, and even at a low 2 percent interest rate on investments, the TVA navigation system was barely breaking even. Ten percent of the valley's best farmland was sacrificed for the reservoirs.[57] Eighty-five percent of flood control benefits are enjoyed by one city—Chattanooga—yet a single dam required the relocation of 3,500 families. Chandler found that without TVA's help, the per capita income of comparable areas in Georgia, Alabama, and Mississippi improved as fast or faster than the Tennessee Valley.

By 1945 water power was not keeping up with demands for electricity, so the TVA began building coalfired and nuclear plants. With only 12 percent of its electricity coming from dams in the late 1970s, the TVA burned more coal—much of it coming from strip mines—than any other electric system in the United States and caused 16 percent of the nation's sulphur dioxide pollution.[58] While building Tellico Dam on the Little Tennessee River the TVA became mired in debate, and a court injunction halted the project because it threatened an endangered fish. The reservoir was eventually filled.

Appointed by President Carter in 1978, S. David Freeman served as TVA board chairman until 1981, stressing energy conservation and aid for solar water heating, attic insulation, wood stoves, and industry powered by waste heat from nuclear power plants. Freeman said, "The dam building era is over. Now we have a more complex job."

FROM SAVING SOIL TO
DAMMING STREAMS

Poor land management led to massive topsoil losses in the 1930s; eastern farms became wastelands of gullies, and Dust Bowl winds literally blew midwestern soil into the halls of Congress. The Soil Conservation Service (SCS) was created as another Depression program and was given the goal of reducing erosion.

Spreading the word about saving the soil, the "district conservationist" of the SCS became a household figure in thousands of rural areas. Steeped in science but at home in the fields, he was a friend to farmers and advised them to contour plow, to grow grass on drainageways, to reduce numbers of cattle in overgrazed pastures, to plant windbreaks, and to grow trees on idle land. The agency also sought to reduce stormwater runoff from unprotected lands (studies of strip mines show that water runs off six times as fast as on nonstripped land). By decreasing the amount of suspended soil in the water, the volume of floodwater is also decreased, and the silt deposits that reduce a stream's capacity are avoided. "Watershed management" was the name given to techniques intended to improve runoff patterns for steadier and cleaner flows. The SCS and its county conservation districts—citizen groups affiliated with the agency—became the leaders in planning and caring for small watersheds.

Good land management resulted in flood control, which gradually became a goal in itself. The SCS later realized that its techniques reduced flood crests after small storms but did little to hold back floods after large storms had saturated even protected soil. So in 1944 the agency started building small dams in the Washita Valley of Oklahoma. After World War II, engineers replaced agronomists and range specialists in SCS policy posts, more structural solutions were proposed, and in the mid-1950s Congress granted a blanket authorization for the construction of small dams averaging fifty feet high with pools of fifty acres.

The SCS fought the Army Corps of Engineers in one of the major water resource debates of the 1950s.[59] The corps recognized that the SCS dams cut the benefits and economic justifications claimed for the large dams, and argued that its own dams offered more protection. Conservationists, opposed to the flooding of large rivers, sided with the SCS. But in the 1960s conservationists began to oppose certain SCS dams, and in the 1970s lawsuits were filed on streams such as Broadhead Creek in Pennsylvania, where Trout Unlimited saved an excellent fishery.

The SCS built more than 4,000 dams. Another 1,224 were approved and an additional 6,000 planned when the program was reevaluated and scaled back in the late 1970s.

Other work of the SCS drew even more criticism than the dams: 9,200 miles of streams were channelized to speed runoff and drain lowlands, and another 11,600 miles of ditches were planned. By 1968 state fish and game agencies and fishermen fought some of these projects, and by 1970 the program drew intense fire from new environmental groups. This "conservation service" was sued, and magazines and newspapers published pictures of SCS draglines and bulldozers digging up streams. Sensitive about its conservation heritage, the agency temporarily halted channelization in 1971 and stopped many proposals. But in the early 1980s some of these were reintroduced, and most of the money in the small-watersheds program was still used for dams and channelization—not for erosion control. The channelization program was then dropped entirely.

THE NONFEDERAL MULTITUDE

Most large water projects were built by federal agencies, but 88 percent of all dams belong to other levels of government or to private owners. Large city projects include dams on the upper Delaware by New York, on the Tuolumne by San Francisco, on the South Fork of the Platte by Denver, on the Owens by Los Angeles, and on the Skagit by Seattle. Thousands of dams, most of them small, were built by fifty thousand public and private utilities nationwide.[60]

In the 1930s California hoped to build a Central Valley Project, but when the state was unable to sell $170 million worth of bonds during the Depression, the CVP was picked up by the Bureau of Reclamation, ever ready to adopt someone else's project. The idea of a state-owned development was later revived, and in the 1960s the State Water Project became the largest of any nonfederal water system. At Oroville on the Feather River, the nation's tallest dam was built to deliver water to distant southern California. To pump the water requires almost as much electricity as all of the people in Los Angeles use.[61]

The New York State Barge Canal is a nonfederal navigation project, but this kind of state project is rare. Most states did not have the competence, money, or need to develop large projects. Most states were not even able to review federal proposals, and plans by the corps or bureau were rubber stamped. This pattern changed when the Water Resources Planning Act of 1965 strengthened state agencies. Dissent began to rise as states became involved. In 1972 Governor Jimmy Carter withdrew support for Spewrell Bluff Dam in Georgia. After economic studies showed that a Kickapoo River dam would benefit few landowners, Wisconsin governor Patrick Lucey stopped construction. In California, the State Water Resources Control Board fought one federal plan to fill New Melones Dam and another plan to divert American River water from its channel through Sacramento.

Most states, however, supported all the federal dam building they could get. When states finally had the money to write their own water plans, many reflected nothing more than the conventional view: build more dams. In the mid-1970s, Pennsylvania still called for Tocks Island Dam on the Delaware and Rowlesburg Dam on the Cheat. The state water plan projected large new demands for irrigation in the wet Susquehanna basin (but it also called for wild and scenic river designations).

With tighter restrictions on federal money in the 1980s, some western states increased their dam building programs. Utah authorized $25 million for water projects, Wyoming collected $4.5 million for water development from a coal severance tax in 1979, and Alaska budgeted oil revenues for Susitna River dams costing billions of dollars. The Texas Water Plan called for dams and Mississippi River diversions to be funded with state oil and gas revenues but was defeated.

Though overshadowed by federal projects since the New Deal, private construction of dams continued, especially for hydropower. In the early 1980s, private dams generated one-half of the United States's hydroelectricity. To entice more developers, the 1978 Public Utility Regulatory Policies Act created incentives for alternate energy such as wind, solar, and water by requiring utilities to buy power from any supplier and to pay "avoided cost"—the cost of alternate generation, usually oil. This requirement seemed to guarantee profits to the renovators of existing dams and to the builders of new ones. The hydro rush of the 1980s was like the Gold Rush of 1849, and applicants raced to the Federal Energy Regulatory Commission (FERC) office to stake claims for permits that gave exclusive rights to study a site for three years, after which developers could apply for construction licenses. The FERC received 1,859 applications in 1981 (compared to 18 in 1978), the heaviest hit areas being California, New England, Pennsylvania, Oregon, and Washington. In 1982 utility companies contested the avoided-cost provision, and the rate of applications decreased, yet private development of hydropower remained the largest reason for new dams.

North America's largest hydroelectric project sprawls across Quebec, where, after long court battles, Cree Indians who had sustained an ancient hunting culture were forced to give up 5,400 square miles of land. Three dams on the La Grande River produce 5,300 megawatts, and 13,700 megawatts (the equivalent of more than ten nuclear power plants) were planned by the year 2000, when an area two times the size of New England was planned to be flooded.[62]

COMPETITION

That the streams would be dammed was rarely questioned until the 1950s, and so utility companies and bureaucracies battled each other in cutthroat competition. If San Francisco had not applied to dam the Hetch Hetchy

Valley, the Pacific Gas and Electric Company probably would have. Private power companies derided the Tennessee Valley Authority as socialism. In the 1930s utilities hired movie stars to campaign against a vote regarding public power in the state of Washington. In retaliation, the Roosevelt-created Bonneville Power Administration hired Woody Guthrie as a "research assistant" and "public relations" consultant. Guthrie hitchhiked to Portland and in less than a month wrote twenty-six ballads touting public power, which easily won.

The corps and the bureau fought each other to spend tax dollars and realize imperial ambitions. Captain H. M. Chittenden of the corps fought the creation of the Reclamation Service, saying that the army could do the job. Franklin D. Roosevelt's powerful interior secretary, Harold Ickes, failed to draw the corps into a proposed department of conservation and said that "the two most powerful intra-governmental lobbies in Washington are the Forest Service and the Army Engineers" and that the corps was "above the law."

The corps and bureau argued over the 2,775-mile-long Missouri River (the Mississippi is only 2,300 miles long). Under the Pick plan, the corps would build five dams for flood control and navigation, but the bureau's Sloan plan called for upstream dams for irrigation and hydropower. Inspired by the TVA, politicians finally proposed a Missouri Valley Authority. Realizing that neither agency might get the work, the corps and bureau endorsed a combined Pick–Sloan plan approving nearly all the projects.

Six major dams now flood six hundred miles of the Missouri; Oahe Dam forms the country's third-largest reservoir. In North Dakota alone, five hundred thousand acres were taken. The Missouri Basin Project proposed 112 dams; 81 were built or under construction in the 1980s.[63]

In 1945 both the corps and bureau were authorized to dam California's Kings River at Pine Flat.[64] After seven years of jockeying for the job, the corps won. On California's American and Stanislaus rivers, differences were settled by allowing the corps to build Folsom and New Melones dams, and the bureau to operate them. Affecting water policy nationwide, the large-versus-small-dam contests between the corps and the SCS preempted attention from other water issues through the 1940s and 1950s.[65]

As of 1980, twenty-five government agencies spent $10 billion a year on water, but they did not work in unison. The Department of Agriculture drained wetlands while the Fish and Wildlife Service in the Department of the Interior tried to preserve them. The Bureau of Reclamation in the Department of the Interior irrigated new farmland while the Department of Agriculture paid farmers to leave the land idle. The Fish and Wildlife Service tried to halt channelization while the Federal Emergency Management Administration paid for bulldozers to plow through streams in attempts to push gravel away after floods.

The Water Resources Planning Act of 1965 created the Federal Water Resources Council to coordinate development and encourage a rational, balanced program. It provided, for the first time since the 1940s, a way for representatives of many governments and agencies to talk and plan together and for an agency that was not building the projects to review them. Under President Reagan, Interior Secretary James Watt disbanded the council in 1983.

The uses of dams have also been in competition. Early dams served single purposes, such as navigation, drinking water, or hydropower, but not mixtures of purposes. For water supply, reservoirs are kept as full as possible with reserve for droughts. But for flood control, an empty reservoir is best, so that the deluge can be caught whenever it comes. Swimmers and boaters need a large reservoir in the summer to cover mud flats. At multipurpose dams the uses compete: once water is drained for thirsty cities or hydropower in the summer, the water is not there for recreation; if reservoirs are emptied in the fall for flood control but no high water comes, then there may not be enough water for irrigation the next summer. Juggling uses is complicated by fish and water quality goals; for example, salmon on some rivers need large flows in the spring to wash smolts to sea and in the fall so adults can swim up the rivers, but these releases may clash with irrigation or hydropower needs.

Yet dams were destined to become multiple purpose. In 1908 the federal Inland Waterways Commission called for integrated development, with hydropower revenues paying for the dams.[66] The Flood Control Act of 1917 included Congress's first mandate that floods and hydropower be considered with navigation. In 1925, Senate Document 308 authorized the corps to study most large rivers, marking the government's initial effort to appraise problems of whole watersheds.

The Great Depression brought an awareness of limits and of the needs for planning. Both concepts led to river preservation in later years, but in the 1930s and 1940s they led only to wholesale damming in the name of resource management. The corps built dams mostly for flood control and navigation, whereas the Bureau of Reclamation built for irrigation and hydroelectric power.

To overcome the conflicts of multiple use, reservoirs were simply built larger, storing water for several uses, expanding economic justifications, and broadening political favor. With Hoover Dam in 1941 the benefits of multiple use were fully realized. The corps's Southeast Basins Study in 1958 called for a further expansion of dam purposes to include navigation, flood control, hydropower, irrigation, municipal supply, waste disposal, industrial supply, recreation, wildlife conservation, lowflow regulation, and soil conservation. This is the so-called bananas list: cynics proclaimed that it included enough categories that a banana plantation in West Virginia could surely be justified. "Framework" studies were written by the corps in the 1960s, each generation of plans recognizing broader goals, more reasons to build dams, further integration of uses, and expanding concerns for social, economic, and environmental impacts.

Multiple use became customary, but multiple means, including solutions other than dams, did not. Floodplain management, water conservation, and other ways of avoiding the need for dams were the last things on the developers' minds. In 1965 President Johnson issued an executive order calling for multiple means toward flood control, and in 1979 President Carter issued policy reforms stressing nonstructural alternatives, but even then, the dam builders enjoyed their largest budgets to date.

Along with competing agencies and conflicting users, neighboring regions fought for rivers. Drier areas diverted water from neighboring basins that were regarded as resource colonies. New York City redirected the Croton River and Catskill streams. Los Angeles took Owens River water, and San Francisco piped the Tuolumne from Yosemite National Park.

In 1931 Supreme Court Justice Oliver Wendell Holmes declared that "a river is more than an amenity; it is a treasure." For this reason, he ruled that the Delaware's water should be divided among states on a basis of need, rather than on the length of stream within each state. Holmes essentially meant that a river is an economic treasure. New York diverted 490 million gallons a day,[67] causing low flows damaging to the Delaware. Holmes's quotation has often been used out of context by river enthusiasts.

In 1963 the Bureau of Reclamation's Pacific Southwest Water Plan stated, "As water becomes more critical in the West, river basin boundaries will become even less rigid in water and land resource development."[68] The bureau proposed to divert northern California rivers to the south and to study Columbia diversions to the Southwest. To export water from Oregon's Rogue River, a pipeline in the ocean was considered. In 1983, one out of five residents in the West depended on water from a source that was more than a hundred miles away[69]—from rivers and lands never seen by many of the people turning the taps.

THE MANY FACES OF
WATER DEVELOPMENT

In different regions, distinctive kinds of water development dominated. In the Northeast, old hydropower dams can be found as often as villages. Flood control reservoirs flood steep-sloped valleys through the Appalachians and the East. Sprawling, shallow reservoirs for flood control and recreation dot the Midwest, and low dams have converted the big river arteries of the heartland into steps for barges. In the Southwest and California, dams for irrigation and for cities plug narrow canyons. In the Northwest, hydroelectric dams block scores of rivers.

And in different eras, the types of water development changed. Navigation projects were among the first to be built: large eastern and midwestern rivers were dredged, then blocked by low dams. While cities grew in the 1800s, reservoirs were constructed for urban water and hydropower. Flood control levees lined the Mississippi in the 1920s, and then the 1930s marked a dramatic turn. Income redistribution through public works became a national economic strategy. The big era of hydropower began with dams on the Tennessee and Columbia. After 1936, flood control reservoirs proliferated. Dams became the most visible symbols of FDR's resource philosophy, and extravagant spending on water projects became a way of politics. River development in the 1930s marked a convergence of the concepts of multiple use, river basin planning, regional development, and government authority.

In the 1940s dams were synonymous with progress, and the rivers were to be conquered with the fervor of a pioneer wielding an axe. When Shasta Dam blocked the Sacramento River in 1944, construction boss Francis Trenholm Crowe said, "That meant we had the river licked. Pinned down, shoulders right on the mat. Hell, that's what we came up here for."[70]

The 1950s and 1960s saw headlong growth in dam construction as projects planned in the 1930s and 1940s were built. Ted Schad, who worked for the Bureau of the Budget, said, "If ever there was an age of dam building, the 40s and 50s were it. In 2,000 years historians will look at these structures the way they look at the pyramids today, and they'll call us 'the dam builders.'" Remote sections of the Rockies, northern California, and parts of the Northwest were among few areas not touched by the developers. In 1956 Congress authorized recreation as a new reason to build dams. Water supply became a priority after an eastern drought in the 1960s when Congress authorized the corps's Northeastern United States Water Supply

Study; however, little construction resulted. By the mid-1960s, conservationists' challenges began to slow the big water projects.

With rising environmental and economic concerns in the 1970s and with awareness of nonstructural alternatives, it seemed that dam construction would nearly stop, but then energy costs soared, and hydropower developers returned to rivers that were passed over before.

THE RESULTS

By 1980 all agencies and private developers had built about fifty thousand dams of twenty-five or more feet in height, each holding at least fifty acre-feet (about sixteen million gallons).[71] Oroville Dam in California rises 770 feet, and the breast of Watkins Dam in Utah stretches for 14.5 miles. Oahe Reservoir on the Missouri River in South Dakota is 250 miles long. Another 1.8 million small reservoirs were built. The Connecticut was changed from a free-flowing river to a staircase of reservoirs. In 1979, 783 federal water projects, including dams and other developments, were under construction and would require $20 billion to finish.

For the future, another 497 projects were authorized. The corps's National Waterways Study in 1981 proposed fifty-eight new or renovated locks and other navigation projects to cost $22.2 billion in 1977 dollars.[72] Two thousand more miles of barge canals were under study, with construction costs projected at $2.5 million a mile. The corps inventoried 1,700 potential new hydroelectric sites. Bureau of Reclamation plans called for more dams, including the unfinished giant of the think-big mentality: Auburn Dam would rise seven hundred feet above California's American River. Hundreds of small dams or channelization projects were planned by the Soil Conservation Service. Several thousand dams or turbine additions were proposed by private developers. The Texas Water Plan included about seventy new reservoirs.

Energy needs—the main reason for dam proposals in the 1980s—could be eclipsed by urban water supply needs in the coming years. If growth in the Southwest continues with current water-consumption rates, supplies will not last, and the water seekers may go farther and farther from home. Consider recent proposals: In the late 1960s southern California's grasp tightened on the Eel River, six hundred miles away, where Dos Rios Dam was planned.[73] Texans hoped for nothing less than to divert the Mississippi. Denver owned water rights to a dozen western Colorado streams and planned to bring them home through ditches across the Eagle's Nest Wilderness and through tunnels beneath the Continental Divide. Arizonans longed for the electricity that Grand Canyon dams could yield. To prime the economic pump of the new state Alaska, boosters and the corps wanted to build Rampart Dam. Like spilled ink, its reservoir would have darkened a waterfowl wilderness the size of Lake Erie. For vanishing wealth in water, the future could bring a relentless search. Where will it end?

The transformation of rivers went mostly unnoticed in a society that supported water development and, for that matter, almost any kind of development, wherever possible. Unconsumed rivers were regarded as wasted. Unused rivers were to be harnessed by those who were strong enough, clever enough, and—in curious discord to the rugged and independent West—by those who could get the government to do the harnessing for them.

The history of water development has been one of progress but also one of destruction. Like the river's building of a floodplain with soil that was eroded from lands upstream, any building is a partner with the tearing down of something else. Historian Daniel Boorstin wrote, "The first charm and virgin promise of America were that it was so different a place. But the fulfillment of modern America would be its power to level times and places, to erase differences between here and there, between now and then. And finally the uniqueness of America would prove to be its ability to erase uniqueness." On the Snake River alone, twenty-four dams were built, flooding a valley at the foot of the Grand Teton, the Marmes Rockshelter—where the oldest human bones in North America had been found, and the second-deepest canyon on the continent.

New river development proposals caused some people to reconsider. Goals that once seemed to be useful had grown to appear extravagant, in what René Dubos called "the absurd development of characteristics that were highly desirable when they first emerged." Where in the statistics of water development does the qualitative support the quantitative? And where is the view of people who stood to lose through the development of rivers?

Why would Congress labor for years over the fate of a river, when only two decades before, the Army Corps of Engineers built dams without so much as an authorization? Why would a secretary of the interior fight for Grand Canyon dams one year and for the preservation of rivers the next? Why would an aqueduct be bombed by angry citizens and a dam in Idaho be blasted into chunks of rubble by a governor?

4

THE BEGINNINGS OF
RIVER PROTECTION

Unwanted side effects came with the dams and the canals. Migrations of fish were stopped, entire ecosystems eliminated, and unique landscapes flooded. Poorly constructed dams were dangerous; a failure at Johnstown, Pennsylvania, killed two thousand people in 1889. Yet even when the early water projects caused problems, there is little record that people knew, cared, or objected. There was no serious protest or nationwide opposition to a dam until a spectacular landscape was to be flooded in a national park.

HETCH HETCHY: FROM BARREN
ROCKS TO CATHEDRAL

More than anyone else, John Muir made the wilderness popular; he praised its spiritual value and encouraged its preservation. Having seen Yosemite Valley under state mismanagement, including the damming of Mirror Lake, he successfully lobbied for the creation of Yosemite National Park in 1890. In 1892, one year after the National Irrigation Congress was formed to support new dams, Muir and twenty-six other people founded the Sierra Club, which would later lead efforts to save rivers.

In the northern part of Yosemite Park, the Tuolumne (too-OL-uh-mee) River crashed over granite, then wound through the untouched meadows of Hetch Hetchy Valley. Glaciated walls decorated by waterfalls surrounded a garden of deep grass, girthy oaks, and evergreens.

47

During his wanderings in the Sierra Nevada, Muir visited Hetch Hetchy and became committed to its protection, writing, "I have always called it the 'Tuolumne Yosemite,' for it is a wonderfully exact counterpart of the Merced Yosemite, not only in its sublime rocks and waterfalls but in the gardens, groves and meadows of its flowery park-like floor." Albert Bierstadt painted the valley, assuring its recognition as a classic American landscape, and the director of the California Geological Survey said, "If there were no Yosemite, the Hetch Hetchy would be fairly entitled to worldwide fame."

One hundred and fifty miles away, and with vastly different motives, San Francisco officials had their own interest in Hetch Hetchy. The city filed a claim for the Tuolumne in 1901, proposing to dam the valley for water supply and hydroelectricity. Because the site was in a national park, no private owners controlled the land or water rights, so none had to be bought. But for the city to tap the public domain, a permit was required from the secretary of the interior, and Congress needed to approve. The stage was set for the first great dam fight and for what historian Roderick Nash called "the first great conservation controversy in American history."[1]

Theodore Roosevelt's first secretary of the interior, E. A. Hitchcock, refused to allow the dam because it would violate the mandate of protecting Yosemite Park as a natural landscape, but the 1906 San Francisco earthquake and fire brought public sympathy as only a natural disaster can deliver, and the city's plea for water assumed humanitarian appeal.

In 1903 Muir had met President Theodore Roosevelt when the two camped out in four inches of fresh snow at Yosemite, and the president said, "This has been the greatest day of my life." In 1907 Muir wrote to Roosevelt, asking him to spare Hetch Hetchy.

The case widened a rift between the "preservationists" and the "utilitarians" that had already begun in the young conservation community. Muir and his supporters argued that the natural landscape had intrinsic worth and that some places should be preserved. This was the national park and wilderness idea, and underlying it was the concept that the earth—at least certain places on it—has values beyond those of hardware and profits. In addition to minerals for industry, trees for houses, and water for cities, the land holds spiritual qualities that people need. Certain places ought to be left alone, especially when Congress had already decided to leave them alone by creating a national park.

Gifford Pinchot—the nation's chief forester, a friend of Roosevelt's, and the man who popularized the term *conservation*—believed that resources should be managed. His view of the public domain as an efficient workshop

SELECTED EVENTS IN CHAPTER 4

1890	Yosemite National Park designated.	1949	Washington state passed Dam Sanctuary Act.
1892	Sierra Club organized.		
1901	San Francisco representatives filed claim for Tuolumne River.	1950	Higley Mountain and Moose River dams in Adirondack Park prohibited.
1905	Wisconsin stopped dams on Brule River.	1952	Namekagon River power project stopped.
1906	General Dam Act passed.		Diversion of Trinity River fought.
1908	Permit issued to dam Hetch Hetchy Valley.	1953	Dam in Blue Valley started.
		1956	Echo Park dams stopped.
	President Roosevelt stopped dam on Rainy River.		President Eisenhower vetoed water projects.
1909	President Roosevelt withdrew 16 rivers from dam permit eligibility.		Smoky Range Dam proposed.
1913	Raker Act passed to dam Hetch Hetchy Valley.		Glen Canyon Dam approved, along with Flaming Gorge, Curecanti, and Navajo dams.
	Owens River aqueduct finished.	1957	Effort started to save Buffalo River.
1916	National Parks Act passed.	1958	Dworshak Dam authorized.
1920	Federal Power Act passed.	1959	Corps proposed Rampart Dam.
	Three dams proposed in Yellowstone National Park.		Seneca Indians lost fight against Kinzua Dam.
1921	Jones–Esch Act passed.	1961	Interior Secretary Udall intervened to try to save Clearwater River.
	International commission recommended dam in Glacier National Park.	1962	Supreme Court ruled in favor of Mayfield Dam.
1922	Izaak Walton League organized.	1963	Glen Canyon flooded.
1923	Permits for Kings River dams denied.		Sierra Club published *The Place No One Knew.*
1924	Owens Valley residents bombed aqueduct.		National Park Service recommended national river status for Buffalo River.
1926	Saint Francis Dam built.		Trinity River dam proposal at the Hoopa Reservation stopped.
1927	Bechler Meadows Dam proposed in Yellowstone National Park.		Corps proposed Potomac River dams.
1928	Hydroelectric plant proposed for Cumberland Falls.	1965	Interior Secretary Udall dropped support for Grand Canyon dam.
	Saint Francis Dam failed.		Kings Canyon National Park expanded to stop dams.
1934	Fish and Wildlife Coordination Act passed.	1967	Rampart Dam stopped.
1936	Kinzua Dam authorized.	1968	Central Arizona Project passed without Grand Canyon dams.
	National Wildlife Federation organized.		Corps dropped plans for dam at Cumberland Falls.
1940	Potomac River dams proposed.	1970	Second Owens Valley aqueduct built.
1941	Tennessee residents fought Douglas Dam.		Clarion River dam proposal stopped.
	Santee–Cooper rivers project built.	1972	Buffalo River named national river.
1942	Corps dropped Clarion River dam proposal.	1973	Lawsuit to save Rainbow Bridge lost.
1943	Bureau of Reclamation proposed Echo Park dams.	1976	Flathead River designated national river.
1946	Residents fought Land Between the Lakes project.		
1947	Grand Canyon dams proposed.		
1948	Glacier View Dam proposed.		
	Indians lost fight against Garrison Dam.		
	Wilderness Society opposed Wilson Dam.		

represented reform from the cut-and-run mentality that had allowed public resources to be depleted for the profits of a few powerful men, but when in doubt, Pinchot favored development: "Conservation demands the welfare of this generation first, and afterward the welfare of generations to follow."

Muir disagreed: "Much is said on questions of this kind about the greatest good for the greatest number . . . but the greatest number is too often found to be number one." For most lands, the preservationists did not disagree with Pinchot's view of management; they simply wanted a few places, such as the national parks, to be left alone.

Pinchot wrote, "Conservation stands emphatically for the development and use of water-power now, without delay." Against Muir he argued, "As to my attitude regarding the proposed use of Hetch Hetchy . . . I am fully persuaded that . . . the injury . . . by substituting a lake for the present swampy floor of the valley . . . is altogether unimportant compared with the benefits to be derived from its use as a reservoir." Disagreement over the two views of conservation had been building, and a showdown would come at Hetch Hetchy.

An advisory board of army engineers discovered four excellent alternatives but stated, "The necessity of preserving all available water in the Valley of California will sooner or later make the demand for the use of Hetch Hetchy as a reservoir practically irresistible." The board reported that Hetch Hetchy was San Francisco's least expensive and only practical solution, though the city of Oakland would tap a cheaper Sierra source, other cities found alternatives in the Sierra, and dams were later built on the Tuolumne below Hetch Hetchy. San Francisco's engineers claimed that the best alternative to the $77 million Hetch Hetchy site would cost $20 million more.

Roosevelt appointed James Garfield, a friend of Gifford Pinchot, as the new interior secretary, and Pinchot advised the dam promoters to renew their permit request.[2] In 1908 the permit was issued, though Roosevelt later wrote to Robert Underwood Johnson, an ally of John Muir's and editor of *Century* magazine, that Hetch Hetchy was "one of those cases where I was extremely doubtful." Now the fate of the valley went to Congress.

Muir and his supporters appealed to the people and started the first great movement to save a landscape from being dammed (though in 1912 the seventy-four-year-old Muir took time out to explore the Amazon). With the help of magazine and newspaper editors, the Hetch Hetchy question was delivered to the public. Many people gave up on saving the valley, but Muir argued fervently, attacking San Francisco by calling it "the Prince of the powers of Darkness" and "Satan and Company." In the conclusion of *The Yosemite*, Muir thundered,

These temple destroyers, devotees of ravaging commercialism, seem to have a perfect contempt for Nature, and, instead of lifting their eyes to the God of the mountains, lift them to the Almighty Dollar.

Dam Hetch Hetchy! As well dam for water-tanks the people's cathedrals and churches, for no holier temple has ever been consecrated by the heart of man.

The preservationists' plea was that national parks should not be sacrificed for special interests and that alternate sites lay outside the park.

While the *New York Times* opposed the dam, the *San Francisco Chronicle* named Muir and the preservationists "hoggish and mushy esthetes." The city argued that people's needs should come first and that the reservoir would enhance the valley, to which Congressman Holvor Steenerson of Minnesota challenged, "You may as well improve upon the lily of the field by handpainting it."

Sponsoring the bill to allow the dam, California congressman John Raker said that the "old barren rocks" had a "cash value" of less than $300,000 but a reservoir was worth millions. Representative Finly Gray from Indiana said, "I admire the beauties of nature and deplore the desecration of God's Creation, yet when the two considerations come in conflict the conservation of nature should yield to the conservation of human welfare, health, and life."

Outlook Magazine countered, "While the Yosemite National Park might very properly be sacrificed to save the lives and health of the citizens of San Francisco, it ought not to be sacrificed to save their dollars."

To protect people from private power monopolies, a "progressive" view that San Francisco would deliver publicly owned power was touted by some congressmen. One of these was William Kent from Marin County, north of San Francisco, who had bought Muir Woods to save it from logging and then persuaded President Roosevelt to designate it a national monument in 1908 to save it from a local water company that planned to condemn the woods for a reservoir.[3] The progressives said that Hetch Hetchy would make citizens "forever free from any danger of being held up in the interest of private profit."[4] Kent and others made certain that the bill allowing the dam prohibited power sales to private utility companies.

Woodrow Wilson appointed Franklin Lane as secretary of the interior in 1913. He had been a lawyer for San Francisco when the city planned the dam. In September, after hearings at which the park supporters were scarcely represented because of short notice, the House passed the Raker Act, 183–43. No western congressman opposed the dam. Having lost in the

House, Robert Underwood Johnson called for a plan to "flood the Senate with letters from influential people." One member received an estimated five thousand letters against the dam. The *New York Times* and hundreds of newspapers nationwide printed editorials against the dam. But San Francisco lobbied quietly and with precision in Washington.

Some senators could not understand why people opposed a dam appearing to promise only public good. On the sixth day of debate, Missouri's James Reed said,

> The Senate of the United States has devoted a full week of time to discussing the disposition of about two square miles of land, located at a point remote from civilization, in the heart of the Sierra Nevada mountains, and possessing an intrinsic value of probably not to exceed four or five hundred dollars. . . . It is merely proposed to put water on these two square miles. Over this trivial matter, the business of the country is halted, the Senate goes into profound debate, the country is thrown into a condition of hysteria, and one would imagine that chaos and old night were about to descend upon the land.

On the morning of the vote a "Special Washington Edition" of the *San Francisco Examiner* greeted congressmen at their desks. Drawings showed idyllic recreation scenes with vacationing families at the reservoir. Late that night senators voted 43–25 to allow the dam. President Woodrow Wilson signed the bill, and the fight was over. As a part of the plan, a second dam, Eleanor, would flood Eleanor Creek, a spectacular Tuolumne tributary also in the park. Because the dam had received so much attention, John Muir said, "The conscience of the whole country has been aroused from sleep," though this was poor satisfaction. Muir died one year later.

John Muir and his supporters did not come close to winning: Presidents Roosevelt and Wilson supported the dam, Interior Secretaries Garfield and Lane approved it, the House committee voted unanimously for it, and the full House and Senate cleared the bill by wide margins. But for the first time, people read articles and editorials pleading to save a landscape, thousands of people wrote to congressmen, and some politicians argued eloquently for preservation.

In *Wilderness and the American Mind*, Roderick Nash wrote,

> Indeed the most significant thing about the controversy over the valley was that it occurred at all. . . . Traditional American assumptions about the use of undeveloped country did not include reserving it in national parks for its recreational, aesthetic, and inspirational values. The emphasis was all the

other way—on civilizing it in the name of progress. What had formerly been the subject of national celebration was made to appear a national tragedy.

The Hetch Hetchy struggle proved that people would become motivated and committed to save a special piece of land. With dam proposals that would cause an absolute loss of tangible property, the stakes were utterly clear. "When a dam is proposed," said Jerry Meral, deputy director of the Department of Water Resources for California in 1982, "it's easy to see what is at stake. All that people have to do is go to the river and look. It's not like a bottle bill for recycling where you can always try again next year."

Construction of O'Shaughnessy Dam in Hetch Hetchy Valley began, though the dam was not completed until 1934. In spite of legal requirements that the hydroelectric power be sold only by public agencies, San Francisco sold it to the Pacific Gas and Electric Company, which owned the transmission lines.

Other river activists would share John Muir's setbacks: technical reports supporting dams; grass roots campaigns beaten by quiet but powerful lobbying of the developers with support of local newspapers; western congressmen voting together for dams; a lack of interest in alternatives; and government officials' and congressmen's refusal to accept the view that the natural river held more than a frivolous recreational value. These same problems would be seen in 1980 during the Stanislaus River debate near John Muir's old battleground.

Public attitudes had a long way to go before the values of a free-flowing river would be widely recognized. If the threat to Yosemite National Park had been logging or commercialization or almost anything but a water project, it might have been stopped. As Ludwik and Eileen Teclaff put it, "Nonuse of wilderness was an accepted (if precariously established) principle by the end of the nineteenth century: nonuse of water was not."[5]

Even with Muir and the preservationists, the struggle was not so much to save a river as to save a national park. Before the Hetch Hetchy proposal, other dams were built on the nearby Stanislaus River at Upper and Lower Strawberry, Utica, Union, Spicer Meadow, and Relief—all flooding outstanding scenic areas but drawing little if any opposition. And at Hetch Hetchy, the river was secondary; it happened to flow through the wilderness valley that looked like Yosemite. The name Tuolumne was seldom even used in the dam fighters' rhetoric. Among the preservationists, the land was the main issue. Rivers for their own values would not receive much attention for many years.

A struggle of Hetch Hetchy's scale would not be repeated for nearly half a century. Few people objected to dams when rivers seemed to be worthless—the continent had no scarcity of running water. In the 1930s dams were one solution to unemployment. World War II and the economic boom immediately following the war spawned few challengers of "progress." Gifford Pinchot's idea of conservation prevailed: the utilitarian view overwhelmed preservation, perhaps more with water management than with other resources. Teddy Roosevelt championed the protection of forests but launched the federal damming of the West with his Bull Moose enthusiasm. Historian Samuel Hays said, "The building of dams and the development of water—especially for irrigation—was regarded as 'conservation.' "[6]

Hetch Hetchy was not a turning point but a cry of dissent in a culture poised for massive river development, a culture that was nearly oblivious to environmental costs. In the name of conservation, the 1902 reclamation act was passed to dam the rivers of the West. The year Hetch Hetchy was lost, Frederick Haynes Newell, an architect of the reclamation program, wrote,

> The achievement of the national government in conserving flood or waste waters and in converting parts of the desert into prosperous farms is both proof and prophecy of what can and should be done on a larger scale. . . . There is every incentive, therefore, for the young man of the present day to seriously and persistently study these matters and to identify himself with the great forward movement which must necessarily take place along these lines.[7]

W. J. McGee, Roosevelt's chief advisor on water programs, wrote that the "Conquest of Water" was "the single step remaining to be taken before Man becomes master over Nature."[8]

Yet after the Census Bureau announced in 1890 that the frontier was closed, some people sensed that the country had lost its youth and that a reminder of the frontier could survive in wild refuges. The Progressive Movement of 1900–1917 gave the government a role that included not only public development of rivers but also the regulation of private water development, and with this came an unrealized boost to river protection. In the Teddy Roosevelt years, scientific management of resources was started, initially justifying development but preparing the way for studies that would address secondary effects of damming rivers. The developers embraced science to support their cause, not realizing the self-destructive element that they had thereby introduced.

It would be half a century after Hetch Hetchy that a consensus, even then vague, would form for the saving of rivers, yet from 1913 to 1965 the seeds of a movement were planted in many places.

PRIVATE POWER AND PUBLIC PARKS

Unlike the dominant American attitude that private ownership of land should be unhampered by government controls, public rights to water and rivers have had long-standing recognition. Although the idea of "public rights" was always slanted toward development—not preservation— nevertheless the use of water could be planned, where we never had the chance with private land. Common rights to large rivers had been established for navigation in the 1800s, and the first decade of the twentieth century brought federal controls on hydroelectricity.

The General Dam Act of 1906 established federal authority to prohibit certain private power dams. Teddy Roosevelt vetoed a dam on Minnesota's Rainy River in 1908. He stated, "The present policy pursued in making these grants is unwise in giving away the property of the people in the flowing waters to individuals or organizations practically unknown, and granting in perpetuity these valuable privileges."[9] Roosevelt later stopped dam builders on Missouri's James River.

At the 1908 White House Conference of Governors on Conservation, New York's Charles Evans Hughes opposed permits for the Morgan and duPont companies to dam the St. Lawrence and other rivers. He said that the sites "should be preserved and held for the benefit of all the people and should not be surrendered to private interest."[10] In his final act to protect natural resources, Roosevelt withdrew sixteen western rivers from permit eligibility in 1909.

The concern of Roosevelt and the governors was not that rivers be protected as free-flowing streams, but that the public receive the best bargain on the hydroelectricity to be produced and that private utilities not gain a monopoly. Realizing the coming importance of electric power, the Inland Waterways Commission called for better public regulation and warned that power costs could control "the daily life of our people to an unprecedented degree."[11] Between 1909 and 1913 President Taft disapproved a dam on Alabama's Coosa River and reserved 135 other rivers until there were controls to protect the public from higher prices and until regulations assured proper planning within the Pinchot concept of efficiency. Many of the permit denials simply saved the rivers so that the government could dam them later.

In sharp contrast, the state of Wisconsin recognized natural river values and passed a law in 1905 stopping dams on the Brule River and another in 1908 to save the Flambeau,[12] but such concern was the exception during that era. Even the limited public rights championed by Roosevelt faced intense opposition by power companies, and the controls would later be compromised by business-oriented administrations.

The Federal Power Act of 1920, born of the Progressive Movement, required dam builders to apply for Federal Power Commission (FPC) permits granting fifty-year leases and offering limited protection of public rights. The FPC, however, was charged with fostering construction and did not consider alternatives. The commission could also allow dams in national parks, and this provision led to the next episode in the protection of rivers.

In 1916 the National Parks Act had stated that "the fundamental purpose of the . . . parks . . . is to conserve the scenery and the natural historic objects and the wildlife therein, and to provide for the enjoyment of the same in such manner and by such means as will leave them unimpaired for the enjoyment of future generations." Several years later the National Parks Association (NPA) was started by Robert Sterling Yard, a friend of park service director Stephen Mather, as a lobby for protection. One of the first tests of the park service and the NPA was to stop the licensing of hydroelectric dams.

In 1921 the parks supporters were successful, and President Wilson signed the Jones–Esch Act banning FPC permits from existing parks but not from future parks. Eventually the act was changed to prohibit licenses in all national parks or monuments, but this simply redirected the dam builders' lobbyists from the FPC office to Congress, where protection could be overridden.

In 1920 Idaho irrigation districts proposed three dams in the Falls River basin of Yellowstone Park. The NPA argued, maybe with too much alarm, that "the granting of even one irrigation privilege in any national park will mark the beginning of a swift end; within five years thereafter all our national parks will be controlled by local irrigationists, and complete commercialization inevitably will follow."[13] The bill allowing the dams passed the Senate but was beaten on the House floor. Taking a slightly different tack, dam supporters proposed to delete the Falls River basin from park boundaries, but this also failed. The case never received the attention given to Hetch Hetchy eight years earlier, but the Yellowstone debate was probably the first successful opposition to a major dam proposal, and it reversed the Hetch Hetchy precedent of allowing a dam in a national park (a distinction often given to the Echo Park case, which came thirty-five years later).

Another proposal was introduced by the Yellowstone Irrigation Association to build a six-foot-high dam at Yellowstone Lake's outlet near Fishing Bridge. Business groups in Livingston, Montana, tried to sidestep opposition by calling the structure a "weir" instead of a "dam," by claiming that the higher level of the lake would make the park more beautiful, and by saying that navigation would be improved on the distant Missouri River. Labeling the scheme a "war on the national parks," the NPA claimed the support of five million members from groups including the American Civic Association, the Boone and Crockett clubs, the Audubon Society, the Sierra Club, the Civic Club of Philadelphia, the American Automobile Association, the Massachusetts Forestry Association, and the National Institute of Architects. This diversity is enough to make modern coalition builders envious. America's most famous landscape architect, Frederick Law Olmsted, spoke out to stop the dam.

With rhetoric equaled by James Watt sixty years later, Interior Secretary Albert Fall in 1922 called the national park defenders "meddlers interfering with the sworn duty of the Secretary of the Interior" and said that the Yellowstone dam was "being taken into politics" and would be built.[14] The same year, Fall received $404,000 from two oil companies in the Teapot Dome Scandal. He was eventually convicted and became the first cabinet officer ever imprisoned for a serious crime committed while in office. Much of President Harding's bad reputation was ascribed to Fall.[15]

Four bills were introduced for the Fishing Bridge Dam, and to fight them, the NPA built on the Hetch Hetchy experience in grass roots organizing. In Montana, opposition to the dam grew, especially from women's clubs, and the sponsoring congressman lost the 1922 election by a 2–1 margin to an antidam candidate, ending the threat.

In 1927 another bill would have allowed Bechler Meadows Dam in Yellowstone. Park superintendent Horace M. Albright, who later became a distinguished National Park Service director, described the basin as one of the park's most interesting primitive areas. The NPA called for the dam's defeat and fought to avoid the "nationally depreciated desolation" of Jackson Lake Reservoir, which had been built by the Reclamation Service on the Snake River at the Tetons. Dozens of groups opposed the Bechler Meadows proposal, and it was killed.

Through all of these debates, it was still parks, not rivers, that were the main issue. About the Yellowstone Lake dam the NPA's Robert Yard said, "Of course we all want this water used in some proper way. One way would be to dam the high fifty-mile Yellowstone Valley north of the Park boundary. But the schemers do not want to do the trick that way, for they would have to purchase the land."[16] In an NPA article about Bechler Meadows Dam, Henry van Dyke wrote, "Let the dam be built, if it is needed. But build it outside the park, lower down, where it will spoil nothing," as if the river outside the park was "nothing." Robert Yard's alternative—Allenspur Dam—was proposed and fought in later years.

Other parks were endangered. In 1921 a joint international commission had recommended an irrigation dam that would turn Glacier National Park's Upper and Lower St. Mary's Lakes—jewels of the northern Rockies—into one reservoir, impounding water ten miles into the park. In 1922 copper miners applied for a Grand Canyon dam at Diamond Creek.

In the southern Sierra, John Muir had drawn his recommended boundaries for a national park, but dam proposals by Los Angeles thwarted protection efforts for decades. Kings Canyon National Park was considered in 1911 and in the 1920s, but the area included the dam sites of Tehipite Valley, shadowed by a granite dome 3,500 feet high, and of Cedar Grove, now a campground. Robert Yard wrote about these sites: "They are both deeper, more rugged, more romantic and in the writer's opinion, far more beautiful than the Hetch Hetchy Valley. . . . The Tehipite Valley is nothing short of the most inspiring chasm in the Sierra. It ranks in its own way with the greatest American spectacles!" With an average depth of 5,700 feet and a maximum depth of 8,240 feet, Kings Canyon is the deepest canyon in the country, exceeding even Hells Canyon of the Snake, the Salmon River canyon, and the Grand Canyon.

The NPA lobbied for a "power proof park," and the San Joaquin Power Company was willing to withdraw applications for dams on Kings River tributaries at Roaring River and Bubbs Creek to allow passage of a park bill in 1922, but the Los Angeles Bureau of Power and Light blocked the additions. Though farmers proposed Kings Canyon dams of their own, Central Valley cities fought the "monstrous and selfish schemes" of Los Angeles and called it "the dictator of central California."[17]

In a rare ruling favoring wild rivers, the FPC denied the permits in 1923, stating that "all said developments are located in whole or in part within the proposed extension of the Sequoia National Park." The FPC also rejected Los Angeles's proposals for the nearby San Joaquin and Kaweah Rivers. Still, the park expansions remained unapproved, and Los Angeles waited for the opportune time to push its plan.

WHOSE RIVER IN THE OWENS VALLEY?

Whereas antidam efforts in the early 1900s were mostly aimed at national parks, violence broke out in the Owens Valley of California over the diversion of water from farms and ranches. With plans to channel Sierra Nevada runoff south, Los Angeles agents had secretly bought land and water rights before Owens Valley residents knew what was happening, and the Reclamation Service, which had supported local irrigation from the Owens River, reversed its stance to favor Los Angeles. After President Theodore Roosevelt's approval of the city's project, expanses of sagebrush were declared a forest reserve to block settlement of lands needed for the city's water system. The aqueduct was finished in 1913.

Southern California businessmen involved in the project knew that it would yield four times the needed amount of water. They bought land in the San Fernando Valley and later collected rich profits from subdivisions when the Owens supply arrived. To store the water, Saint Francis Dam was hurriedly built in 1926, but two years later it broke, killing four hundred people.

Where seven hundred thousand cattle and sheep had grazed in the Owens Valley during the 1870s, the farms and ranches were now scorched. Few people questioned the city's legal claim to the water, but the moral right to turn the farmers' homeland into a desert was another matter.[18]

Armed residents took control of an irrigation canal that was to be closed for the aqueduct, and they pushed the city's grading equipment into the water. At 1:00 A.M. on May 21, 1924, dynamite blasted an aqueduct spillway, and water poured onto the desert. Forty people from Inyo County scattered from the site, and the Owens Valley war began. Dead cats were thrown into the city's water; when more than twelve holes were blasted in the aqueduct, Los Angeles officials stationed armed guards with orders to kill. Legal battles were fought, and the city eventually passed a $12 million bond issue to buy more land. When only 1 percent of the property remained in private ownership, the fighting ceased.

This is one of few water projects that bred violence, and it should not be confused with river protection. The residents' interest was not in saving the river. The questions were, Who would enjoy the wealth and livelihoods delivered by the water? And, How much would the local people be paid?

Having dried up the river, Los Angeles began pumping groundwater during a 1929 drought. After completion of a second aqueduct in 1970, pumping increased. The seventy-five-square-mile Owens Lake became a dust pit. New fights over the eastern Sierra water began, and the aqueduct was bombed again during a drought in 1976. Statewide concern focused on the evaporation of Mono Lake, a unique refuge for wildlife, as Los Angeles intercepted the water that had filled the landlocked lake near Yosemite.

SAVING THE SPECTACULAR

Another episode during the 1920s, although scarcely publicized, marked an important success for river protection and a milestone of private investment. In Kentucky, the Cumberland River plunges over the East's largest waterfall except Niagara. Cumberland Falls's moonbow—the only one in the world known to regularly appear—is a white "rainbow" during clear nights. In 1928 private developers proposed to divert the water around the falls for hydroelectric power. Robert Blair, a local businessman, organized the Cumberland Falls Preservation Association and persuaded T. Coleman duPont to buy the falls and surrounding land for $400,000 and deed it to the state with strings attached: "Said property shall not be used . . . for the production of hydroelectric energy." The purchase is one of the outstanding examples of private money being used to save a river. In the 1950s another hydroelectric plan was announced by the Army Corps of Engineers, but Blair reactivated his association, and in 1968 the corps dropped the project.[19] With the Cumberland, river protection expanded beyond national parks to include this spectacular falls.

RIVERS FOR FISH

The saving of Cumberland Falls was exceptional during the Harding and Hoover eras, which were otherwise flush for private hydroelectric developers. Support for government dams was also growing indomitably. Dams were viewed as a progressive part of responsible government, economic advancement, and resource management. Through the 1920s and 1930s, magazines, including *Scientific American*, published articles full of technological hype about dams but without thought to the land that was flooded, the changes in the environment, or other effects.

Yet river protection slowly spread from concern for national parks to broader interests in fish and wildlife. Outdoor reporter Miller Freeman wrote about power dams in the July 16, 1925, *Seattle Star*. "We all remember when the railroads were very nearly the government of this country. This has been in a measure corrected, but a new evil has arisen overnight. . . . The Federal Power Commission is a creature of the power interests. . . . Would it not be well for the public to slow up a bit in its insistence on development of natural resources so far in advance of our needs?"[20]

Founded in 1922, the Izaak Walton League was the first conservation group to attract a large membership and to campaign for protection of rivers and fish. When the league's influence declined in the late 1940s, the National Wildlife Federation, formed in 1936, took over this role.

In the 1930s and 1940s, leaders of young conservation groups objected to the eradication of salmon on the Columbia River. With more success, Oregon fishermen fought dams proposed for the Rogue and McKenzie Rivers. In North Carolina, the U.S. Biological Survey, the Izaak Walton League, and the Audubon Society argued for protection of aquatic habitat and fought a corps project for reservoirs and diversions of South Carolina's Santee River to the Cooper River, which was nevertheless built in 1941.[21]

The Izaak Walton League tried to save the Upper Mississippi River Wildlife and Bird Refuge from the corps's dredging of a nine-foot-deep channel with dams and locks for 564 miles to Minneapolis. Although the conservationists failed to stop the dams, they won some concessions to protect habitat during construction.

The Fish and Wildlife Coordination Act of 1934 required federal dam builders to consult with the Fish and Wildlife Service in the Department of the Interior, the first major law to protect wildlife from water projects. Another act in 1958 reinforced this role.

River conservation in the first two decades of the century had been to save parks, and now in the 1930s and 1940s it recognized few values beyond fish and wildlife. Most of this concern was further limited to fishing and hunting. For example, the lower Colorado was a poor sport fishing river, so Kenneth A. Reid, director of the Izaak Walton League, supported Hoover Dam, calling the river "too thin to plow and too thick to drink."

STATE PARK RIVERS

Opposition to dams expanded to state parks at Pennsylvania's Clarion River in 1940. Proposed as the eighth flood control reservoir in an Army Corps of Engineers system to protect Pittsburgh, Mill Creek Dam would have flooded 103 acres of rare virgin hemlock in Cook Forest State Park.

After local conservationists fought the dam, the National Resources Planning Board—created by Franklin D. Roosevelt to strive for water policy reform—hired Bernard Frank, a specialist in watershed management, to study the corps's proposal. He reported that with reservoir flooding and resulting wind damage to remaining trees, 85 percent of the virgin forest would die within ten years, and he recommended two smaller dams outside the park. The Pennsylvania Federation of Sportsmen's Clubs joined to save the park, and even the mayor of Pittsburgh wrote to the Bureau of the Budget that "this monument of nature" had "social and aesthetic values which would justify a modest increase in expense." In 1942 the chief of engineers ordered that alternate plans be drawn, but these were not economic.[22] The corps returned to the Clarion in 1970 to propose a larger dam at St. Petersburg, but this was also stopped.

AT HOME IN THE VALLEY

In the 1940s dam builders faced a different kind of opposition, so basic to the American way of life. People began fighting to save their homes and farms. Along the French Broad River, residents fought the Tennessee Valley Authority (TVA) over Douglas Dam, though most of the publicity was given to the loss of potential marble mines.[23] As with other dam proposals of the early 1940s, government officials said that the project was needed for the war effort, and it was built. In the media, including the popular film *Wild River*, local people were characterized as backward hillbillies with no understanding of progress, yet in 1941 the Tennessee Farm Bureau presidents wrote, "Could not . . . other power sites [be] found that would not result in such profound economic and social disturbance and maladjustments to people resident in the reservoir areas . . . ? There is no price that can compensate people for these values in a home and a farm."[24]

In 1946 people along the Cumberland River below Nashville fought a proposed TVA dam and supported two smaller Army Corps of Engineers dams. The Lower Cumberland Association stated that the farmland to be flooded was seven times more valuable than the power to be produced, but the TVA built the project anyway and much of the homeowners' property is now a part of the Land Between the Lakes recreation area[25] (dubbed "Land Under the Lakes" by critics). As of the late 1940s, TVA reported that 13,638 families had been moved for reservoirs and that 593,651 acres would be flooded. Landowners, however, were unorganized, the dambuilding momentum continued, and most people remained oblivious to the values of free-flowing rivers. TVA director David Lilienthal wrote in 1953, "For the first time in the history of the nation, the resources of a river were not only to be 'envisioned in their entirety'; they were to be developed in that unity which nature herself regards her resources."[26]

The landowners' view was shown in a painting by Lowell Hayes titled *A TVA Commonplace*, shown at the Smithsonian Institution in 1982. One side of an eight-by-eight-foot panel showed homes, barns, fences, children playing, cows grazing, boys fishing, and other details of rural life. The opposite side of the panel showed a landless sea with the caption "In the greater Tennessee Valley the TVA has done much to eradicate rural poverty."

Mountain people did not want to be evicted, but neither did they fight with force or believe that they could stop the government. Elsie Spurgeon, one of three hundred residents who was forced to move in the late 1930s for Youghiogheny Dam in Pennsylvania said, "People just didn't think they had any say in the matter."

But in the 1940s, residents of Kansas's Blue Valley organized against a dam, marking a new determination to save homes and farms. Tuttle Creek Dam had been authorized for corps construction and would flood fifty thousand acres of farmland and nine villages housing four thousand people. Residents delayed the proposal for a decade, but after a flood in 1951, Kansas City lobbied for construction. By this time some planners were arguing for small headwaters dams instead of large downriver dams;[27] Blue Valley gave national publicity to the debate. *Reader's Digest* published an article by Elmer T. Peterson called "Big-Dam Foolishness," and the same title was later used for one of the first books opposing dams. *Farm Journal* called Blue Valley "one of the richest valleys in Kansas."[28] Unlike most other angry but despairing landowners, the Kansas people testified at hearings where they asked why their lands should be sacrificed for more industry on Kansas City's floodplain. The corps answered that to defer would be "dangerous" because levees that the corps had constructed downstream would be "deathtraps" without the dam.[29] With an election campaign then unequaled in dam fights, local people ran a candidate for Congress against a fourth-term Republican incumbent, and even against the momentum of Eisenhower's victory, the dam fighters won, electing the district's first Democrat in a century. But it was too late. In 1952 Harry Truman said, "Nobody can save the valley." Campaigning for president, Dwight Eisenhower said, "I sympathize with citizens who object to Federal encroachment in their affairs," but he did not stop construction, which began in 1953.

The next year, Kansans fought another dam at Glen Elder, where the local newspaper editor wrote, "The people are against it, but it seems there's nothing we can do about it, because the higher-ups have ordained that the dam must be built." Landowners were speaking out against government projects, but a sense of hopelessness still prevailed. On Montana's South Fork of the Flathead, Hungry Horse Dam went unopposed, a local resident saying, "Everybody just figured it would go through. You didn't hear anything about it." In Missouri, the Ozark Protective Association delayed dams on the Current River until preservation programs succeeded in the mid-

1960s, but this was exceptional, and landowners would not consistently win until the 1970s.

A BROADER APPEAL

The Potomac River attracted a larger base of opposition to river destruction in the 1940s when the corps identified twenty-five dam sites within the basin. Seneca Dam would flood thirty-five miles between Washington and Harpers Ferry. Three dams would block gorges within the Washington area, and others would impound the Shenandoah River. The main purpose was to dilute pollution and improve the city's water supply.

Fishing groups, including the Izaak Walton League and the League of Maryland Sportsmen, fought the plan and were joined by the National Capitol Park and Planning Commission and other groups. Frederick Law Olmsted, Jr., argued for protection of the Chesapeake and Ohio Canal, historic sites, gorges, islands, and forests, making the Potomac one of the first cases in which historic sites and the more commonplace features of the natural environment were emphasized as reasons to save a river. Farmers and landowners joined, 1,200 of them crowding angrily to a meeting called by the corps. Railroads fought the plan because their tracks would be eliminated. Few cases had attracted such solid opposition, and probably none had drawn such diverse opponents. The corps settled back and waited for a better time to reintroduce the plan.[30]

STILL NOT SACRED

In spite of the preservation precedent set at Yellowstone and Kings Canyon, proposals for dams in national parks did not die easily. Designation of Kings Canyon Park in 1940 left important dam sites unprotected. Facing its postwar population boom in 1949, Los Angeles renewed an FPC application for six Kings Canyon dams: Zumwalt Meadows, Sentinel, Paradise Valley, Tehipite Valley, Cedar Grove, and the Middle Fork–South Fork confluence, all with magnificent scenery. Park superintendent E. T. Scoyen wrote, "No proposal ever made relative to any national park ever carried the seeds of such vast destruction as is now faced by Kings Canyon."[31] Martin Litton opposed the dams in a *Los Angeles Times* article, writing that with an average depth of 5,700 feet, Kings Canyon is "easily the deepest canyon of the Western Hemisphere if not the entire globe. . . . For many Californians it would be hard to believe that another Hetch Hetchy can ever happen." By this time Central Valley farmers had bought water from another dam on the Kings River, and fearing that the hydroelectric plan would jeopardize irrigation, they joined the park supporters in fighting Los Angeles.

Several sites were in the national park and could not be dammed without congressional approval. After alternatives were studied, the dam plans were withdrawn, and in 1965 Tehipite Valley and Cedar Grove were finally added to the park, ending forty-five years of threats to the upper Kings River.

Other parks were also threatened. The National Parks Association had testified in 1937 against the Big Thompson Aqueduct to be tunneled under Rocky Mountain National Park, but Interior Secretary Ickes reluctantly approved it.[32] In 1949 the Mining City Dam on Kentucky's Green River at Mammoth Cave National Park was proposed to flood the Echo, Styx, and Roaring Rivers—unique underground streams and habitat of blind fish—but was stopped.

In Montana, conservationists faced the Army Corps of Engineers' first major threat to a national park river. As one unit of a seven-reservoir plan for the upper Columbia basin, Glacier View Dam, proposed in 1948, would flood 19,460 acres in Glacier National Park and twenty-five miles of the North Fork of the Flathead for flood control and power. Promoters argued that with the dam, industry could move inland from the coast and not be so vulnerable to enemy attack.[33] The project was opposed by the Sierra Club in their largest dam fight since Hetch Hetchy, by the National Parks Association, and by the Wilderness Society.

Newton B. Drury, National Park Service director, had been praised for saving the parks from wholesale development in the name of national security during World War II, and about Glacier View he said, "Eight thousand acres of virgin forest would be flooded, including one of the finest ponderosa pine stands in North America. . . . Threatened with permanent destruction . . . is an extraordinarily fine sample of original America."[34] The Sierra Club's David Brower, not one to support dams, called for development of an alternate site on Montana's Clark Fork River at Knowles, "because adequate development there could end the threat of upstream dams that would encroach on a national park, on a wilderness area, and on lands of high scenic and resource values that should be dedicated." The sites at Glacier View, Knowles, and Paradise (another Clark Fork proposal) were not developed, but Hungry Horse Dam, near Glacier National Park on the South Fork of the Flathead, destroyed a wild river that local people said was the best in a region of stunning streams.

In 1956 the corps proposed Smoky Range Dam on the North Fork of the Flathead as an alternate to Glacier View. Opposition culminated in national wild and scenic river designation for the Flathead in 1976, ending three decades of dam proposals on this crystal-clear river, one of the nation's finest for whitewater canoeing and camping. Canadian logging and coal mining continued to threaten the Flathead's remarkable water quality.

WILDERNESS, WEST AND EAST

Though not receiving congressional protection until 1964, some of the finest untouched areas of the West had been set aside as wilderness and primitive areas by the Forest Service. Dams were proposed in some of these, and river conservationists expanded their influence beyond the parks. In 1948 the Wilderness Society's Howard Zahniser testified against Wilson Dam, planned for flood control on the North Fork of the Sun River in Montana's Bob Marshall Wilderness: "We desperately need a national inventory of outdoor recreation needs, carried on with a determination to plan all our resource development programs in the light of the data from such an inventory."[35] The dam was not built, and the inventory eventually led to a nationwide recreation study and recommendations for a national rivers system. Other dams were proposed but not built in wild sections of Utah's Uinta Mountains and in Colorado's Flat Tops Wilderness.

The largest protected wilderness in the East became the target of dam builders in 1945. In the Adirondack Park, "forever wild" by order of the New York state constitution, the state Water Resources Commission proposed Higley Mountain Dam to flood the Moose River and the Adirondacks' best deer yarding area. The project was one of the first dam controversies to appear on billboards, on television, and in the Supreme Court. Statewide, voters finally killed the dam by plugging a loophole in the constitution. The commission proposed another Moose River site to flood four thousand acres at Panther Mountain. This was also voted down, and in 1950 the governor signed a bill banning the dam.

With fears that New York City's water supply would run short, threats to Adirondack rivers increased in the 1950s. Gooley Dam would have flooded sixteen thousand acres of the park and a reach of the Hudson River that John Kauffmann in *Flow East* called the "grandest of all whitewater runs in the East." The Adirondack Hudson River Association promoted alternatives for New York City, including water metering to cut waste. A bill was eventually passed unanimously and signed by the governor banning any dam on the upper Hudson.

In the Adirondacks and in national parks, it was for water development more than land development that the laws protecting the parks were challenged. Whereas the damming of the Hudson was plausible, the strip-mining of the Adirondacks' Mt. Marcy would have been anathema. But through public debate, the rivers were gaining status earlier given only to special lands. Describing the importance of the Hudson, an Adirondack ranger said that the river was "part of the soul of the Adirondacks. To dam it up and destroy it would be like bulldozing off the high peaks." The conventional wisdom was gradually accepting that, like mountains, rivers were worth saving. Widespread recognition of the value of deserts and wetlands later followed the same pattern.

A GREATER SENSE OF LOSS

Opposition to dams through the 1940s was sporadic and based mainly on the saving of outstanding valleys, but a new consciousness about rivers and dams was taking hold. In April 1952, Dr. Julian A. Steyermark wrote in *Scientific Monthly* about the destruction of "valuable scientific records" by corps projects; for example, Bull Shoals Dam on Missouri's White River eliminated a rare species of mulberry from the state. An article in *Science* stated that four hundred archaeological sites were buried by Bull Shoals. In a 1949 *Harper's* magazine, Robert deRoos and Arthur A. Maas wrote one of the first powerful exposés against the corps: "The Lobby That Can't Be Licked." In 1952 an *American Forests* article criticized the corps's damming of the Angelina River in Texas, where two hundred thousand acres of productive forests were lost, and the flooding of twenty-two thousand acres of timber along the South Fork of the Flathead.

Criticism against dams expanded from specific cases to generic issues, though the criticism did not hit hard and make much difference until the 1970s. In 1950, Bernard Frank and Anthony Netboy wrote in *Water, Land, and People*, "Finally, despite the expenditure of hundreds of millions of dollars annually for damming, dredging, cleansing, and otherwise stabilizing and normalizing our major rivers, we do not seem perceptibly to be reducing floods, siltation, or contamination." In March 1951, E. Laurence Palmer wrote in *Nature* magazine,

> Dams are not undisguised blessings. . . . We must frankly admit that we as a
> group support the building of a given dam for a specific purpose, and are

willing to sacrifice certain other things when we do this. In spite of what the
politicians tell us, we cannot build a power dam that will be of maximum
use for flood control, for irrigation and also provide superior facilities for
recreation and for wildlife.

A 1954 *Audubon* article reported that with desalting plants and atomic
power, "scientific progress" may make big dams obsolete.

In 1950 the President's Water Resources Policy Commission addressed
the irreversible effects of dams, stating, "There is a sobering finality in the
construction of a river basin development, and it behooves us to be sure we
are right before we go ahead."[36] Under a contract to write history for the
corps, Michael C. Robinson stated that by the 1950s, "Dams came to be
regarded as despoilers of immense expanses of beautiful landscape, valuable
forests and plant habitat, as well as historic and archaeological sites." But,
Robinson added, "The Corps was in a position to shrug off a few setbacks
at the hands of conservationists and other critics. Due to its huge inventory
of authorized projects, resources and emphasis could be shifted elsewhere
and plans kept on the shelf until the political climate was more favorable."

THE EISENHOWER SLOWDOWN

Eisenhower reversed the New Deal philosophy of government spending
and public hydroelectric power. He referred to the TVA as "creeping socialism." The Bureau of the Budget sent the president a memo stating that big
dams had been "spectacular but exceedingly costly" and that reclamation
projects had been authorized to meet "political demands."[37] Eisenhower
vetoed two rivers and harbors authorization bills. Ted Schad, who drafted
the veto messages while working for the Bureau of the Budget, said, "Many
of the projects had no reports prepared, and we wanted to see cost sharing.
Federal money was being given for levees on the lower Mississippi with no
local cost sharing at all; it was one of the biggest ripoffs I can think of, and
it drained wetlands too."[38] Congress sustained the two vetoes, then passed
a bill in 1958 excluding most of the uneconomic projects. Pointing out that
executive policies change like the wind, Schad added, "Through the following years all the bad projects were added back in."

Eisenhower stressed a federal "partnership" with state and private-
developer building projects but maintained a "no new starts" policy for the
corps and Bureau of Reclamation (with several major exceptions, including

Echo Park and Kinzua dams). Schad said, "None of this was in the sense of preserving rivers—it was promoting private investment."

For Hells Canyon of the Snake River, the Eisenhower administration turned its back on corps and Bureau of Reclamation plans and approved three Idaho Power Company dams—Brownlee, Oxbow, and Hells Canyon—flooding the best rapids of the country's second-deepest canyon, hundreds of miles of salmon habitat, and a whitewater run that outfitter Martin Litton said "was comparable in many ways to the Grand Canyon itself." Some conservationists supported the dams as alternatives to an even more destructive Bureau of Reclamation proposal at the Nez Perce site that would have blocked both the Salmon and the Snake Rivers.

In retaliation against Eisenhower's "no new starts" policy, the Senate formed a select committee to press for business as usual. Ted Schad was chosen to write the committee's report. "I approached it as a professional job," Schad said, "but some senators were like dogs at my heels saying, 'When are you going to get to the need for new projects?'" The report found pollution—not Eisenhower's austerity—to be the largest water resource problem.

ECHO PARK

The national attention brought by Hetch Hetchy was not repeated until Echo Park was to be flooded. In northern Colorado near the Utah border, the Green and Yampa Rivers meet in red sandstone canyons. Just below the confluence is an oasis of cottonwoods, called Echo Park because cliffs echo voices perfectly. Steamboat Rock rises two thousand feet straight from the water. Just below lies Whirlpool Canyon; above is Ladore Canyon of the Green and a wilderness reach of the Yampa. The Green River is larger than the Colorado, where the two later meet, and the Yampa was the Colorado basin's only large undammed river until Stagecoach Dam was built in the 1980s.

Because of dinosaur skeletons trapped in sediment, Woodrow Wilson designated eighty acres as Dinosaur National Monument in 1915. A national monument is protected like a national park, the main difference being that Congress designates a park, whereas a president designates a monument. Franklin Roosevelt enlarged the monument in 1938 to protect about one hundred miles of the Green and Yampa canyons.

As part of the Upper Colorado River Storage Project calling for nine dams, the Bureau of Reclamation in 1943 proposed two reservoirs to flood most of the monument's canyons so that upper-basin states could withdraw irrigation water and still deliver a prescribed amount to California, Nevada, and Arizona. Echo Park Dam, 525 feet high, was proposed as the upstream version of Hoover Dam, with revenues from hydroelectricity to pay for irrigation.

National Park Service director Newton Drury opposed the dams. When Interior Secretary Oscar Chapman said that he supported the sites because of their low evaporation rates, Drury asked, "How about the evaporation rate of the national parks and monuments?" In 1950 Chapman approved Echo Park Dam in a memorandum to the Bureau of Reclamation and the park service. In the style of Pinchot, Chapman stated that his choice was "in the interest of the greatest public good."[39] Drury resigned. Chapman also supported using the Everglades as a bombing range—a proposal that even the Defense Department rejected. In *Echo Park Controversy*, Owen Stratton and Phillip Sirotkin suggested that western democratic congressmen, expecting to lose their elections if the dam were stopped, spoke to President Truman. The president said, "It has always been my opinion that food for coming generations is much more important than bones of the Mesozoic period."[40] (The dinosaurs were not even in the threatened area.) Spectacular wild canyons were about to be lost, and most people did not even know that the place existed.

The debate became the conservation issue of the 1950s, bringing the question of national parks and wild rivers to the attention of more people than any earlier case. Devereux Butcher, director of the National Parks Association, wrote about the threat and gained allies. Authors Bernard DeVoto and Wallace Stegner brought an unprecedented quality of journalism to the cause of river protection. Ulysses S. Grant III, a retired army engineer and president of the American Planning and Civic Association, argued against the dams. The Wilderness Society's Howard Zahniser made some of his strongest pleas for wildlands protection, and David Brower—the first full-time director of the Sierra Club—built his rising career on the saving of this place.

Born in 1912, two years before John Muir died, Brower grew up in Berkeley, California, and became an avid mountaineer. While hiking on Pilot Knob in 1933 he met photographer Ansel Adams, who later proposed to his fellow Sierra Club board members that Brower be hired as executive secretary, but the board declined. In World War II Brower taught climbing to soldiers and served as an intelligence officer, earning three battle stars and a Bronze Star. He returned to California and worked as an editor for the University of California Press. In 1952, climbing partner Richard Leonard proposed Brower as the first full-time executive director of the Sierra Club. This time the board approved.[41]

The commitments of most conservation leaders began with outdoor activities. For Brower these were hiking and climbing. His river traveling was limited to a few desert canyons, but fighting dams is what built Brower's reputation and started an important part of the environmental movement.

As Sierra Club executive director, Brower's first major effort was to save Echo Park, which presented a new challenge requiring opposition to the Department of the Interior. The old club leadership was inclined to accept the dams, but influenced by Brower, the board now decided to fight. Brower became known for his adamant views on park protection, leading an activist element of the club that thrived on conflict and sought publicity in national campaigns. In *Voices for the Wilderness*, Brower wrote, "Polite conservationists leave no mark except the scars on the land," and, "When a living heritage is being put to death—perpetual, eternal, permanent death— there is no fairness in giving the attacker and the savior equal time."

The club did not object to the Upper Colorado River Storage Project because such opposition would alienate many congressmen, but it sought an amendment to eliminate the Echo Park dams. As Elmo Richardson wrote in *Dams, Parks and Politics*, "The burden of these polemics was tact-fully more pro-park than it was anti-dam." Brower wrote, "The Club does not oppose a sound upper Colorado project that does not adversely affect Parks, Monuments, or Dedicated Wilderness."[42] The conservationists encouraged alternatives to Echo Park—one of these they would later deeply regret.

Dam opponents again thought that they were fighting for the entire park system; if a dam were built in Dinosaur, the precedent would support old proposals at Glacier, Kings Canyon, and the Grand Canyon. The original upper Colorado basin plan plotted projects in a dozen parks, but Echo Park was the most serious and imminent threat to the system since Hetch Hetchy. Congressman Wayne Aspinall verified the conservationists' concern when he said, "If we let them knock out Echo Park Dam, we'll hand them a tool they'll use for the next hundred years."[43]

Ted Schad, working on Echo Park Dam as a budget analyst for the Bureau of Reclamation, denied the importance of the precedent: "The bureau was not trying to eliminate the parks. It was just a good power proj-ect, and the bureau had an old water reservation for the dam."

In the *Saturday Evening Post*, Bernard DeVoto alerted the nation and said that Dinosaur was important "as wilderness that is preserved intact."[44] DeVoto blasted the dam many times in his column in *Harper's*.[45] In *Speaking for Nature*, Paul Brooks wrote that DeVoto "may well have been the most potent one-man force for the conservation of nature in the mid-twentieth century."

Wyoming Senator Joseph C. O'Mahoney argued for the dam in *Collier's*: "Water, precious and priceless water, actually is being wasted. It is being allowed to flow on down the Colorado River, over the wonderworking Hoover Dam and finally into the Gulf of California." He stressed that the upper-basin congressmen favored the dam and that the opposition had "an incidental and sentimental reason." He wrote that many dinosaurs may have "died in uncontrolled floods" and that the river's "dangerous rapids" would be "eliminated." He added, "The basic issue here is between the sentimental and aesthetic feelings of some people, mostly outside the area, and the welfare of the several hundred thousand who live there."[46]

The *Denver Post* charged that the entire preservationist attitude was unwestern, but Utah-born DeVoto advised westerners not to criticize easterners "too loudly or too obnoxiously. You might make them so mad that they would stop paying for your water developments." He added, "Massachusetts will pay a larger part of the cost of any dam in the project than Colorado will."[47]

In *Collier's*, Ulysses S. Grant III called for substitute measures that would allow the upper Colorado project to be completed without Echo Park Dam, writing that it would be a tragedy to give up the canyons for "a few acre-feet of water and a few kilowatt hours." His alternatives included Flaming Gorge Dam on the Green (later built) and Cross Mountain on the Yampa (opposed by conservationists and stopped in the 1980s).

In 1955 the *Salt Lake Tribune* wrote, "Echo Dam would turn a hidden wilderness area into a great Scenic Resource." The paper printed an illustration of the proposed reservoir, and editors asked. "What has been obliterated? Between 200 and 300 feet of talus at the base of cliffs rising 2,000 feet and higher—adding much and detracting nothing from the scenery." The Mormons' *Deseret News* called the conservationists' view "romantic tripe."[48]

To generate public support, and to record "what once was" if the dam were built, Wallace Stegner edited *This Is Dinosaur: Echo Park Country and Its Magic Rivers*, writing, "It will not be only the buffalo and the trumpeter swan who need sanctuaries. Our own species is going to need them too. It needs them now." Publisher Alfred Knopf sent copies of the book to all congressmen.

Collier's stressed that this was no local project: "One third, for example, would be paid by the taxpayers of New York, Ohio, Pennsylvania, Illinois and Michigan." *Newsweek's* column about the dam was titled "Pork, Unlimited."[49]

A defense plant, once given as a reason for the dam, was planned for the Ohio River instead. Interior Secretary Chapman reversed his earlier decision, now stating that the dam was "absolutely not necessary." The election of 1952, however, brought Eisenhower's Douglas McKay, a Chevrolet dealer from Salem, Oregon, as secretary of the interior, and contrary to the president's "no new starts" policy, McKay renewed the dam's approval and called the conservationists "long-haired punks."[50] Dam supporters calling themselves the "Aqualantes" campaigned with a Bureau of Reclamation film and a brochure titled "Echo Park—Tomorrow's Playground for Millions of Americans."

David Brower and Howard Zahniser organized support and publicity. Zahniser persuaded a St. Louis chemical manufacturer to fund the cause.[51] Conservationists printed a pamphlet titled "Will You DAM the Scenic Wild Canyons of Our National Park System?" and produced a film that was shown nationwide. In one of the first cases in which river traveling was used to gain political support, the conservationists offered raft trips to show people that the canyons were worth saving, and the number of people floating at Dinosaur grew from 47 in 1950 to 912 in 1954.

The Hoover Commission Task Force on Water and Power reported that the upper Colorado project was a glaring example of subsidies, poor planning, and dubious management. Conservationists took a new attack aimed at costs, which embarrassed Republicans and angered easterners. Even Governor J. Bracken Lee of Utah was hesitant to support the dams because they would add to the "terrific" federal deficit.[52]

At congressional hearings, David Brower held up photographs of Hetch Hetchy before and after it was dammed and said, "If we heed the lesson learned from the tragedy of the misplaced dam in Hetch Hetchy, we can prevent a far more disastrous stumble in Dinosaur National Monument."[53] The conservationists were almost alone because National Park Service employees and Geological Survey scientists, being in the same department as the Bureau of Reclamation, were not allowed to testify.

Southern California was the conservationists' paradoxical ally. Not only would upper Colorado dams cut flows, causing less hydroelectric generation at Hoover Dam, but delays in upstream impounding would also give California more time to use its extra share of the Colorado. However, help from the West Coast was not worth much; dam supporters were quick to associate the environmental groups with the hated California interests that for years had competed with other states for water, and animosity burned hotter.

Echo Park Dam bills passed interior committees of both houses, but mail ran 80–1 against the project and editorials in many papers attacked the dam. Floor action was postponed, giving Brower and the others time to rally.

Hearings in 1955 brought bureau officials, governors, congressmen, water users, utilities, and chambers of commerce touting the dam. Navaho Indians supported the dam after they were promised a tribal irrigation project to be built at Navajo Dam on the San Juan River. Fighting Echo Park Dam were conservationists, eastern congressmen, and educational groups. Minnesota canoeist and author Sigurd Olson asked if "we might not destroy the very things that have made life in America worth cherishing and defending?"

Without belaboring the issues of parks and aesthetics, David Brower exposed a Bureau of Reclamation error in arithmetic about reservoir evaporation and proved that more water would be lost than was reported and that alternate sites would lose less. He said that it "would be making a great mistake to rely upon the figures presented by the Bureau of Reclamation when they cannot add, subtract, multiply, or divide."[54] The bureau had called evaporation the "fundamental issue" for favoring Echo Park, but after Brower's testimony, the evaporation figures were twice revised downward.

In April 1955, Oregon senator Richard Neuberger, in a courageous step for a westerner, offered an amendment to delete Echo Park Dam. Senator Hubert Humphrey supported him, gaining more mileage out of John Muir's defeat by saying, "Where once there was the beautiful Hetch Hetchy Valley . . . there is now the stark, drab reservoir of O'Shaughnessy Dam."[55] The amendment failed, but in the House, Pennsylvania's John Saylor—"Big John"—led the way toward defeat of the dam.

Saylor was one of the first and strongest modern conservationists in the House, later sponsoring the Wilderness Act and the Wild and Scenic Rivers Act. Saylor opposed pork barrel because it could not be justified. Unlike many of his Republican contemporaries, he favored spending for social needs such as education. Help came when Governor Johnson of Colorado called the dam atrocious.

Facing Saylor's insurmountable objections, and fearing that nothing would be passed if the dam were included, the House Committee on Interior and Insular Affairs endorsed the project without Echo Park Dam. For future insurance, the conservationists had lawmakers add a phrase in the Colorado River Storage Project Act of April 11, 1956: "It is the intention of Congress that no dam or reservoir constructed under this Act shall be within any national park or monument." Seventeen years later, at Echo Park's alternate site, David Brower would sue the Bureau of Reclamation over this provision.

With Echo Park the dam fighters proved that they could master the political process and mobilize support. Although David Brower went on to a long and remarkable career, Frank Graham, Jr., wrote in *Audubon* that Echo Park was Brower's "most spectacular success." Some people even say that Echo Park was the birth of the environmental movement or, as John McPhee wrote, "the turning point at which conservation became something more than contour plowing."[56] Roderick Nash wrote that at Echo Park "the American wilderness movement had its finest hour to that date."

Unlike the Hetch Hetchy debate, many more organizations and supporters were available to save Echo Park (the coalition included thirty groups), river supporters raised technical arguments, and congressional leadership was strong. No newspapers campaigned as effectively as had the San Francisco papers for Hetch Hetchy, and Senator Neuberger and Governor Johnson broke the western bloc for the dam.

As with Hetch Hetchy, the point was still to save a park. Few people fought the philosophy of big water development or the loss of wild rivers outside the national park system. This view had served conservationists well, but its limitations were soon to be seen. The irony of saving Echo Park was that Glen Canyon would be dammed.

FIGHTING FOR A FISHERY

Even though Washington state law required fish ladders or hatcheries with new dams, Tacoma City Light built five dams with neither ladders nor hatcheries, while offering the lowest residential electricity rates in the nation and selling even cheaper power to Kaiser Aluminum, Boise–Cascade, and other industries. In the early 1950s, Tacoma proposed Mayfield Dam on the Cowlitz River.

Fishermen objected, but sports columnist Elliot Metcalf of the *Tacoma News Tribune* answered with the boosterism of that era. "Forget your worry, sportsmen . . . rise to move Tacoma ahead to better things industrially and economically. . . . It is inevitable as death that the power productive Cowlitz will be harnessed for the good of all, not set aside for the minority, or few."[57]

Residents near the site joined sport and commercial fishermen, and state agencies attempted to enforce the Dam Sanctuary Act of 1949, which banned dams in Washington's lower Columbia basin. The license was denied by an FPC examiner, who found that the project was not adapted to "beneficial uses," including recreation, and that the need to preserve fish outweighed the need for power. But the FPC granted the license anyway. The state director of fisheries sued and for eight years won court victories ending at the U.S. Supreme Court in 1958, where after a poor presentation by the state attorney general, who had supported the dam before his election, earlier decisions were reversed. Tacoma began building the dam while fishermen appealed to voters statewide in an antidam initiative. They won, but in 1962 the state supreme court ruled that the vote could not stop construction.

Mayfield Dam was finished, but the state required Tacoma City Light to build a hatchery costing $20 million—more than the cost of the turbines and generators. Plagued with diseases, fish required treatment three times to keep them alive to spawn, and the hatchery failed to meet its goals 75 percent of the time.

Even though the Cowlitz was lost, the episode heightened awareness about salmon. A commitment grew through the 1960s, but not as fast as the dams. Fishermen again lost in California, where they fought a Bureau of Reclamation dam and diversion on the Trinity River in 1952, but on the Namekagon River, Wisconsin convinced the FPC to stop a hydroelectric dam because of fisheries, scenic beauty, and recreational values.[58]

THE KINZUA MUD

While park supporters and fishermen fought dams in the West and Midwest, the Seneca Nation of the Iroquois Confederacy tried to save the last Indian lands in Pennsylvania.

In 1794 President George Washington signed the Pickering Treaty—the oldest Indian treaty—granting the Seneca under Chief Cornplanter 30,189 acres along the Allegheny River, including the village of Kinzua (meaning "fish on spear"), and stating that the Indians' land "shall remain theirs, until they choose to sell the same to the people of the United States, who have the right to purchase." The Senecas did not trust the government and refused to sign until the Society of Friends (the Quakers) guaranteed the president's word.

In 1936 Congress authorized the Army Corps of Engineers to build Kinzua Dam on Seneca lands so that floods could be controlled at Pittsburgh, two hundred miles downstream. Indians objected. One sent a

Christmas card to Herbert Vogel, district engineer of the corps, wishing him all the blessings of the new year to which "he might be rightfully entitled." Having fourteen other dams in their upper Ohio basin plan (which was similar to the Pittsburgh Flood Commission plan written in 1908), the corps procrastinated on the troublesome Kinzua.

But civic leaders in Pittsburgh campaigned for the dam in 1955, and support grew a year later after a flood caused $2 million of damage at Warren, eight miles below the prospective dam site. When the corps recommended funding for the project, Congressman John Saylor said, "Apparently you have become so calloused and so crass that the breaking of the oldest treaty in the United States is a matter of little concern to you,"[59] but the local congressman wanted the dam, and Eisenhower approved funding. The condemnation of Seneca lands and the relocation of several hundred Indians was scheduled to begin.

Backing their word from 160 years before, the Quakers tried to save the reservation. They recommended that the Seneca hire Dr. Arthur E. Morgan to study alternatives. Morgan had designed the Miami River Project—America's first comprehensive flood control project and a landmark of hydrologic planning—and served as the first chairman of the Tennessee Valley Authority. In 1956 Indian president Cornelius Seneca met with Morgan, who agreed to help but advised acceptance of the dam if no alternative could be found.

With Barton Jones, former TVA chief design engineer, Morgan identified several options that would divert flood water to a glacial depression in the nearby Conewango basin. Morgan reported that more water could be stored and that low-flow augmentation would be improved through the Conewango plan, costing less than Kinzua Dam.

The corps hired the "independent" engineering firm of Tippetts-Abbett-McCarthy-Stratton to review the alternative. Morgan objected because the firm's founder was a former corps engineer, three of four partners had worked for the corps, and for twenty years the corps had been the firm's major client.[60] The consultants reported that the alternative was feasible but would cost $91 million more than Kinzua, would flood more land, and require relocation of more people. Morgan was not allowed to review the appraisal and said that his plans were misrepresented. He was so enraged by ridicule from congressmen and the corps that he wrote *Dams and Other Disasters*—a book criticizing the corps—as the last major project of his career.

The Seneca had filed suit, and sympathy for them grew during the next two years. A song called "Cornplanter, Can You Swim?"—about the flooding of the chief's grave—was broadcast. But editors of the *Pittsburgh Press* wrote that the Indians deserved no more consideration than 2,500 white people who had been moved for the nearby Conemaugh Dam. The editors had no sympathy for the view that "Indians were so poorly treated by white men that we shouldn't take their lands now—even to save ourselves from flood disaster." In 1957 the district court ruled that Congress had been informed of the treaty and had intended to take the lands regardless. In 1959 the Supreme Court denied an injunction request.

The 180-foot-high dam was finished in 1965, flooding the Allegheny River and the Indian villages of Jennesadaga and Kinzua. The Seneca were moved from riverfront homes to southern New York, where each family could buy subdivided plots of one to three acres. On these, ranch houses were built. The graves of Cornplanter and three thousand other Indians were relocated.

Public opinion changed later. Concern for Indian rights grew in the 1960s and 1970s as some people heeded a Seneca leader's advice: "Why feel guilty about what happened in the nineteenth century? Pay closer attention to what you are still doing to us." Folk singer Buffy Saint Marie sang of the "liberty bell, as it rang with a thud over Kinzua mud." Pittsburgh's largest newspaper no longer referred to people concerned about America's oldest treaty as "bleeding hearts." A few years later, more arguments would have been added to the Indians' case. The Allegheny had been a magnificent Appalachian river, clean, undeveloped, and full of fish, but to save it for its river qualities had not been a part of the fight against the dam.

The Allegheny battle was outstanding, but the history of dam building is littered with projects that took the last shreds of Indian homelands. Authorized in 1944 as part of the Pick–Sloan Plan for the Missouri River, Garrison Dam in North Dakota displaced 1,544 Indians. The business council of three tribes opposed the dam, but seeing that it would be built, the Indians asked for access to electric power, for pasture along the reservoir, for the use of timber from the reservoir area, and for a bridge so that neighbors could see each other without traveling hundreds of miles around the impoundment. Angered by a splinter group of Indians fighting the plan, General Pick of the corps withdrew from negotiations. The Indians were required to move out of the protected and fertile river valley and were relocated on the high plains, where there were no usable water supplies. They received few of the compromise benefits they had requested. A 1948 photograph shows the Indian chairman weeping as Interior Secretary J. A. Krug signs the contract for the land.[61]

By the 1960s, dam proposals on Indian lands were fought and won. A

Bureau of Reclamation proposal to dam California's Trinity River on the Hoopa Reservation was stopped in 1963. On the Middle Fork of the Eel in California, Dos Rios Dam was halted, in part because it would flood the Round Valley Reservation. With changing attitudes and the melding of Indian rights and resource issues, Orme Dam in Arizona and Copper Creek Dam in Washington were stopped in the late 1970s.

THE POTOMAC AGAIN

In 1963 the corps revitalized its Potomac River plan and called for sixteen dams (and also, in an unusual move, for preservation of the Cacapon River). Fighting with vigor until now reserved for places like Yellowstone and Kings Canyon, the National Parks Association published *Analysis of the Potomac River Basin Report*, one of the first places in which Supreme Court Justice William O. Douglas spoke against dams. He led a hike on the historic Chesapeake and Ohio Canal, argued for pollution control instead of dilution, and called the dams' thirty-nine thousand kilowatts of power "trivial." A federal task force finally recommended small dams instead. Only one large dam was built. The defeat of the dams led to the restoration of the Chesapeake and Ohio Canal and to President Johnson's proposal for a Potomac national river with open space, trails, and pollution abatement, but the proposal was defeated because of landowner opposition.[62]

THE WEST'S LARGEST MISTAKE

Glen Canyon was called "incomparably beautiful" (Richard C. Bradley), "extraordinarily majestic" (Wiley and Gottlieb), and "a place of haunting beauty" (William Wyant). Wallace Stegner wrote that the canyon was "almost absolutely serene. . . . Its walls are the monolithic Navajo sandstone . . . fantastically eroded by silt side canyons, alcoves, grottos green with redbud and maiden-hair and with springs of sweet water."[63] Above all, Glen Canyon was "The Place No One Knew," and with a river awareness rarely expressed in the early dam fights, photographer Eliot Porter wrote, "The architect, the life-giver, and the moderator of Glen Canyon is the Colorado River." The dam site was in Arizona, upstream from Grand Canyon.

In 1916 the first survey of the Colorado had identified a Glen Canyon dam site, but its Navajo Sandstone—the red showpiece of southwestern national parks—is porous and absorptive. In 1954 the interior secretary stated that "the poorly cemented and relatively weak condition" of Glen Canyon rock caused "some concern" that foundations could not support a dam higher than seven hundred feet. The Bureau of Reclamation opposed Echo Park alternatives, but this view changed as politics required. In 1955—the year before Congress banned Echo Park Dam—an Interior Department geologist stated that Glen Canyon was an excellent site for a dam.

When arguing against Echo Park Dam, David Brower had said, "If the river disappeared in its course through Dinosaur, or was somehow unavailable, a sound upper Colorado storage project could be developed elsewhere." Glen Canyon was the Bureau of Reclamation's "elsewhere," and because it was not a national park or monument, the dam was scarcely opposed.

When the authorization reached Congress in 1956, Florida Congressman James Haley argued that the site was unsafe. He dropped a piece of canyon shale into a glass of water, and Congress watched the rock disintegrate. Supporting the dam, Arizona's Stewart Udall dropped his own shale in a glass and said that he would drink the water when he finished his speech.[64] The Bureau of Reclamation later estimated seepage losses of 15 percent at the reservoir.

Some senators wanted conservationists to fight the entire Upper Colorado River Storage Project, but the act faced no firm opposition, and it passed in 1956. The bureau was authorized to build Glen Canyon Dam, Flaming Gorge Dam in Wyoming, Curecanti Dam in Colorado, and Navajo Dam in New Mexico.

Soon after Congress's vote, the Interior Department's Geological Survey stated that the Colorado River could be regulated by thirty million acre-feet of storage, already held by existing dams (mostly by Hoover Dam). Glen Canyon would increase the total to nearly twice the needed amount. The Geological Survey's report stated that the gain in regulation would be largely offset by a corresponding increase in evaporation and that "storage development may be approaching, if not exceeding, the useful limit."[65] Other proposals by the bureau would bring total storage to eighty-six million acre-feet—nearly three times the needed amount, causing evaporation of 13 percent of the river's supply. The storage needs of the dam could have been met by amending the Colorado compact to allow for upper basin storage credits at Hoover Dam, but the hydroelectric plant at Glen Canyon was to be the upper basin's "cash register," with revenue from nine hundred thousand kilowatts to fund irrigation in the headwater states.

Started in 1956, the dam rose 710 feet, its five million cubic yards of concrete exceeding those of Hoover Dam. In 1963 the gates were closed to fill Lake Powell, eventually flooding 180 miles of Colorado River canyons and scores of tributaries, including the Escalante River and small canyons named Twilight, Mystery, Cathedral, and Music Temple. A Bureau of Reclamation brochure named the reservoir the "Jewel of the Colorado" and stated,

> To have a deep blue lake
> Where no lake was before
> Seems to bring man
> A little closer to God.

"We didn't know how much devastation would occur," said river outfitter Martin Litton in 1983. "With a national park, there was a constituency that we didn't have with Glen Canyon. We weren't thinking of potential parks. Looking back, I'd say Echo Park was less valuable than Glen Canyon. We tried to fight the dam, but we were tired. We didn't know our own strength. We didn't realize the snowball we had started at Echo Park."[66]

In 1983 Stewart Udall said, "The Sierra Club fought for the middle-sized fish and let the big one get away. If I could switch it, I'd have Glen Canyon be the national park and build the dam at Echo Park." Floating through Glen Canyon just before its flooding is one of the experiences that changed Udall's goals to include river conservation as well as development.

Never having seen what was at stake, David Brower also rafted through Glen Canyon before its flooding, and he later called this canyon the greatest loss of wilderness in his lifetime. In a 1982 *Audubon* interview Brower said, "My failure to act still haunts me. It was the greatest sin I have ever committed." In *The Place No One Knew*, Brower wrote, "Glen Canyon died in 1963. . . . Neither you nor I, nor anyone else, knew it well enough to insist that at all costs it should endure." This book of Eliot Porter photographs was a milestone celebrating a lost place and documenting a remarkable, extinct landscape. With its powerful message that a place must be known to be saved, it created an entire movement for wilderness awareness and publicity. Other award-winning Sierra Club books designed by Brower followed, showing threatened landscapes and pressing people into action at the Redwoods, the North Cascades, and the Grand Canyon.

Richard Leonard, honorary president of the Sierra Club in 1984, said, "Dave Brower and Martin Litton feel that it was wrong to let Glen Canyon be built. But I think we were right at the time. We couldn't stop Dinosaur and Glen Canyon both. If we hadn't fought at Dinosaur we would have lost the National Park system. If we would have fought at Glen Canyon people would have been fed up with conservationists stopping everything."[67]

Edward Abbey wrote of Glen Canyon in *Desert Solitaire*: "To grasp the nature of the crime that was committed imagine the Taj Mahal or Chartres Cathedral buried in mud until only the spires remain visible. With this difference; those man-made celebrations of human aspiration could conceivably be reconstructed while Glen Canyon was a living thing, irreplaceable, which can never be recovered through any human agency."

Attitudes about rivers and dams had been slowly changing, and Glen Canyon polarized two views. In *Encounters with the Archdruid* by John McPhee, Commissioner of Reclamation Floyd Dominy was quoted as saying, "The unregulated Colorado was a son of a bitch. It wasn't any good. It was in flood or in trickle"; of the reservoir he said, "It is the most beautiful lake in the world." About the same lake, Edward Abbey wrote in *The Monkey Wrench Gang* "Instead of a river he looked down on a motionless body of murky green effluent, dead, stagnant, dull, a scum of oil floating on the surface. On the canyon was a coating of dried silt and mineral salts, like a bathtub ring, recorded high-water mark. Lake Powell: storage pond, silt trap, evaporation tank and lagoon." In the memory and mythology of western river people, there are the three greatest losses: Hetch Hetchy, Glen Canyon, and the Stanislaus, flooded in 1982.

The Glen Canyon loss gave David Brower and the conservationists the determination to stop the Bureau of Reclamation's next proposal—dams in the Grand Canyon. And with utter clarity, Glen Canyon showed that rivers in addition to those flowing through national parks deserved protection.

REGARDLESS OF THE LAW

Rainbow Bridge is a 160-acre national monument in the upper recesses of Glen Canyon. The largest-known natural bridge on earth, this sandstone arch could cover the Capitol dome in Washington. In defeating Echo Park Dam, conservationists made certain that the law prohibited the flooding of any national park or monument, but a full Lake Powell would be forty-eight feet deep beneath the bridge, possibly undermining its foundation.[68] The Bureau of Reclamation proposed a $25 million barrier dam to hold back the reservoir, but despite Interior Secretary Udall's urging, Congress funded other water projects instead.

In 1970 a suit was filed by Friends of the Earth (an organization formed by David Brower when he was ousted from the Sierra Club after disagreements over his opposition to a nuclear power plant), the Wasatch Mountain Club, and river outfitter Ken Sleight to prevent the flooding of Rainbow

Bridge. In 1973 District Court Judge Willis Ritter ordered the government "to take forthwith such actions as were necessary to prevent any waters of Lake Powell and the Glen Canyon unit from entering within the boundaries of Rainbow Bridge National Monument." He added, "It was pretty sneaky of Congress to pass a law and then ignore it completely."[69]

To keep Rainbow Bridge dry, Lake Powell's depth would need to be reduced one hundred feet, cutting storage capacity in half and losing annual hydroelectric revenues of several million dollars. The lower level would also save two hundred miles of canyons from inundation, including parts of the Colorado's Cataract Canyon and the proposed Escalante Wilderness. This was perhaps the first time a serious effort was made to stop the filling of a reservoir behind a dam that was already built.

Conservationists held that the upper basin's lost storage capacity could be acquired in a paper transaction amending the basin compact so that some of Lake Mead's water would be shared, and that evaporative losses would be cut with a smaller reservoir. But a water resource attorney remarked that "pigs will fly" before Congress would tamper with the compact that had divided the basin in two.

The Supreme Court ruled that congressional action in denying funds for the barrier dam took precedence over the Upper Colorado River Storage Project Act, which prohibited Rainbow Bridge's flooding. Lake Powell would be filled to the brim.

THE ULTIMATE SITE

Glen Canyon was unknown, but millions had seen the Colorado in the Grand Canyon. In a legendary journey, John Wesley Powell led the first known boating expedition through the canyon, and he wrote, "The glories and the beauties of form, color and sound unite in the Grand Canyon. . . . It is a region more difficult to traverse than the Alps or the Himalayas, but if strength and courage are sufficient for the task, by a year's toil a concept of sublimity can be obtained never again to be equalled on the hither side of Paradise."

The canyon became a symbol of scenery and wilderness; in 1874 Congress approved $10,000 to buy a Thomas Moran painting of the canyon for the Senate lobby. To protect the canyon was a goal of John Muir's, and Teddy Roosevelt had stood at the rim and said, "Leave it as it is. You cannot improve on it. The ages have been at work on it, and man can only mar it." In 1908 Roosevelt declared part of the canyon a national monument.

More than three million people a year visited there in the 1970s, and during each season fourteen thousand people float the river that Powell had so perilously explored.

Part of the 280-mile-long canyon became a national park in 1919, but not before Arizona congressman Carl Hyden deleted large areas for grazing and mining. Water interests also tried to allow dams. The bill from which the 1919 act was derived had been reported from committee with provisions that the Reclamation Service could use the park for a reservoir, but on the Senate floor in 1918, a condition was added that dams must be "consistent with the primary purposes of the said park."[70]

As a part of the Central Arizona Project (CAP), in 1947 the Bureau of Reclamation proposed two Grand Canyon dams to generate 2.1 million kilowatts of power needed to lift water from the Colorado River to Arizona cities. A Bridge Canyon site would impound ninety-three miles of the river, including twenty-seven miles beside Grand Canyon National Monument and thirteen miles in the national park. The Marble Canyon site would flood the upper reaches of the canyon. Only about one-third of the Colorado in the Grand Canyon would remain free flowing, with no access to the river between the dams. Lava Falls, regarded by some people as the most exciting rapid in the country, would be under 214 feet of water, and Havasu Creek—a paradise to many—would be eighty-five feet under.

In 1947 the Sierra Club directors approved of the Bridge Canyon Dam, providing certain changes were made, but the leadership voted the next year against any dam in the national monument or park. Some conservationists thought that the only way to prevent Bridge Canyon Dam was to allow Marble Canyon Dam outside the park, but under David Brower the club abandoned the earlier prejudice of protecting only national park rivers, and it opposed both dams when the bureau reintroduced them in the 1960s.

The arguments against Echo Park Dam were repeated with new fervor. The dam fighters said that all parks could be commercialized if the Grand Canyon were dammed, and in fact, threats to the parks had proliferated: a Buffalo River dam in Grand Teton Park, the Wawona Project in Yosemite, Rio Grande dams in Big Bend Park, and Moab Dam in Arches National Monument.

Conservationists brought more analysis to the Grand Canyon case than any earlier dam fight. From the two reservoirs, two hundred thousand acre-feet of water—almost enough to supply Detroit—would evaporate, leaving bicarbonates, chlorides, and sulfates of sodium, calcium, and magnesium in an already-saline river. The Geological Survey reported that the reservoirs would result in "no significant gain in net regulation."[71] Using government data, the Sierra Club calculated that the dams would be full of silt in 60 to 160 years, and uneconomic much sooner. The bureau listed a life of 163 years for Bridge Canyon Reservoir if sediment-catching dams were not built on tributaries, 250 years with the catchment dams.

Because the dams would serve urban growth at Phoenix, John Saylor, ranking Republican on the House Interior and Insular Affairs Committee, said,

> The Federal reclamation program was begun over half a century ago for the basic purpose of reclaiming the arid, barren lands of the West in order to make them more productive. In the ensuing decades, and particularly in the past few years, the policies and programs of the bureaucrats in the Bureau of Reclamation have wandered so far afield from this basic goal that it seems reclamation has become of only incidental importance. . . . A reclamation program is needed to reclaim the Bureau of Reclamation for its original purpose before it is too late.[72]

The Sierra Club argued that cheaper power could be generated at coal-fired or nuclear plants and stated, "The day may be near when atomic energy will begin to produce really inexpensive electricity," and, "Coal-fired generation plants would use a fuel that is plentiful in the region and would leave Grand Canyon National Park inviolate."[73] Later recognizing the narrowness of this view, David Brower said, "We thought that strip mines were not of scenic importance to the Grand Canyon."

The dams' approval hinged partly on Secretary of the Interior Stewart Udall, the great-grandson of John D. Lee, for whom Lee's Ferry just below Glen Canyon was named. Udall was the son of a judge, and after becoming a lawyer and congressman he was appointed by President Kennedy to the interior job. At the suggestion of author Wallace Stegner, Udall wrote *The Quiet Crisis* early in his term. The book carried a strong conservation message but reflected the view still prevalent in 1961 that water development was a positive part of conservation. About the New Deal dam-building programs Udall wrote, "This is a new kind of American empire building; its goal was the common good . . . and its most visible symbols were the huge dams that began to rise from the bedrock of such rivers as the Colorado, the Tennessee, and the Sacramento." Udall's term as interior secretary ran eight years, exceeded only by that of Harold Ickes, who served nearly thirteen years under Roosevelt and Truman. The Grand Canyon dams presented a dilemma for Udall and his brother, Morris, who succeeded to Stewart's seat in Congress. Both believed in conservation, yet both were Arizonans knowing that water development takes political priority.

Speaking to the Senate Subcommittee on Irrigation and Reclamation, Stewart Udall recognized the need to protect parks but said, "It should be noted that such a reservoir invasion would be a peripheral one which would occur in the most remote and inaccessible area of the park. It should be further noted that 98 percent of the land area in the park would remain in its natural condition."[74] He argued that "the pristine natural condition of the river has already been permanently altered by the construction of upstream dams which regulate the flow of the river." This prodam argument that the river was regulated and therefore not worth saving was not accepted by Congress or by policy makers of the national rivers system. Udall told the Senate, "A fresh water lake could provide boat-type access to a region . . . that would otherwise be available for only the most limited use." His opponents argued that the Grand Canyon reservoirs would be like bathtubs with mud rings, vertical shorelines, and cliffs magnifying motorboat noise. The National Park Service under Stewart Udall took no strong stands against the dams.

Led by David Brower and the Sierra Club, the conservationists mounted the largest campaign yet to protect wild lands. They produced brochures, bulletins, films, news releases, and a book of color photographs with a narrative by François Leydet about a Grand Canyon journey and the dams. In an unprecedented move among conservation groups, Brower spent $15,000 for a full-page advertisement in the *New York Times* and also bought a page in the *San Francisco Chronicle*. Addressing Udall's argument that more people would see the canyon from motorboats, the ads stated, "Should we also flood the Sistine Chapel so tourists can get nearer the ceiling?" After these ads, the Internal Revenue Service revoked the club's tax-exempt status, but club membership doubled in a surge of growth not exceeded until environmentalists rallied in outrage against Interior Secretary James Watt in 1981.

The conservationists did not oppose the whole Central Arizona Project, only the Grand Canyon dams. Yet broader questions indicated growing concerns related to water: Should Phoenix become another Los Angeles? Are artificial rivers for the development of arid lands the most economic use of national resources? Would the money benefit the people more if it were invested elsewhere?

Two utilities in Arizona and one in Los Angeles favored coal-burning power plants as alternatives to dams, and Stewart Udall's Indian policy supported a power plant on the Navaho reservation. In 1965 Udall dropped his support for one of the dams, and in 1967 he proposed that the coal plants be built instead of either dam.

What changed Udall's mind? "Taking the trip down the river," he answered in 1983. "There was a lot of pressure from my Arizona constituents and my brother and so forth—we had to have a dam. But when I came off the river, I knew we were going to abandon the dams." Udall had become involved in other river-saving efforts and in a proposal for a national system of protected waterways. He said, "How could I be for scenic rivers and build a dam in the Grand Canyon?"[75]

Central Arizona Project supporters decided to drop the controversial dams in order to save the rest of the project. In September 1968, President Johnson signed the CAP law without the Grand Canyon dams. Conservationists, concerned with pollution, later fought coal-fired power plants, running another full-page newspaper advertisement stating that strip mining on the Navaho's Black Mesa was "Like Ripping Apart St. Peter's in Order to Sell the Marble." But the coal was mined, and the pollution from the Four Corners power plants is one of the few man-made features visible from outer space.

In saving the Colorado in the Grand Canyon, the conservationists gained new strength and confirmed that they were a political force. The debate led to broader concerns about energy, coal and nuclear power, air pollution, and urban sprawl, and at the end of the Grand Canyon effort the environmental community was at the brink of a nationwide movement, poised to plunge into issues encompassing the totality of life in America. After the CAP fight, Morris Udall became a leader in environmental legislation, and in 1972 he wrote, "There was little to tell us in 1963 that the great ecology–environment movement would take center stage by the end of the decade. In retrospect, it is clear that the battle of the Grand Canyon dams was a central, symbolic event which played a major role in awakening environmental awareness in America.[76]

At a 1977 conference about river recreation, historian Roderick Nash stated that Boulder Dam's

> completion in 1935 was a reason for universal jubilation in the United States. A wild river had been tamed. The engineers were heros, and as Lake Mead began to fill, a proud nation proclaimed Boulder Dam the eighth wonder of the civilized world.
>
> Thirty years later the tables were almost totally turned. Again engineers proposed a dam on the Colorado River—upstream from Hoover Dam in the Grand Canyon. But this time the engineers did not seem to be the agents of progress that they had in the 1930s. For a great many Americans the Colorado River in the Grand Canyon was not a monster to be shackled

and put to work for the economy but something valuable in its own right
and already working to enhance the quality of American life. . . . In 1968
the cheers that forty years before greeted the authorization of Boulder Dam
now sounded in support of the defeat of the Grand Canyon dam projects.

Yet, looking at other rivers being dammed, it still seemed that, beyond
the national parks, not much was really sacred. In *Goodbye to a River* John
Graves wrote about his final canoe journey on Texas's Brazos River before
it was dammed: "Maybe you save a Dinosaur Monument from time to time,
but in between such salvations you lose ten Brazoses." Dozens of wild and
scenic rivers were still being destroyed: the Kootenai in Montana, the upper
Rogue in Oregon, the Feather in California, the Gauley in West Virginia,
the Allegheny in Pennsylvania, and the Coosawattee in Georgia (which
inspired *Deliverance*, though the movie was filmed on the Chattooga). Dam
builders thrived in a refuge from would-be opponents who never knew that
these places existed.

But conservation leaders made the Grand Canyon a nationwide issue,
and the Colorado River was supported more than any river so far. Not only
the park but also the rapids and the water-based geological process were
reasons to fight dams. As free-flowing streams became scarce, the river protection movement was on the verge of a giant step. Values were to be recognized in many rivers, in all regions.

In 1975 Congress extended national park boundaries to include most
of the Grand Canyon, but in 1982 Arizona congressman Eldon Rudd introduced a new bill for dams. Brandt Calkin of the Sierra Club said, "I'm not
concerned for this year or next, but I'm still concerned. I've seen too many
of these things come back. It seems like all of our victories are temporary,
all our defeats permanent."

The Grand Canyon victory has remained solid. Other decisions for
permanence in river protection would spring from the loss of a spectacular
wild river in Idaho.

THE SEEDS OF PERMANENCE

Forty-nine new dams were proposed for the Columbia basin in the 1950s.
Libby Dam on the Kootenai River was stalled by Canada, railroads, and
local conservationists but was later built, and it flooded ninety-eight miles
of river stretching into British Columbia. John Day Dam on the Columbia
was delayed by private versus public power disputes but built. In the incred-

ibly wild and beautiful Clearwater basin of Idaho, Penny Cliffs Dam was proposed to flood the Clearwater, Selway, and Lochsa rivers, but first Bruce's Eddy Dam (now called Dworshak) was planned as one of America's tallest dams, on the Clearwater's North Fork.

Fishing and conservation groups fought Bruce's Eddy Dam, which would destroy forty-eight miles of excellent steelhead and salmon habitat and one of the state's most important elk ranges. The dam had been delayed by Eisenhower's rivers and harbors veto in 1956, but in spite of opposition by the Idaho Fish and Game Department, the dam was authorized in 1958 at the insistence of Senator Henry C. Dworshak, who argued that Idaho never received its share of corps spending.

In 1961 dam opponents asked Interior Secretary Stewart Udall to intervene. With the Grand Canyon dams, Udall was "caught in the politics" of his own state and of his own agency—the Bureau of Reclamation— which would do the building. But Bruce's Eddy was an Army Corps of Engineers dam, and the Interior Department had nothing to lose.

Udall was impressed by the fishermen's arguments and by the wildness of the place, but it was too late. The most he could do was work with congressmen who added an amendment—stricken before the vote—to prohibit additional Clearwater dams. However, the Clearwater case led Udall to reconsider nothing less than the philosophy of dam building, and he suddenly became committed to balancing the federal water program.

The Clearwater case alerted Udall and others that one dam could cause enormous losses of fish and wildlife, significant to the entire northern Rockies region. But in Alaska, a dam was proposed that would have continental effects by destroying a river that supported more waterfowl breeding than all national wildlife refuges combined.

THE SIZE OF LAKE ERIE

The Yukon River was without national park status and without the household recognition of a Grand Canyon, yet it became a nationwide environmental issue because of Rampart Dam. Hetch Hetchy had been the first great conservation battle in the nation; Rampart was the first in Alaska.

Echo Park had exemplified the threat dams posed to national parks— the first reason to save rivers. The second main reason was wildlife protection, and Rampart represented the ultimate in wildlife destruction. The debate over the proposed dam was thus a culmination of wildlife protection efforts.

The two-thousand-mile-long Yukon is the sixth-largest river in North America, penetrating wild mountains, dark forests of spruce, and subarctic plains grazed by caribou and ranged by wolves. The Yukon Flats are a maze of sloughs and thirty-six thousand lakes, where the river and its islands are eighty miles wide. River travelers must use a compass to find their way through.

Below the 180-mile-long Flats are the Ramparts—a deep canyon where the Army Corps of Engineers proposed the dam in 1959. Five hundred and thirty feet high and 4,700 feet wide, the dam would form the largest reservoir ever built, 280 miles long and flooding 10,200 square miles—larger than Lake Erie or New Jersey. With a patriotic flare, Harold L. Moats of the corps's Alaska office said to the Alaska Rural Electric Cooperative Association, "Rampart Canyon, the big one, is Alaska's most valuable resource, and as it is developed, Alaska will take her rightful place in the family of states contributing richly to the economy of the nation and to the welfare of the whole free world."[77]

Alaska's economy had suffered after a 1950s military boom collapsed. Taxes threatened to strangle the new state, and the corps's $3 billion for Rampart looked like a solution. Rampart would be the country's costliest dam ever, having as its sole purpose the generation of five thousand megawatts of electricity. Promoters hoped that the aluminum industry, which needed vast amounts of electricity, would move north. Senator Ernest Gruening boosted the project: "Alaska is confronted with the task of catching up after years of federal neglect." His staff called the area worthless, containing "not more than ten flush toilets. [In fact it had none.] Search the whole world and it would be difficult to find an equivalent area with so little to be lost through flooding."[78]

Native groups did not agree. About 1,500 Athapascan Indians and a few hundred white people lived in the reservoir area, and twice that number lived along the river below the dam site. The natives' *Tundra Times* reported that all but one village from the head of the reservoir to the Bering Sea were against the dam. The livelihood of other natives in Alaska and 3,500 in the Yukon Territory would be affected or eliminated by the loss of salmon.

The corps was required to ask for comments from federal agencies, including the Fish and Wildlife Service in the Department of the Interior, where biologists reported, "Nowhere in the history of water development in North America have the fish and wildlife losses anticipated to result from a single project been so overwhelming." They projected elimination of 1.6 percent of all North American ducks; 12,800 geese; 10,000 cranes; 20,000 grebes; a total destruction of the salmon run for thousands of miles of rivers and streams above the dam; and a loss of furbearers that accounted for 7 percent of the total state harvest. Altogether, 1.5 million waterfowl migrated south from the Flats—more than the annual production of all other national wildlife refuges in 1964. Wildlife losses would extend 750 miles to the Bering Sea because of lack of seasonal flooding, which maintains the wetlands, renourishes the soil, and rejuvenates the willows—food for twelve thousand moose.

Alerted by the Fish and Wildlife Service studies and by a few lonely Alaskans fighting the dam, conservationists and duck hunters argued not only that the wildlife should be saved but also that the power would be too expensive and would be thirty times the amount used in the state. Devil's Canyon on the Susitna River was supported by some conservationists as an alternative—a site that was threatened in 1984.

Rampart supporters asked, "Who ever heard of a duck drowning?" and because the reservoir would require twenty years to fill, they said, "The ducks and animals have twenty years to move out of the area." State politicians who opposed the dam lost elections. After a University of Alaska faculty member questioned the building of the dam, a member of the state House of Representatives suggested cutting university appropriations.

At the North American Wildlife and Natural Resources Conference in 1963, Dr. Ira N. Gabrielson of the Wildlife Management Institute warned that Rampart was about to be rushed through Congress and that the dam "is synonymous with resources destruction." Fifteen organizations in the Natural Resources Council of America pooled $25,000 for a study documenting the case against Rampart; this move showed the growing role of scientists in fighting dams.[79]

In 1967 Interior Secretary Udall released a report on Rampart. Beyond the impacts on wildlife, the Interior Department stated that the power would not be used and that the timber industry would lose the equivalent of three years of total Alaska production. Udall's recommendation that the dam not be built was a setback to the corps. Alaska Governor Walter Hickel, who had backed the dam, was appointed as interior secretary under Richard Nixon, but when oil was discovered on the North Slope in 1968, the development interests turned all their attention to the Trans-Alaska Pipeline. Under President Carter, the 8.5-million-acre Yukon Flats National Wildlife Refuge was designated, ending all planning for the dam.

The argument that rivers should be saved for fish and wildlife had failed on the Mississippi, Cowlitz, Trinity, Santee, and Clearwater Rivers, but here on the faraway Yukon, conservationists won. Effects of the project were simply too ruinous to be dismissed as "frivolous" concerns about fish.

Along with the park savers, landowners, and fish and wildlife supporters, one more group of river activists came together in the 1960s, not in the
mile-deep canyons of the West or the howling wilderness of the north, but
in the gentle hills of Arkansas.

THE RIVER PEOPLE

In northern Arkansas there are wild lands, rocky cliffs, clean water, quick
rapids, smallmouth bass, and bubbling springs that attracted people who
were aware of the many complex values of a river. The Buffalo River supporters were canoeists, and the very nature of their interest led to concerns
that crossed boundaries and combined issues. Because they traveled on
nearly the whole river, they were interested in the entire length, not just
farms and not just fish. The free flow of the river was not just compatible,
it was essential to what they did. They used both the water and the shores.
After paddling the river from top to bottom, it was easier to see the ecological and philosophical concepts of the river as one lively unit, like an organ-
ism with all parts connected.

Newspaper reporter George Wells wrote in the *Pine Bluff Commercial*,
"It was largely due to the availability of these canoes that more people were
exposed closeup to the beauty of the Buffalo and joined the crusade to 'save'
it from the dam."[80] Wells's writing includes one of the first references to
"river people."

Harold Alexander, who worked for the Arkansas Fish and Game
Department and expanded an interest in fisheries to encompass many river
values, wrote, "A stream is a living thing. It moves, dances and shimmers in
the sun. It furnishes opportunities for enjoyment and its beauty moves men's
souls. Like the condor, the whooping crane and the wolf, the streams of
America are on the road to oblivion." In 1957 Alexander wrote an Arkansas
Audubon Society resolution against the corps's Gilbert Dam, which would
flood forty-seven miles of the Buffalo. The next year, Alexander asked for
help from Paul Bruce Dowling of the Nature Conservancy, who recommended that the National Park Service consider federal protection for the
river. Citizen leader Dr. Neil Compton asked Senator Fulbright to persuade
the park service to do a study, which was started with a $7,000 budget.

Compton tried to enlist nationwide support for the Buffalo. He traveled to California to meet with David Brower of the Sierra Club in 1962,
but that was during the Grand Canyon debate, and Compton reported, "It
was my belief that we would not be able to generate enough interest under

this label or with the high annual dues levied by the Sierra Club." Instead, Compton and others formed the Ozark Society, bringing national attention to the Buffalo in 1962 when William O. Douglas joined them on a canoe trip and called the Buffalo "a national treasure too beautiful to die." Park service planners recommended national river status in 1963, following the model of the Current River, which they had studied several years earlier (see Chapter 6).

The Buffalo is one of few cases in which a river controversy broke into violence. Canoeists were shot at after being stopped by trees that had been cut to block their path. Barbed wire was strung across the stream. A fight at a local basketball game was blamed on the Buffalo River issue. When a student chapter of the Ozark Society advertised a "coeducational float," a local sheriff saw a chance to discredit the Ozark group, and he staged a raid to expose his idea of immorality. But instead of finding the canoeists' camp, he stumbled onto an outing of the Landsman's Society—a group of local lawyers and realtors, who were fined for possession of untaxed whiskey.[81]

Governor Orval Faubus opposed the dam in 1965, temporarily ending the threat. Senator Fulbright introduced a national river bill, but in spite of opposition to the dam by the next two governors the bill languished because the representative from the local district still backed the dam. In the spirit of *This Is Dinosaur*, a book of photographs by Kenneth Smith titled *Buffalo River Country* was published in 1967 as a call for preservation. In 1972 the dam was finally banned when Congress designated the Buffalo as a national river.

Canoeists had become one of the important groups in river protection. Led by Randy Carter—author of whitewater guidebooks—they stopped the corps's Salem Church Dam on the Rappahannock River in Virginia. In the nationwide movement to save rivers in the 1970s, river runners were a prime force in creating the American Rivers Conservation Council and in fighting dams on the St. John and Stanislaus, where they brought awareness of river values to a new peak.

THE BURDEN OF PROOF

A different view of rivers and water development had grown from Hetch Hetchy to include other national park rivers: the Yellowstone, Kings, Flathead, Green, Yampa, and Colorado. The new view expanded to state parks and wilderness areas along the Clarion, Hudson, and Sun Rivers. With mixed success and failure, fishermen worked to protect their best streams:

the Rogue, Cowlitz, Namekagon, and Clearwater. The commitment to build dams was attacked by landowners in Kansas's Blue Valley and by Indians along the Allegheny. For the Potomac, diverse interests joined to protect the river. The Yukon was saved for wildlife; the Buffalo was saved by canoeists. To justify dams, the burden of proof was shifting from the conservationists to the developers. Sydney Howe of the Conservation Foundation wrote, "Few, if any of our institutions face a greater crisis of confidence than does the public works establishment."

Beyond the political thicket, the smallest seeds were planted for a spiritual outlook toward the rivers. The phrase "reverence for life" occurred to Albert Schweitzer as he stood on the deck of a steamer going up Africa's Ogovve River. The land ethic described by Aldo Leopold began to gain acceptance and would be expanded to waters. In the years to come, some people felt a spiritual importance in the rivers and tried to describe this in a society not anxious to listen.

By the mid-1960s the four main groups of river conservationists—park supporters, fishermen, landowners, and canoeists—were growing in power, and their concerns were reaching more people. The reasons to protect rivers were growing, overlapping, and attracting supporters, and through the bitter losses and the precedent-setting successes, a movement was born to save the rivers that were left.

5

THE MOVEMENT TO SAVE RIVERS

A revolution in attitudes about rivers moved through the country and touched every stream. The late 1960s and early 1970s brought powerful ingredients for change: a growing sense of scarcity, the environmental movement, activism by conservationists and landowners, applications of science and economics coupled with publicity, recreational use, and tight money—all contributing to a national movement to save threatened rivers.

The sense of scarcity came when people realized that thousands of dams had been built but free-flowing rivers were rare. All of the Columbia in the United States was dammed except for a fifty-two mile section, inaccessible because of the Hanford nuclear power reservation, and even there Ben Franklin Dam was proposed. In California, 1,300 dams blocked every major river but one, and huge second-generation dams such as New Melones and New Don Pedro were planned to flood out the old dams. Still foreseeing scarcities, the water developers searched with the zeal of the desperate. Cities fearing shortages sent their engineers hundreds of miles away to claim new supplies.

The environmental movement galvanized support for river protection, it expanded awareness, and it brought new expertise. The message of Earth Day, April 22, 1970, reached almost everyone. An easy place to see the problem was at a dam site where one action, often funded by the taxpayers themselves, caused destruction that was immediate, obvious, and vulnerable to citizen outrage. New laws, especially the National Environmental Policy Act, gave citizens unprecedented influence.

Patriotism, fear, and hopelessness were no longer reasons to accept plans of the Army Corps of Engineers or other builders. Antigovernment activism became accepted. The type of landowners who had trembled

SELECTED EVENTS IN CHAPTER 5

1964   Construction started on Cross Florida Barge Canal.
Delaware Valley Conservation Association fought Sunfish Pond power project.

1967   Conservationists and William O. Douglas protested Red River Dam.
Environmental Defense Fund organized.
Supreme Court ruled on Hells Canyon dams.

1969   National Environmental Policy Act passed Congress.

1970   Environmental Defense Fund sued to stop Gillham Dam.
Earth Day held on April 22.
Natural Resources Defense Council organized.
Save the Delaware Coalition opposed Tocks Island Dam.

1971   Cross Florida Barge Canal halted.
Environmental Defense Fund sued to stop Oakley Dam.

1972   Environmental Policy Center organized.
Environmental Defense Fund sued to delay Tellico Dam.

1973   Governor Jimmy Carter halted work on Sprewrell Bluff Dam.
Friends of the River sponsored statewide initiative against New Melones Dam.
Snail darter discovered in Little Tennessee River.
Environmental Policy Center published *Disasters in Water Development*.

1974   License issued for New River dams.
Natural Resources Defense Council sued to delay Auburn Dam.
Friends of the St. John organized.

1975   Oakley Dam halted.
Governor Wendell Ford opposed Red River Dam. Hells Canyon National Recreation Area stopped dam proposals.
Delaware River Basin Commission recommended deauthorization of Tocks Island Dam.
Earthquake reached 5.9 on Richter scale near Auburn Dam site.

1976   New River designated national river.
Teton Dam ruptured.
Irrigation districts and San Francisco applied for permits to dam Tuolumne River.
First national conference for river conservation held.

1977   Corps recommended that Cross Florida Barge Canal be terminated.

1978   National Parks and Recreation Act passed.
Supreme Court ruled to stop Tellico Dam.

1979   Interior Secretary Andrus announced that Auburn Dam would need to be reauthorized.
Congress approved Tellico Dam.
Friends of the River opposed filling of reservoir at New Melones Dam.

1980   Dickey–Lincoln dams deauthorized.

1981   Orme Dam stopped.
Tuolumne River Preservation Trust organized.

1982   Reservoir at New Melones Dam filled.

1984   Tuolumne River designated a national river.

before the agencies condemning land now fought back. Even small dam proposals stirred up people willing to battle a bureaucracy and the local chamber of commerce.

Scientists proved that water projects were wreaking havoc and upsetting entire ecosystems. Economists calculated enormous costs in dollars and cents. Journalists got the word out. The issues of river protection made headlines in magazines, in newspapers, and on television. National publicity, begun by John Muir in *Century* magazine, was resumed in *Harper's*, *Collier's*, the *Atlantic*, the *New Yorker*, *Reader's Digest*, *American Forests*, *Outdoor Life*, and other magazines after the mid-1950s, peaking in the 1970s. Some of this attention responded to public interest, and some created interest.

Support for development was shaken by a proliferation of dam fiascos hurting dozens of communities, and people's protests were like ripples overlapping in a pool. Instead of gaining popular support with new dams, the builders were losing it. Many people saw exorbitant costs, unsafe construction, exterminated wildlife, and the relocation of families pushed from their homes by a force that seemed like war. A consensus was building in a group including millions more people than the park supporters and fishermen of the first dam fights.

In the 1970s, use of rivers boomed with canoeists, kayakers, and rafters. Even beer and cigar commercials featured whitewater boaters. Tourism took many Americans to the scenic rivers of the mountains, and people saw what was at stake. Once they experienced a wild river—any wild river—people could understand conservationists wanting to save a similar place. Paddlers and river guides became activists, and like the hikers and climbers of the 1950s who matured into the wilderness preservationists of the 1960s, these river runners forced their way into the political process.

The growing strength of the river conservationists was met by waning strength among dam builders. By the 1970s most of the economic projects were finished, and the water developers were left with proposals difficult to justify.

The river protection movement grew in tangled relationships of issues, places, and people. Two main directions evolved: the fighting of dams described in this chapter, and the start of a national wild and scenic rivers system. National river designation, which prohibits the construction of more dams, is covered in Chapter 6.

THE NEW LAW AND THE CASSATOT

More than anything else, the National Environmental Policy Act (NEPA) of 1969 changed the way federal actions affecting the environment were decided, and the Cassatot in Arkansas was the first case in which people used the new law to try to save a river.

The National Environmental Policy Act requires that an environmental impact statement be written before a federal agency can build, license, or participate in a project likely to harm the environment. For dams, canals, highways, and other developments, the statement describes the project, the impacts, and the alternatives. The law does not demand that the destruction be stopped, only that the statement be prepared. Yet the act's sponsors reasoned that if agencies were required to think about problems, publicize them, and be held accountable, then projects would improve. The new law set the nation on a course painful to those who had been profiting from the status quo but hopeful to people seeking change. Under a contract from the Army Corps of Engineers, historian Jeffrey Stine wrote, "The Corps was now faced with dealing with an environmental community with much more power."[1] To advise the president and coordinate federal programs, the NEPA created the Council on Environmental Quality, which also helped to stop some water projects. The dam-building agencies, however, would have bypassed the new law if citizen groups had let them.

The Environmental Defense Fund (EDF) was organized in 1967 to fight environmental destruction through the courts. Cofounder Victor Yannacone said that the worst environmental problems were from "allegedly public-interest agencies such as the U.S. Department of Agriculture, the U.S. Army Corps of Engineers and many state and regional development agencies."[2] The group's first major victory was the banning of DDT—a cause that signified to many people the beginnings of the environmental movement itself. Scores of times nationwide, the EDF sued the government for inadequate environmental impact statements. The Natural Resources Defense Council, formed in 1970, worked in similar ways to protect the environment through the courts.

Gillham Dam on the Cassatot had been authorized in 1958 mainly for hydropower, but this use was dropped and flood control inserted. After completion of other dams, flood control could not be justified, so the corps credited 70 percent of benefits to water supply, though the Interior Department found that Gillham and several other ongoing projects could meet four times the region's needs in the year 2080. For this, the 13.8-mile-long reservoir would destroy the last large stream in the Ouachita Mountains.

In 1970 the EDF and other groups filed suit against the dam. With the land acquired, access roads built, and spillway finished, construction was one-third complete, yet the 160-foot-high dam itself was not yet built. The corps argued that an impact statement was not needed because construction was started, but a district court judge disagreed, ruling in 1971 that NEPA compliance was mandatory no matter when the project was begun. Addressing an aspect of planning that had for years been regarded as deficient by policy analysts, the judge ruled that NEPA required consideration of alternatives to the dam, and he stated, "The most glaring deficiency in this respect is the failure to set forth and fully describe the alternative of leaving the Cassatot alone. . . . Then, if the decision-makers choose to ignore such factors, they will be doing so with their eyes wide open." Environmental Defense Fund attorneys called the case a landmark because it was the first final order under the NEPA to stop a dam.

After the corps released a twelve-pound impact statement in 1972, a federal court ended the injunction. The dam was finished, but the National Environmental Policy Act stood as a threat to other projects.

For river conservation, a new turning point was in sight. The NEPA had been passed because of a broadening view of environmental protection; it then in turn forced agencies to consider the environment, broadening the view further. With the availability of new analytic tools and a more sophisticated awareness of ecology, the dam fights of the future would be organized less around the philosophical and romantic views of wilderness, parks, and rivers and more around scientific studies showing ecological damage, quantifiable impacts, social injustice, and financial costs.

RIVERS AS ECOSYSTEMS: THE OKLAWAHA

In 1875 poet Sidney Lanier called Florida's Oklawaha River "the sweetest water-lane in the world." With a sandy bottom, the tea-colored river twists through a mile-wide valley of hydric hammock ecosystems and forest homes of panthers, black bears, otters, and bobcats. Herons, ducks, and shorebirds feed along the river's edge. Alligators and turtles sun themselves. The Silver River, an Oklawaha tributary, runs full of fish and crystal clear from Florida's largest spring—a $200 million-a-year tourist attraction where *Cross Creek* was filmed. The Oklawaha is one of Florida's two wild rivers and was recommended for national protection by the Interior Department in its first national wild and scenic rivers proposal of 1963.

In 1825 Congress considered a canal to cut across Florida so that shippers could avoid West Indies pirates. Later studies to connect the Atlantic and Gulf coasts through the Oklawaha basin appeared in 1913 and 1924, but high costs led the corps to recommend against construction. Franklin D. Roosevelt proposed a canal to make jobs, but not until World War II and fears of German submarines did Congress authorize the Cross Florida Barge Canal, to run 107 miles up the Oklawaha and across Florida's central hump to the Gulf of Mexico near the mouth of another outstanding river— the Withlacoochee. The canal would be dug 150 feet wide and 12 feet deep, draining the river and slicing into the Ocala dome—a groundwater reservoir forming the largest single water storage basin in the nation. Rodman and Eureka dams would flood 27,350 acres of wild swamp. Forty-five miles of the Oklawaha would be eliminated by dams, ditching, or draining.[3] John F. Kennedy was convinced that his support for the canal would win Florida votes, and in 1960 he said, "If elected, I will cooperate in making this project a reality." The corps revised the benefit–cost ratio by adding benefits and slashing 12 percent from costs, even though five bridges were added and even though the national index for construction had risen 15 percent since 1958. But on paper the canal looked good with a new ratio of 1.17–1, and Congress approved it in 1964.

Unlike earlier dam fights to save national parks or wildlife, this struggle was launched to save the river itself. Marjorie Carr of Florida Defenders of the Environment (FDE) said, "The environmental threat of the Cross Florida Barge Canal that first caught our attention was the destruction of the Oklawaha River." The FDE tried to get the canal rerouted away from the Oklawaha, but Lyndon Johnson turned the first spade of earth in 1964 and contractors dug a six-mile-long ditch through the lower river. Rodman Dam was built in 1968 to flood sixteen miles of river. In 1968 the FDE approached the Environmental Defense Fund, and while the canal was delayed in court, other events were changing an entire attitude, nationwide.

Earth Day came in 1970, and *Time* magazine named the environment the issue of the year. A Gallup poll found that environmental problems were regarded as the second most important issue of the decade (the Vietnam war was first). But also in 1970, Lieutenant General F. J. Clarke, chief of the Army Corps of Engineers, said, "With our country growing the way it is, we cannot simply sit back and let nature take its course."

The conservationists were moving beyond ideology and developing political savvy, following the advice of James Nathan Miller, who wrote, "Conservationists must band their presently fractionalized forces into tough and demanding legislative lobbies. By properly mobilizing their enormous potential power, they can force our state and national lawmakers to treat the land not merely as a machine to be made more efficient, but also as a place for ourselves, and even our grandchildren, to live in." Miller brought professional journalism to the cause of river protection, continuing a tradition set by Wallace Stegner and Bernard DeVoto in the mid-1950s, but reaching many more people because he wrote for *Reader's Digest.*

At the same time, scientists were becoming involved in environmental causes nationwide, changing the whole complexion of conservation toward greater professionalism.[4] In the case of the Oklawaha, the FDE sponsored environmental and economic studies of the Cross Florida Canal, enlisting the aid of dozens of volunteer scientists, who stressed ecology more than in any dam fight so far. The case reflected the environmental movement by recognizing the entire ecosystem and the effects of a project on the web of life, including support systems such as water supplies of entire cities and regions.

Economists with the FDE charged that the corps's claims for barge traffic were overestimated: for oil products the corps projected an increase of 80 percent per capita, when in fact consumption would decrease. Five million dollars were claimed as benefits from two shippers that would not use the canal. Twenty-four percent of the benefits counted for recreation were for lakes that would be weed filled. Without this padding of numbers, the ratio would not have allowed construction.[5]

The western section of the canal—sometimes ninety feet deep—would fill with groundwater. Hydrologists found that ocean salt and pollution from boats would mix with underground supplies, perhaps contaminating the drinking water of many towns. Fluctuating levels in canal locks would be reflected in nearby springs (the canal would pass only five miles from Silver Spring). The conservationists gained broad support when people saw that more than wildlife was affected. Real estate developers and city officials— earlier anticipating an economic boom from the canal—agreed that ground- water was more important. As Marjorie Carr said, "The canal was in competition with new growth." The FDE's 150-page analysis, signed by 150 scientists, was used in the EDF lawsuit and helped to influence Interior Secretary Walter Hickel to call for a moratorium on construction in January 1970. (Like Dworshak and Rampart dams, this is another example of a corps project being fair game to the Interior Department, whereas Bureau of Rec- lamation dams such as Teton Dam went unchecked.)

The conservationists won when a federal judge halted the $210-mil- lion project, one-third completed in January 1971. Bob Teeters, the corps's representative on an Oklawaha task force, said, "The canal fight showed the Army Corps that NEPA was for real. The decision shocked a lot of people in the corps, and led to better analysis in the 'statement of findings' that the corps did after the Rivers and Harbors Act of 1970. There's nothing like writing down the balance to realize what's happening."[6] With a recommendation from his Council on Environmental Quality, President Nixon signed an executive order to stop construction. He called the Oklawaha "a national treasure" and sought to "prevent a past mistake from causing permanent damage."

The Canal Authority—a local promotion group—called the president's action unconstitutional. In February 1974, a federal judge agreed that the president could not by himself halt the canal, but stated that construction should not proceed until a new environmental impact statement was written. In 1976, pressured by Florida conservationists and influenced by studies by state agencies, the governor and state cabinet voted 6–1 for deauthorization. Governor Reubin Askew later said, "I favor restoring the Oklawaha."

In February 1977, in a landmark decision to stop a project, Chief of Engineers J. W. Morris recommended that the canal be "terminated" due to "marginal" economic justification and "adverse environmental impacts."

The canal is important as a case in which river development was halted after construction had begun and in which a dam was built but its reservoir remained unfilled. The FDE estimated that the Rodman Dam section could be restored for the cost of reservoir weed control through only a five-year period. Without restoration, operation of locks, dams, and a six-mile-long canal for motorboats would require $250,000 a year. Without dissent, federal and state agencies agreed to the largest restoration ever considered for a river. They would drain Rodman, restore sixteen miles of river channel, remove the unfilled Eureka Dam, and repair the western end of the canal. In May 1977, President Carter called for legislation to deauthorize the canal, to begin a national river study of the Oklawaha, and to restore the damaged sections.

Only a few years before, saving a river had been a new concept, but on the Oklawaha, officials, including the president, were recommending that dams be dismantled and rivers be reclaimed. A federal task force in 1978 recommended $25 million for restoration; the money was not approved, however, and the dams remain in place.

Water development had been slowed in the 1960s, and now it was almost stopped in the 1970s. A few large projects would still be built, but only after costly fights that further sapped the momentum of development.

JIMMY CARTER'S RIVER: THE FLINT

Few people start out with an interest in rivers. They start with one river— one place that they grow to know and care about, one that later leads them to other streams. Jimmy Carter's river was the Flint.

Georgia conservationists asked Carter to stop Spewrell Bluff Dam, authorized in 1963 for corps construction. The 211-foot-high dam would flood twenty-eight miles of the Flint as it wound through hill country south of Atlanta. Prized by fishermen, canoeists, and naturalists, the river was ranked the top resource of the state by the Georgia Natural Areas Council. This was the only river whose fall line—the rocky drop separating the piedmont and the coastal plain—remained undammed. With a technique started at Echo Park, river supporters promoted the Flint through raft and canoe trips, winning supporters by simply showing the place to people. In 1972 Carter decided to see for himself what was at stake, and after his canoe trip he said, "If we are going to destroy all this natural beauty, we better make sure that what we get in return is worth the price."[7] Carter told his staff to study the project. He received six thousand letters in support of the Flint and called them "enough to get any politician's attention."

Under corps policy, a governor's disapproval halts a project, and this is what Carter did. In October 1973 he stated,

> It became obvious to me that none of the [corps's] claims were true. The report was primarily promotional literature supporting construction. Population figures . . . had been strangely doubled. Flood control benefits had been increased by a factor of 287 percent since the initial estimates. In just a few months, the Corps more than quadrupled the economic benefits from recreation, and federal recreational advantages computed by the Corps were 1,650 percent more than those originally computed by the National Park Service.

The project had been justified for flood control, recreation, and hydropower, but Carter pointed out that only 12 percent of the flood control benefits were for existing development; the rest were for increased floodplain use. About $1 million of yearly benefits were for increased farm production in counties where $4 million was paid annually to farmers to keep fifty thousand acres idle. Electric power reserves were an adequate 16.9 percent without the dam. Eight underused recreational lakes sat within sixty miles. Nearly all state and federal recreation agencies opposed the dam, and a state survey showed a "gigantic present deficit" of recreational opportunities along streams.

The governor recommended that a river park be created and "that the apparent bias of the Corps of Engineers in favor of dam construction be assessed by the General Accounting Office, by the Congress, and by other responsible agencies—in this project, and other similar projects now planned or to be considered in the future. The construction of unwarranted dams and other projects at public expense should be prevented."[8]

Spewrell Bluff remained an inactive project but was reconsidered in a metropolitan Atlanta water supply study in 1981. The river still lacks long-term protection.

The Flint is one of the best examples of a dam stopped by a governor. The case molded Carter's commitment to river protection and led to reforms during his presidency, though he would find that changing federal policy and stopping dams in the West would be more difficult than saving the Flint.

SAVING A PARK AT THE SANGAMON

In Illinois conservationists combined the proven politics of saving parks with the economic analysis that became one of the most important requirements for river protection in the 1970s.

Oakley Dam was authorized in 1962 for flood control, water supply, and other uses. The proposal drew little attention until the corps enlarged plans in 1966 to flood part of Allerton Park—1,500 acres registered as a national natural landmark, with virgin woodland given to the University of Illinois for research and public use as a nature reserve. The Committee to Save Allerton Park was formed one year later, and arguments and alternatives were developed with analysis by economists and scientists from the university. *Battle for the Sangamon*, a ninety-three-page booklet, was one of the most effective citizen reports against a dam. The committee argued that a 21,000-acre greenbelt would offer cheaper and better flood protection than the dam, that sewage should be treated instead of diluted, and that groundwater could be pumped economically.[9]

The EDF sued in 1971 to delay the corps because of an incomplete environmental statement, and in 1973 the Washington-based Environmental Policy Center included Oakley among thirteen proposals that would be the worst "disasters in water development."

After the cost climbed to four times the authorized level, the General Accounting Office in 1975 questioned the corps's claims, and the governor opposed the dam, temporarily ending the threat. John Marlin had worked to stop Oakley, emerging as a master of local political processes. Through the 1970s he organized landowners to halt other dams in the Midwest.

Michael Robinson, a historian under contract with the corps, wrote that the Sangamon case was one of the most outstanding in showing that

environmentalists had "marshalled economic resources, professional expertise, and political skill."[10] As in earlier dam fights, the main cause first
attracting Sangamon supporters was the saving of a park, but with the Sangamon, technical and economic analyses of the project were paramount.
River conservationists had refined their rationale for the protection of park
lands, fish and wildlife, recreation, environmental quality, and now economic values. To this arsenal of arguments, landowners brought new power.

THE RED RIVER AND THE
MOUNTAIN FARMERS

Conservationists wanting to save the natural environment and landowners
wanting to save their homes combined efforts along the Red River in Kentucky. The North Fork, used by a million people a year for hiking, geological study, and canoeing, flows from Daniel Boone National Forest, where
eighty-four rock arches were called a "geological art gallery." Below the
gorge the river winds through a valley of Appalachian farms. Authorized by
Congress in 1962, the 141-foot-high Red River Dam would flood 1,500
acres and fifteen miles of the North Fork, including fourteen rare or endangered plant species. The American Association for the Advancement of Science opposed the dam, stating that it would destroy "a unique natural area
of geological, botanical, and zoological significance, valuable in research and
instruction." With thirty-one archaeological sites, the area may hold more
Indian petroglyphs than anywhere else in the East.

Residents and the Kentucky chapter of the Sierra Club held a protest
hike in 1967, when Justice William O. Douglas led six hundred people
through the gorge and urged them to write to congressmen. Douglas had
already traveled to the Allagash to speak against Rankin Rapids Dam and to
the Buffalo to fight Gilbert Dam. Through the late 1960s and the 1970s he
became one of the best-known public figures speaking out against dams at
the Sangamon, Sunfish Pond in New Jersey, and the Little Tennessee.

Dam opponents pushed for an alternate site five miles downstream.
The corps agreed to this site in 1969 but also raised the height of the dam
so that much of the gorge would still be flooded. The conservationists now
fought the alternative, thinking that because they had won once, they could
win again. With support from conservation groups in eighteen states, the
Red River Gorge Legal Defense Fund sued and won time to turn the politics around.

Unlike the Green, Colorado, or Yukon, where the river was important to the entire nation and could be saved in spite of local politicians, the Red River needed backing at home, so dam fighters organized in Kentucky and collected forty-four thousand signatures on a petition to the governor. One local couple—H. B. Farmer and his wife—wrote three hundred letters, and two thousand people protested at the state capitol. Organizer Chuck Hoffman said, "The Red River was the closest thing to a movement that Kentucky ever had."[11] The dam was impossible to ignore.

Opponents argued against flood control because only eighty-seven homes in Clay City, below the dam, had ever been damaged by floods. Ten of twelve cities to use the new water supply denied wanting it. The Environmental Protection Agency found that the water was too high in iron and manganese during some months, and questioned the water supply benefits. The corps counted flatwater recreation as a benefit, but existing river recreation was considered intangible and was not recorded among costs.[12]

In August 1975 the General Accounting Office stated that recreation and flood control figures were "overstated" and that water supply was "included without an adequate assessment." The GAO recommended that the corps recalculate benefits. The planning stopped when Governor Wendell Ford announced his opposition. The river was designated by Congress for a national wild and scenic river study in 1978, but has not been designated.

Red River supporters, seeing threats to other streams, in the mid-1970s formed the Kentucky Rivers Coalition, one of the strongest statewide river groups. They listed rivers worth protecting, then worked with other groups to save the most threatened. "There was a lack of experience in many of the out-of-the-way places," Chuck Hoffman said, "and the coalition was able to pool leadership so that there was enough to operate."

The Red River showed that landowners were no longer reluctant to fight the government. Residents were no longer dismissed as vested interests or as an uneducated minority against progress. The 1960s had brought growing awareness of folklore (especially in Appalachia), a rekindled interest in rural self-sufficiency, sympathy for the individual against the government, and a revitalized image of the landowner as a taxpayer. Whereas "outsiders" with the national conservation groups had led dam fights in the West, conservationists in the East would stand behind united landowners, effectively influencing local politics and capitalizing on the antigovernment sentiment of the late 1970s.

Most of the major dam fights of the 1970s were fought by local and statewide groups, but one site remained where the nationwide conservation community would rise powerfully again to save a dark canyon in one of the most isolated corners of the country.

THE SNAKE AND THE
SECOND-DEEPEST CANYON

In the early 1830s Captain Benjamin L. E. Bonneville wrote of the Snake River's Hells Canyon: "Nothing we had ever gazed upon in any other region could for a moment compare in wild majesty and impressive sternness with the series of scenes which here at every turn astonished our senses and filled us with awe and delight." Since then the 1,056-mile-long Snake has been dammed twenty-four times for hydropower and irrigation of Idaho drylands. Three dams blocked upper Hells Canyon, but below them a reach of nearly 100 miles remained as the continent's second-deepest canyon, averaging 5,500 feet from rim to river. (Some people contend that Hells Canyon is the deepest canyon.) Alpine peaks rise 8,000 feet above a cactus-spotted floor. The river was home to steelhead and ten-foot-long great white sturgeon—the largest freshwater fish in North America. A surrounding wilderness supported elk and bear. With two major rapids and many small ones, the canyon became popular as the largest river for whitewater trips in the nation (at its mouth the Snake carries three times the flow of the Colorado.) Luna Leopold of the University of California, who developed an intricate process for measuring the uniqueness of canyons, ranked Hells Canyon behind only the Grand Canyon.

When the Pacific Northwest Power Company applied to impound the remaining canyon of the Snake, the only question was which dam to build.[13] An eight-hundred-foot-high Nez Perce site was favored by the Federal Power Commission (FPC) because the dam would block both the Salmon and Snake Rivers. This was later abandoned for the High Mountain Sheep site, just above the mouth of the Salmon, to spare that river's anadromous fish. A license was issued in 1964 for High Mountain Sheep and its fifty-eight-mile-long reservoir but was contested. In 1967 the Supreme Court ruled on the case of which dam should be built, and William O. Douglas wrote the decision. Not limiting himself to the question of alternate dams, Douglas stated, "The grant of authority . . . does not, of course, turn simply on whether the project will be beneficial to the licensee. . . . The test is whether the project will be in the public interest. . . . The Commission must hold more hearings on the subject of whether any dams should be built at all, not just on which one."[14] Douglas called for study of power needs, public interest in wild rivers, and fish and wildlife. The case was a landmark because it held the FPC accountable for more than power production, and it recognized the values of a wild river. Douglas did not stop the dam but cleared the way for someone who would.

Like David Brower, Brock Evans had not traveled much on rivers, but during one weekend he sat alongside the Snake at Lewiston below Hells Canyon and felt "the power, the feeling, the tugs and the murmurs, the enchantment. The river had a life of its own. Lower Granite Dam flooded that site soon after, but the Snake in Hells Canyon would become a big river in my life."[15] Evans had grown up in the Midwest, then worked as a lawyer in Seattle. After volunteering with the Sierra Club, he left his law office, which represented power companies building dams, and became the Sierra Club's Northwest representative. "Soon I was visited by an emissary out of darkest Idaho," Evans recalled. Floyd Harvey, a jet boat pilot on the Snake, asked Evans to fight for Hells Canyon. Douglas had created an opportunity and Evans jumped on it, filing an appeal against the FPC and mailing it twenty minutes before midnight on the due date.

Evans recalled, "At the hearing in Portland there were twenty-seven lawyers in a circle, and after two hours of testimony for the dam, the judge, up in his seat high above us, asked with the greatest contempt, 'Does the Sierra Club really want to add to this?' Well, we did, and three long bitter years of hearings followed, giving us precious delay. Before the fight was over, there was no more contempt, but respect. We forever changed the balance of power." While courts heard the appeal, conservationists formed the Hells Canyon Preservation Council with the ambitious goal of reversing the politics of water in three states whose modern existence depended on dams.

Cecil Andrus was elected governor of Idaho in 1970 and said that there would be no more dams in Hells Canyon "unless it's over my dead body." Wildlife biologist John Craighead rowed Interior Secretary Walter Hickel down the river. Brock Evans and river guide Verne Huser took freshman senator Bob Packwood through the canyon, and he introduced legislation to ban the dams.[16] Idaho senator Frank Church sponsored a preservation bill that passed, but John Saylor's companion bill failed in the House.

At more hearings in 1971 the power companies argued that Hells Canyon was one of the few remaining sites for large hydropower development in the Northwest and that their project would produce as much electricity as the whole TVA system. Conservationists argued for better use of existing dams: the Bonneville Power Administration had scheduled sixty new generators at federal dams and nine at private dams. Archaeologists said that two hundred important sites would be flooded. The Oregon Wildlife Commission opposed the dams because elk and deer needed the canyon for winter range. Craig Markham of the Central Cascades Conservation Council testified, "If we are incapable of surviving without hydroelectric power from Hells Canyon, then we are incapable of surviving."

National media covered the issue, additional conservation groups supported the river, and in 1973 all the senators from Idaho and Oregon, bordering the river, were ready to vote for protection. In 1975 the governors of Oregon, Idaho, and Washington all opposed the dam.

Cliff Merritt of the Wilderness Society, Brock Evans, and others discussed making the middle Snake a national wild river. "But why not do more?" Evans asked. They drew boundaries of surrounding wilderness in the Seven Devils Mountains in Idaho and the Wallawas in Oregon and lobbied for a bill reaching far beyond the river. In December 1975, President Ford signed legislation prohibiting the dam, adding the Snake and 28.5 miles of Idaho's Rapid River to the national wild and scenic rivers system, and creating a 662,000-acre Hells Canyon National Recreation Area "to assure that the natural beauty, historical and archaeological values of the Hells Canyon area and the 71-mile segment of the Snake River . . . are preserved for this and future generations."

Brock Evans wrote,

> Some day I want to return to Hells Canyon, to lie beside the river and listen to its music, to feel the breeze and watch the grand play of light and form, rock upon rock down the gorge, to watch eagles wheel and arc high above the rim. I may wander up one of the side valleys high into the alpine country far above the river and stroll among the flowers and quiet forests and great peaks. And I will remember, with great joy, that the canyon is safe now, safe forever, because enough people loved and cared enough to rush into the breach and turn a lost cause into a stunning victory. This new recreation area is one of the gifts we now leave to future generations. When more Americans come to know Hells Canyon, they will realize that it is one of the most beautiful victories environmentalists have ever enjoyed.[17]

Urgent threats to places like the Grand Canyon had awakened the nation and built the environmental movement in the 1960s, and the Hells Canyon debate followed the patterns of the big western dam fights. But after 1976 this kind of action was rare. With the rise of the environmental movement and conservation groups' involvement in air pollution, toxic wastes, nuclear power, and other issues, less time was spent on single places. It became the policy of national environmental leaders to choose one strategic route to accomplish as much as possible, and so some threatened places were passed over and controversial rivers were sometimes sacrificed. If a river was considered a political liability to a bill protecting a dozen areas, politicians dropped it. This happened with both the Stanislaus and Tuolumne Rivers in California. In 1981 Sierra Club director Michael McCloskey said,

> In the fifties and sixties things were so slow that programs were site-specific. But by the seventies we realized we couldn't work on one site at a time. We had to package areas by states and to work on generic effects. In Alaska, wilderness and wild rivers were packaged together. Maybe we'll return to rifle shooting at single places, but only if the political situation deteriorates so much that we have to.[18]

By the mid-1970s, then, river protection depended on the local and state levels, aided but not led by the national organizations. Whereas earlier, national groups had been important in drawing wider attention and in taking dam fights out of the local political arena, where dam supporters were the strongest, now the smaller groups had the determination, skills, and influence to achieve complex goals. Local organizations, aided by two new support groups in Washington—the American Rivers Conservation Council and the Environmental Policy Center—now filled much of the space left by the big national groups.

LEAVING THE OLDEST RIVER ALONE

Lacking the big-gorge grandeur of Hells Canyon, the New River is extraordinary in its Appalachian way: it is the oldest river in America; next to the Nile, it is the oldest in the world. Like the middle Snake, the New was threatened by a licensed power dam, and these rivers were the first cases in which national river status was granted in spite of power companies that were ready to build.

The Appalachian Power Company, a subsidiary of the American Electric Power Company, the nation's largest corporate utility, received an FPC license in 1974 for two dams to flood 44 river miles, 212 tributary miles, and forty-two thousand acres, displacing 2,800 people from the North and South Forks of the New. Local people organized as they had done along the Red River. Five thousand attended a festival that followed a citizen organizers' rule—celebrate what you are trying to save (similar gatherings were later held to fight dams on the Little Tennessee, Stanislaus, Yampa, Ocoee, and Staunton). Partly because the power company sponsoring the dams was from Virginia, no elected official in North Carolina supported the project at the height of the campaign. The legislature added the New to the state's wild and scenic rivers system, but as in the Cowlitz case, courts found that the federal license overrode state law.

With heavy lobbying in Washington, river supporters and the state convinced Interior Secretary Thomas Kleppe to name twenty-six miles of the South Fork of the New in the national rivers system in 1976, but the power company appealed and the court ruled that only Congress could revoke the FPC permit. A bill to designate the New in the national rivers system was finally passed and signed by President Ford.[19]

The New is an example of state government working to save a river, of the need for national protection, and of teamwork between local people and the American Rivers Conservation Council (see Chapter 6). The New was also an indicator of changing times and attitudes. For North Carolina and the eastern mountains, the Appalachian Regional Commission had in 1964 touted recreational values from reservoirs while listing none from rivers. But in 1978 North Carolina advertised in national magazines: "Come see the state that kept the world's second oldest river from dying of unnatural causes. . . . Except for North Carolina, the prehistoric river would be just another man-made lake by now."

Saving the New was a landmark case, as conservationists stopped a utility company's dam even after land had been bought. But could river people halt a big federal project, one ready for construction, supported by four states, promoted by a river basin commission, and considered by some to be crucial to cities no less than Philadelphia and New York?

SERVING THE PEOPLE WITHOUT THE DAM: THE DELAWARE

After two hurricanes devastated parts of the Delaware basin in 1955, the corps studied the river under new guidelines, and Tocks Island Dam, sixty-two miles from New York City and seventy-five from Philadelphia, was proposed as a model of contemporary planning. Interior Secretary Stewart Udall pressed for Water Resources Council approval, calling Tocks Island the "Grand Coulee Dam" of the Delaware.[20] In 1962 Congress authorized the 160-foot-high dam and thirty-seven-mile-long reservoir, to stretch up to Port Jervis, New York.

The original authorization was mainly for flood control, but after the 1961–1965 drought, water supply benefits were increased, and during a ten-year delay due to lack of funds, the corps combated inflation by adding recreational benefits until these accounted for nearly half of the justification. The reservoir would be surrounded by the East's largest national recreation area under park service management.

In 1964 residents formed the Delaware Valley Conservation Association, and 604 landowners filed a class action suit to stop the dam, but the case was dismissed. In a seemingly unrelated effort, conservationists fought a power company's plan to pump Delaware water up Kittatinny Ridge for pumped storage power generation at Sunfish Pond (similar to a proposal that conservationists had recently beaten at Storm King above the Hudson). When the power company dropped the plan, the conservationists, inspired by their success, turned to Tocks Island. The Save the Delaware Coalition was started in 1970 as a union of landowners and conservationists.

The corps bought and reduced two-hundred-year-old stone farmhouses to rubble, enraging people who hadn't cared that much about ecology and recreation at the river. The coalition demanded protection under the Archaeological and Historic Preservation Act of 1974, which required agencies to identify and "mitigate" the loss of historic sites. The Historic Preservation Act of 1966 also called for federal agencies to protect sites named on the National Register of Historic Places. Action under these laws delayed, but did not stop, Tocks Island Dam, New Melones Dam, and other projects.[21] When squatters who had moved into homes that had been abandoned for the reservoir ignored orders to leave, armed U.S. marshals appeared without warning before dawn, gave the people five minutes to evacuate, then demolished the houses and everything in them with bulldozers.[22] The heavy-handed tactics turned more people against the project. Local people won an injunction to delay the razing of Zion Church because it was on the national register.

In a procedure that had become standard, the Environmental Defense Fund sued, saying that an eight-page impact statement for a $300 million project was incomplete. A longer statement was written. Freshman congressman Pete duPont of Delaware still tried to halt funds but wrote of the "frustration of trying to convince half of my 434 colleagues that a dam that had been under study for ten years needed further study."

Fighting duPont on the floor of Congress, Texan Jim Wright said, "We cannot keep people from intruding upon the earth. And the interests of people must come first. Nature sometimes, as in this case, needs the corrective surgery of intelligent man, under the injunction given to us in the book of Genesis, to subdue the earth and husband its resources."[23]

Appropriations passed the House in 1971, but in the Senate New Jersey's Clifford Case demanded study by independent scientists, leading to an interagency review. A crucial blow to the dam builders came in a report by the corps's consultants. Because of farm and poultry runoff and other pollution, eutrophication (overfertilization) would cause algae to grow, endangering water supplies and reservoir recreation (similar studies helped stop a Kickapoo River dam in Wisconsin). The President's Council on Environmental Quality called for a moratorium on construction until waste sources were controlled. Leo Eisel of the EDF developed nonstructural alternatives for flood control and proposed water conservation and the pumping of floodwaters to offstream reservoirs for storage. When other studies indicated that existing water supplies in New Jersey could be expanded at 20 percent less cost than the dam, the New Jersey governor abandoned Tocks, followed by the governors of New York and Delaware. Only Pennsylvania, arguing that Philadelphia needed the water, continued to back the dam. In a 3–1 vote, the Delaware River Basin Commission recommended deauthorization in 1975.

A debate had been staged between landscape architecture and recreation management students at Penn State University in 1970: to build the dam and national recreation area or not to. The National Park Service, army corps, and Save the Delaware Coalition participated. The winner was a splinter group opposing the dam but supporting the recreation area, and this is exactly what the park service did. Ten thousand acres that would have been flooded were added as recreation land. This was one of few times when river and flatwater recreation were given equal consideration in the assessment of people's needs.

Not satisfied that the dam's inactive status would last, Congressman Peter Kostmayer from Pennsylvania pushed to make the Delaware a national wild and scenic river, and the National Parks and Recreation Act of 1978 designated 110 miles for protection. To reactivate the dam now, Congress must override the national rivers system.

In 1980 the Pennsylvania Department of Environmental Resources estimated that Philadelphia would demand more water after the year 2000. The agency opposed the abandoning of Tocks Island Dam unless other alternatives were successful, including unlikely reductions in New York's diversions from Delaware headwaters and construction of at least four dams on smaller streams.

The gentle-flowing Delaware, with its fishing pools, canoeing reaches, and patchwork of fields and woods, is what motivated conservationists, but it was environmental impact statements and historic preservation requirements that enabled people to delay dam construction. The dam was finally beaten through technical studies of water quality and water supply alternatives, and protection gained through the national wild and scenic rivers system.

Because the proposed dam was close to large cities, the Tocks Island debate reached people who had never followed a river controversy, and the case heightened interest in alternatives to large dams. Pete duPont wrote, "After years of subsidizing inefficient water management projects, the Congress is beginning to scrutinize the value of these investments. . . . The government must embrace new, flexible alternatives to the big dam." Pointing out that New York City, with no residential water metering, wastes more than one-half the amount supplied by all of its Delaware basin reservoirs, the EDF urged the river basin commission to adopt a conservation plan. Finally in 1979 the commission called for a 15 percent reduction in water use through leak detection and other measures. Yet the commission recommended reconsideration of Tocks Island after the year 2000.

THE INDIANS WIN

The Seneca Indians lost their lands along Pennsylvania's Allegheny River in 1965, but when Arizona politicians called for a dam on the Verde River, the times had changed. Authorized in 1968 as part of the Central Arizona Project (CAP), Orme Dam was to be built near Phoenix to store water pumped from the Colorado River and to control floods. Twenty-five miles of the Verde and Salt Rivers would be flooded, including a section of the Salt used for inner-tubing by thirty thousand people each week in summer, and including 70 percent of the Yavapai's Fort McDowell Reservation.

In the late 1800s the Yavapai had been relocated and imprisoned, but some of the Indians managed to return to ancestral lands, where a reservation was eventually established by executive order. After Roosevelt Dam was built in 1911, valley farmers repeatedly tried to gain control of the Indians' land and water, the greatest threat coming from the Orme Dam proposal. Subdivisions in suburban Phoenix were built near river channels, and when these subdivisions flooded in 1980, water lobbyists blamed the Yavapai for delaying construction of the dam. An Arizona Republic editorial stated that with Orme the Indians could develop recreation facilities, but the tribe voted 101–1 against the dam, one Indian saying, "If Phoenix wants so much water, why don't they move to the ocean?"[24]

The Yavapai delayed the project with lawsuits while other opposition grew. Environmental groups led by the Maricopa Audubon Society opposed destruction of some of the finest desert streamside in the Southwest, including habitat for three pairs of endangered southern bald eagles, endangered Yuma clapper rails, zone-tailed hawks, and black-hawks. President Carter proposed elimination of Orme but later allowed funding provided alternatives were first studied.

In 1981 Interior Secretary Watt accepted recommendations from the Bureau of Reclamation and the corps to build New Waddell Dam near Phoenix and to reconstruct other dams instead of building Orme. The Indians held new power and used it on other rivers, such as the Skagit in Washington, where they blocked Copper Creek Dam because it would stop the migration of salmon, and the Kootenai in Montana, where they fought to protect a religious site from a hydroelectric project.[25]

DISASTER AT TETON

While many people remained oblivious to the problems of Indians and bald eagles at sites like Orme, another dam caught the attention of anybody who watched television.

Trout Unlimited and other conservation groups had sued to stop the Bureau of Reclamation from damming Idaho's Teton River, prized for cutthroat trout, west of Grand Teton National Park. Wildlife biologist Frank Craighead spoke out against Teton Dam, and it was rated by the Environmental Policy Center as one of the nation's thirteen worst water projects. An injunction delayed work, but the dam's political support in Idaho could not be eroded.

Construction had just been completed when two leaks, common to earth-filled dams, appeared downstream from the Teton site on June 3, 1976. The next day, a leak was found three hundred feet from the dam. Early in the morning on June 5, workers spotted two unquestionably dangerous leaks: one at the abutment and another at the foot of the dam, where water erupted at twenty-two thousand gallons a minute. At 10:00 A.M. the dam's right abutment ruptured. A hole grew rapidly, sucking fill from the embankment and washing it through the cavity. A hideous whirlpool drained water from the reservoir while on both sides of the dam men on bulldozers pushed dirt into the hole but accomplished nothing. The crews fled only minutes before their equipment was devoured and flushed through the whirlpool.

At 11:57 A.M. the dam burst. The newly filled, seventeen-mile-long reservoir descended as a twenty-foot-high wave upon the Teton River valley and killed eleven people, scoured one-hundred thousand acres of farmland, obliterated thousands of buildings, drowned sixteen thousand head of livestock, and washed away toxic chemicals that had been stored on the floodplain. The catastrophe caused $1 billion in damages and drove twenty-five thousand residents from their homes.

Scientists who had studied the site were not surprised. Geologists with the Department of the Interior's Geological Survey—the parent agency of the Bureau of Reclamation—had warned the bureau about earthquake faults and weak bedrock. David Schleicher of the Geological Survey had suggested that "we consider a series of strategically placed motion-picture cameras to document the process of catastrophic flooding." During the conservationists' court case, Shirley Pytlak, a former geologist for the Bureau of Reclamation, testified that the rhyolite bedrock was dangerously porous, but bureau officials assured that they would pump cement grouting into the cavities.[26] A memo alerting the Bureau of Reclamation to safety problems was delayed for six months, to be made "more objective," according to Harold Prostka of the Geological Survey.

This was one more case in which the power of the Bureau of Reclamation within the Interior Department was evident. The National Park Service, the Geological Survey, the Bureau of Land Management, the Fish and Wildlife Service, and the Bureau of Outdoor Recreation were all overpowered in dam fights, including those at Echo Park, Glen Canyon, Grand Canyon, Auburn, and the Stanislaus.

After the disaster the Bureau of Reclamation circulated a question-and-answer paper: "With the benefit of hindsight, is there anything that Reclamation might have done to prevent this disaster?" The answer was, "Nothing."

The Committee on Government Operations thought differently, stating in a September 23, 1976, report,

> Pressures to build Federal water resource projects have been so great in some cases that the Bureau of Reclamation officials have been blinded to dangers and hazards presented by some projects. In the case of the Teton Dam, great human and economic costs have been the price of succumbing to those pressures. . . . Once physical construction has commenced, the decision to halt construction is no longer an option available to the Bureau, and safety

problems, regardless of their magnitude, are generally met with unques-
tioned reliance on the Bureau's ability to "engineer" workable solutions.
The Teton Dam is a prime example of fulfilling the momentum to build at
any cost.

The committee stated that the bureau had been "deficient in the geologic
examination of the site" and "in resolving satisfactorily the warning of safety
hazards," and it had "failed to comply with prescribed safety precautions
during the course of the filling of the reservoir."

Not since 1928, when Los Angeles's Saint Francis Dam burst and killed
four hundred people, had dam safety received so much attention. After
Teton, dam fighters added safety to their bundle of arguments. While fighting a Snoqualmie River dam in Washington, opponents pointed out that
the site's geology was the same as at Hansen Dam on Washington's Cedar
River, where a weak foundation prevented complete filling.[27] Gathright
Dam on Virginia's Jackson River was opposed in part because of porous
bedrock. In 1977 President Carter ordered all federal dam-building agencies
to review safety practices. With other dams proposed and under construction near large cities, nuclear power plants, and military bases, concerns for
safety took a toll in the dam fights to come.

ONE DAM TOO FAR

Nowhere in the nation has the debate and conflict over water raged as much
as in California. With two-thirds of California's water in the north and two-
thirds of its people in the south, the politics of water are tense and volatile.
Here are the most powerful water developers and the most active river protectors. The dams are among the largest and most costly, and the rivers
among the most scenic and popular.

As a part of the Bureau of Reclamation's Central Valley Project,
Auburn Dam was an engineer's dream: the world's largest double-curvature
thin-arch dam, curved in width and height, something like the side of a
teacup. The superior physics of this shape rather than its mass of earth or
concrete was intended to hold back a six hundred-foot wall of water. The
dam would have been the fifth tallest in the United States, by far the most
expensive, and closer to a large city than any other high dam. It would plug
the American River and flood forty-eight miles of the North and Middle
Forks—wild canyons thirty-two miles above Sacramento. Fifty-six percent
of the alleged benefits were for irrigation, though the dam would add only

one-fifth to existing Folsom Dam supplies, most of which remain undelivered thirty years after construction. At best, 25 percent of capital costs would be recovered from irrigators, the difference to be paid by electricity users and taxpayers.

In 1974 the Natural Resources Defense Council sued to delay the project because of an incomplete environmental statement. A judge halted canal construction but allowed work on the dam's foundation to continue. A citizens group formed, arguing that if 6 percent interest were charged, a $3.5 billion deficit would result in fifty years, and that the dam would provide for only 1 percent of California's water needs and 0.3 percent of its electricity. Local congressman Harold "Bizz" Johnson, however, had labored for the dam most of his life, and he chaired the House Public Works Committee; as another congressman said, "If Bizz says he wants the Auburn Dam built, it will be built."

In August 1975 the story was forever changed when the Sierra foothills, thought to be seismically quiet, lurched with an earthquake of 5.9 on the Richter scale, rattling windows for sixty miles around Oroville. The state had recently built Oroville Dam, a 770-foot pile of earth (some geologists think that the dam and its reservoir caused the earthquake). Oroville Dam was unharmed, but this side-of-a-teacup Auburn Dam could be different. Although $200 million had already been spent, work was stopped, making Auburn the nation's largest project to be halted after construction had begun. The Association of Engineering Geologists reported that the dam could "crack over thousands of feet horizontally and hundreds of feet vertically" and "would be unsafe even in a moderate earthquake." Bureau of Reclamation studies required by California stated that "complete failure" of the dam would flood 750,000 people, five military bases, and the state capital.[28]

Two months in office, President Carter called Auburn economically marginal and added it to a list of water projects to be scrapped. The Bureau of Reclamation defended the design, but when Teton Dam burst, the bureau's credibility went with it. At a 1977 hearing, members of Friends of the River, a California river protection group, released a Geological Survey memo identifying an active fault that had shifted three feet near the dam in the last seventy thousand years.

The Interior Department began the most extensive seismic studies ever done for a water project. After one hundred miles of trenching, geologists found that Auburn and seventy existing dams were near potentially damaging faults. Interior Secretary Andrus recommended a new design to withstand a foundation shift of five inches, though the Geological Survey had recommended three feet.

While technicians grappled with the safety issue, attitudes changed. New water policies of the president emphasized sound economics and discouraged the heavy subsidies epitomized by Auburn. Governor Brown's administration built the best water conservation program in the nation and defended wild rivers. The state Department of Water Resources compared capital costs of water from Auburn to the costs of other large dams: Shasta at $415 an acre-foot, Oroville at $901, and Auburn at $3,072. Auburn would preempt money from other projects; Assistant Interior Secretary Guy Martin wrote to Andrus: "If you decide to proceed with Auburn, it will completely dominate the water and power construction budget for the next ten years." He cautioned that the entire Auburn unit would cost more than all bureau funds spent in California since the 1930s and that the cost would be ten times that originally authorized by Congress. "Construction of Auburn would only drive the CVP account further into the red."[29]

The American River supported 14 percent of California's king salmon and five million user-days of recreation in Sacramento, but Auburn's Folsom South Canal would reduce the river to ankle depth to divert water to farms and other cities. A state official warned, "It's the same as Owens Valley—one part of California is trying to take water now used by other people."

Secretary Andrus stated that reauthorization was needed for work to resume, and the project receded under more studies. Replacing Andrus, James Watt called for fewer controls on federal irrigation water. To recommend Auburn, however, would have been absolute hypocrisy from an administration that cut domestic programs to the bone. The final decision rests with Congress, where Bizz Johnson's replacement, Eugene Chappie, said, "I intend to push for Auburn."

Realizing that the dam would not be dead if farmers still wanted its water, Friends of the River and the Brown administration promoted water conservation, citing federal reports that millions of acre-feet of irrigation water could be saved. Local groups supported a park system for the American River canyons, with their rapids, trails, and archaeological sites. Yet Michael Catino, acting regional director for the Bureau of Reclamation, said in 1981, "We would have a difficult time recommending deauthorization. Nearly $400 million will be sunk, which is a lot to write off as a poor investment."[30] Auburn may have needed only another politician with the disposition and power that Bizz Johnson had. Bureau staff offered tours of the site and waited for the politics to change. "You try to stay in readiness for the day you get green-lighted," Catino said. In 1983 reclamation commissioner Robert Broadbent said that the dam was not dead. "We're trying to find new sponsors for the project."[31] Bills were introduced in 1983 to reauthorize the dam at $2.2 billion.

A July 19, 1984, memorandum from Assistant Interior Secretary G. Ray Arnett cited the need to protect the fishery and recreational values of the American River below the Auburn site (a national river) as well as the fisheries of San Francisco Bay and the Sacramento Delta. Reserving water for these uses would make Auburn Dam even less feasible.

Auburn remained unresolved, but it may have signaled a change in attitudes about technological wonders and a turning point in our reliance on engineering fixes. The size and intricate engineering of this dam were used as an argument, not for its construction, but against it. In this respect it was similar to the Supersonic Transport. The studies still went on, and the price went up—$10 million a month when inflation was high—the dam's viability receding in a new era of limits.

At Auburn, the Bureau of Reclamation pushed the Central Valley Project one dam too far, into the economic wasteland of a dead investment. The Tennessee Valley Authority also fell prey to building too much, but unlike the bureau, it would be rescued by some of the most ludicrous lawmaking ever affecting a river.

THE FATE OF THE LITTLE TENNESSEE

The Tennessee Valley Authority had dammed the Tennessee and most of the Little Tennessee, but above the mouth of the Tellico River a thirty-three-mile section survived as one of the best trout rivers in the East and the only large, clean river in the state. Three hundred and forty farms populated the wide valley. William O. Douglas wrote that the Little Tennessee was "one of God's finest free-flowing rivers. . . . It is one of our best float streams because of its many islands for camping and because of its rainbow trout that run up to fifteen pounds."[32]

The valley was one of few sites known to be occupied continuously for ten thousand years, and a TVA study credited it with "world-wide significance."[33] The National Indian Youth Council wrote, "The Cherokee capital of Echota was located there. Echota was more than an old tribal town, it is the heart of what it means to be a Cherokee. It was called 'the mother town' or the 'beloved town.' . . . Echota, then, is a sacred place, the Cherokee Jerusalem. . . . The destruction of the Tellico Valley is to Indians as the flooding of the entire state of Israel would be to Christians."[34] Supporting the Indians, author Peter Matthiessen wrote, "Is there a human being who does not revere his homeland, even though he may not return?"[35] The valley also included the Indian town of Tennase, from which the state's name was derived. Toskeegee was a neighboring village where Sequoyah, the author of the Cherokee alphabet, was born in 1760.

In 1966 the TVA approved funding for Tellico Dam, to be built at the confluence of the Little Tennessee and Tellico Rivers. Tennessee Valley Authority director Aubrey Wagner said that the dam would be one of the agency's best power projects. But it would produce only twenty-three megawatts—less than 0.1 percent of TVA's capacity. The dam would provide no flood control, and it did not even meet Department of the Interior standards for safety. Recreation was credited for 40 percent of the benefits, though twenty-four other large reservoirs are within sixty miles, and the Tennessee basin has more flatwater shoreline than the Great Lakes. Sixteen thousand acres of prime farmland were eliminated. Twenty percent of the claimed benefits were for real estate sales; much of the thirty-eight thousand acres bought (some of it through condemnation) from farmers would be sold to lakeside industrial developers at a TVA profit, leading Michael Frome to write in *American Forests*, "It is not the business of the federal government to take the role of real estate developer." Fishermen and conservationists fought the dam in the late 1960s, and the EDF took the case to court in 1972 but only delayed construction.

While snorkeling in 1973 in the section of the river to be dammed, a University of Tennessee zoologist discovered a three-inch-long fish previously unknown. Named the snail darter because it eats snails, the fish was placed on the Department of the Interior's endangered species list in 1975, one year after the Endangered Species Act required federal protection of species near extinction. While $20 million was being spent to save another endangered creature—a vulture called the California condor—$103 million of government funds were being used for a land speculation project that could exterminate the snail darter; the TVA speeded construction with round-the-clock shifts.

National conservation groups considered fighting the dam but knew that it would be difficult to stop a project already under construction and having solid congressional support. Worst of all, they feared that the Endangered Species Act would be rescinded as an example of environmental extremism. But what they decided did not really matter, because Zygmunt Plater, a faculty member of the University of Tennessee law school, filed a lawsuit of his own.

The district court in Knoxville ruled against Plater, saying that Tellico was almost finished and the Congress's funding indicated its desire to complete the project (this was the same opinion given about Rainbow Bridge ten years earlier). Plater appealed, and Judge Anthony Celebrezze granted an injunction, stating, "Whether a dam is fifty percent or ninety percent completed is irrelevant in calculating the social and scientific costs attributable to the disappearance of a unique form of life."[36] In 1978 the Supreme Court agreed, ruling that the law required that the fish be saved but suggesting that Congress could change the law.

Politicians immediately assailed the environmental restriction. Senator William Scott from Virginia quoted from the Bible, saying that God gave humans dominion "over every creeping thing that creepeth upon the earth." Senator Jake Garn from Utah said that there was no justification for calling the acts of humans unnatural, because "beavers build dams too." Not wanting to sponsor legislation directly counter to the Endangered Species Act, Senator Howard Baker from Tennessee sponsored a bill creating a cabinet-level committee to review federal projects conflicting with the act. Congress empowered the committee to waive requirements if there were no reasonable alternatives or if the benefits of the project clearly outweighed those of alternatives. Environmentalists called this the "God committee."

The committee met in December 1978, and Charles Schultze, chairman of the President's Council of Economic Advisors, said that Tellico Dam's "costs clearly outweigh the benefits. It would be difficult to say there are no reasonable and prudent alternatives to this project. . . . Here is a project that is 95 percent complete, and if one takes just the cost of finishing it against the total project benefits, it doesn't pay, which says something about the original design."

Interior Secretary Cecil Andrus—a committee member—wrote to House Speaker Thomas P. O'Neill with the committee's arguments against finishing the dam: costs outweighed benefits, safety standards were not met, recreation benefits were inflated, hydropower would be insignificant, land uses other than a flooded valley would generate more income, and transplants of the snail darter to the Hiwassee River might not live. Tennessee Valley Authority chairman S. David Freeman agreed that use of the free-flowing river "has larger intangible benefits" and would provide more jobs than the dam.

Howard Baker responded with a bill to eliminate the committee that had been his own creation. When this failed, he sought to exempt Tellico Dam from the Endangered Species Act but lost again.

Few congressmen were on the floor on June 18, 1979, and most were

Appropriations Committee members awaiting routine action on the energy and water development bill. House rules prohibit the use of an appropriations bill to change an existing law, so Congressman John Duncan, from the Tellico area, orchestrated an effort with fellow congressmen. He quietly placed an amendment in the hopper, then deftly stopped the clerk's reading of the measure just before the important paragraph. Another member interrupted, saying that the minority had reviewed the amendment and accepted it. Tom Bevill, chairman of the Appropriations Subcommittee on Energy and Water Development, stood and spoke for the Democratic majority: "We have no objection." Immediately, a voice vote was taken and the amendment passed. All of this required forty-two seconds. The *Congressional Record* printed the paragraph not read on the floor: the TVA would finish Tellico Dam and fill it notwithstanding the Endangered Species Act and "all other laws."

California's Paul McCloskey led an effort to rescind the amendment, McCloskey himself having been present but fooled by Duncan's scheme. The Senate voted 53–45 to remove the House amendment, but then the House restored the Tellico approval. On September 10 the Senate debated the measure again. Baker called Tellico "an unfortunate symbol of environmental extremism." Dam opponents had the votes, but Baker walked the aisles, and in the last minute changed the votes of six senators. The dam won, 48–44.

Everyone expected President Carter to veto the uneconomic and destructive water developments he had opposed ever since Spewrell Bluff. Some White House staff members told environmentalists to lobby Congress to uphold a veto, but other White House staff needed political currency to trade for the Panama Canal Treaty and the creation of a department of education. The president signed the Tellico approval and said, "Even if I vetoed this bill, Tellico exemptions would be proposed repeatedly in the future." On the same day, Congressman Bevill had attached a Tellico rider on a funding bill that Carter would have had even more difficulty vetoing. Twelve hours after the president's signature, TVA bulldozers were finishing the dam. The gates were closed and the valley was flooded in December 1979.

Robert Cahn wrote in *Audubon*:

> More than a half-century ago, because of a congressional decision, conservationists lost a multi-year battle to stop the first dam's being built within a national park (Hetch Hetchy Dam in Yosemite). But a lesson was learned. No dam has been built since within any national park. Perhaps we can learn

a similar lesson from the snail darter. Perhaps this will be the last time (as well as the first) that we consciously sacrifice a species or a habitat for political reasons.[37]

Conservation leaders who had steered clear of Tellico saw the final outcome as proof that the case was an unnecessary risk to the Endangered Species Act (since the debate the snail darter has been found in other rivers). Michael McCloskey of the Sierra Club was concerned that "river saving will be stigmatized as a loser issue."

But in 1983 Zygmunt Plater defended his work:

It was not a mistake. We had the facts, the economic case, and the law on our side. If we had not pressed it, we would have been writing off the Endangered Species Act anyway—admitting that there was no way for rationality to run the system. Carter could have vetoed the bill. All he had to do was to take on Congressman Jim Wright in front of the American public and say that the issue was not that of a little fish. The media and the politicians sold the public a bill of goods about the snail darter. The real issue was that Tellico wasted money as a land speculation project.[38]

Tellico again proved a point known since the EDF tried to save the Cassatot: lawsuits must be part of a larger strategy and not an end in themselves. If the politics are not changed from prodam to proriver, Congress will simply pass whatever new laws are needed to build the dams. The Little Tennessee was a great loss, but in its wake came a great success.

THE NEW BREED

Without the more tangible goals of saving parks, homes, fish, or money, New Englanders working for the St. John River in Maine brought the river protection movement a long step closer to the simple goal of saving a river for the river's sake. This may be the best example so far in which the stream's specialties were the central issue. "Up there you had the river and that's all it took," said Bill Painter, director of the American Rivers Conservation Council.

Named by Samuel de Champlain in 1604 on the feast of John the Baptist, the river is more like a Canadian waterway than any other in the United States. Wild, clean, crowded by spruce, it is the habitat of moose, lynx, otter, marten, beaver, eagles, and osprey. From its source near Quebec, the St. John runs unblocked and undeveloped for more than 100 miles. Only three primitive bridges spanned the water. Most land is owned by lumber companies. The Appalachian Mountain Club's New England Canoeing Guide states that the upper 120 miles of the St. John have "no equal in the Eastern United States in the number and diversity of wilderness canoe trips which can be made." The region is considered one of the finest for brook trout in the country.

Canoeist, river activist, and lawyer Tom Arnold wrote,

> There is a magical moment on every St. John trip. When you push off from shore for the first time, you know that nothing lies ahead but paddling, floating, watching the sun and clouds, hearing the wind and river, and that each day your senses will open like flowers to the sun and absorb more of what is around you. The St. John is the only free-flowing river in New England that is long enough for this to happen.

For that matter, it is the longest undeveloped river in the East.

In the 1950s the Army Corps of Engineers proposed the Rankin Rapids hydroelectric dam to back water up the St. John and thirty-five miles up the Allagash River—a tributary and a favorite stream of river guides and fishermen. Fought by Maine conservationists, Senator Edmund Muskie, and Interior Secretary Stewart Udall, the dam was dropped. Udall recalled, "Senator Muskie was very astute on this; he was trying to balance things in Maine, so he moved the dam site upriver to Dickey, where the Allagash wouldn't be affected."[39] But the cost of saving the Allagash was that the St. John would be dammed farther upstream—a compromise that Muskie honored from his position as chairman of the Environmental and Public Works Committee. The senator's environmental record was otherwise excellent—he led efforts for the Clean Water Act of 1972—and so he was rankled by environmentalists' criticism of his support for Dickey–Lincoln. He believed that public hydroelectric power—never developed in a large New England project—would be good for Maine, and he echoed local boosters who hoped for construction jobs and an economic boom.

The dams had been authorized in 1966, but New England utilities lobbied successfully against funding until the 1973 oil embargo brought gasoline shortages and unexpected fuel price hikes. The dams were supported by twenty-two of twenty-five New England congressmen, including liberals who argued for public power in the same way that progressives such as William Kent had argued for the dam at Hetch Hetchy in 1913.

Dickey Dam would be the country's sixth largest, 340 feet high and 9,260 feet long. With a small dam downstream at Lincoln, the project would flood eighty-nine thousand acres, 55 miles of the St. John, 223 miles of tributaries, and thirty lakes and ponds. For peaking use, 830 megawatts of power would be generated for two and a half hours a day and exported to Boston and southern New England, 450 miles away. The dam would produce less power than a small coal-fired plant and would serve about 1.5 percent of New England's needs.[40]

Tom Arnold called New England conservationists together to organize Friends of the St. John in 1974. Within a month he collected a coalition of twenty groups and $3,000. By organizing people and lobbying in Washington, Arnold proved that one person can make a difference in saving rivers. "If you'd taken Tom Arnold out of that fight, I'm not sure what you would have had," said Bill Painter. And many other people worked for the river: thirty thousand brochures were mailed by the Natural Resources Council of Maine, and the L. L. Bean store in Freeport became an information center for the dam fighters.

Friends of the St. John argued that the wild river was worth saving, that the dams were not worth the cost (eventually estimated at $1 billion), and that energy conservation was cheaper. Flood control benefits were reduced when a new corps levee protected the town of Fort Kent. To operate the dams would employ only sixty-eight people, the jobs costing $15 million each if other benefits were not counted. Recreation on a pool with 6,000 acres of mudflats was branded absurd when Maine had three thousand natural lakes, many of them underused and nearly all of them closer to population centers. The corps assigned river recreation no value in the benefit–cost analysis, but as author Joel Garreau wrote of the St. John, "recreational wilderness is more scarce than Middle Eastern oil."[41] In a state economically dependent on logs, 110,000 acres of forests would be flooded. The New England Rivers Center—another group led by Arnold—found that new attic insulation would make available forty-three times the energy for the same price as the dams.

President Carter added Dickey–Lincoln to a list of water projects to be cut but then, influenced by Senator Muskie, deleted it. When the corps prepared an environmental statement, botanists discovered twenty rare plants along the river, including the Furbish lousewort and Josselyn sedge, which qualified for protection as endangered species.

It took five years of lobbying by Tom Arnold and others, but by 1979 most New England congressmen opposed the project as a waste of taxpayers' money. Congressmen Robert Edgar from Pennsylvania and James Cleveland from New Hampshire led an effort to deauthorize the dams and won a committee vote—the first time that the House Public Works Committee acted to stop a project on which substantial funds had been spent. After Edmund Muskie left the Senate to become secretary of state, the deauthorization bill passed in 1980. The corps began a new study of only the Lincoln Dam, which would flood eleven miles of the river in a lower section not as highly valued.

This was one of the first cases in which alternatives of energy conservation were publicized, dovetailing with the movements for nondestructive energy development, such as solar power. Other projects had been stopped even after earth moving had begun, but no other dam nearing construction had been deauthorized.

The St. John showed the growing strength of a new breed of river conservationists. They were people who traveled the rivers—canoeists, kayakers, and rafters—and the river was the center of their activity. The canoeists who saved the Buffalo marked a beginning of this movement in the 1960s, but with the Snake, New, Delaware, and now the St. John more than any other case so far, the river was recognized as valuable in its own right. People argued economics, but that was just political pragmatism. As Bill Painter said, "That's not the big issue in our hearts. We're not losing sleep because tax money is wasted but because it's used to destroy something we love. Dam fights always start with somebody who cares about that place." A spiritual side to river protection, not unlike John Muir's feeling for the wilderness, surfaced in the river protection movement, and nowhere was this dimension seen more vividly than on the Stanislaus River in California.

A HOLY PLACE

First authorized in 1944, New Melones Dam was to be built in the Sierra Nevada foothills north of Yosemite for flood control. In 1962, irrigation, hydropower, recreation, and fish and wildlife enhancement were added, and the proposal was enlarged to call for America's fourth-tallest dam. Twenty-six miles of the Stanislaus River would be buried; the upper nine miles were a wilderness and contained the deepest limestone canyon on the West Coast, with hundreds of archaeological and historic sites, thirty caves, rich wildlife habitat, and exciting rapids. By the mid-1970s the Stanislaus canyon was probably the second most boated whitewater in America, with forty-nine thousand floaters a year, including more handicapped people than any other river or wilderness. Here was a river having the finest of wild and recreational values, but the plans for its damming were drawn.

Whereas other people had written off the canyon to the army corps project, canoeist Jerry Meral paddled the river in 1967 and, like Tom Arnold on the St. John one year earlier, decided that the stream was worth saving. After futile attempts through the state resources secretary and a petition drive in which river supporters collected a hundred thousand signatures for President Nixon, Meral organized Friends of the River (FOR) in 1973 to campaign for a statewide initiative to stop the dam, already under construction. Other statewide votes had been taken to save rivers: the Cowlitz in Washington, which won but was dammed anyway, and the Hudson in New York, which won and was saved.

Many people saw New Melones as merely a local issue, but FOR propelled it to state and then national attention. Meral persuaded Mark Dubois, who had grown to know and love the Stanislaus while guiding raft trips, to work on the campaign. Helped by thousands of volunteers, the river people faced prodam advertising, funded by the contractors building the dam, that urged voters to "Save the River, Vote No on 17," which was a vote for the dam. Friends of the River narrowly lost, and a poll afterward found that 60 percent of the people intended to vote against the dam but were confused by the advertising.

Emerging from the campaign a charismatic leader, Mark Dubois led new efforts, all generating support and bringing the issues of river protection to more people, but failing to stop New Melones. Much of the campaign was funded by rafting outfitters, and some of the FOR leaders had discovered the river while working as guides. The group came within one committee vote of clearing a state wild and scenic river bill for legislative action.

Seeing no need to drown the whitewater until contracts were sold for irrigation supplies, the state Water Resources Control Board had blocked the filling of the reservoir even though the dam would be built. In a precedent-setting decision, the Supreme Court found that the state could dictate operations of a federal project provided that these conformed to Congress's authorization. But further court delays and district court decisions undercut the water board's decisions.

In the most dramatic case of direct action to save an American river, Mark Dubois chained himself to bedrock near the rising water's edge while the reservoir was filling in 1979. Search parties on foot and in boats and helicopters could not find Dubois. If the dam were filled much more, he would be drowned. In a letter to corps colonel Donald O'Shea, Dubois had stated, "Part of my spirit dies as the reservoir fills and floods the lower Stanislaus Canyon. . . . The life of the 9 million year old Stanislaus Canyon is far more significant than my short tenure on this planet."

Governor Jerry Brown sent a telegram to President Carter urging him to save Dubois and the river, and the corps released water to lower the level. Then FOR lobbyist Patricia Schifferle convinced Congressman Don Edwards to introduce legislation to name the Stanislaus a national river. With volunteer help from professional planners and a team of twelve people, FOR and the American Rivers Conservation Council completed the only citizen-prepared wild and scenic river study for a national river candidate. Economist and assistant resources secretary Guy Phillips prepared a study showing that the dam would yield a subsidy of $1 million to each of four hundred farmers over the next fifty years and that a partly filled reservoir sparing the upper canyon would fulfill most intended purposes and would be more economic than a full reservoir.

With a "row for the river" to San Francisco, a sixty-mile walk to Sacramento, political rallies, and river trips for scores of writers, newspeople, and politicians, FOR sought to make the Stanislaus the most publicized loss of wilderness in America, and they may have succeeded. Articles appeared in the *New York Times, Newsweek, American Forests, Audubon, Sports Afield*, a dozen other magazines, nearly all of the environmental publications, and California newspapers. Television brought the chaining incident to a nationwide audience, which for the first time saw that someone was willing to risk his life for a river. Again and again, FOR launched grass roots campaigns, and people wrote thousands of letters. On commercial river trips, guides stopped for breaks and customers wrote their congressmen. More than in any previous struggle to save a river, raft trips were used to publicize what was at stake and to promote protection.

Dam supporters derided the controversy as "recreation versus food," but with economic studies and growing sophistication, the river people stressed that the sacrifice of the canyon was not needed, did not pay, and violated the law. Water developers saw the Stanislaus as symbolic—since New Melones was already built, to leave the reservoir unfilled would shake the entire water development establishment.

An intense campaign for the national river designation fell two votes short of committee approval in 1980. When President Carter lost to Ronald Reagan, the last hope was gone. High runoff in 1982 and 1983 filled the reservoir, drowning a river that thousands of people had worked for years to save.

The Stanislaus case is filled with unequaled commitments and offers a whole chapter in the evolution of attitudes about rivers. The motivation of those fighting New Melones Dam went beyond the saving of parks and homes, beyond recreation, economics, and ecology. Like the St. John, the river was recognized as valuable for its own sake. Unlike the St. John, the Stanislaus was a people's river, known by millions through the media and known firsthand by hundreds of thousands of people who took raft trips. As Paul Brooks wrote, "It is obvious that we fight to preserve only what we have come to love and understand."

What was it that moved so many people? "It's not kilowatt hours or recreation days," Mark Dubois said. "It cannot be counted, but it is still a value that is important and real to many people. On trips I usually ask people to try to go and sit alone. They return with a glow on their faces. This canyon feeds people's spirits. They touch something that they haven't touched anywhere else."

Many people became involved who did not do that much with rivers—they had no particular concern. The river, alone, was enough. Jerry Meral said, "You had the anglers and the boaters and others, and then you had the people who just liked rivers. On the Stanislaus, they included many of the people who worked the hardest."

The Stanislaus was regarded as a thing of wonderful power, beauty, and life. Alexander Gaguine of FOR said, "This river has done a lot for people. Trying to keep up with the demand for more water or more power does not uplift people, but spending a day in the Stanislaus River canyon often does. The experience can raise people's spirits or bring out feelings of wonder and joy. The Stanislaus becomes a very real part of their home, whether people are there for three days or three months." The Stanislaus brought out feelings of reverence for the natural world, where rivers are a source of life and a center of attention. The river was a sacred and holy place. Gaguine said, "Europe has its great cathedrals, but in America it is our own great natural landscape which uplifts our spirits and souls as individuals and as a whole nation. What will inspire us when the holy places are gone?"[42]

The reverence given to the Stanislaus could show a new regard for rivers. In many of the earlier dam fights, it was not so much the rivers as it was the parks, fish, and homes that people wanted to save. Then, with the environmentalism of the 1970s, people saw that the stream and ecological concerns were inseparable, and the movement came closer to that of saving rivers for themselves. With increased river travel by canoeists, rafters, and kayakers, a river culture was quietly born. People began to talk more about the joy, the wonder, and the spirituality brought by rivers. What they wanted to save would remain enigmatic and lost for words because it was so tied up in feelings and emotions condemned from public debate. Dubois, Gaguine, and others tried to describe the importance of their river, though they usually resorted to guiding people in rafts because the only thing that really worked was to experience the river personally. Why save a river? Because it is the unspoiled Eden, right here, available to all. Why save a river? Because it is a river.

One of the few North American precedents for this commitment to rivers lies in the Indians' ancient concept of holy and powerful places. Now, in a culture so responsive to economic gain and technology—in a society poorly prepared to face people who are spiritually committed to the earth— the rivers movement adopted the ideas of stewardship, responsibility, reverence for life, and spirituality in new ways that reached many people as they camped in canyons like the Stanislaus and as the fights against dams were dragged through Congress and publicized to the nation.

RETURN TO THE TUOLUMNE

Hetch Hetchy Valley of the Tuolumne was the site of the nation's first major dam fight, and in 1982 this river became the subject of the greatest controversy in river protection. On a section below Yosemite National Park, more remarkable natural and recreational values were threatened than anywhere else in the country. The twenty-seven-mile-long canyon between O'Shaughnessy Dam and New Don Pedro Reservoir includes some of the country's most challenging but regularly used whitewater. Tuolumne raft trips offer the height of outdoor adventure along with the peace of canyon camping only four hours from San Francisco and eight hours from Los Angeles.

The canyon houses two hundred species of birds and animals, including the bobcat, black bear, and spotted owl. Yosemite Park's two largest deer herds winter in the canyon. Gold Rush relics and 250 archaeological sites from the Miwok Indians lie along the river. Many fishermen consider the Tuolumne the Sierra's best trout stream, and the state estimates that the river yields a thousand pounds of fish per acre, three times the amount of the best fishing reservoir in California. Congress designated the Tuolumne for a wild and scenic river study in 1975, and eighty-three miles were recommended for protection by the Carter administration.

In 1976 San Francisco and the Modesto and Turlock irrigation districts applied for federal permits to dam the lower canyon and to divert flows from the upper canyon for hydroelectricity. The $900 million project would destroy twenty-seven miles of the Tuolumne and seven miles of the Clavey River to produce 390 megawatts—less than 0.5 percent of California's projected electrical supplies in 1992. Additional plans called for dams on the South and Middle forks.

In 1978 Tuolumne County voters opposed the project by a two-thirds margin, and under Governor Jerry Brown the state supported wild and scenic river status. In 1981 the California Energy Commission reported that new reservoirs for power were fifth priority for meeting energy needs and that conservation, geothermal development, existing reservoirs, cogeneration, and interstate transfers of power could meet needs to 1992. Public Utilities Commission president John Bryson said, "The small increments of new supply that could be provided by additional damming of the Tuolumne are outweighed by the natural values associated with the protection of the remaining stretches of that beautiful canyon." The frail case for power production came from irrigation districts where electricity rates were among the lowest in the nation.[43] An economic analysis by Richard B. Norgaard of the University of California concluded that the project would cost more than it would earn.

In December 1982, editors of the *Los Angeles Times* wrote, "We think that a strong case has been made for permanent protection of one of the few relatively unspoiled rivers left in California. . . . California has nearly exhausted its supply of wild rivers to meet the water needs of its farms and cities."[44] On January 29, 1983, the *Los Angeles Times* stated, "The loss of one of the few remaining semi-free rivers within reach of millions of Californians is too high a price for the sake of lower power bills for a few thousand customers." San Francisco reversed its position and supported protection of the Tuolumne.

After the national river study moratorium expired in 1982, the Federal Energy Regulatory Commission issued permits for the planning of the dams. The sponsors spent $5 million on plans and hired Lee White—former chairman of the Federal Power Commission—to plead their case. In 1983 the irrigation districts spent $140,000 a month lobbying for their dams.

Realizing that the temporary protection would expire, Jerry Meral, who now headed the Planning and Conservation League of California, and others had formed the Tuolumne River Preservation Trust in 1981 and hired John Amodio to run the campaign to save the Tuolumne. Amodio had led the fight to expand Redwood National Park, and he brought political experience and a determination to gain broadbased support. "We needed to avoid polarization," he said. "We built our arguments on the concept of balanced use—*they* were the extremists, wanting to dedicate the river to hydroelectric power when it was already providing for many needs." The river's three dams already provided water for one of twelve homes in the state, for irrigation, and for hydroelectric power. Even the organization's name—a trust—was aimed at conservative people. The board of directors included some members who had even supported New Melones Dam. A $100-a-plate dinner at San Francisco's Meridian Hotel was attended by the political elite wearing tuxedos. The event, which earned $20,000, honored actor Richard Chamberlain, among others.

Chamberlain had rafted the river and met Don Briggs—a guide and longtime Friends of the River activist—who encouraged Chamberlain to become involved. He lobbied for two days in Washington and testified eloquently before congressional committees. "To my eyes, God seems to have lavished a special abundance of living gifts on this river. We have the power to destroy it. But never, never in our wildest imagination can we ever recreate it." To save the Tuolumne became the priority issue of the American Rivers Conservation Council, which hired lobbyist David Dickson—a river guide and former Friends of the River staff member.

Senator Alan Cranston had favored protection for years, and after Senator Pete Wilson received more mail about the Tuolumne than about any other issue, he supported national river status also. The trust and other groups gained wide support in the House, where the effort was led by Tuolumne area congressman Richard Lehman, John Siberling of Ohio, and Sala Burton of San Francisco, who took her husband Phillip's seat when he died in 1983. Fresno congressman Tony Coelho, in support of the dams, was isolated despite his powerful party position, which allowed him to control funding for Democratic campaigns.

National river status for the Tuolumne was attached to the California Wilderness Bill, which passed and was signed in September 1984. Capitalizing on the experience and support gathered during the Stanislaus battle, the river people won this extraordinary victory against great odds and again showed the strength of the river conservation movement by saving one of America's most valuable wild rivers.

THE CENTER OF THE MOVEMENT

In the 1970s the saving of rivers had grown from isolated dam fights to a major environmental issue. Certain problems were common to all the threatened rivers, and as awareness grew, people joined together. Conservationists became adept in science and economics, and a center for lobbying was established in Washington, D.C. Leading the way in much of this movement was Brent Blackwelder.

The son of a minister, Blackwelder was living in Washington and earning a doctorate in philosophy when he volunteered with Friends of the Earth in 1970. He had not been an avid canoeist or fisherman, but set out to stop the government from channelizing streams. Explaining his motivation, he said, "One picture of a channelization disaster was all it took." During the 1970 election campaign, Blackwelder worked for the League of Conservation Voters to defeat House Public Works Committee chairman Fallon. "That election showed me that if you know what you're doing, you can win," Blackwelder recalled with the optimism that would carry him through the dark tunnels of dozens of struggles to save rivers.

Blackwelder and others who had worked for Friends of the Earth formed the Environmental Policy Center (EPC) in 1972 specifically to lobby Congress, and ten years later the group employed more lobbyists than any other public interest organization in Washington. As the first lobbyist to work full time on river protection, Blackwelder fought Dickey–Lincoln dams, Tocks Island Dam, and many others. American Rivers Conservation Council (ARCC) director Bill Painter said, "Brent was the real genius at involving everybody whose ox was to be gored, and in gaining that broad base of opposition to water projects." He circulated information and told people along one river to talk to people along another river. Dam fighters who were flailing away on their own began to find each other and to form coalitions.

Why does Blackwelder do this work? He says simply that special places are being destroyed for no good reason, and at public expense. Bill Painter said, "Brent thinks that those water projects are wrong, just ethically and politically wrong. He's zealous, but you have to get outraged to fight what we're dealing with."

In 1973 the EPC, ARCC, and other groups published *Disasters in Water Development*, a booklet documenting the reasons why thirteen of the nation's worst water projects should not be built and calling people to action as no single publication had ever done. In 1976 the EPC and ARCC sponsored the first national conference for river conservationists in Washington. Just as the wilderness conferences that started in 1949 had drawn preservationists together and given them a forum, the "Dam Fighters Conference" brought river protectors together more than ever before. From the plains of Nebraska, the canyons of California, the valleys of Appalachia, law offices in Boston, universities in Florida, and Indian reservations in Arizona, two hundred people came, and they found that river protection was a common goal. Renamed the National Conference on Rivers, the meeting drew several hundred people every spring to hear the latest news, to join in workshops about political skills, and to testify at appropriations committee hearings. It was the event of the year for river activists.

With Peter Carlson at the EPC, Blackwelder helped to stop 140 dams, canals, and channelization projects by 1983, saving taxpayers $20 billion in the process. He said that the keys to success are

> strong local groups, good information, coalitions, connections to national organizations, and knowing how to influence congressmen. If all else fails, elect new representatives. The French Broad River in North Carolina is a case where the people organized and elected new local officials when the ones they had wouldn't fight the TVA dams that were proposed. Then the feds saw the handwriting on the wall and backed off. The media makes all the difference. We've built and built the coverage, and as our name became known, the reporters started coming here whenever some controversy came up.

Through all of these river conflicts, patterns had developed. Where conservationists started early enough, they almost always won. When the corps started a study for Keating Dam on the West Branch of the Susquehanna in Pennsylvania, environmental groups made a strong showing, and authorization was never recommended. No more authorizations slipped in ahead of the opposition. Coalitions of conservation groups were essential, and by the late 1970s, support from economic, business, labor, social, and education organizations was needed for the conservationists' political success.

Except for national parks and a few other special cases, river conservationists learned that all water politics is local. Organizations in Washington did much to help, but streams were won or lost in towns and counties where congressmen depended on votes.

Party politics was riddled with exceptions on the subject of river conservation and water development. Herbert Hoover, for example, fought the establishment of the TVA but fathered Hoover Dam. Dwight Eisenhower cut federal water project funding but supported Echo Park Dam and private dams in Hells Canyon. John F. Kennedy approved dams in the New Deal style of Democrats since Franklin Roosevelt, but he also encouraged conservation. Lyndon Johnson tipped this balance slightly toward conservation. With individuals who supported river development and others who supported river preservation, each party, particularly before 1970, has had enough champions to show any general analysis to be questionable. But a complex and imperfect pattern did evolve: Republican congressmen were less enthusiastic than Democrats about dams and public works projects, though they were under the same political pressures to bring money home from Washington and build dams with it. Republican administrations were more likely to cut funding for public works projects, though they were flatly unreceptive to river conservation as a positive initiative. Democrats faced a difficult dilemma. Steeped in the New Deal tradition of federal spending for public works and dependent on social welfare causes, they also sought the votes of conservationists. Though water developers and river savers were opposites, both represented "liberal" causes. What resulted was a remarkable effort to do everything—sometimes touted as balanced use—involving both continued destruction of rivers through federal projects and a newly popular saving of rivers, but only when conservationists launched powerful campaigns.

Another new pattern was that politicians' decisions were leveraged by technical studies. Although the Grand Canyon had been won by virtue of the place involved, it was a consultant's study of eutrophication that helped to kill Tocks Island Dam and a hydrologist's study of groundwater that helped to halt the Cross Florida Barge Canal. Use of the Environmental Policy Act and its requirement for environmental impact statements became a formula for delaying projects; seven hundred suits regarding all kinds of environmental issues were taken to court in five years.[45] Given time, the dam fighters turned the politics around by exposing hidden costs that had never been counted.

The late 1960s and early 1970s had seen a growing influence of science and economics, bringing hard data that were more convincing in a political forum than the old arguments for wilderness and national park ideals, wildlife, and philosophical views of nature. This shift was partly due to growing sophistication in the sciences, with new emphasis on the ability to apply scientific techniques and knowledge to everyday problems. Furthermore, scientists were now becoming personally involved in river protection; politicians were growing more receptive to stringent analysis when their decisions were placed in the public spotlight; and, perhaps most important, conservationists now saw that if they were to save more than the most sublime of natural wonders, they must oppose developers on the developers' terms—through economic arguments and through analysis that showed negative effects on the lives of average citizens.

Yet, curiously, the rationale to save rivers was also working in the opposite direction at the same time. People were becoming involved with rivers and supporting them for their own sake. Though the arguments put forth to Congress grew more analytical and scientific, the old river-saving rationale, which some have called "romantic," was growing—not shrinking—among the general public. More people were becoming more committed simply because they loved rivers.

Beyond the major river controversies, attitudes had changed. People had regarded the stream through the center of town as a storm sewer, but now they were cleaning it up and turning a cluttered riverfront into a park. Programs for pollution control and open space preservation improved waterways, and residents took new pride in their surroundings. Oregon's Willamette River, once a fetid dump for paper mills and cities, was reclaimed under Governor Tom McCall and became a community asset, a blue ribbon through the farmland. People had turned their backs on waterways since the demise of river navigation and since the first pollution killed the fish, but now, from the Potomac to the Sacramento, people flocked toward the water to bicycle, walk, swim, and paddle. Growing interest in protecting entire watersheds brought concern about logging, highway construction, and urban sprawl.

The aesthetics of water were changing. A corps brochure still stated, "The man-made lake behind a dam can often be an environmental enhancement. A lake not only offers an interesting change in scenery, but provides for recreation such as boating, swimming and water-skiing not found in many free-flowing rivers." But many people had come to see reservoirs as drowned rivers, mud ringed, monotonous, and lifeless in comparison to the streams, valleys, and canyons that had disappeared.

River protection had come from small groups of people striving to save a park or homeland to large groups fighting for many things. In addition to the controversies that drew national attention, people fought to protect scores of streams from small dams by the Soil Conservation Service, from channelization, and from land development. People were motivated not only by their individual interests in one river but also by a wider awareness of rivers as the best of nature, even as holy places with spiritual values earlier reserved for cathedrals.

These fights against dams and canals were only part of the movement to save rivers. Beginning in the 1950s, a few people had realized that instead of constant opposition to development, a positive approach was needed. Recognition of river values was crucial in making antidam decisions final. Otherwise the builders would simply return when the politics changed. Since 1824 Congress had passed laws to develop thousands of streams, and now a law was needed to save some of the best of what remained.

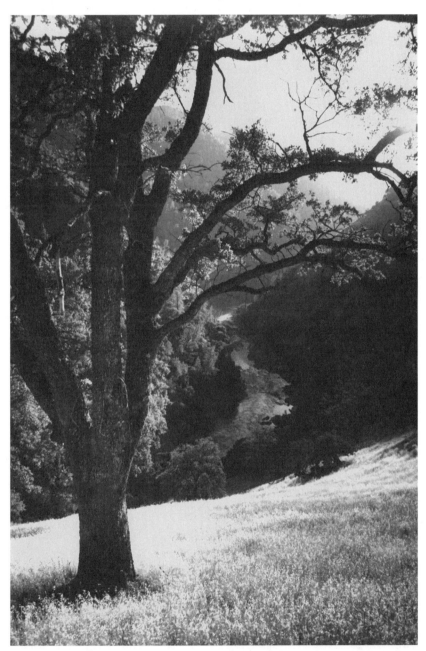

The Tuolumne River in California was the site of John Muir's battle to save Hetch Hetchy Valley. This scene lies downstream from there and in 1984 was the location of a hydroelectric proposal that would have dammed or de-watered a remaining wild section of the river.

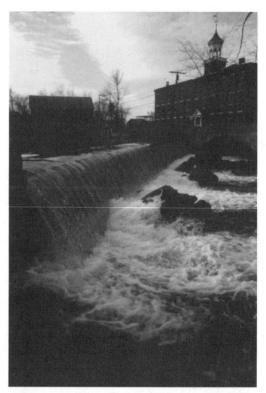

Billerica Dam on the Concord River was built in 1847. Henry David Thoreau looked forward to the day when the dam would be leveled and the river would "run clear again."

After the first great controversy about protecting a river in America, Hetch Hetchy Valley of the Tuolumne River was flooded by this water supply reservoir for San Francisco.

A hydroelectric dam at Cumberland Falls in Kentucky was stopped in 1928, indicating that concern for river protection was reaching beyond established parks.

Grand Coulee Dam on the Columbia River in Washington was the quintessential New Deal water project. It was built for economic development but flooded 137 miles of river and eliminated 1,000 miles of salmon habitat.

The Bureau of Reclamation planned Echo Park Dam for this area of the Yampa River in Colorado, sparking intense opposition by conservationists who acted to protect Dinosaur National Monument and the national park system.

An epic dam fight was won at the Grand Canyon when David Brower and others slowed the momentum to build large dams in the West.

In the 1940s and again in 1963 the Army Corps of Engineers called for multiple dams to be built on the Potomac River, including sites such as this near Harper's Ferry. Confronted by citizen opposition, the Corps built only one of the dams.

For 280 miles the Yukon River would have been flooded by Ramparts Dam, proposed in 1959. Wildlife agencies and organizations stopped the plan that would have created a reservoir larger than Lake Erie.

As Governor of Georgia, Jimmy Carter halted the construction of Spewrell Bluff Dam on the Flint River in 1973, a case that awakened his concern for rivers and wasteful water projects.

A hydroelectric dam would have flooded the Snake River here at Wild Sheep Rapid in Hells Canyon, but conservationists blocked approval at the last minute and protected the Snake as a national wild and scenic river in 1975.

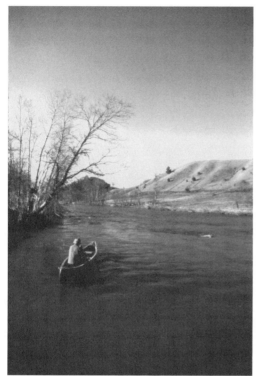

State action was inadequate to stop a power company from damming the South Fork of the New River in North Carolina, so it was added to the national wild and scenic rivers system in 1976.

The Delaware River above Tocks Island was almost certain to be dammed by the Army Corps of Engineers, but growing support to protect the river resulted in national wild and scenic river designation in 1978.

The North Fork of the American River flows with intricate rapids through a wilderness canyon only an hour's drive from Sacramento.

The Bureau of Reclamation's excavation and foundation for Auburn Dam on the American River just below the North and Middle Fork confluence was halted after a nearby earthquake raised safety questions in 1975. For thirty years Friends of the River continued to fend off dam proposals at this site.

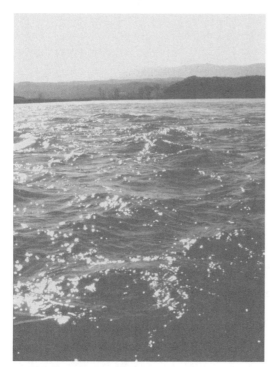

At the Little Tennessee River a small fish called the snail darter ignited the nation's first great endangered species debate. Tellico Dam flooded this site in 1979.

On the Saint John River in Maine, Dickey–Lincoln Dam was opposed in the 1970s and finally deauthorized in 1980, sparing the wildest river in the East.

Rankin Rapids Dam was stopped on the Allagash River of Maine in the 1950s and the river received national protection in 1970. Thirty years later river advocates criticized the state for poor management of the Allagash.

The Norden Dam proposal on Nebraska's Niobrara River was halted in 1983, and the river was nationally protected in 1991.

Widespread dredging was planned for the Atchafalaya, America's largest hardwood swamp in Louisiana. Part of President Jimmy Carter's "hit list," the project was scaled back and much of the river was protected.

A large copper mine proposal threatened the Tatshenshini River in British Columbia, but a successful international campaign protected the area as the largest nature preserve in the world.

The era of big-dam construction came to a halt at the Kings River in California where a large irrigation dam was stopped in 1988.

At the Greenbrier River of West Virginia, local people and conservationists stopped a flood control dam in the 1980s, further confirming that the age of big-dam construction was over, at least for a while.

The Klamath River in California was added to the national wild and scenic rivers system in 1981, but diversions for irrigation resulted in low flows that killed 33,000 salmon in 2002.

Celebrating the 200th anniversary of the Lewis and Clark expedition, American Rivers worked to restore healthy flows to the upper Missouri River in 2004.

While floodplain zoning supposedly protects lowlands from new development, loopholes in the federal flood insurance program allow new homes to be built in areas obviously prone to high water here along the Pearl River in Mississippi.

Here along the West Branch of the Susquehanna in Pennsylvania, polluted runoff is the main problem with mine drainage killing all the fish in this otherwise scenic section of river.

Edwards Dam on the Kennebec River in Augusta, Maine, was removed in 1999, re-opening the lower river for the migration of ten species of anadromous fish.

With some of the finest salmon habitat in the United States, the Elwha River on Washington's Olympic Peninsula will begin to be restored with the removal of two large dams, slated to happen in 2007.

In this facility at Lower Granite Dam on the Snake River in Washington, the Army Corps of Engineers captures young salmon and loads them onto barges for motorized transport past eight dams. Undergoing this treatment for decades, the fish are now nearly extinct.

The Salmon River of Idaho offers superb spawning habitat for salmon and steelhead that would migrate up the Columbia and Snake Rivers if the fish could only survive the hazards of dams built in their way. The removal of four dams on the lower Snake would make the fishes' journey possible and could be done economically while increasing jobs in the region.

6

NATIONAL RIVERS

Even though they moved west after college, the Craighead brothers never escaped the outdoor memories of growing up along the Potomac River and in the Appalachians. "As kids we canoed and swam in the Potomac," John remembered. "Up at the Seneca Breaks we caught small-mouth bass and drank from the river. Bald eagles nested there."[1]

After studying wildlife biology, John and Frank Craighead settled in Montana and Wyoming, where they became the authorities on the grizzly bear, even seeking out the temperamental giants of the northern Rockies in their winter dens. Yet, part of the Potomac stayed with those two scientists: they were river lovers. They rafted upper Hells Canyon of the Snake, now dammed. Even in winter they ran Idaho's Salmon, called the River of No Return by Lewis and Clark in 1805. They traveled and made films on the Middle Fork of the Salmon, where they first publicized the term *wild river*. Then came an adventure that would change the course of river protection: they returned home.

"Years after we had moved west we went back and saw the Potomac. The water was polluted, it wasn't anything like what we had known," John said. A homeland—the place of growing up, good times, and first impressions—may be a universal love, and seeing the loss of that place has moved many people to act. "I realized that we still had wild rivers in the West, but we wouldn't for long if we didn't do something to save them."

Fighting the Army Corps of Engineers' Spruce Park Dam for the Middle Fork of the Flathead in Montana (an alternative to Glacier View Dam, stopped in the 1940s), John Craighead wrote that conservationists should have a rivers program of their own instead of always acting on the defensive. In a 1957 issue of *Montana Wildlife* magazine he wrote about classifying rivers and protecting the least developed.[2] Adding to the wilderness preservation idea that had taken hold among conservationists since Aldo Leopold's work thirty years before, Craighead wrote, "Rivers and their watersheds are inseparable, and to maintain wild areas we must preserve the rivers that drain them." Wild rivers were a "species now close to extinction" and were needed "for recreation and education of future generations." With analysis of the rivers' potential for dams versus undeveloped use, Craighead believed that irreplaceable streams and landscapes could be saved while still meeting the needs for water.

At a Montana State University conference in 1957, John Craighead promoted his river protection idea, writing later in *Naturalist* magazine:

> Today it is still possible to challenge and to enjoy a wild river, but already they are a rarity. Only a few such rivers exist and these are threatened by an expanding, groping civilization, public indifference and bureaucratic sluggishness. In spite of the durability of rock-walled canyons and the surging power of cataracting water, the wild river is a fragile thing—the most fragile portion of wilderness country. A dam can still its turbulent flow, a road eternally change the river bank, and a logging operation completely alter the watershed.[3]

Craighead wrote that wild rivers are needed as "benchmarks" for comparison of environmental changes. In an earlier issue of *Naturalist*, Frank Craighead had described a system of river classification including wild rivers, semiwild rivers, semiharnessed rivers, and harnessed rivers. He reasoned that once rivers were categorized, people would see the scarcity of quality streams and realize the need to protect them.

"I had worked on the wilderness legislation with Olaus Murie, Howard Zahniser, Stewart Brandborg, and others," John Craighead recalled, "but they were not interested in rivers. They were most interested in specific areas of wilderness, many of them without rivers because the lands were at high altitudes. The more I became involved, the clearer it became that we needed a national river preservation system based on the wilderness system but separate from it."

STARTING WITH THE CURRENT

Like the Craighead brothers, Paul Bruce Dowling was a wildlife biologist and had spent part of his youth in the Appalachians of central Pennsylvania. He moved to Missouri, where fishing from flatboats had been a tradition for

generations on the spring-fed Current and Jacks Fork Rivers. Dam proposals at Blair Creek and Doniphan were temporarily beaten in the 1940s, and
the state government—one of the most progressive in natural area preservation—supported protection of the two rivers in 1950. In one of the first
cases in which the development of river recreation was promoted as an
alternative to reservoirs, the Current River Protective Association proposed
a river park with public ownership of recreation sites.

As secretary of the Missouri chapter of the Nature Conservancy in the
mid-1950s, Bruce Dowling wrote to Senator Stuart Symington asking for a
federal study of the Current and Jacks Fork. In 1983 Dowling remembered,
"I had floated those rivers when I was a wildlife biologist with the state, and
through a Nature Conservancy inventory we realized that many of the rare
plant communities were along the streams of the Ozarks. Across the country
we had national parks, and here I saw the potential for "national rivers"—
maybe ten or twenty of the unique gems, free-flowing streams representing
the different physiographic regions.[4]

In 1956 the National Park Service proposed a national recreation area
along the Current and nearby Eleven Point River, where local people had
also fought dams. The park service then wrote another report, recommended an Ozark Rivers national monument, and held hearings at which
Dowling testified that in 1957 the Missouri chapter of the Nature Conservancy had "introduced the idea of 'national rivers' as a designation appropriate to the Current River."[5] This is perhaps the first official reference to
"national rivers."

Ted Swem, director of park service planning, said, "We hoped that the
Current River proposal would be prototypical, and that we could come
forth with other river proposals."[6] In 1959 the park service studied Montana's Missouri River below Fort Benton, but the river protection plan was
shelved because of infighting among federal agencies. For Maine's Allagash,
the park service proposed a national recreation area, but this was vetoed by
the state, which feared federal controls. The Suwannee in Florida and Georgia was also studied.

Within the Interior Department, resource planners John Kauffmann
and Stanford Young thought that a whole set of rivers should be protected.
Swem recalled, "After studying the Current, the Allagash, and the Missouri,
we began talking about the possibility of a system of rivers." In addition to
Craighead and Dowling, citizen advocates for river protection were Sigurd
Olson in Minnesota, whom Stewart Udall called one of the "great philoso-
phers" of wild rivers; Joe Penfold of the Izaak Walton League; Bud Jordahl
in Wisconsin; and Leonard Hall in Missouri. Swem said, "I can't say that

SELECTED EVENTS IN CHAPTER 6

1905 Wisconsin protected Brule River.
1908 Wisconsin protected Flambeau River.
1915 Oregon protected certain streams and waterfalls.
1950 Missouri supported protection of Current River.
1956 National Park Service proposed national recreation area along Current and Eleven Point Rivers.
1957 John Craighead wrote about wild river protection.
     Paul Bruce Dowling introduced idea of national rivers.
1959 Craighead brothers testified for federally protected rivers system at Senate select committee hearing.
     National Park Service studied protection of Missouri River.
1960 Interior Department supported protection of free-flowing streams.
     Senate select committee supported system of protected rivers.
1961 Stewart Udall became secretary of the interior.
     National Park Service recommended national recreation area for the Allagash River.
     Outdoor Recreation Resources Review Commission supported protection of free-flowing rivers.
1963 Stewart Udall supported protection of Current River.
1964 National Park Service prepared potential list of national rivers.
     First wild rivers bill drafted.
1965 Wisconsin passed first wild and scenic rivers act.
1966 Maine designated Allagash Wilderness Waterway.
1968 Tennessee, Ohio, and Maryland started state rivers systems.
     National Wild and Scenic Rivers Act passed.
1972 Lower Saint Croix added to the national rivers system.
     California designated state rivers for protection.

1973 American Rivers Conservation Council organized.
1974 North Carolina designated New River for protection.
     Chattooga River added to national rivers system.
1975 Snake River in Hells Canyon designated national river.
     Twenty-nine rivers designated for national river study.
     Nationwide rivers inventory started.
1976 American Rivers Conservation Council fought to save New River.
     Flathead, Obed, and Missouri Rivers added to national rivers system.
1978 General Accounting Office criticized rivers program.
     National Parks and Recreation Act passed, designating Delaware and six other rivers.
1979 President Carter issued directive to protect inventoried rivers on federal lands.
1980 Twenty-six Alaskan rivers added to national system.
     Salmon River added to national system.
1981 Interior Secretary Andrus designated northern California rivers in national system.
1982 Development moratorium expired for eleven national study rivers.
1983 Federal judge determined designation of northern California rivers invalid.
     Governor Brennan of Maine protected sixteen rivers in state system.
     Bills introduced to delete national rivers.
1984 Appeals court restored national status to northern California rivers.
     Tuolumne, Illinois, Owyhee, Verde, and Au Sable rivers added to the national system.

any one person had the idea. There were many people in different roles, and they were all crucial."

FROM DAMMING RIVERS
TO SAVING THEM

To thwart President Eisenhower's policies against federal projects, the Senate formed a Select Committee on National Water Resources. The committee planned to retaliate with policies of its own and with new dam proposals that would end the impasse and move on with development. Ted Schad, director of the committee's staff, had served in a fascinating variety of jobs. As a Bureau of Reclamation budget director he had justified Echo Park and other dams, but at the same time he had also served as a volunteer representing a Seattle climbing and hiking group on a Department of the Interior advisory committee. There he met Howard Zahniser of the Wilderness Society. "Zahniser convinced me that Echo Park should not be built," Schad recalled in 1983. After transferring to the Bureau of the Budget, Schad wrote Eisenhower's rivers and harbors veto messages.

At one of Ted Schad's Senate select committee field hearings in 1959, the Craighead brothers called for a system of federally protected rivers. They urged that the newly formed Outdoor Recreation Resources Review Commission begin a system of river evaluation. The Fish and Wildlife Service in the Interior Department reported to the select committee that some rivers are most valuable if left unaltered,[7] and in 1960 interior officials wrote to the Committee on Interior and Insular Affairs: "There still remain in various sections of the country natural free-flowing streams whose integrity might be preserved in the face of the water-control onslaught if conscientious planning to this end were applied."

Armed with these recommendations, Schad proposed in the Senate select committee's report "that certain streams be preserved in their free-flowing condition because their natural scenic, scientific, aesthetic, and recreational values outweigh their value for water development and control purposes now and in the future."[8] Examples were listed: the Allagash, Current, and Eleven Point, and the Rogue in Oregon. Some senators on the select committee may not even have noticed Schad's wild river recommendation—it was one of many in the report. The committee adopted the report without discussion of the river protection idea, and this became the government's first major proposal for a national rivers system.

Through the late 1950s, debates had been held about wilderness and how much of it was needed, leading to broader questions about recreation that no one could answer. So the Outdoor Recreation Resources Review Commission was created to prepare the nation's first thorough study of recreation needs. Arthur Davis, one of the study report's authors, said, "Water was one of the building blocks for recreation. 'Scenic river' was not a brand new term, and in the water area it was a parallel to the wilderness idea."[9] The commission issued *Outdoor Recreation for America*, stating, "Certain rivers of unusual scientific, esthetic, and recreation value should be allowed to remain in their free-flowing state and natural setting without man-made alterations."[10]

By 1961 Craighead's idea of classifying and protecting rivers had matured, and Dowling's idea of national rivers gained support. The Current River would be saved, and a growing collection of river proposals was incorporated into government reports. Interior Department planners, enthusiastic about river protection, waited only for a secretary who was ready to act.

THE SECRETARY WITH TWO VIEWS

"As a congressman in the 1960s I was prodam," Stewart Udall said in 1983. "I voted for the upper Colorado project that flooded Glen Canyon. I instinctively identified my values more with the Sierra Club than with dam building, except that I was from Arizona, and so you had to be for water. You couldn't go to Congress and be against dams."[11]

On a field trip, rarely allowed by interior committee chairman Wayne Aspinall, Udall and his family were one of the last groups to float through Glen Canyon. "I got off the river with very mixed feelings. I didn't feel guilt stricken, but I kept saying to myself that we hadn't done a very good job in the West of achieving balance. In deciding where to put dams we had made mistakes. So I began to have doubts."

In 1961 President Kennedy appointed Udall secretary of the interior. "Suddenly I had the national responsibility, and that put on my shoulders the burden of thinking for the nation and not just for Arizona, which is what a congressman would do when it comes to water. My thinking gradually changed in the early sixties at the same time that I was testifying for dams."

Udall personified the upheaval happening in water development philosophy. He had supported dams that were the epitome of river destruction and that rallied conservationists to the cause of river protection. But with the help of people who were working to save their rivers, by experiencing these waterways personally from a canoe or a raft, and with a statesman's regard for his job, Udall saw the need for balance and preservation. This man stood uniquely as a river developer and a river saver both, bearing the complications and compromises inherent in the holding of two opposite views at once.

> Three major things happened during my first year. Senator Muskie got a little floatplane and we went up to canoe the Allagash. He was anxious to leave the river alone, and it was threatened by the Rankin Rapids Dam. So the Allagash was identified as one of the finest wild rivers in the eastern part of the country, and the fact that people in Maine wanted to save it left an impression on me, particularly when I saw it, when I canoed it. I had never been canoeing really; we didn't have that many rivers in Arizona. Senator Muskie knew that Maine couldn't afford to buy land, yet the state wanted to do the job themselves, so we matched their funds with federal funds. We preserved a river for about $3 million.

Udall, unequivocally a man of the desert, saw something new, something worth saving in the soggy bogs feeding this wild river of the far eastern, far northern United States.

"Then later that summer we were looking at new parks and seashores. It was an explosive period for that, and I made it a policy to go out and see the places in order to throw the spotlight on the proposals." On a Current River canoe trip Udall met George Hartzog, whom he later appointed director of the National Park Service.

> We were all enthused about making the Current a national park, but since we were really preserving the river, we called it the national scenic riverways.
>
> The third thing was even more of a catalyst. There was a big fight over an Idaho dam called Bruce's Eddy, now called Dworshak, on the Clearwater. The conservationists opposing it came to me and wanted me to help in the fight. I got involved, and it dramatized for me the flaws and misconceptions in the dam-building philosophy of the New Deal. The values were changing, and if that dam were considered in 1964 it never would have been authorized. So for me, this is where the kernel of the idea for the wild and scenic river bill came from.

Udall sought an amendment banning additional Clearwater dams. This failed, but the concept would be resurrected for nothing less than an entire system of rivers.

In *The Quiet Crisis*, Udall articulated his new view of river protection:

> Generations to follow will judge us by our success in preserving in their natural state certain rivers having superior outdoor recreation values. The Allagash of Maine, the Suwannee of Florida, the Rogue of Oregon, the Salmon of Idaho, the Buffalo of Arkansas, and the Ozark Mountain rivers in the State of Missouri are some of the waterways that should be kept as clean, wild rivers—a part of a rich outdoor heritage.

After Udall boated on the Allagash and Current, Senator Gaylord Nelson of Wisconsin invited him to canoe the Saint Croix, and Bob Harrigan, a canoeist who had pioneered many runs in the Appalachians, guided him on the Potomac and Shenandoah.

"Big things under Kennedy were the national seashores, Canyonlands National Park, and the Ozark rivers, but the wilderness bill was the landmark legislation. As it came closer to law, my thinking began to turn more toward rivers legislation that would complement and be another kind of wilderness bill, and we started studies in interior." Udall asked Frank Craighead, who worked for the Fish and Wildlife Service, to prepare a paper on river classification. Udall acted on the key recommendation of the Outdoor Recreation Resources Review Commission by creating the Bureau of Outdoor Recreation, and he wrote to Orville Freeman, secretary of the Department of Agriculture, to organize a wild and scenic rivers study team. In 1964 planners led by Stanford Young collected a list of 650 rivers for consideration, reduced it to 67, then announced 22 rivers for detailed field study.

New national park proposals were attacked by critics who were against "locking up" resources, so to sidestep political hazards, interior officials were receptive to innovative land protection. The naming of national recreation areas (most of the early ones surrounded large reservoirs), national seashores, lakeshores, and rivers was a way to expand the federal recreation estate without the restrictions of national park status that ignited the wrath of hunters and private landowners. Ted Swem said, "Although the national monument classification was justified for the Ozark rivers, it was obvious that the proposal would not be authorized if hunting was prohibited. So we suggested the national scenic riverways classification."

While the idea of a rivers system was being explored, the political support to protect the Current River had matured. With Udall's recommendations, President Kennedy called for Current River protection in his conservation message to the Senate Select Committee on National Water Resources in 1961. At hearings in 1963 Udall said, "It would be difficult to find an area where so much beauty and variety of natural features can be preserved by setting aside so little." Also in 1963 Gaylord Nelson introduced a bill to make the Saint Croix a national river (he had helped convince the Northern States Power Company to sell to the government seventy miles along both sides of the river where a power dam had been planned). Nelson's bill passed the Senate but stalled in the House. John Saylor and others went to work, and in 1964 the Ozark National Scenic Riverways were designated as the first national rivers, for "conserving and interpreting unique scenic and other natural values, including preservation of portions of Current River and Jacks Fork River as free-flowing streams." During the same year, the Wilderness Act passed—a law requiring that certain public lands remain without development or logging, though a loophole not yet used allows water projects if the president approves. Conservation leaders, political momentum on their side, looked to their next opportunity.

"John Craighead had left all this material on my desk," recalled Stewart Brandborg, then director of the Wilderness Society. Howard Zahniser had talked about a system of "wilderness rivers," and, Brandborg said, "The idea of wild rivers was deep in the hearts of the old Wilderness Society leaders."

Comparing wilderness preservation to rivers preservation, Stewart Udall said,

> The wilderness concept began with Aldo Leopold and other foresters back in the twenties. The Wilderness Society was formed in the thirties. They said we needed a law, and wrestled around in the fifties, and the first bill was introduced in 1957. The wilderness concept had this forty-year gestation period. With wild and scenic rivers it was just a few years. It came on strong, even though there was no national constituency. The momentum of the wilderness bill had a tide moving, and sometimes you see two waves, and you jump on the second wave and ride it in. The timing was just perfect. President Johnson's chief of domestic affairs kept saying, "Johnson wants new legislation," and I told him about the wild and scenic rivers idea and he said, "That sounds great, get it ready."

In 1964 the first wild and scenic rivers bill was called the "Wild Rivers Act," focusing on the extraordinary rivers of the West, but the bill was later broadened to include "scenic" and "recreation" rivers. President Johnson called for approval of a rivers bill in his 1965 State of the Union address:

> We will continue to conserve the water and power for tomorrow's needs with well-planned reservoirs and power dams. But the time has also come

to identify and preserve free-flowing stretches of our great rivers before growth and development have made the beauty of the unspoiled waterway a memory.

Udall vividly remembered his former committee chairman's reaction:

> After Johnson's message, Wayne Aspinall walked off the floor and told a reporter that wild rivers were the craziest idea he ever heard of. He thought I was off my rocker by then on a lot of things. Since Senator Frank Church had been involved on the Clearwater, he decided to take his life into his own hands and sponsor the wild and scenic rivers bill in the Senate. He was bold; he was from Idaho, and this was controversial. He was splitting from the other side. I remember going to John Saylor—he was in complete agreement with the rivers idea—and about Aspinall's comment Saylor said, "We'll just wear him down."
>
> In 1965 we got the bill passed overwhelmingly in the Senate, where Senators Church and Nelson were strong supporters. They said, "The country wants wild and scenic rivers." It left Aspinall with the question, Was he going to be arbitrary and obstruct the will of the country? Then Saylor started nagging him, "Wayne, better get some hearings going or things are going to get mighty unpleasant around here."

Howard Zahniser was Saylor's personal friend, and he had stressed that the rivers idea paralleled the wilderness law but was broader because it included all types of rivers and could mobilize people nationwide. Stewart Brandborg remembered, "That's all you had to say to Saylor."

The rivers act would be one of Saylor's greatest conservation accomplishments. Others included the Wilderness Act, the defeats of the Echo Park and Grand Canyon dams, the preservation of the Current and Jacks Fork, and the saving of Hells Canyon. From Johnstown, Pennsylvania, known for devastating floods, Saylor was an anomaly—a small-town politician who was also a lifetime member of the Sierra Club. He gave sacks of home-grown potatoes as Christmas presents to friends. He was pleased to see the popularization of conservation in the late 1960s but did not subscribe to the new environmentalism. Addressing "boys and girls" on Earth Day at Penn State University in 1970, he said, "I don't buy this antigrowth idea. We need growth to pay for the environmental improvements that have to be made. You can't build a sewage treatment plant unless people have money to pay for it." A champion of new parks and traditional conservation, he was a master at congressional dealing and arm twisting in the old style.

In 1967, after carefully compromising the bill so that most water developments would not be threatened, Aspinall introduced the most complex legislation. What converted Aspinall? "He must have owed Saylor some real big favors," Stewart Brandborg said in 1983. (Aspinall received support for five dams in Colorado, three of which the Bureau of Reclamation did not even recommend, authorized in 1968 as part of the Central Arizona Project.)

The national rivers bill called for three classes of rivers: wild, scenic, and recreational. The wilderness idea of preserving the "glamour" rivers of the West was broadened, and Secretary Udall said, "Rivers should be saved in all parts of the country." National conservation groups, canoe clubs, and dam fighters packed hearings in 1968. The Saint Croix, Eleven Point, and Little Miami—all in the Midwest—received the most support. Stanford Young of the Interior Department said, "Mostly the motivation was against dams. The problems of riparian development were not yet perceived because they weren't dramatic." Testimony for the rivers bill included opposition to dams on the Eleven Point, the Saint Croix, and the Little Miami in Ohio. The Middle Fork of the Feather in California was included, though two dam sites proposed by the Richvale Irrigation District had been approved by the state.

But the federal water development agencies saw that the act stopped no dams that they really wanted. Tennessee Valley Authority chairman Aubrey J. Wagner objected to protection of the French Broad River and the Little Tennessee, including the Tellico Dam site, because "planning and construction of water control and development projects have progressed to a point which would make it inappropriate to include these streams." The spectacular Green River in Wyoming was deleted because of an irrigation dam site at Kendall. A Seattle City Light representative testified against the upper Skagit, where Copper Creek Dam was planned to flood the river's only remaining whitewater. The Tocks Island Regional Advisory Council supported Delaware protection but only above the Tocks Island Dam site. Residents stopped wild and scenic designation of Potomac tributaries in West Virginia. Landowners along the Shenandoah objected, expressing fears that would grow in the next decade. Mrs. John Locke Burns, Jr., said, "When I read these scenic and wild river bills, I am almost made to feel that no longer does the right to ownership exist." All of these river sections were deleted. The National Reclamation Association flatly opposed the bills: "The concept does not conform to the principles of multipurpose development."

The acting secretary of the army was more subtle: "The Nation can

well afford to forego the development of streams of unusual natural beauty.
. . . But for very few of these have studies been made which provide an
adequate basis for a wise decision." Because the bill would block dam proposals on the Salmon and Middle Fork of the Clearwater, several senators,
led by Len Jordan of Idaho, dissented from the interior committee and
stated, "The combined runoff of the Salmon and Clearwater Rivers is
greater than the total runoff of the Colorado River and the combined
hydroelectric potential is greater than Grand Coulee or greater than all
hydroelectric potential on the entire Colorado River."[12]

Congressman Sam Steiger from Arizona flatly said, "Under the guise
of protecting scenic values, this legislation will stifle progress, inhibit economic development and incur a staggering expenditure."[13]

But Stewart Udall knew what he was doing. He said, "We had the
momentum, and the dam people who didn't like it just weren't in a frame
of mind to fight it. 1 had been pretty good to them, giving them some of
the things they wanted, including dams. So 1 looked them in the eye and
said we're going to balance things off."

A SYSTEM OF THEIR OWN

Support was strong as the conservation movement matured and the environmental movement of the 1970s approached. Robert Eastman, who
became director of the rivers program said, "Back then, if you had a good
idea, you could put it to work. The people were concerned about conservation. They wanted to protect natural places. Secretaries Udall and Freeman
wanted to push programs, and Presidents Kennedy and Johnson were
receptive. There was money to do things without having to take it out of
someone else's program. Times were good and people didn't mind spending
funds on parks and rivers."

Stewart Udall said, "Some people think that environmental protection
began with Earth Day in 1970, but a lot of action led up to that." Although
the early 1970s did see the greatest advances in fighting pollution and in
governmental reform regarding the environment, the 1960s were a remarkable age for natural areas protection.

Reflecting on the parks and the new systems of wilderness, seashores,
and national rivers, Ted Swem said of the 1960s, "I don't know if we'll ever
have a period like that again."

Because 1968 was an election year, action on the rivers bill was delayed
until many people thought it was too late. The House refused to suspend

rules to allow the bill to bypass committees and go straight to the floor. The interior committee quit meeting, but Wayne Aspinall agreed to poll his members, who had dispersed across the states, and they agreed to release the bill on September 6. On September 12 the House voted 265–7 in favor of the bill. On October 2, the Senate approved and President Johnson signed the National Wild and Scenic Rivers Act, designating parts of eight rivers and identifying twenty-seven others for study and possible inclusion.

The act states:

> It is hereby declared to be the policy of the United States that certain selected rivers of the Nation which, with their immediate environments, possess outstandingly remarkable scenic, recreational, geologic, fish and wildlife, historic, cultural, or other similar values, shall be preserved in free-flowing condition, and that they and their immediate environments shall be protected for the benefit and enjoyment of present and future generations. The Congress declares that the established national policy of dams and other construction at appropriate sections of the rivers of the United States needs to be complemented by a policy that would preserve other selected rivers or sections thereof in their free-flowing condition to protect the water quality of such rivers and to fulfill other vital national conservation purposes.[14]

Although the bill drafted by the Interior Department had simply named one category of national river, the final version called for three classes: wild rivers are "vestiges of primitive America"; scenic rivers have "shorelines or watersheds still largely primitive and shorelines largely undeveloped but accessible in places by roads"; and recreational rivers "are readily accessible by roads" and "may have some development along their shorelines." Conservationists thought the three classes made a stronger bill, but the classes also introduced troublesome complexity. Some people thought that a "wild" river had to include dangerous whitewater. Others thought that a "recreational" river would always bring crowds of tourists and busloads of people from cities. Debates often center on the semantics of classification, diverting attention from more important questions, such as, Should the river be protected from dams or not?

The original twelve "instant" rivers and tributaries were the Middle Fork of the Clearwater and its tributaries the Lochsa and the Selway for 85 miles in Idaho (including the Penny Cliffs dam site); the Eleven Point for 44 miles in Missouri; the Middle Fork of the Feather for 154 miles in California; the Rio Grande for 53 miles and its tributary Red River for 4 miles in New Mexico; the Rogue for 85 miles in Oregon; the Saint Croix and tributary Namekagon for 200 miles in Wisconsin and Minnesota; the Middle Fork of the Salmon for 104 miles in Idaho; and the Wolf for 25 miles in Wisconsin.

The act prohibits dams or other federal projects that would damage the river. Shoreline protection is encouraged through local zoning, public acquisition, or management of government lands. Instead of expensive and unpopular land buying, the act encourages the use of easements—partial ownership, including development rights, thus allowing residents to stay and keep their property. Land may not be condemned if more than half of the acreage in the corridor is publicly owned, or if acquisition (including easements) would exceed 320 acres a mile—an average of one-quarter mile from each shore. In many cases, far less than this amount would be bought, but landowners along some rivers would mistakenly think that all lands one-quarter mile from the water would be acquired.

To add a river to the system, Congress first votes for a study of the river. The National Park Service or Forest Service collects information, meets with people, writes a report, receives reviews, decides if the river qualifies and how it should be classified, and recommends an agency to manage it. After approval by the Office of Management and Budget and the president, the recommendation goes to Congress, where a vote is normally needed for designation. However, an alternate route can be followed: for state-legislated scenic rivers a governor can request the secretary of the interior for national designation, requiring an environmental impact statement but no vote by Congress. The act also calls for the Interior Department planners to help the states in protecting rivers through state systems and other alternatives.

RESCUING THE PROGRAM

As the Craigheads had envisioned thirteen years before, river supporters now had a program of their own. With a positive alternative, they could take the initiative and did not have to be "against" everything. Yet the movement had far to go. River supporters were busy with rearguard battles and could not get ahead of the dam builders enough to work for long-term preservation. At Interior Secretary Walter Hickel's direction, the Bureau of Outdoor Recreation studied controversial projects of the corps (but not of the Bureau of Reclamation) and helped to stop Salem Church Dam on Virginia's Rappahannock River, but a recommendation to make the stream a national river went nowhere.

In 1972 the rivers act was amended to add the lower Saint Croix, but otherwise the system languished. Few studies, essential for congressional action, were completed. The rivers program lacked the constituency enjoyed by the wilderness supporters, and in many ways saving rivers was more difficult. Stanford Young said, "Rivers are so much more controversial than blocks of land; many people are dependent upon the rivers." Unlike the western high country, rivers and their valleys appeal to a chorus of competing users. Bottomland timber is often the best, and roads follow floodplains. Most streams are partly bordered by private lands, and whether or not government acquisition was proposed as part of a national river proposal, residents feared condemnation. The alternative—land use control— was likewise anathema, especially if coming from the state or federal government instead of the local level. Water developers with countless schemes wanted the rivers for themselves. Because of implied water quality controls, towns upstream from potential designations joined in fighting protection. State and local governments resented federal involvement even though the act allowed states to administer rivers without federal managers.

Rivers remained a secondary concern of the national environmental groups, which were busy with wilderness, parks, wildlife, water quality, and air pollution. Michael McCloskey, executive director of the Sierra Club, said in 1981, "We're interested in saving substantial tracts of land that include rivers, but we're not enamored with the linear aspects. To us in the West, that's too confined an approach. Even John Muir didn't want strips up the streams, but the whole watershed. It's against the grain for us to be real happy with corridors. With wilderness, we get the whole package."[15]

Gaylord Nelson—environmental leader for twenty years in the Senate, where he was the initiator of Earth Day in 1970—was chairman of the Wilderness Society in 1983. "Much of the conservation activity has revolved around the issues of public lands, not rivers," he said. "The original founders of the Wilderness Society were thinking mainly about land issues."

"The rivers have taken short shrift," said Brock Evans of the Sierra Club and later of the National Audubon Society. "The conservation groups budget their work on rivers within the category of public lands, and as a result, the rivers don't get the attention they deserve." State groups were formed, such as Ohio's Rivers Unlimited in 1972 and California's Friends of the River in 1973, but no group protected rivers nationwide or lobbied for the national system. In articles in the American Whitewater Affiliation's journal, Jerry Meral and others called for a national rivers organization.

In March 1973, thirty-three conservationists, including Mike Fremont from Ohio, Jerry Mallett from Colorado, Claude Terry from Georgia, Rafe Pomerance (later director of Friends of the Earth), Jerry Meral (founder of

Friends of the River), David Foreman (founder of Earth First), and others met in Denver at the invitation of Phil LaLena of Colorado to form the American Rivers Conservation Council (ARCC). Brent Blackwelder, working for the Environmental Policy Institute, served as chairman of the board of ARCC for many years.

"We debated about what to do," Blackwelder remembered in 1983. "Should we fight dam proposals or support scenic river designations? We decided to work for scenic river protection, but some of the most logical choices are slated for damming, and if we didn't fight the developers, there would be no scenic rivers to protect. So we've always focused on getting rivers in the system and also on stopping dams." Other goals were to see deauthorization of certain water projects, establishment of state river systems, an increase in interest rates charged for water projects, and elimination of recreation benefits justifying new dams. The Salmon River—the longest river outside Alaska with only one minor dam—was one of few streams named for special action, though its protection would for years be an elusive goal.

Mike Fremont remembered, "Eventually we got to where we knew money was needed to kick this thing off, and Brent threw a hundred bucks down. Everybody pitched in and we had a few thousand dollars to start an operation." A director to be paid $400 a month was difficult to find, but eventually the board hired Bill Painter, who had worked on the original Environmental Teach-in at the University of Michigan in 1969.

Painter recalled the council's early days when he and Blackwelder shared a one-room office packed full of paper and ringing telephones on a side street southeast of the Capitol.

> Money was always a struggle, and I spent a lot of time learning the ropes on the Hill. I knew how to run a little ragtag outfit, but the lobbying—that I had to pick up from Brent. We got a newsletter rolling and I went to work trying to get more rivers in the national system.
>
> While I was trying to do that, Brent was in the thick of two dozen scrapes between the Environmental Policy Center and the army corps. That was before the tide was turned on bad projects—they were coming from everyplace and it was an overwhelming job—Dickey–Lincoln, Salem Church, Teton, Garrison, Tenn–Tom. I could have done nothing but help Brent on each daily political crisis, but I saw that if ARCC was to have an identity, we had to get rivers in the national system. Considering how Brent was overworked, and how important it was to fight those turkey water projects, saying no to him was about the most difficult part of the job.

The efforts of Painter and others paid off. In 1974 the Chattooga River in North Carolina, South Carolina, and Georgia was designated as a national river. In January 1975, a package of twenty-nine rivers for new studies passed Congress. Painter said,

> My biggest satisfaction was working with people out there who loved their rivers. Matt Bailey was an older guy along the North Fork of the American in California. He wanted to save that river but he didn't know what to do. Being able to help was a real good feeling. We added the river to the 1975 study act, and eventually it was designated. I didn't get out of Washington much, but I fell in love with those rivers by just looking at the pictures people sent in. Then when Congress recessed, Brent and I went on a tour. Neither of us was married or had families then. We went around the country and people showed us their streams, and there's nothing like seeing a river through the eyes of somebody who really cares about it.

In 1974 ARCC lobbied and helped to win a stronger federal flood insurance program to protect river frontage through floodplain zoning. On the last day of 1975 the Hells Canyon National Recreation Area Act was passed, adding the middle Snake and the Rapid River in Idaho to the national rivers system and deauthorizing Asotin Dam, which had been planned for lower Hells Canyon (Asotin would later be proposed by private utilities).

In Painter's four years at ARCC, the New River in North Carolina was a big project. He recalled,

> The fight against those two dams had gone on for years, and somebody had already figured out that they ought to designate the river. If I were going to pick out a river, the upper New wouldn't be the one to grab me—it's real nice, but not biologically unique or anything like that. I guess it's easy to fall prey to the big gorges, but Chuck Clusen of the Sierra Club and Brent said that this one was important, and after a while I saw why: the national rivers system was mostly made up of rivers that no one else wanted for dams, but here was a case where we had to fight water developers on their own ground. The dam was already licensed by the Federal Power Commission; national designation was the only way to save it. It seemed like a tough one to win, but the local people were organized and we went to work.

Painter developed a formula that would prove effective on other rivers:

> We helped frame the campaign so it would sell in Congress. The local people were emphasizing the river, but I began to emphasize the Appalachian

cultural history and the farmers who would have to move. There were people who traced their deeds to the king of England, and I played that stuff up. We quit calling it a hydroelectric project and called it a pumped storage project—all it would do was store power. And we found out in the FPC files that there were alternate sites that would affect less land and fewer people. We ran into the argument that the river didn't qualify for the national system, but the cultural angle made it, and when the New was designated in 1976, it was a huge success. We had won a river that would otherwise have been dammed.

In 1976 the North, Middle, and South forks of Montana's Flathead were designated, including the Glacier View Dam site fought in the 1940s, the Spruce Park site fought by the Craigheads in the 1950s, and the Smoky Range site fought in the 1960s. The Obed of Tennessee was included where the Tennessee Valley Authority had studied a dam site. On the upper Missouri, where Interior Department planners had proposed national protection in the early 1960s, 149 miles were finally protected. (Except for the Suwannee, this completed protection for all of the prototype rivers that had been recommended before the National Wild and Scenic Rivers Act was passed.) Three rivers had been added through governors' requests: Ohio's Little Miami and Little Beaver, and Maine's Allagash, which had been proposed by the Interior Department as a national recreation area in 1961. By 1977, 1,655 miles on nineteen river sections were designated.

When Bill Painter became director of the Conservation Society of Southern Vermont, Howard Brown, who had analyzed water development for the Congressional Research Service, became the second ARCC director, bringing a knowledge of water policy that was important during the Carter years.

Through the late 1970s many national river proposals in the East and Midwest were stalled by landowners fearing condemnation of their property. Eminent domain was used in some of the first designations, such as the Current and Saint Croix, but by 1976 the thrust of protection was mostly on zoning. Yet it did not matter that officials emphatically assured people that they would not be evicted; the specter of a land grab could not be erased.

People blamed national designation for increased recreation, but activity was booming on other rivers too: Pennsylvania's Youghiogheny, not in any scenic rivers system, carried 5,000 floaters in 1968 and 150,000 in 1982. Even though it was in the national system, Ohio's Little Beaver received no increase in use. In 1976 Maurice Arnold, director of the Bureau of Outdoor

Recreation in the Northeast, said, "All good rivers will eventually see an increase in use, but through the rivers program, we have a chance to manage that use and avoid problems."

Although ARCC's lobbying paid dividends, the rivers system did not grow much, and a national river study required a tedious five to seven years. Reports were sometimes stalled at the Office of Management and Budget for years. In 1978 the General Accounting Office published *Federal Protection and Preservation of Wild and Scenic Rivers Is Slow and Costly*, stating, "The national system is growing slowly, and processes for adding rivers are not functioning well."[16]

Howard Brown of ARCC agreed: "The way the system has been set up to protect rivers makes it agonizingly slow, and the results are disappointing. A wilderness area or national park can go through Congress once, but wild and scenic rivers must make two trips—once for a study, then for designation. Twenty-eight rivers are protected now, but the number should be closer to a hundred." To speed protection, Brown supported incentives for state action and more emphasis on easements.[17]

Even though easements had been recommended as early as 1963, when author William H. Whyte testified for national protection of the Current, little was done. "The river managers and park superintendents always opposed easements," said Bob Eastman of the park service, "but the first thing a new superintendent looks at is a map, and he wants to see a solid block of green—to own everything and to keep the job simple. We can't afford to do that today."

Overcoming all the difficulties, San Francisco representative Phillip Burton, chairman of the House Interior and Insular Affairs Subcommittee, led passage of the National Parks and Recreation Act of 1978, one of the most comprehensive natural area preservation laws ever enacted. The act designated the section of the Delaware threatened by Tocks Island Dam and also protected the Skagit, lower Rio Grande, North Fork of the American, Pere Marquette, Missouri, and Saint Joe Rivers. Both the number of rivers and the mileage in the national system increased by 40 percent, and seventeen new study rivers were named. With other sections addressing national parks, wilderness, and recreation, Burton's bill approved 144 projects in forty-four states; it was dubbed "parks barrel" by both supporters and critics, who recognized the act's resemblance to pork barrel bills that had authorized dams and canals all over the country. Reflecting on the river protection movement of the 1970s, Stewart Udall said, "The American Rivers Conservation Council has been the major, effective voice for preserving America's rivers."

REACHING FURTHER

Except for the original inventory done by interior planners under Stanford Young, the process of national river selection was largely one of political hit-and-miss. No one knew how many rivers had the qualities needed for the national system or where they were, so in 1975 the Department of the Interior's Bureau of Outdoor Recreation (changed under President Carter to the Heritage, Conservation, and Recreation Service) began a nationwide rivers inventory to provide data as a guide for recommending new national river candidates, and for other uses by agencies and citizens. A point system was devised to compare amounts of development on one river to another. After studying topographic maps, surveys, and people's comments, planners listed the rivers with the highest number of points.

Covering all states but Montana, where the governor halted work owing to fears of federal controls, Department of Interior planners found that 61,700 miles on 1,524 river sections were relatively undeveloped and met standards of the national rivers system. Not counting Alaska, this is less than 2 percent of the nation's river miles.[18]

Adding teeth to the inventory, President Carter in 1979 directed federal agencies to assess the listed rivers flowing through federal lands and to recommend either designation, further study, or other uses. A memorandum to department heads stated, "The agency is encouraged . . . to prepare legislation to designate the river as part of the Wild and Scenic Rivers System if appropriate." The president directed agencies to avoid or mitigate adverse effects on the inventoried rivers, thus giving those streams some protection without the long congressional process of designation.

A few agencies followed the directive. The Forest Service considered the inventory when writing land management plans for each national forest. Unfortunately, the agency with perhaps the most important role—the Federal Energy Regulatory Commission (FERC)—did not consult with the National Park Service, which inherited the Heritage, Conservation, and Recreation Service's duties when it was disbanded in 1981. The Reagan administration ignored the inventory, but it proved to be useful anyway. For example, when Alabama highway planners noticed that a new road project was near a listed river, they wrote to Bern Collins of the National Park Service for guidance and special construction procedures. "The inventory is simply treated as information," said Collins, "and some agencies are finding that the rivers can be protected by choosing development alternatives."

In 1980, twenty-six Alaskan rivers were designated, adding 3,071 miles for 43 percent of the national rivers system in 1984. And after years of debate, 125 miles of the Salmon River were added to the system. Both the Alaskan and Salmon actions were pushed by President Carter and rode through Congress as part of larger land protection bills.

The last advance for rivers under Carter was the federal protection of streams already in California's state rivers system. This was important because of a dam proposed on the Middle Fork of the Eel.

To divert water south, the Army Corps of Engineers and Los Angeles had in the 1960s planned Dos Rios Dam, which would eliminate the state's largest summer steelhead run, drown the town of Covelo housing two thousand people, bury much of the Yuki Indians' reservation, and flood thirty miles of popular whitewater. A bill signed by Governor Reagan in 1972 designated northern California rivers, including the Eel, in the state scenic rivers system. This halted Dos Rios Dam but invited reconsideration in 1984. Seeking better protection for four thousand miles of the northern rivers, Governor Brown requested national river designation in 1979. Federal designation makes it more difficult for the powerful southern California and San Joaquin Valley political bloc—a state majority—to rescind protection, and it means better management of logging on national forest river frontage, unregulated under the state's forest management law. Included in the proposal were the Smith, California's only major undammed river and one of the nation's outstanding scenic streams; the Klamath, one of the largest West Coast rivers south of Canada and one of the world's greatest producers of steelhead trout; the Scott and Salmon, undeveloped Klamath tributaries; the Trinity, the largest Klamath tributary; and the Eel, with three forks running in a special beauty of grasslands, woodlands, and whitewater. All are vital to a multimillion-dollar fishing industry off the California coast, to Indians, and to sport anglers. Designation of 1,235 miles of streams (excluding several thousand miles of small tributaries requested by Governor Brown) was signed by Interior Secretary Cecil Andrus only nineteen hours before he left office in 1981. This single action increased the national rivers system by almost 25 percent and protected three adjacent rivers, establishing a wild and scenic rivers "region."[19]

To rescind federal protection, southern water agencies and northern timber companies sued, arguing that typescript rather than printed notices of the environmental impact statement did not meet requirements and that management plans were not in force (these were not required for other rivers). Earl Blaise, board chairman of southern California's Metropolitan Water District, said, "Even though I do not feel there is any rush to develop the Eel, I always felt the option should be there if the state needed the water."

Saying that an environmental report's review period had been one day too short, a federal judge in 1983 declared Andrus's designation invalid, but this decision was overturned in 1984 when an appeals court restored national status after finding the objections to be "insignificant" and "trivial." Meanwhile, the Metropolitan Water District of southern California lobbied for a bill to allow state legislatures to subtract rivers from the national system—support that the *Los Angeles Times* called "a desperation move that seems unlikely to get the Metropolitan Water District anything except a reputation as a bureaucracy that cares about nothing else in California as long as its customers' faucets make a splash when they are turned on." Bills to rescind state protection of the Eel have been introduced in the state assembly, where a majority of southern Californians could open the way for Dos Rios Dam if the river loses its federal protection.

The ARCC lobbied for bills to protect forty fishing rivers in 1980 and eight Oregon rivers in 1982 and for incentives for state programs in 1983, but these failed to pass. Under President Reagan and Interior Secretary James Watt, the rivers program was nearly eliminated; rivers and trails appropriations were cut from $3.6 million in 1981 to $1.67 million in 1983. The Heritage, Conservation, and Recreation Service, responsible for the program, was eliminated, with some functions being assumed by the National Park Service. Whereas previous administrations had recommended designations, Watt's directives declared the streams "eligible but not suitable" if private land was included or if developers objected. The Carter directives were mostly ignored. The FERC was encouraged to grant private permits for dams, with applications streamlined to cut "red tape."

In the Department of Agriculture, the Forest Service—usually less protective than the National Park Service—offered the only river proposals, recommending designation of eight streams for 505 miles, but the president's Office of Management and Budget cut the list to 245 miles by eliminating private land and possible dam sites. Of 165 miles studied on Michigan's Au Sable River, only 74 were recommended by the Forest Service, and only 23 miles passed the Office of Management and Budget.[20] The administration also recommended elimination of the park service's technical assistance to states and local governments striving to protect rivers, but Congress insisted on some funds to keep the program alive.

Worst of all, by 1982 the development moratorium for eleven rivers had expired, because there had been no congressional action after the five-year study period. Chris Brown, the new director of ARCC, asked for an extension of the moratorium and testified that his organization "feels strongly that the fate of these rivers should not be decided by congressional default." Most important was the Tuolumne in California, where San Francisco and irrigation districts had applied to the FERC to build five dams that would eliminate one of the nation's premier whitewater runs and a superb trout fishery. Oregon's Illinois and Colorado's Gunnison were also threatened by hydroelectric proposals. A bill to extend protection failed, leaving the FERC free to license dams.

In 1984 wilderness bills that came to a vote added five rivers to the national system: the Tuolumne, which had been one of the wildest but most imminently threatened rivers in the history of the national rivers system; the Illinois in Oregon, where a hydroelectric project had been proposed; the Owyhee in eastern Oregon; the Verde in Arizona; and twenty-three miles of the Au Sable in Michigan. Four new study rivers were also named.

In 1985 a 7.5-mile segment of the Loxahatchee River became Florida's first national wild and scenic river. But in the same year the Reagan administration recommended designation of only 173.7 out of 1,604 miles of rivers that had been studied and found eligible for the national wild and scenic rivers system. To protect rivers in the national system—never an easy job— became increasingly difficult in the 1980s, with opposition by landowners, a hydroelectric boom, and neglect or outright hostility on the part of the federal government itself. Chris Brown said, "We need to look harder at alternatives to national designation."

BEYOND THE NATIONAL SYSTEM

Although state wild and scenic rivers programs must clear some of the same political hurdles as the national system, state designations were the main alternative. A pioneer in river protection, Wisconsin outlawed power dams on the Brule River in 1905 and on the Flambeau in 1908. For scenery and recreation, the Oregon legislature denied water diversions from certain streams and waterfalls in 1915, and dams that would interfere with salmon were stopped on the Rogue River (the corps's Lost Creek Dam was later built anyway). Minnesota bought easements in 1919 to halt subdivisions along a 150-mile section of river. To save steelhead, California banned dams on the Klamath in 1924. To save salmon, Washington passed a law to prohibit dams in parts of the Columbia basin but was overruled by the Federal Power Commission during the Cowlitz River debate. In 1965 Wisconsin passed the nation's first wild and scenic rivers act to protect the Pine, Popple, and Pike rivers, and Montana designated rivers for recreational use.[21] Maine formed an Allagash Authority in 1963 to develop preservation plans and in 1966 designated the Allagash Wilderness Waterway. Ohio, Tennessee, and Maryland started scenic river systems in 1968. In 1974 North Carolina designated the New River to help stop power dams.

Some states adopted their own scenic rivers systems as alternatives to the federal program; others saw state action as a way to protect even more rivers than the federal government could ever hope to do. In 1972 the California scenic rivers law named 4,006 miles of waterway on fifty-nine streams—the largest state system. The act prohibits dams, including one planned for the Middle Fork of the Eel, and in spite of heavy influence by the timber industry, it restricts riverfront logging on nonfederal lands. The Minnesota system requires riverfront zoning by local governments following state standards. By talking to each landowner, planners built political support and avoided the opposition that undercut programs in other states. One of these was Maryland, where state land use regulations along the upper Youghiogheny were met by hostile mountain residents who retaliated by blocking access, threatening fishermen, and shooting at kayakers who launched from a bridge pier. Rarely were rivers designated when a dam was planned, but Pennsylvania stopped a utility's pumped storage project by naming Stony Creek a state river.

By 1983, thirty states had wild and scenic river systems or had designated individual rivers totaling 269 waterways for 13,674 miles. Most programs are in the East, protection varying from a toothless list to a ban on dams and a requirement for local zoning.[22] In 1983 Stewart Udall said, "Within about four years of the federal act, many states had passed their own rivers bills, and nothing pleased me more. Today the states don't have wilderness acts, but they do have wild and scenic rivers acts."

Governor Joseph Brennan of Maine won the 1983 River Conservation of the Year Award from ARCC after he issued an executive order protecting 1,500 miles on sixteen rivers. The designation prohibiting state support of dams came after a National Park Service study that identified the most valuable streams. Included are the nation's only ten stretches of river with a natural population of Atlantic salmon. The order denied approval of two hydroelectric projects but allowed approval of an important site on the West Branch of the Penobscot.

To avoid antigovernment feelings, alternatives to even the state programs are sometimes sought. Along Montana's Blackfoot River, residents had an inherent bias against federal protection, so a coalition was formed among ranchers, timber companies (Champion International and two ranchers own 75 percent of the frontage), county planners, the state, Trout Unlimited, and citizens, aided by the federal Bureau of Outdoor Recreation. Landowners allowed recreation on their property, and state agencies maintained the sites. To save open space, the Nature Conservancy bought $20,000 worth of easements where land acquisition would have cost $15 million. The program does not prohibit dams that were once proposed.

Formed in 1973 by the Maine legislature, the Saco River Corridor Commission regulates land use in a 1,000-foot-wide strip along the river. Most construction is banned on the hundred-year floodplain, buildings are located 100 feet back from the water, and standards are set for logging within 250 feet. With representatives from each of twenty communities, the commission avoids antistate sentiment yet is more stable and capable than local government. In Minnesota, eight counties formed the Mississippi Headwaters Board to protect 466 miles of river.

State and local protection has been effective where national designation was not wanted, but to stop federal water projects, to prohibit federal permits for private hydroelectric dams, and to save rivers on federal land, national designation is still needed.

WINNING AND LOSING

By the end of 1985, sixty-six major rivers, including a total of 170 named rivers and tributaries, were in the national wild and scenic rivers system of 7,250 miles. Twelve of the rivers were administered by states. Ninety-two rivers had been named for study, and fifty-five studies had been completed. Nineteen of these rivers were designated, and thirteen were recommended but not acted on.

Similar in some ways to the wild and scenic rivers, another official designation—"national river"—was established by Congress for the Buffalo River in Arkansas and the New River Gorge in West Virginia (the Current and Jacks Fork in Missouri were the first streams to be called national rivers). Stanford Young of the National Park Service wrote that the national rivers are "elongated national parks," where the government acquires wide corridors of land. A national recreation area on the Big South Fork of the Cumberland in Kentucky protects the river through a unique arrangement: After the Devil's Jump Dam proposal was defeated, the river was designated in 1974 in a rivers and harbors bill, which normally authorizes only dams and developments. The Army Corps of Engineers bought land and built recreation facilities, which were later turned over to the park service.

In 1983 Stewart Udall said that he was "very pleased" with the wild and scenic rivers system. "We really didn't know how successful the program would be." John Craighead said, "I never expected it to grow so much."

Not everyone is satisfied. In 1981 David Sumner wrote in *Sierra* that the national system "consists of token remnants rather than a true system."[23] With about seven thousand miles protected, the system is not in even near the same league as the national parks. Even the national wildlife refuge system had 772 units.

"I don't think the rivers program ever really came into its own," said Bob Eastman, retired from the Interior Department in 1983. "It was overshadowed in the early years by the wilderness program and was troubled in later years by political problems and budget cuts."

Stanford Young, also retired in 1983, said, "I predict that the national rivers system will have its ups and downs but that in time it will grow just as the national parks system, wilderness system, and wildlife refuge system have grown. The river protection concept is important to too many people to be denied. Money will be found to get the job done once the river constituency gets its act together. It's merely a matter of time."

The system may grow on federal lands, where hundreds of outstanding rivers are vulnerable to hydroelectric proposals, and on rivers near the people, since water quality has improved in some streams. In the early 1980s, new organizations, including the American Wilderness Alliance and the National Organization for River Sports, worked to save rivers.

The ARCC—still a small organization—grew as a leader of the river movement. The group lobbied for new legislation to aid local and state programs through federal loans for open space acquisition and to protect state-designated rivers from hydroelectric dams licensed by the FERC. Working on the Gauley River, the ARCC helped to organize a local group in West Virginia, and it fought a corps hydroelectric proposal to divert water from three miles of one of the most challenging whitewater runs in the country.

Even though the prospects for large new dams by the federal government subsided, other threats increased. By monitoring hydropower permit requests in 1983, ARCC found nine applications that would affect national rivers in Washington and California. In violation of the wild and scenic rivers act, the FERC issued a permit for a dam on the federally designated Suiattle River in Washington. The ARCC appealed.

In Alaska, the state senate unanimously passed a resolution in 1983 asking Congress to delete Birch and Beaver Creeks from the national system so miners could dredge gold. Legislation was introduced to rescind federal protection for the Rio Grande in Texas, raising questions of long-term security for national rivers. One act of Congress designated them, and another can delete them. Would the national system be simply a savings account where rivers are banked for future development? "Not if people keep supporting the rivers," said Chris Brown. "The real challenge is to get the message out to people about these rivers. People take them for granted. We're sitting on a mountain of opportunity, but if we don't mobilize support for some of the rivers soon, they'll be lost to hydroelectric dams and other developments."

Conservationists hoped that there will always be new designations of national parks and wilderness areas, but there was not likely to be another expansion of parks like that of the 1960s, and wilderness protection also peaked as the agencies and Congress tried to resolve RARE II (Roadless Area Review and Evaluation)—a government effort to "round out" the wilderness system. Rivers were the frontier program, and much remained to be done. The wild and scenic system had the necessary political flexibility, and if properly presented in new ways, it might have overcome the resistance to federal involvement and to the "locking up" of resources. It could appeal to a broad constituency, including landowners and urban open space users. Also, if river groups such as the American Rivers Conservation Council combined more effectively with fishermen, who in the past were often the backbone of rivers protection, a new, powerful effort might have speeded action. Rivers had the potential to be a major natural area protection program in the years to come.[24]

The national wild and scenic rivers system had gone partway toward establishing the balance of federal water management, but only 0.2 percent of the nation's streams were protected—about three and a half yards per mile—and the threats to even those did not go away. River conservationists had fought individual dams from Hetch Hetchy to the Stanislaus. Although the national wild and scenic rivers system added a positive alternative to dams, it was still limited to individual streams, the saving of each requiring a major campaign. To save rivers on a larger scale, the basic politics and policies for destroying them had to be changed.

7

POLITICS AND PROBLEMS OF
WATER DEVELOPMENT

The people who worked to save rivers were motivated by special places, but what they encountered was an acquisitive brand of politics known as pork barrel. The name dates from the Old South, where planters served up barrels of salted pork as bonuses to slaves, who rushed to get as much as they could. By 1879 the term *pork barrel* was used by congressmen to refer to public works projects that were not really needed. The rule became "You vote for my project and I'll vote for yours," and the mutual bond delivered billions of tax dollars to local districts with little regard for efficiency except in terms of reelection. It is what Senator Daniel Patrick Moynihan called "a chaotic and idiosyncratic system of economic and resource development, producing a random array of benefits more responsive to the vagaries of seniority in the U.S. Congress than anything else."[1]

Votes on one water project were not only swapped indiscriminately for votes on another, they were also used as currency to buy votes on altogether different issues. President Kennedy signed the Arkansas River Barge Canal bill for Senator Robert Kerr's vote on a tax bill, and President Carter traded his approval of Tellico Dam for a Panama Canal treaty.

Senator William Proxmire explained why water projects are so vulnerable to the pork barrel process: "The question that's always raised against incumbents is: 'What have you done? You haven't done anything.' One thing you can point to that people can understand, see, touch, feel, is a public works project. Labor likes it, management likes it, it may even be named after you. Only the taxpayers pay for it—but the taxpayers in your district pay only a tiny fraction."[2] For many congressmen, especially from the South

183

SELECTED EVENTS IN CHAPTER 7

1914   Reclamation law allowed twenty years to pay back irrigation costs.

1926   Reclamation law allowed forty years to pay back irrigation costs.

1934   Wildlife Coordination Act passed.

1936   Flood Control Act required calculation of cost–benefit ratios.

1939   Reclamation law allowed ten years with no repayment for irrigation costs.

1944   Flood Control Act authorized drainage projects.

1950   Uniform guidelines established for cost–benefit ratios.

1961   Benefits allowed for dilution of pollution.

1962   Senate Document 97 set new guidelines for cost–benefit ratios.

1965   Water Resources Council formed.

1972   Benefits for dilution of pollution disallowed.
Texas Water Plan proposed.
Buffalo Creek Dam collapsed.
National Dam Inspection Act passed.

1973   National Water Commission called for cost sharing and controls on floodplain development.
Principles and standards for water projects established.
Montana Water Use Act passed.

1974   General Accounting Office study critical of cost–benefit ratio calculations.
Railroads and conservationists sued against Lock and Dam 26.

1976   Lawsuit delayed Tennessee Tombigbee Canal construction.
National Wildlife Federation sued to stop Russell Dam.

1977   Tacoa Falls Dam failed.
President Carter called for dam inspections.
National Audubon Society sued to stop Garrison Diversion.

1978   Public Utility Regulatory Policies Act created incentives for hydropower.
Yellowstone River water allocated to in-stream uses.

1980   User fees for barges started.
Arizona passed groundwater management law.

1981   General Accounting Office study critical of subsidies included in water projects.

1982   Reclamation Reform Act passed.
Utility companies challenged "avoided cost" requirements.

1983   Bucks County residents rejected Delaware River diversion.
Payment in Kind program subsidized large farms.

and the West, water projects have clocked more mileage toward power and prestige than any pursuit of long-range solutions to people's problems.

During election year of each congressional session, two kinds of water development bills are normally passed: an authorization bill to initially approve projects, and an appropriation bill to pass out the money. Army Corps of Engineers activities are authorized through omnibus rivers and harbors bills approving many projects at once. Bureau of Reclamation projects are often passed singly, but some "projects" include a dozen or more dams. If enough projects are stacked into one bill, none of the congressmen benefiting are likely to vote against it, and with the threat of retaliation, criticism from other congressmen is scarce.

The direct beneficiaries are often an undemocratic few. In Oregon, 80 percent of the flood control benefits from Applegate Dam went to speculators owning undeveloped floodplains that appreciated at taxpayer expense. In Colorado, the Fruitland Mesa Project would have cost $1.2 million for each of sixty-nine farms. Barge companies, whose freight is 60 percent oil and coal products, enjoy locks, dams, and canals that were built at no cost to them while railroads and trucks paid at least a part of their own way. To bankers, a new dam means that old mortgages will be paid off after people are forced to abandon their homes, and new mortgages will be financed at higher rates. To western farmers, reclamation projects mean paying $3.50 an acre-foot for water that costs the government $80 an acre-foot to produce. These are the people who lobby for the projects and contribute to politicians who will push the votes and paperwork through. As water policy analyst Gilbert White more tactfully stated, "National efficiency usually has been mixed with local aspiration in promoting new projects."[3]

Not everybody agrees with the negative overtones the name pork barrel gives to the politics of water projects. Congressman Jim Wright wrote, "The term is both inappropriate and misleading. The connotation it conjures of slimy manipulation and backstage connivery—or the impression that the water developments authorized in these measures are really somehow unneeded—simply does not square with the facts." Even Stewart Udall wrote, "To call such projects 'pork barrel,' as they have so often and inappropriately been termed, is not only misleading—it is downright deceit."[4] Many agree that projects are needed, but water management professionals call for case-by-case study based on uniform guidelines, not on politicians' logrolling.

Political watchers say that the "iron triangle" is what makes many of the water projects possible. At one corner are the agencies: the Bureau of

Reclamation, the Army Corps of Engineers, and a few others. Congress is at the second corner, and local promoters are at the third. Although a project can be conceived at any corner, most start with the local promoters. Those who will benefit organize support, brass-band the idea, sell it to the newspaper editor, and meet with their congressman. Votes and contributions are explicit. The congressman requests a study by the corps or bureau, or sometimes he goes straight to lawmakers with an authorization amendment. All three corners of the triangle need each other: if the corps has no projects, it has no work, so corps officials meet with local business leaders and encourage them to become political. Ultimately, part of the contract for building the dam, or part of the wealth that it creates, will likely be funneled back to the congressman's campaign. To stop a water project, river supporters must break in and control one or more of the three corners.

The projects do not necessarily go where they are needed: they go to the districts of certain influential politicians. Several chairmen of public works and appropriations committees are essential to the delivery of projects, because these men call meetings, schedule hearings, draft proposals, select staff, and push a dam through or hold it up. They have been incorrigible spenders for their districts. The two senior members of the Senate Appropriations Subcommittee on Public Works received the highest and second-highest amount of corps spending in 1976, chairman John Stennis from Mississippi luring sixteen times the median level to his state. The top five states in corps spending (Mississippi, Washington, Missouri, Kentucky, and Louisiana) received 46 percent of the corps budget in 1976, and all but one of these states were represented on the subcommittee.[5]

Votes may depend on congressmen bringing home federal dollars, but why not federal largesse for hospitals and schools? Arthur Davis, who worked for the Bureau of the Budget in the Eisenhower years, said in 1983, "If the money is going to be given away, give it for something worthwhile. But there were few choices about what to give to the West. Back in the fifties it didn't need the other facilities, so it was given water projects." Likewise, eastern flood control dams had front-page appeal, and the momentum to build continued long after critical needs had been met.

In *Under the Influence*, Congressman Jim Weaver was quoted: "You know, in the old days, in the New Deal, a dam was the hope. It was! The dam sites were then worth something. You could produce power and some other things, and there was the hope of jobs. Now these people, these old pork-barreling congressmen, their minds were made up in the thirties when people were desperate, you've got to remember that. And so they're *still* for that dam, even if it's absolutely valueless."

"The water development agencies want to stay in business," said Brent Blackwelder of the Environmental Policy Institute, "and that means funding for the status quo." Without new laws, new expertise, and new commitments, the corps can not rebuild city water lines, construct sewage treatment plants, repair bridges, fill potholes, or renovate mass transit.

One way to control pork barrel is to require approval of full funding at a project's outset instead of authorizing year-by-year allowances. The difference in figures is often in multiples of ten. Other reformers called for states and beneficiaries to pay greater shares of the costs, the theory being that anybody who has to pay will discriminate between the good and the worthless. In 1983 the National Taxpayers' Union lobbied to squeeze out uneconomic projects with a balanced-budget amendment that would stop Congress from spending more than it receives. Congressman Robert Edgar advocated a capital outlay budget that would make dams and canals compete with schools and hospitals for federal dollars.

COLLECTING THE FACTS AND
JUGGLING THE NUMBERS

Water projects are governed by the pork barrel system and also by a somewhat economic approach that started with the Flood Control Act of 1936, which required that benefits "to whomsoever they accrue" exceed costs. To determine if some people will gain more than everybody will pay, facts are collected. The first uniform guidelines for calculating benefits and costs were in the 1950 "Green Book," revised in 1952 by the Bureau of the Budget. In 1962 Senate Document 97 offered new guidelines. In 1965 the Water Resources Council was created as a cabinet-level group to coordinate water development, and in 1973 it issued "principles and standards" as new benefit–cost criteria.[6] Cases such as Tellico Dam showed that politics—not professional water management—is what finally counts, but in an era of growing accountability lawmakers found it difficult to run roughshod over tough benefit–cost analysis.

So instead of opposing only individual projects, the people fighting dams in the 1970s turned increasingly to economics. Though benefit–cost analysis was intended to eliminate political debate, the analysis itself led to endless argument, and in 1976 the Congressional Research Service stated, "Probably the most frequently voiced criticism of benefit–cost analysis is that because of its singular economic criterion it ignores environmental and other effects which cannot be monetarily quantified." In *Strategies of Ameri-*

can Water Management, Gilbert White wrote, "The ecological view was at a disadvantage in having little evidence to put up against the more confident engineering predictions of practical outcomes in water flow, power production, or visitor days at recreation sites." Dissatisfied that the emphasis was always on plans while ignoring performance, White sought study of water projects after they were built to see if they did what the builders claimed they would do.

Americans are committed to numbers—the census is a national event, bank books are consulted daily, and calculators are built pocket-size—but the economic justification for spending billions of taxpayer dollars was ludicrous, even in the narrow context that excluded social and environmental effects. Of 380 projects studied by Senator William Proxmire's office, 220 were found not to be justified by normal business standards. The senator said, "I have consistently found that projects with an alleged benefit-cost ratio of less than two-to-one provide returns less than their cost."[7] Even accepting the Army Corps of Engineers' figures, Proxmire stated that of 178 major projects studied, 83 had cost overruns of 100 percent or more.

Resource economist Robert Haveman at the University of Wisconsin studied one hundred benefit–cost ratios of the corps and estimated that only 25 percent would survive rigorous analysis and that half of these would not be cost-effective if environmental damages were counted.

A General Accounting Office (GAO) survey in 1974 found nineteen instances in which benefit–cost calculations were incorrect or unsubstantiated, the errors favoring construction in all cases but one.[8] For Lost Creek Dam on the Rogue River, the corps counted hypothetical hydroelectric benefits that might be added in the future. Fishing use to be eliminated by the dam was not deducted from recreation benefits, and irrigation benefits were claimed though the irrigation facilities were to be built in a different project. Overstatement of benefits totaled nearly $50 million, equaling 40 percent of costs, and corrections would expose the dam as unfeasible. For Pattonville Lake on Missouri's Grand River, $1.1 million were claimed for agricultural production, but the Department of Agriculture estimated a $1 million cost due to inundation of land.

Audits of forty-four corps projects were prepared by the accounting firm of Price, Waterhouse and Company, which found that the amounts of money charged for water were decreased, creating more demand for it. Repayment periods for reimbursable costs were extended beyond the legal fifty years. In 1981 the GAO reported that the corps used fifteen-year-old cost information to set 1980 water prices for the Willamette River Basin Project.[9]

"Area redevelopment" is tallied as a project benefit, sometimes meaning that active farms are condemned and then resold to the highest bidder. New dams are touted for the jobs they create, the costs of labor being turned around as an employment "benefit." However, when engineer Bruce Hannon and economist Roger Bezdek at the Univenity of Illinois studied employment from five government programs, they found that corps construction yielded the fewest jobs—national health insurance, social security, sewage plants, tax relief, and mass transit brought more jobs per dollar spent.[10]

The discretion of cost–benefit ratios can begin with something as basic as population. For Stonewall Jackson Dam on the West Fork River in West Virginia, the corps projected that the populations of Weston and Clarksburg would grow 173 percent and 91 percent, respectively, in the next fifty years, though the Department of Labor expected only a 9.6 percent increase for the towns in the next thirty years.

Recreation benefits—popular especially in the 1960s—have padded projects' appeal. The corps claimed that recreation at Grove Reservoir in Kansas would exceed that of Yellowstone National Park. Logan Dam, proposed for Ohio's Clear Creek, was intended for flood control, but to justify it the corps claimed 76 percent of the benefits for recreation. Meramec Park Dam in Missouri would have flooded a popular recreation river, a state park, a wildlife management area, and Onondaga Cave, which attracts several hundred thousand people a year. Half of the recreation benefits justifying the dam were for "sightseeing" by people who would do nothing but look at the corps's work.

Benefits for diluting pollution were allowed in 1961. They accounted for 40 percent of the justification of Gathright Dam in Virginia, most of the dilution serving a Westvaco paper mill. Dilution claims were disallowed in 1972, but because Stonewall Jackson Dam was authorized earlier, the corps still credited 36 percent of the benefits to dilution, a claim not valid anyway because ten sewage treatment plants had been built since the corps collected its data. Water quality improves below some dams, but below others it is ruined. In 1981 tens of thousands of fish were killed below Conowingo Dam on the Susquehanna River because of low oxygen levels.

Benefits and costs are calculated for one hundred years, and interest is charged on the cost. Anyone who has bought a home knows that even at low interest rates, interest through the life of the mortgage can be larger than the principal. By manipulating the interest rate, projects can be made to appear more or less economic. During the 1950s the corps used a 2.5 percent rate. After 1968 Congress required a rate of about 5 percent—still far below the cost of borrowing money. In 1973 the Water Resources Council's principles and standards set a rate adjusted to that of fifty-year bonds, which was 6⅞ percent that year. But the new rates did not apply to already authorized projects, and the sponsors basked in a refuge from real-world economics. Only about half of these projects would have had adequate benefit–cost ratios at the new rates.[11]

To determine the value of proposed hydroelectric dams, the corps compares the difference between the cost of the project and the cost of the cheapest alternative. For Dickey–Lincoln dams in Maine, an interest rate of 8¾ percent was used to calculate the cost of oil-fired power, which was then compared to the cost of the dams; the dams, however, had been assigned a lower interest rate. At the proposed Oakley Dam in Illinois, the corps charged a higher rate for alternate water supplies because they would be locally sponsored and more risky. Manipulations of interest rates bolstered many projects' failing bills of economic health.

Another question of costs is, Who pays? As a "nonreimbursable" cost, the government pays for large flood control reservoirs. For levees, channelization, and small dams, the government pays for construction but not land acquisition, operation, or maintenance. Local governments pay for a part of municipal water supplies as a "reimbursable" cost. For Bureau of Reclamation projects, the irrigators are supposed to pay back construction, operation, and maintenance costs, but no interest. Hydroelectric costs are reimbursed from power sales. Navigation costs were all paid by the government until 1980, when a tax was levied on fuel for towboats using the projects. Federal agencies are to collect interest payments from municipal and industrial water buyers, but according to a 1981 GAO study, the rates do not always reflect government costs. Titled *Reforming Interest Provisions in Federal Water Laws Could Save Millions,* the study report stated that "on four projects of 100 reviewed, GAO calculated more than $667 million in tax-payer-provided interest subsidies. The total amount of interest subsidies for all Federal water projects is in the billions of dollars."

Cost sharing by the states has been proposed many times. In 1973 the prestigious National Water Commission stated, "Cost sharing requirements would be effective in eliminating political pressures from a group seeking a project for no other reason than that they expect it to be paid for by the federal treasury."

President Carter proposed that states pay 10 percent of costs, but Colorado governor Richard Lamm and author Michael McCarthy wrote in *The Angry West,* "To saddle the West with costs never anticipated and never agreed upon is a serious enough matter. . . . A sudden shift to 25 percent front end state financing would mean, simply, no projects—at least for the forseeable future." President Reagan proposed even larger shares to be paid by the states, and in 1980 the GAO found that without legal changes, the Bureau of Reclamation and the Soil Conservation Service "have the legal authority to require non-Federal entities to share a larger percent of project costs."[12]

Beyond economic considerations affecting all kinds of projects, challenges grew against four of the main purposes of water development: flood control, hydroelectric power, navigation, and irrigation.

SPECULATION ON THE FLOODPLAIN

Whereas original authorizations in the 1930s called for federal dams to meet national needs, practice soon established that any flood control was a "national" need. Concerning a better definition, Luna Leopold and Thomas Maddock wrote in *The Flood Control Controversy*, "The truth of the matter is that no one wants such a definition. . . . What is wanted at local levels is a program that will permit unhindered development of the flood plain through federally conducted works." The policy of protecting existing development, no matter how provincial, expanded further to the support of real estate speculation and new construction along the rivers.

The 1966 Task Force on Federal Flood Control Policy noted that in the 1940s only 10 percent of the corps's flood control benefits came from protecting future floodplain development, but in the 1960s more than 40 percent of the benefits were attributed to development that was only a gleam in realtors' eyes. In 1965 the Bureau of the Budget questioned the policy of claiming up to 50 percent of benefits from nonexistent development.[13] Two-thirds of Days Creek Dam's benefits in Oregon were for future development. Opponents to Gillham Dam on Arkansas's Cassatot River pointed out that 74 percent of the original benefits were for flood control, but no significant development existed for forty-nine miles below the dam. Federal judge G. Thomas Eisele accused the corps of "circular reasoning." The dam would make possible new development that would justify the dam. A realtor estimated that Red River Dam in Kentucky would cause floodplain property to jump in value from $750 to $6,000 an acre.[14] River conservationists maintained that with only 5 percent of the nation's land being floodplain, there were other places to build and no need to subsidize river-bottom speculators.

The proposed Lincoln and Oakley reservoirs showed another problem:

they would flood more farmland than they would protect. Hillsdale Dam in Kansas would flood fourteen thousand acres to protect seven thousand. In 1974 the Department of Agriculture wrote that more than three hundred thousand acres of farmland were lost per year under reservoirs.[15]

Levees and channelization were criticized for aggravating flood hazards above and below the projects. In *Science* magazine, Charles Belt, Jr., wrote that Mississippi floods in 1972 crested at record heights in St. Louis even though the volume of water was only that of a thirty-year flood. Levees and wing dams forced a smaller amount of water to rise higher.[16]

The Flood Control Act of 1944 authorized major drainage projects as a part of flood control, and one hundred million acres were drained.[17] The wetlands no longer absorbed flood waters, and faster runoff caused erosion. A 90 percent reduction in fish was found in channelized waters of North Carolina, and the streams still have not recovered.[18] Ninety miles of Florida's Kissimmee River were straightened to fifty-two miles, resulting in a loss of 95 percent of the river's wildlife habitat and the ecological and hydrologic destruction of Lake Okeechobee, affecting much of southern Florida.

In spite of $15 billion spent for flood control by 1982, damages continued to climb ($3.4 billion in 1975), and 90 percent of disaster relief was for flood damage. Critics argued that nothing was as certain as death and floods and that flood control projects lull people into a false sense of security: levees in Wilkes-Barre, Pennsylvania, were overtopped in 1972, forcing 80,000 people from their homes, and in South Dakota, Pactola Reservoir had been built only fourteen miles above Rapid City, but when fourteen inches of rain fell below the dam, a flood killed 236 people. The Task Force on Federal Flood Control Policy in 1966 and the National Water Commission in 1973 stated that by avoiding new floodplain construction, people could avoid flood damage without more channelization and dams.[19]

WHO OWNS THE POWER OF THE RIVER?

Whereas much attention is given to the power produced at dams, it also requires power to build dams. Auburn Dam would use the equivalent of about twelve million barrels of oil, and if built in the mid-1980s it would have owed an energy debt until 2016. Economists at the University of Illinois studied the energy use of six major federal programs and found corps projects to be the most consumptive, far exceeding expenditures for health, railroads, mass transit, water treatment, and education. Because dams are often far from cities, 10 percent or more of the electricity is lost in transmission.

Small hydroelectric development, defined by the Department of Energy as fifteen megawatts or less, has been backed as a soft-path approach to new energy. The Public Utilities Regulatory Policies Act of 1978 (PURPA) required that utility companies bought electric power from producers at alternative sources such as hydroelectric dams and windmills and that the utilities paid the same rate as they paid for their costliest source of power (usually oil). The 1978 law was interpreted by the Federal Energy Regulatory Commission (FERC) to include power not only from existing dams but also from new dams. A boom in applications to build small dams resulted.

Provided enough water is left in the stream for fish and the ecosystem, environmental effects from small hydroelectric projects may be slight. But as the kilowatts add up, so do the impacts. By 1983 in California alone, sixty-two new projects had been proposed for rivers eligible for the national wild and scenic rivers system. Two thousand miles of streams in the Sierra Nevada would have been affected if the FERC had approved all pending applications. The Sierra Club's Russell Shay said, "Proposals are being made for new dams and diversions . . . with potentially devastating effects on fisheries, wildlife, wilderness, recreation and water quality. Even though they are small projects, the building of any large proportion of them would drastically alter the face of the West." Fish and Game biologist Phil Pister commented on the diversion of Sierra Nevada streams: "It comes down to the logic that it's awfully hard to go fishing or grow trees in a pipe."[20]

In the remote Salmon River basin of Idaho, sixty-three hydroelectric projects were proposed. Even though the dams would be on tributaries, they would have blocked the flow of nutrients, starved bottom life, and depleted fish numbers farther downstream. The Nez Perce Indians, Idaho Wildlife Federation, and others appealed and asked for an environmental review of the cumulative rather than the isolated effects of the dams.[21]

In 1980 a Bureau of Reclamation booklet stated, "The Bureau of Reclamation is researching and developing the potential of hydroelectric power in the West. Some new reservoir sites can and will be developed. However, there is considerable additional capacity at existing dams and facilities. Even without building new dams, hydroelectric production can be greatly increased."[22]

Side effects of repairing or adding turbines to existing dams can likewise be great. Diversion of water sometimes leaves a dry streambed, and releases at a power plant may alternate from a trickle when water is being stored to a small flood when power is generated. Hundreds of proposals in New England called for new generation at existing dams. The American Rivers Conservation Council reported that half of the renovations would involve diversions through penstocks or long pipes, sometimes dewatering streams for a thousand feet. On the Colorado River, new turbines at Glen Canyon Dam caused erratically high flows, eroding Grand Canyon beaches.

The Army Corps of Engineers reported that, nationwide, 641 large hydropower dams were feasible. Important proposals were pending on the Tuolumne in California, the West Branch Penobscot and Kennebec in Maine, the Snake below Hells Canyon, and the Gauley and Blackwater in West Virginia.

"In the sixties it looked like we were going to save a lot of streams," said Stanford Young, leader of the first national rivers study. "Then came the rush for hydro dams. Now it looks like it will be tougher to keep rivers free, and we'll have to fight for places we thought we had already saved."

Preliminary permits to study dam sites are often granted by the FERC without concern for power needs or environmental questions. People can hire a lawyer and intervene, hoping to reverse a federal decision, but they are usually unsuccessful because the permit allows only a feasibility study. When a construction license is later requested, people can intervene again, but by then, millions of dollars might have been spent by the developer. So it is difficult to fight the preliminary permit because the data are not collected, and difficult to fight a final permit because the sponsor is so committed. Since 1935, the FERC has approved nine hundred hydropower applications. In 1983 FERC commissioner Georgiana Sheldon said, "Since license applications for new projects contain many special conditions to provide for environmental protection, it has not been necessary for the commission to deny any license applications for environmental reasons." The FERC has denied several.

Among FERC reviewing agencies, only the Fish and Wildlife Service regularly commented on applications, and it was swamped with work. The FERC was supposed to consider the overall public interest and deny a permit if nonpower values were more important, but the agency nearly always viewed its role as promoting maximum development. River basin plans, which the commission was directed to follow, did not exist for many rivers, and where they did, the plans often parroted old development proposals. Citizen appeals through Congress and the administration could influence the FERC, and some dam fights, such as those at New River and Hells Canyon, were won when Congress passed laws superceding FERC licenses.

State-required permits could also control new dams. "In California, it's the state that's holding the lid on," said Greg Thomas of the Natural Resources Defense Council in 1982. But California's concern faded with the passing of the Brown administration. Water quality permits, often administered by the states, were sometimes needed for dams and could stop projects that the FERC would otherwise approve.

In 1982 utility companies challenged the legal requirement that utilities must buy power from small hydroelectric developers, leaving the feasibility of some projects in doubt. Appeals were pending, but regardless, hydroelectric power remained a reason to dam rivers. Chris Brown of ARCC said, "Through helter-skelter hydro development we may see a great setback in the river conservation work of the last twenty years."

TAXPAYERS PUSH BARGES

Belching smoke as they churned on the Ohio and Mississippi, the riverboats of Mark Twain's day made commerce possible through the heartland, and the pilot—wise to the ways of the currents—was a national hero. Those boats are gone, the slap of paddle wheels replaced by the drone of diesel engines, and the rivers that the early pilots knew are also gone. Now twenty-six thousand miles of river are channelized or dammed for barges.

Until 1980, all construction, operation, and maintenance for river navigation was done by the government at a subsidy of more than $400 million a year,[23] giving barge companies an advantage over railroads, which paid for their own tracks and even paid taxes on their rights of way.

The lower Mississippi, Ohio, Monongahela, and some other rivers warranted the federal investment, but new barge routes seem like the stream Mark Twain described in *The Guilded Age*: "Goose Run, if deepened, and widened, and straightened, and made a little longer, would be one of the greatest rivers in our western country."

In the 1950s "Kirwan's ditch," named after Congressman Michael Kirwan, was proposed to canalize the Beaver and Mahoning Rivers between Pittsburgh and Lake Erie. The $1-billion project was never built.[24] The Cross Florida Barge Canal was also stopped, but opponents were not successful with Lock and Dam 26 or with the Tennessee–Tombigbee Waterway.

At Alton, Illinois, the corps planned in the late 1970s to replace Lock and Dam 26 with two 1,200-foot-long locks, deepening the draft from 9 to 12 feet at a cost of $400 million. Environmental groups against the expansion found support from the railroads, which funded the opposition (this unlikely alliance also fought the Tennessee–Tombigbee Waterway and coal slurry pipelines in Montana). In 1974 conservationists, twenty-one railroads, and a taxpayers' group sued because the corps was acting only on a 1909 authorization for maintenance and emergency repairs (70 percent of the Ohio River's locks had already been enlarged to an unauthorized size).[25]

The groups argued that Lock and Dam 26 was the first step in dredging a deeper channel 670 miles to Minneapolis, which would cost $10 billion and wreak ecological havoc on the river and three hundred thousand acres of state and federal wildlife and recreation lands. Twenty-nine dams already covered riffles above St. Louis, and additional wing dams, built out from the shore to direct the flow to midstream, caused silting and partial filling of the river between the dams, smothering two hundred square miles of rich backwaters. (On sections of the Missouri River, bank and channel work has caused the loss of 50 percent of the river's surface area.) The deeper channel and the dumping of dredged silt and gravel would aggravate problems, and barge traffic would churn more sediments and destroy the bottom life, basic to the food chain.

While the corps stated that only Lock and Dam 26 was planned, Assistant Interior Secretary Nathaniel Reed said, "When you notice a camel's nose poking through your tent flap, you are wise to conclude that out there is a whole camel, rear-end and all." Federal judge Charles Richey found the corps's contention "unworthy of belief."[26] Thus delayed, the corps went to Congress for authorization, and the focus of the debate shifted to proposals that the barge companies pay for improvements.

Presidents Franklin Roosevelt, Eisenhower, Kennedy, Johnson, and Nixon all had proposed that barge companies pay part of the costs of locks and dams. Supporters of user fees argued that navigation benefits are not shared widely enough to warrant taxpayers' investments. For Kirwan's ditch, the corps had calculated a benefit–cost ratio of 2.5–1, but an Arthur D. Little study commissioned by the army found that savings to shippers were fourteen times greater than to the public. Economist Robert Haveman found a return of forty-four cents on the dollar from the Illinois River Canal.[27] Barry Allen at Ramapo College in New Jersey found that among fifty-two dredging projects for barges, only 17 percent showed positive ratios.

Barge promoters cited that on a ton-mile basis, moving freight by barge is the most energy-efficient way. But a 1974 study by Anthony Sebald at the University of Illinois found that because of the meandering of rivers, barges travel four miles to trains' three, and that the barge promoters' rail data covered the entire country, including climbs over the Rocky Mountains, where barges do not go. Sebald concluded that railroads are more energy efficient than barges by 10 to 23 percent. A U.S. Department of Commerce and Department of Transportation study of Lock and Dam 26 indicated that if barge operators paid fees, more traffic would shift to railroads.[28]

The enlarged lock and dam was authorized anyway, but with it Congress required the first user fees for barges. A Department of Transportation study had suggested a thirty-four- to thirty-eight-cent tax per gallon on towboat fuel. Congress agreed on four cents a gallon starting in 1980, increasing to ten cents in 1985, to be used for new construction. This was 6 percent of projected construction costs for the next five years and included nothing for operation and maintenance.

THE COSTLIEST DITCH OF THEM ALL

The Tennessee–Tombigbee Waterway in Alabama and Mississippi is the exemplar of federal spending for canals. Through the influence of southern congressmen, the project was authorized in 1946, even though the corps recommended against it. The 232-mile-long canal cost about $4 billion— America's most expensive water project ever. To link the Tennessee River to the Gulf of Mexico required a twenty-seven-mile-long cut through mountains, five dams, and two and one-half times the excavation of the Panama Canal. Once a biological treasure, 217 miles of the Tombigbee River were dredged. The canal affects 115 species of fish and 51 species of mussels; 7 of which were considered for the endangered species list. The joining of the two rivers will serve not only barges but also a parasitic lamprey and the nuisance water milfoil, which are expected to migrate through the locks. Fifty-one valleys next to the canal are dumps for dredged soil, yet a 1974 corps brochure claimed that "greater attraction will be provided for waterfowl from the Mississippi and Atlantic flyways." The canal cut 800 miles off the route of barges—70 percent of which are expected to carry coal, though the GAO reported that coal supposedly to be floated down the canal from Tennessee exceeds the recoverable reserves in the area to be served.[29] Two hundred and fifty families were relocated.

Costs for disposal, grading, and revegetation of soil were not counted in the 1976 benefit–cost ratio, which barely slipped through at 1.1–1. Several companies listed as future shippers on the canal had no intention of using it.[30] By one estimate published in the *New York Times*, railroads would lose $70 million a year. A *Times* editorial, "The Engineering of Deceit," stated that beneficiaries included a power plant that was to get coal in amounts it could not burn.[31]

In 1971 an Environmental Defense Fund lawsuit delayed the project, and in 1976 the fund, a railroad, and other groups charged that the waterway, authorized for a 170-foot width, was being dug 300 feet wide. The court delayed construction while opposition grew.[32]

In the budget-cutting 1980s, the Tenn–Tom price tag was a miasma to supporters, who won their appropriations by only two votes in the Senate and ten in the House. Brent Blackwelder credits the approval to the political leverage of John Stennis, ranking Democrat on the Senate Armed Services Committee; Jamie Whitten, chairman of the House Appropriations Committee; and Tom Bevill, chairman of the House Appropriations Subcommittee on Public Works—all from Mississippi or Alabama.

Other navigation projects accused of being costly and damaging included the Arkansas River Canal to float barges 516 miles from the Mississippi to Catoosa, Oklahoma. On the Ohio River, less turnover of water in expanded impoundments caused pollution; the Environmental Protection Agency estimated a 30 percent loss in waste assimilation capacity at Markland Dam near Cincinnati. Ohio River farmlands and roads were eroded after the larger dams were built, but courts found the corps not responsible. On Texas's 550-mile-long Trinity River, proposed channelization would cut off 180 meanders, shrinking the route to 335 miles at a 1977 cost of $2 billion. Wallsville Barrier Dam—one of three impoundments—would eliminate twelve thousand acres of estuary, but the canal was twice defeated in referendums. Some navigation projects were built at exorbitant costs and scarcely used; in the mid-1970s half of the federal operation and maintenance costs for navigation went to rivers carrying only 3 percent of the freight.[33]

While new projects received bonus appropriations, old locks such as those on Pennsylvania's Monongahela River deteriorated. In 1983 the corps's National Waterways Study stated that $5.2 to $12 billion may have been needed by 2003 for navigation; the largest problem was aging locks. The corps planned to spend $7.5 billion on canals from 1983 to 1988. Now that most feasible flood control dams had been built, maintenance for navigation, which in 1824 was the corps's first role with rivers, returned as the agency's main job.

RE-CLAIMING NOTHING

With the Reclamation Act of 1902, Congress intended that irrigators repay the government for the irrigation projects, and Bureau of Reclamation brochures still claim that 80 percent of costs are reimbursed by water users: "The Reclamation program has been and continues to be one of the soundest investments possible. . . ." But in 1981 the GAO reviewed six bureau projects and found that each provided a subsidy of more than 92 percent, some at 97 percent, and concluded, "The original rationale for building the Federal projects and increasing the subsidy was based on early twentieth century goals for the settlement of the West and for regional development. Those goals have been reached and the projects should now be reevaluated in the light of current economic and social conditions." The office explained, "Irrigators are receiving a large subsidy because much of the money allocated for constructing the irrigation facilities is scheduled to be repaid by someone other than the beneficiaries." Farmers pay 5 to 10 percent of the cost of much of the irrigation water, consumers of electricity pay 33 percent, and the taxpayer pays the rest.[34]

The bureau does not base water charges on the government's cost, but on the "ability to pay." Contracts under this clause sell water at $3.50 an acre-foot. The GAO reported that the government's cost of providing the water was $54 to $130 an acre-foot. In the Fryingpan–Arkansas Project, diverting water through the Continental Divide from the Fryingpan River to the Arkansas River, the bureau estimated that the Colorado farmers could pay $.27 an acre-foot, but GAO found the ability to be $14.91. In the Pollock–Herreid Project in South Dakota, $3.10 an acre-foot was paid for water costing $130 to deliver. The GAO stated that farmers could pay from three to fifty times more than they were charged.

Hydroelectric and irrigation purposes were intertwined. A Bureau of Reclamation dam was proposed in the 1960s for Montana's Big Hole River, where $14 million of costs were nonreimbursable for uses such as flood control, $8 million would be paid by irrigators, and the remaining $63 million would be paid by power sales generated elsewhere at Missouri River dams. A 1962 audit, however, showed that the power revenues for the Missouri dams were nearly $2 million short of paying interest on the Missouri projects alone, not counting the debt that the Big Hole Dam would amass. With no other funds coming in, taxpayers would be saddled with irrigation costs. The dam has not been built.[35]

Army Corps of Engineers dams were criticized for low interest rates, but with bureau projects, farmers pay no interest at all, and even at rates far below market value the interest on a fifty-year project exceeds capital costs. The GAO stated, "Repayments for irrigation are presented to the Congress as full repayment. Since no interest is charged, however, these payments actually cover less than 10 percent of the Federal government's actual cost."

Congress first required reimbursement for water projects in ten years. Irrigators could not do this, so the law was changed in 1914 to twenty years, in 1926 to forty years, and in 1939 to allow ten years with no payback after project completion. Operation and maintenance costs are supposed to be reimbursed, but farmers at the corps's Lucky Peak Reservoir in Idaho and industries at reclamation's Glendo Reservoir in Wyoming were not charged.

Until Carter's presidency, contracts for sale of water ran forty years with no increases to reflect rising operations costs. For the Bonneville Unit of the Central Utah Project, an Interior Department audit reported that a 1965 repayment agreement precludes government recovery of about $198 million that should have been reimbursed. In 1981 an Interior Department audit of the Central Valley Project—the Bureau of Reclamation's largest—revealed $79,000 a day in losses. Unless hydroelectric rates were raised, the project would be a financial basket case facing an $8.8-billion deficit by 2038—the intended break-even year. In 1983 Robert Broadbent, commissioner of reclamation, blamed the Central Valley Project deficit on old contracts: "We need to have new contracts to raise the price of water. But you have to remember that about 98 percent of these are contracts for long-term water. The Reclamation Reform Act of 1982 attempts to do something about that. It says that in four and a half years all people will enter into new contracts to pay at least full operation and maintenance charges." But, the commissioner added, "I'm sure those people are going to litigate. They say it's unconstitutional; you can't take away a contract right. The court will have to decide who's right. I don't know if it will stand up in court. Someone's got to keep their word." About the Central Valley Project deficit Broadbent said, "It'll come out of the taxpayer—the general appropriations."

On the question of subsidies Broadbent said, "The benefits of reclamation far exceed the costs. Look at Hoover Dam. The $10 billion has been spent, and today on reclamation farmland we produce about 10 percent of the cash food and fiber products of the country. We spend more on the subway system here in Washington than on reclamation."[36]

The way many westerners see it, the subsidies are needed for farmers to stay in business. Richard Lamm and Michael McCarthy wrote, "If the West's half-finished projects are abandoned and if Washington's 'no-new starts' mandate continues to hold, sooner or later it will cripple the farmers. No farmer can afford to pay $100 an acre foot. No farmer can bid with Exxon."[37] They argued that Army Corps of Engineers' projects "generally are completely non-reimbursable." In reference to proposed pricing changes, they argued that even though authorized water projects would total more than $30 billion of additional spending, the rules of the game should not be changed halfway through.

Former congressional budget office director Alice Rivlin said,

> These subsidies encourage wasteful use of water in regions that may no longer need subsidized development. They also distort farmers' decisions about which crops to grow. . . . Market gluts can occur, driving the market values of those commodities downward, in turn prompting the government to raise values artificially by means of price supports. . . . Under current policy, the federal government will invest roughly $3.8 billion from 1983 through 1987 in irrigation facilities. Of this amount, roughly $75 million would be recovered with charges now in place.

In 1983 the government's "Payment in Kind" (PIK) program gave surplus crops to farmers so they would not grow more crops. The GAO surveyed farms and found that cotton growers in California received the largest PIK subsidies, followed by California rice growers—two of the most water-intensive crops, already heavily subsidized by the Bureau of Reclamation. Twenty-one irrigated cotton farms received free crops worth $27 million in 1983. Seven farms each received crops valued at more than $2 million, despite the Agricultural Act of 1949, which states that one farmer should receive a maximum of $50,000 worth of surpluses.[35]

The subsidies, interest payments, and deficits have much to do with river protection. Unless the water is sold cheaply enough for farmers to buy, the bureau cannot "justify" the building of more dams. Even at bargain rates, some water cannot be sold; the GAO reported that federal reservoirs hold fifteen million acre-feet that is uncontracted for, some of it for many years.

A FRONTIER NO MORE

Some crops, needing a certain climate, can be grown only through irrigation in California and the Southwest, but other crops were grown elsewhere before the federal government subsidized irrigation. After 1950, eastern and southern farmers went out of business as crop production shifted. Through the twenty years following World War II, cotton acreage dropped by one-third in the South but increased 300 percent on lands watered by the Bureau of Reclamation. Fruit and nut acreage fell 50 percent in the north but grew 237 percent on reclamation lands. Bean acreage dropped by 449,000 acres across the country while it doubled on farms served by reclamation. Charles Howe and William Easter of Resources for the Future wrote, "Reclamation has probably replaced 5 to 18 million acres elsewhere" and that perhaps 180,000 farm workers lost their jobs in nonwestern regions.[39] Rain-soaked fields in Louisiana were abandoned while California farmers flooded dry-lands for rice. Grown close to seaports, much of this heavily subsidized crop is exported to Korea. Old animosities between the eastern and western United States may be renewed.

Reclamation advocates at the turn of the century had faced easterners' criticism, but Congressman Oscar Underwood of Alabama argued, "These lands are being opened to all the people, whether they be residents of the East, South, or West. The farm boys of the East want farms where they can . . . build homes without being driven into the already overcrowded cities to seek employment." Historian Frederick Jackson Turner called the struggle of West versus East one of "democracy against privileged classes."[40]

But at a 1966 conference of the American Society of Civil Engineers, Pennsylvania's environmental resources secretary Maurice Goddard said that the East

> is handed the crumbs and the cake goes west. It seems just plain ridiculous to us to keep placing eastern farm land in the "Soil Bank" while continuing to bring additional marginal western lands into production through subsidized water development. Why not bring eastern land, where the people are and where the rainfall is plentiful, back into production?

Commissioner of Reclamation Floyd Dominy answered, "Let me deny emphatically that there is an East–West conflict." Then he proceeded to stress the need to fund his program: "Important schemes will be required that will dwarf any of those in existence today. But this is a challenge that must be met if growth and development of these United States are to continue."[41]

This novel version of civil war intensified when New York City faced default and Mayor Ed Koch compared his city's needs to those of corporate farmers in California and to realtors in Arizona and Texas: "We're still fighting the old formulas that give most of the money for water projects to the South and the arid West."[42]

In 1976 the *National Journal* reported, "Federal tax and spending policies were causing a massive flow of wealth from the Northeast and Midwest to the fast growing southern and western regions of the nation . . . and eroded the tax bases of many state and local governments in the East and

Midwest." From 1950 to 1976, the Northeast received slightly more than 6 percent of the national water resources funds spent by the corps and the bureau, while the West received more than 48 percent and the South 28 percent. For municipal and industrial supplies, the corps spent only $34.2 million in the New England and North Atlantic regions, compared to $214.3 million in the Southwest. All Bureau of Reclamation funds are spent on the West.

The desert notwithstanding, water costing $2 in Utah costs up to $13 in Pennsylvania, and people in Boston pay four times the Phoenix rate. The Central Arizona Project will receive more water development money than the sixteen states from Minnesota to Maine, but 70 percent of the crops grown in Arizona—including cotton, which is one of the largest consumers of water—have been classified as surplus and eligible for price supports.

Why didn't eastern politicians object to paying for projects that hurt their constituents? Gaylord Nelson answered,

> When I went on the interior committee in 1963 I was the only member from east of the Mississippi, and I wasn't from very far east of it. The committees are controlled by the beneficiaries, and the political lifeblood of western politicians is water. All the westerners become experts; if you find one who isn't, he's an accident and he won't be there for long. An eastern congressman can't get up on the floor and talk intelligently against them, and who wants to look stupid? So you have the prowater experts on one side and ignorance and lack of interest on the other side.[43]

In 1977 President Carter said, "The current pattern of water project distribution is contributing to the federal dollar drain out of the heavily populated Northeast where economic stimulus is needed."[44]

In 1983 Brent Blackwelder said, "Now that the West is settled and developed, water users should pay their way." Eastern tax dollars were redistributed to the frontier to lure settlers, but in the 1980s the Northeast and Midwest reeled from economic recession, and their urban water systems decayed for lack of funds to repair them.

FROM FAMILY FARMS TO
CORPORATE CONGLOMERATES

Thomas Jefferson said, "The small landowners are the most precious part of the state,"[45] and on their behalf Congress, in passing the Newlands Reclamation Act in 1902, recognized that western agriculture would have to be subsidized. Yet lawmakers and Theodore Roosevelt were determined that reclamation would serve family farmers, not speculators like those who had corrupted irrigation planning to that date. Roosevelt said, "The money is being spent to build up the little man of the West so that no big man from East or West can come in to get a monopoly in the water or land." In 1905 F. H. Newell, active in drafting the reclamation law, said, "The object of the Reclamation Act is not so much to irrigate the land as it is to make homes."

Guarding against tax dollars feeding the fortunes of big businesses, the act required that a farmer buying government-supplied water own no more than 160 acres. In 1916 this was interpreted to mean 320 acres for a husband and wife and eventually 640 acres for a family of four, which could farm 1,280 acres if they also leased land. To get the water, farmers had to live on their farms, but in 1910 it was ruled that owners could live within fifty miles, and in 1916 the residency rule was required only of the initial applicant.[46] Even these diluted requirements were ignored, large areas such as California's Imperial Valley were excepted, and owners found loopholes as simple as deeding lands to business partners.

In 1924 a committee of special advisors on reclamation reported, "The Government reclamation program had in a measure failed to accomplish the human and economic purposes for which it was created."[47] In 1978 the Department of the Interior estimated that corporations—not family farmers—collected $150 million in irrigation subsidies in California alone. In one area farms averaged 2,200 acres,[48] though the Department of Agriculture found that the efficient size for a one-man farm in California was 200 to 400 acres.

About 145,000 farms used Bureau of Reclamation water in the 1970s, 96 percent meeting the acreage provision. Owners of "excess" lands (more than allowed under the "160 acre" limitation) included J. G. Boswell Co., with 133,228 acres; Southern Pacific Land Co. (Southern Pacific Railroad), with 106,680; and Tenneco West, Inc., with 64,941. In 1977, 1.3 million acres of excess land were held by 5,288 owners, 85 percent of them in California and Arizona. An Interior Department study indicated that less than 1 percent of the irrigators controlled 20 percent of lands served by reclamation. In the Central Valley of California the subsidy was worth $1,000 an acre, and in the Westlands District the subsidy was worth about $3.4 million for a typical 2,200-acre farm.

To reform the reclamation act, Congressman George Miller of northern California championed the cause of small farmers and water reformers. In 1981, calling water contracts for the southern Central Valley of California "an almost perfect example of socialism for the rich," he sponsored a bill to eliminate the "ability to pay" discount and to charge at least 2 percent interest. Miller said, "The Administration has correctly criticized many federal programs which have grown uncontrollable at great cost to the taxpayer. Irrigation is an example where the subsidies just grew and grew, and now we find billions of dollars in taxpayers' money used to subsidize some of the wealthiest agricultural interests in this country." Agribusiness lobbied heavily for continued subsidies.[49]

The National Farmers Union stated that if the excess lands were cut to tracts of 320 acres, 4,012 farmers would have new opportunities, and if the excess acreage were cut to the average farm size of 105 acres (in 1977), excess lands would serve 12,226 families. Family farm supporters with National Land for People supported a bill limiting eligibility for reclamation water to 640 acres.

The Reclamation Reform Act of 1982 raised the acreage limit from 160 acres for an individual to 960 for a family and granted unlimited leasing. People or corporations holding excess acreage may still receive federal water but will pay interest of 7.5 percent for water used on the excess acres. Residency requirements were repealed, and water conservation plans were required.

The new law gave large agribusiness most of what they wanted. The restrictions against nonfamily farmers are gone. The National Wildlife Federation's Edward Osann said, "Without the stipulations that reclamation have a social purpose by benefiting family farmers, the justification for the subsidy is gone." Only 1 percent of America's farms and 2 percent of the farmland are served by the bureau. With its 90 percent subsidies, the program does not pay its way. It never did.

WATER MINING

Groundwater is inseparably tied to rivers; 30 percent of streamflow comes from underground sources. The abuse of groundwater means the eventual abuse of rivers when dams are built to replace exhausted groundwater supplies. The federal Water Resources Council estimated that 33,000 trillion to 59,000 trillion gallons of water lie underground—fifty years of surface runoff. About half the population drinks from wells numbering in the millions, but 68 percent of all groundwater withdrawn is for irrigation. Of all irrigation supplies, 35 percent are from groundwater. In California, 48 percent of all water used was from underground—more groundwater than was used in all eastern regions combined.

To overdraft is to pump out more water than seeps in, and this happens at a nationwide rate of twenty-one billion gallons a day.[50] In the Central Valley of California, soils have compacted where water was overdrafted, and lands have subsided as much as thirty feet. With less water, farmers drill wells deeper, and energy costs climb. During California's drought in 1977, twenty-eight thousand new wells were drilled. Eventually wells go deep enough to draw salt water that intrudes from deep formations or from the ocean in regions such as New York's Long Island and Texas's Gulf Coast.

Critically overdrafted, the Ogallala aquifer, on the plains from Nebraska south to Texas, supplied drinking water for two million people and irrigated ten million acres. The annual pumping of more water than flows in the Colorado River caused a three-foot-per-year drop in the aquifer's water level, which has been lowered a total of seven hundred feet in some places. Farms near Lubbock, Texas, have been abandoned in what could be a preview of the future; Texas A & M University reported that irrigation in the Texas Panhandle would begin a severe decline by 1985 if no water was imported from other regions.[51] On average, the Ogallala had forty years of life left if the pumping continued, and without the groundwater, the region may return to dry wheat fields, grazing lands, or forage for wildlife.

At a 1972 cost of $20 billion, the Texas Water Plan was proposed to import water from the Mississippi River, but other states were not enthusiastic. The governor of Arkansas sent the governor of Texas a jar of water and a note: "This is all you're going to get." Packed with problems, including those of damming Texas rivers, the plan was defeated by a coalition of environmentalists and schoolteachers (because the proposed funds would otherwise go to education).[52]

Arizonans overdrafted 2.2 billion acre-feet a year—46 percent of their total consumption—and the water table dropped as much as twenty feet a year while developers, miners, and farmers race each other to the bottom of the well.[53] Some farmers were retiring because of declining water tables; as energy costs escalated, fewer could afford to pump. To gain water rights, the city of Tucson bought twelve thousand acres from farmers, and mining companies bought another eight thousand acres. Arizona will see continued urban growth but less farming, which consumed 89 percent of the water but produced only 3 percent of the personal income in the 1980s.

The overdraft was one of the main reasons for the Central Arizona Project (CAP), designed to pump Colorado River water to the Phoenix and Tucson areas at a cost of $1.6 billion. Although the system was designed to carry 1.2 million acre-feet, only 500,000 acre-feet were to be available in 1990, decreasing to 284,000 acre-feet by 2030 because of additional withdrawals from new projects in Colorado and Utah. A centerpiece of the CAP was to have been Orme Dam, which was fought by Yavapai Indians. Charleston Dam on the San Pedro River would have flooded nesting sites of five pairs of endangered gray hawks. Hooker Dam on New Mexico's Gila River would have flooded six miles into the nation's first designated wilderness area, set aside in 1924 through the work of Aldo Leopold. The four dams and canals would evaporate 10 percent of the water—enough for a city of five hundred thousand. Also authorized under the CAP, but not for Arizonans' use, were five dams in Colorado: Dolores, Animas–La Plata, Dallas Creek, San Miguel, and West Divide. These were added at the insistence of Congressman Wayne Aspinall. Some of the dams had less than a 1–1 benefit–cost ratio, and all became controversial in the 1970s. Only Dolores and Dallas Creek were recommended by the Bureau of Reclamation and scheduled for completion. Under the combined attacks of Indians, taxpayer groups, and environmentalists, the Arizona dams were deferred and the bureau sought alternatives.

Arizona was among the top ten states in per capita water consumption, and even with the Colorado River supplies, groundwater overdraft will likely be reduced by only two-thirds. Conservation of water could do much more to cut the overdraft, but as former Tucson city council member Barbara L. Weymann said, "People have brought their old environments with them here and they resent being told they're in the middle of the desert."[54]

In 1977 Arizona formed a Groundwater Management Study Commission, which recommended strict controls. Facing the threat of fewer water projects during the Carter administration, the state passed one of the nation's best groundwater management laws in 1980, requiring conservation of water. Other groundwater regulations had been adopted by Minnesota in 1937 and in Florida in 1957. In California's Central Valley, however, where groundwater was overdrawn at a rate of 1.5 million acre-feet a year, anybody could drill any number of wells and pump without regard for the loss of a neighbor's well and without consideration of the public costs of diverting rivers to replace the depleted underground supplies. New dams were the agricultural industry's answer to disappearing groundwater.

Underground pollution by toxic wastes was the most publicized environmental problem of the early 1980s. Thousands of water supplies were eliminated. The California State Health Department reported that 35 percent of the wells in the Central Valley were polluted with the pesticide

DBCP. The Environmental Protection Agency estimated that three-fourths of the chemical waste dumps were leaking and that a hundred million Americans might be threatened by contaminated groundwater.

Even if the government strengthened programs to stop the dumping and the leaking of dangerous wastes, much damage would still be permanent. The pollution of underground water may cause a reversal of the trend to favor wells over rivers as a water source. Though the rivers have been polluted in the past, some are improving, whereas ruined groundwater supplies will remain ruined for an unknown number of generations. Stopping the pollution of surface water was an important national goal in the early 1970s, but the concern has suffered from budget cuts since then. Groundwater pollution may make cleaning up the rivers more important than ever.

LEAVING THE WATER IN

The threats to rivers include more than dams, channelization, and pollution. Diversions have ruined thousands of stream miles. Fish, wildlife, recreation, hydropower, and navigation are in-stream uses that suffer, the worst case being a dry riverbed. Other problems are warm water, silt, salt, algae, and pesticides and herbicides from returned irrigation water.

In the mid-1800s, some people recognized in-stream flow problems below dams. Catskill Falls, painted by Thomas Cole, had become a tourist attraction, but visitor George Curtis wrote, "In fact, if your romantic nerves can stand the steady truth, the Catskill Falls is turned on to accommodate poets and parties of pleasure." For twenty-five cents, a boy opened a sluice to let the water fall.[55] Modern plans to "mitigate" the loss of canoeing and rafting runs are just as contrived: to replace the Stanislaus whitewater, the corps proposed to dynamite channels and add boulders to another section of the river. Most boaters did not support the proposal, and it was dropped.

One of the first Bureau of Reclamation dams was built in 1906 on the Truckee River below Lake Tahoe, cutting the flow in half, eliminating world-record cutthroat trout, and shrinking the Paiute Indians' Pyramid Lake in Nevada. The lake level dropped eighty feet, and the Indians lost much of their livelihood.[56] The cui-ui, a fish found only in Pyramid Lake, is a living fossil but likely to become extinct as 9.8 billion gallons of water are diverted yearly for irrigation.

Below dams, rivers are affected by artificial releases, which sometimes improve the flow, as when water is added during dry months, but which often cause damage. Many hydroelectric dams release radically fluctuating amounts of water; irrigation and water supply dams may release only an anemic trickle.

How much in-stream flow is needed? An amount called Q 7–10 is often required, meaning that diversions may not cause a stream to drop below the amount of water in the lowest seven-day period likely to occur each ten years. Yet this minimum flow is only one element of in-stream needs and is often barely enough to keep the streambed wet. Seasonal variation is needed, the right temperatures are important, and even floods are essential to a stream's health.

In 1979 the Water Resources Council published estimates of the percentages of streamflows needed by fish and wildlife, ranging between 60 percent and 88 percent of a river's flow.[57] Most conflicts about in-stream uses are in the West, where vast quantities are withdrawn for irrigation.

A project with extreme problems was the Garrison Diversion, where the Bureau of Reclamation planned to channel Missouri River water across the plains and return polluted runoff to Canada's Souris River and the Red River of the North, thereby incidentally connecting the Mississippi basin with Hudson Bay. For irrigation of 250,000 acres in North Dakota, Garrison's canals and other facilities would take 220,000 acres out of agricultural production. Twelve national wildlife refuges would be damaged, including one that was started to mitigate losses that occurred when the Missouri was dammed. Sixty thousand acres of marshes and wetlands—already drained at the rate of 300,000 acres a year nationwide—would be destroyed. Waterfowl losses in North Dakota—which produces more waterfowl than any state but Alaska—were projected at 350,000 a year (original benefit–cost ratios were negative until "benefits" for wildlife were added). Fewer than a thousand farms would benefit at $800,000 each, leading Senator William Proxmire to call the project "sheer, unadulterated pork." The Canadian government protested and requested a moratorium on construction. The National Audubon Society sued in 1977 and delayed work.[58] After considering halting the project, the Carter administration approved a smaller version not affecting Canada. The Reagan administration proceeded with the plan, but in 1984 Congress required further studies before additional construction was approved.

Because of a Mexican treaty guaranteeing in-stream flows for Mexican irrigation, the United States built the world's largest desalting plant to improve the lower Colorado River, which Mexicans cannot fully use because of ten million tons of salt a year. The $365-million plant was paid for by taxpayers, even though half of the salt was caused by upstream water projects that divert flows for irrigators[59]—when fields are flooded, salts in the soil dissolve in the water, which then flows back into the river.

Even the water quality in reservoirs can be harmed by new dams. Russell Dam on the Savannah River of Georgia and South Carolina was fought because of outstanding wildlife, fishery, and canoeing values, but construction nevertheless began in the late 1970s. The project will flood the only remaining undammed section of the upper river, where the riffles and current are needed to recharge oxygen between other reservoirs. In 1976 the National Wildlife Federation sued to stop construction. The district court ruled that dams can be point sources of pollution—a decision that may affect many dams in the future by requiring compliance with water quality regulations, but no injunction was granted for Russell.

Water for fish is the first thing sacrificed during droughts. When New York needed water in the mid-1960s, the minimum releases to the Delaware River were cut back even further. The Bureau of Reclamation diverted 80 percent of northern California's Trinity River to the south, causing an 80 percent loss of salmon and steelhead. And the bureau had planned yet more dams for northern California. As regional spokesman James Cook put it, "There are long arguments on whether fish or people will get the water, but when the nut gets tight, people are going to get the water." A Congressional Research Service study of the Missouri River stated that with minimum flows reserved for fish and wildlife, the basin will be short of water by the year 2000. Power plants, coal slurry pipelines, and oil shale processing create new demands on in-stream flows in eastern Montana and western Colorado.

On the Youghiogheny River in western Pennsylvania there has been little concern about shortages, but any more permits to withdraw water would not allow enough dilution of industrial and municipal waste. In a 1983 vote, Bucks County, Pennsylvania, residents rejected a plan to divert Delaware River water for the Limerick nuclear power plant. Sponsors of the referendum hoped to reverse decisions of the Delaware River Basin Commission to allow withdrawal of 95 million gallons of water a day.

For years, in-stream requirements were ignored in the operation of dams, but some states now require water withdrawal permits and regard in-stream flows as a "beneficial use"—a recognition reserved in earlier years mainly for irrigation. Wisconsin officials can deny a permit for a dam if it would damage aesthetic values, and in Vermont a dam can be stopped if it will hurt recreation, scenery, fish, wildlife, or the natural flow below the dam. Oregon has denied dam approvals in order to protect salmon and steelhead.

Yet some states still say that to keep cattle healthy is a beneficial use of a river, but to keep fish alive is not. Activities that need even more water, such as rafting, can rarely compete with irrigation. The high flows needed for the natural maintenance of river channels and for the formation of islands are rarely considered. States such as California that consider fish and wildlife usually regard them as less important than cities, industries, and farms.

Montana's in-stream reservation for the Yellowstone River was a path-breaking case. Headwaters of the river are in Yellowstone National Park, and upper reaches are superb trout water with spectacular scenery. In 1930 the U.S. Fish and Wildlife Service coded the Yellowstone and some other Montana streams as "blue-ribbon" trout waters—one of the first classifications given to rivers. There are no large dams on the river, and except for six diversion dams, the 670-mile-long Yellowstone would be the longest undammed river in the country outside Alaska.

In the lower basin, the Fort Union coal formation holds forty-three billion tons of strippable reserves, and with synthetic fuel potential and coal slurry pipelines, water demands could reach 2.6 million acre-feet a year, more than the river can provide while still meeting irrigation and municipal needs. Faced with coal development proposals, the state passed the Montana Water Use Act of 1973, for the first time allowing state agencies to reserve in-stream flows for fish, wildlife, and recreation. The following year the state banned further withdrawals until water was allocated. On the basis of studies of cutthroat trout on tributaries, the hydraulics creating the islands needed by Canada geese, the rising flow that triggers fish spawning, and much more, the Department of Fish and Game applied for nearly all remaining water in the river.[60]

After weeks of hearings at which coal developers attacked the Fish and Game Department's position, the Board of Natural Resources and Conservation in 1978 allocated about 62 percent of the average flow on the lower river and 76 percent in upstream reaches to in-stream uses. This was considered a success for in-stream values, and fish and game official Jim Posewitz wrote, "What we have done in our complicated way is decreed that the Yellowstone can still flow free."

Ironically, the recognition of in-stream needs may lead to even more dam proposals; water developers may treat the low-flow requirements as one more reason to store water, and the Yellowstone allocations could lead to growing pressure for Allenspur Dam near Yellowstone National Park. In 1979 Assistant Interior Secretary Robert Herbst said, "The pressure for dam building is going to grow with in-stream reservations."[61] It may be axiomatic that to protect both in-stream values on the lower ends of rivers and free-flowing reaches up above, in-stream regulations must be coupled with dam prohibitions such as the wild and scenic rivers act.

MAKING UP FOR LOSSES

To protect fish and wildlife, whether from in-stream flow reductions or from flooding by reservoirs, the Wildlife Coordination Act of 1934 was the first major law requiring that agencies consult with the Department of the Interior's Fish and Wildlife Service. But this agency and state fish and game departments had little leverage to require adequate releases. For example, the Idaho Fish and Game Department was overruled in an attempt to save a trout fishery below a corps dam on the Boise River in the late 1950s. But through the Fish and Wildlife Service review, Interior Secretary Stewart Udall was able to stop Rampart Dam on the Yukon River, and the Interior Department has helped to stall a power company's damming of Canaan Valley in West Virginia.

To make up for fish and wildlife losses where the projects are built, federal agencies were required to prepare "mitigation" plans to replace whatever is to be lost. This often meant the trading of a wild fishery for an inferior hatchery. Dam plans often excluded money for mitigation; the Bureau of Reclamation's Oahe Dam in South Dakota took 100,000 acres of river bottom, and twenty years later mitigation was still incomplete. In the South, where corps projects resulted in 1,236,045 acres of lost habitat, the Fish and Wildlife Service requested 877,078 acres of mitigation acreage—111,300 acres were authorized, and only 33,800 acres were purchased. Although many people were not interested in these wildlife losses, other secondary effects of water development were not easily ignored.

THE ROAD TO BABYLON

Just as the Sumerians along the Tigris and Euphrates Rivers were plagued with salted soil when their civilization collapsed some three thousand years ago, farmland of the American West suffers from excessive salinity. As irrigation water flows through the soil, it picks up salt and then deposits it on other fields. Many fields are underlain with impervious clay where the water is trapped; when it evaporates it leaves salts behind in growing concentrations, making it difficult for plants to take in moisture and get oxygen. Salt buildup in parts of California's Central Valley is 1.5 tons per acre annually.

The Bureau of Reclamation stated that more than four hundred thousand acres are affected, and more than one million acres "may become a barren salt flat." In 1979, $31 million in farm goods were lost, and $300 million per year were expected to be lost by the year 2000.[62]

The Bureau of Reclamation proposed to sewer the California farm-land—a solution that promised yet more problems. The three-hundred-mile-long San Luis Drain would carry salty water to the San Francisco Bay at a 1979 cost of $750 million and with unknown costs of bay pollution. Agricultural drainage including dissolved minerals, pesticides, and herbicides already polluted the Kesterson National Wildlife Refuge in the Central Valley, where the Fish and Wildlife Service reported that up to 40 percent of hatched birds suffered birth defects, most of these dying. The water would kill most fish in two days.

Evaporation from reservoirs is another secondary effect of dams. Called "the river's storage charge" by Bureau of Reclamation officials, evaporation from Lake Mead equals seven feet off the top of the reservoir each year. Interior Secretary Cecil Andrus said, "Water projects don't create water, they move it around and sometimes lose some in the process."[63] All large reservoirs in the West evaporate eleven billion gallons daily—enough for about 40 percent of the nation's public water supply.[64] Evaporation intensifies the problems of salt, which remains behind. Water users argue that less water evaporates than would flow down the river and "waste to sea" if it were not for dams. But in the Colorado and some other basins, the flow is already evened out through normal years, and more dams would add only evaporative losses.

Other secondary debts of water projects are easier to see. After most Colorado River floods were stopped below Hoover Dam, plants grew in the riverbed at Needles, California, and silt piled up, raising the river bottom and requiring that one hundred families be moved out and that a levee be raised. Total expenses for the Colorado River Front Work and Levee System were $70 million, but the area was flooded again in 1983. Gavins Point Dam on the Missouri River caused rising groundwater to flood basements in the town of Niobrara, where six hundred people had to be moved at a government expense of $14.2 million.

SAFETY LAST

Older dams are showing wear and tear. The TVA bought Nolichucky Dam from the Tennessee Eastern Electric Power Company in 1945. Silt filled 77 percent of the reservoir, and the dam's cracked concrete required $2.5 million worth of safety improvements.[65] Budgets show increasing spending to repair dams and to correct damages that they cause. On Kentucky's Cumberland River, Wolf Creek Dam creates the largest reservoir in the East, but water seeped through the dam and required repairs costing more than the original project. Twenty-seven provisions in the 1979 omnibus water development bill were to correct problems caused by projects already built. In 1983 the corps's maintenance budget exceeded its construction budget.

In 1972 Buffalo Creek Dam, made of coal waste, collapsed and killed 125 people in West Virginia. Three hundred and fifty major dam failures have occurred in the United States, fifteen of them since 1972, most being privately owned dams. Public safety will require climbing costs for generations.

The National Dam Inspection Act of 1972 directed the Army Corps of Engineers to inspect all 50,000 large dams, 40 percent of them located where their failure would imperil life and property. No money was released until 1977, however, when President Carter, spurred by the Tacoa Falls failure, which killed thirty-nine people in Georgia, ordered the inspections. Of 9,000 dams that the corps checked in populated areas, nearly one-third were unsafe, and 130 posed imminent danger, but many of the dam owners could not be found. Much of the inspection job is left to states. In Pennsylvania, two inspectors were responsible for 3,000 dams.

Old dams were part of the "infrastructure crisis" given front-page attention in 1982 as people became aware of the backlog of crumbling roads, bridges, water mains, sewer lines, and subways. Old public works were neglected. As an assistant secretary for housing and urban development stated in *Newsweek*, "Have you ever seen a politician presiding over a ribbon-cutting for an old sewer line that was repaired?" Billions of dollars still shower new projects having nothing but political appeal.

Many scoffed at the chance of sabotage or wartime destruction of dams. Yet consider what our own nation has done: In World War II, American bombers destroyed Ruhr Valley dams, as Wing Commander Guy P. Gibson wrote in the Atlantic, "Cars speeded along the roads in front of this great wave of water which was chasing them and going faster than they could even hope to go. . . . Until quietly and rather quickly there was no longer anything except the water. . . . The floods raced on, carrying with them as they went viaducts, railways, bridges, and everything that stood in their path."[66] In Korea, only days before peace, American planes bombed North Korean dams to damage the economy of that country.

By the mid-1970s, river conservationists and others had built a powerful case against the pork barrel politics of water development. No longer were they fighting against only Echo Park Dam as one part of the Upper Colorado Basin Storage Project, or Grand Canyon dams as one part of the Central Arizona Project; rather, they were addressing complex, deep-rooted problems: unfair subsidies, wildlife impacts, energy consumption, salinity, international needs, Indians' rights, and more. Campaigns had been won to save certain rivers, and now people had succeeded in using science and economics, in capitalizing on everyone's concern for safety, and in exposing an anachronistic political system. But could the politics of water development be changed?

8

A NEW ERA

On horseback and by canoe, George Washington explored the Appalachians for possible canal routes, including the Youghiogheny, Cheat, and Casselman Rivers. He believed that western settlement depended on water development. But Thomas Jefferson said, "Talk of making a canal of 350 miles through the wilderness—it is little short of madness."[1] Andrew Jackson, president in 1830, touted river development and defended the Army Corps of Engineers: "In improving the navigation of our rivers, bays, and harbors . . . this corps forms an essential reliance." Following Jackson, President Martin Van Buren thought waterway projects were unconstitutional, and in 1839 he halted them.[2]

President John Tyler put the corps back to work on the Ohio River in 1842, and about river development and the West he said, "The great importance of these subjects to posterity . . . and the security of the whole country in time of war cannot escape observation." In 1844 President James Polk stopped all of the corps's river work. Presidents Zachary Taylor and Millard Fillmore supported projects in 1848 and 1852, but Congress disagreed. Then when Congress pushed water development in 1853, President Franklin Pierce fought appropriations, but his vetoes were overridden.

In 1882 Chester A. Arthur refused to sign one of the first water development bills recognized as pork barrel. The president pointed out that each state was scrambling for federal money and that "as the bill becomes more objectionable it secures more support." Congress overrode the veto.[3]

President Theodore Roosevelt, in many ways a great conservationist, approved Hetch Hetchy Dam. He created the Reclamation Service and touched off a half century of wild-river damming by calling to "make the

SELECTED EVENTS IN CHAPTER 8

1830   President Jackson supported river development.

1839   President Van Buren halted water projects.

1842   President Tyler supported corps projects.

1844   President Polk stopped corps projects.

1848   President Taylor supported water projects.

1852   President Fillmore supported water projects.

1853   President Pierce fought water project appropriations.

1882   President Arthur unsuccessfully vetoed water projects.

1936   Flood Control Act passed under President Franklin Roosevelt.

1941   National Resources Planning Board formed.

1949   President Truman supported Echo Park Dam.

1955   Hoover Commission proposed water project reforms.

1956   President Eisenhower vetoed water project bills.

1960   President Kennedy supported Cross Florida Barge Canal.

1968   President Johnson signed National Wild and Scenic Rivers Act.

1973   National Water Commission proposed reforms.

1977   President Carter announced "hit list." President Carter approved compromise water projects appropriations bill.

1978   President Carter announced new water policy. President Carter vetoed water projects appropriations bill. "Potholes" bill for water projects stopped by Congressman Edgar and others.

1979   President Carter approved water projects bill including Tellico Dam.

1981   President Reagan appointed James Watt as secretary of the interior. First major water projects deauthorization bill passed.

1983   Jobs bill passed with funds for water development.

streams . . . of the arid regions useful by irrigation works for water storage."
President Woodrow Wilson also approved Hetch Hetchy.

President Harding applied no breaks to private dam development in
the Northwest despite growing evidence that fisheries were being eradi-
cated, but he opposed building a dam in Yellowstone National Park. President Herbert Hoover took steps to control water pollution and Alaskan
salmon fishing, but he also expanded river navigation and championed the
authorization of Hoover Dam, a milestone of river development.

Under President Franklin D. Roosevelt the greatest age of dam building began with the flood control acts of 1936 and 1937, the Works Progress
Administration, the TVA, and the Columbia River dams for hydropower
and jobs.

President Harry Truman supported Echo Park Dam, deriding the
importance of "dinosaur bones" even though these had nothing to do with
the controversy. He raised water power to a prime goal, "a subject close to
my heart and vital to the future of the nation." To accelerate the damming
of the Columbia he proposed a Columbia Valley Authority.[4]

President Dwight Eisenhower promoted state and federal "partnership," with the government encouraging private and state dam builders. In
his first State of the Union message he said, "This combined effort will
advance the development of the great river valleys of our nation and the
power they can generate." While Eisenhower's policies allowed free reign
to private river developers, his "partnership" was an undisguised euphe-
mism for limited federal construction. He opposed federal water development on principle referring to the TVA as "creeping socialism." Despite his
approval of Echo Park Dam, the Bureau of Reclamation's budget plummeted from $364 million in 1950 to $165 million in 1955. Eisenhower
adopted a "no new starts" policy for federal projects and twice vetoed
omnibus water development bills. But Ted Schad, author of the veto messages, said in 1983, "The vetoes didn't really have anything to do with the
preservation of rivers." Bringing new analysis to the planning of water projects that had been hustled with a minimum of critique, Eisenhower's
Bureau of the Budget set economic standards designed to cut federal spending. It was the first serious attempt to stop projects on the basis of economic
criteria, which some viewed as placing New Deal development policies on
the chopping block. The Eisenhower analysts' approach preceded a curious
blend of environmental liberalism and fiscal conservatism that would mature
in twenty years.

President John F. Kennedy was a liberal conservationist but also a New
Deal developer. He used water projects as political currency, supporting the

Cross Florida Barge Canal to garner Florida votes. Although Kennedy's personal support for environmental protection focused on the seashores, he backed Interior Secretary Stewart Udall on many issues and was the first president to call for a national system of protected rivers.

President Lyndon Johnson said that "material progress is only the foundation on which we will build a richer life of mind and spirit." His rhetoric was at once prodevelopment and proconservation, but it was more than any other president had given to river preservation. The dam-building momentum slowed as the best projects were completed, the Vietnam war preempted money, and conservationists gained strength. Johnson told the Water Resources Council to raise the interest rate charged to water projects, and he ignored the Bureau of Reclamation in congressional messages that emphasized parks, rivers, and pollution control.[5] He signed the National Wild and Scenic Rivers Act, establishing the first major national program for river preservation and nailing the coffins of dam proposals on the Eleven Point, Feather, and Saint Croix rivers.

President Richard Nixon was attacked for anticonservationist views—exemplified, for instance, in his support for the Supersonic Transport—but he signed the National Environmental Policy Act, which provided unprecedented and unexpected means for the Natural Resources Defense Council, the Environmental Defense Fund, and other groups to sue and delay dam projects long enough to stop some of them politically. Nixon's characteristic of exceeding his authority benefited river protection: he halted the Cross Florida Barge Canal even though courts later ruled that he did not have the authority to do so. His controversial impoundment of funds delayed several destructive water developments, including the Central Arizona Project. But, saying, "There is too much pork in this barrel,"[6] he also canceled the building of sewage treatment plants. When Nixon's staff prepared a "filthy fifty" list of project terminations, political advisors seeking cooperation from Congress convinced the president to scrap the list, and the projects went uncontested.

THE HIT LIST

Among presidents, Jimmy Carter was the greatest rivers enthusiast. Unlike the motivations of Van Buren, Polk, Pierce, Arthur, Eisenhower, and Nixon, Carter's reasons for stopping water projects were more than fiscal and political conservatism. He had canoed on the Chattooga River in Georgia. As governor, he had canoed the Flint River and halted Spewrell Bluff

Dam. Eisenhower golfed, Ford skied, and Carter paddled. On a presidential vacation in 1978 he rafted the Middle Fork of the Salmon in Idaho. Campaigning for president, he said, "I will halt the construction of unnecessary dams by the Corps of Engineers." A campaign paper stated, "Each new project must be subjected to careful study. . . . We must realize that the federal government's dam building era is coming to an end. Most beneficial projects have been built."[7] Even after New Melones Dam was completed, but before the reservoir was filled, Carter said that if Congress passed a bill granting national protection to the Stanislaus River, he would sign it.

Carter appointed Cecil Andrus secretary of the interior. As governor of Idaho, Andrus had fought the lower Hells Canyon dams. He had supported the Bureau of Reclamation's Teton Dam, then presided as governor during its impressive failure. When questioned by congressmen, Andrus said, "We are coming to the end of the dam-building era in America."[8] Guy Martin, who as Alaska's natural resources commissioner had reversed decisions to allow oil drilling in rich estuaries, was Andrus's assistant secretary in charge of the Bureau of Reclamation. Robert Herbst, responsible for one of the best state scenic river programs when he was Minnesota's commissioner of resources, became the assistant secretary for fish, wildlife, and parks, in charge of the national rivers system. Leo Eisel, a former EDF engineer and scientist, was appointed to head the Water Resources Council. With these men came an unprecedented opportunity to reform water development and to save rivers.

In February 1977, one month after his inauguration, Carter announced a "hit list" of water projects. His staff had reviewed 341 proposals and recommended that 32 be scrutinized and possibly cut. Carter then recommended deletion of $289 million for 19 projects having economic, environmental, or safety problems.

Included was California's Auburn Dam on an earthquake fault above Sacramento. Oklahoma's Lukfata Dam would cover 10,000 acres of timber for one catfish farm and the town of Idabel, population six thousand, which would receive enough water for one hundred thousand. The Cache River Basin Project would ditch two hundred miles of Arkansas's rivers and streams so that soybeans could replace 110,000 acres of wetlands and hardwood forests—the continent's largest wintering ground for mallard ducks. The Bayous Chene, Boeuf, and Black Project in the Atchafalaya River basin would dry up thousands of acres of Louisiana wetlands so that two oil rig manufacturers could assemble rigs inland and float them to the Gulf, rather than assemble them on open water.

Meramec Park Dam would be cut, and the Central Arizona Project would be modified. Parts of the Central Utah Project, designed to divert water from the Uinta Mountains to the Salt Lake City area, would be halted to save twenty-three thousand acres of land and two hundred miles of streams. The Garrison Diversion in the Dakotas would be stopped, saving the Cheyenne Lake National Wildlife Refuge and seven others, and avoiding the pollution of the James, Souris, and Red Rivers, about which Canadians were enraged. Applegate Dam in Oregon would be cut, where four-fifths of the flood control benefits were for speculative development and fifty miles of salmon streams would be blocked.

Carter scrapped the Savery–Pot Hook and Fruitland Mesa projects in Colorado, each to benefit less than 100 farm families at a cost of $1 million or more per farm while adding brine to the already-salty Colorado River. And more: Narrows Dam in Colorado would provide water to the equivalent of 230 farm families, but required relocation of 216; Platte River flows would be cut by 11 percent, eliminating high spring runoff crucial to habitat of the endangered whooping crane. Thirteen of fifteen irrigation districts in the area opposed the project, and a landowners group stated, "If they took the money they wanted to spend on Narrows and put it in a trust fund, they could pay the farms that would supposedly benefit $5,000 per year, every year, forever." Carter considered stopping other projects but allowed them to proceed, including the Dolores Project, which would flood fifteen miles of river, reduce in-stream flows, add salts to the Colorado, and eliminate elk and deer herds. Who but people with the most vested of interests would not support Carter in stopping this barrel-bottom crop of projects?

Former commissioner of reclamation Ellis Armstrong called the administration's decision makers "uninformed amateurs."[9] In halting these environmental and economic boondoggles, Carter threw pork barrel politics into a ferment.

Unfortunately for the president, he had not discussed the cuts with some important congressional leaders. At the American Rivers Conservation Council's conference in 1980, Secretary Andrus said that he did not know that the list had been announced when a reporter asked him for comments. Adding to difficulties, the announcement came during the worst western drought in years.

Jimmy Carter was not playing the game the way congressmen were accustomed to play, and their reaction was vitriolic. Most congressmen beyond Missouri accused Carter of declaring "war on the West." Even environmentally conscious members such as Arizona's Morris Udall and Colorado's Gary Hart complained—projects in their states were included.

President Carter encountered a classic dilemma of Democrats engaged in river protection: party members remained philosophically committed to the New Deal ideal of income redistribution, and they remained politically dependent on the beneficiaries of federal water projects. Age-old party solidarity recognized water projects as sacred cows of a sort, and members who split from that platform often paid a high price in lost cooperation. Where they could, the Democrats sought to represent conservation as a liberal cause that was a companion to other social causes holding no appeal for Republicans. *Where they could* is the crucial phrase. Even with an administration strongly in support of river protection, even with a Democratic Congress, even with all the advances in river protection in recent years, the reform of water development appeared to remain subservient to the powerful political support of the water development lobby.

The *Denver Post* accused Carter of "vengeful opposition" because the West did not vote for him in 1976. Colorado governor Richard Lamm called the hit list "a study in federal arrogance . . . riddled with antiwestern prejudice and wrapped in ignorance."[10] He argued that federal projects had already been built for California, and that Colorado needed its dams to use its 34 percent share of the Colorado River.

Westerners argued that the federal projects were needed so that farmers and ranchers, consuming 90 percent of the water used in the West, could stay in business. Meanwhile, farmers were amiably selling their water to energy companies: for the Intermountain Power Project in Utah, farmers sold $10-per-acre-foot water for $1,750 an acre-foot, yielding $3 million to one rancher. Along Utah's Sevier River, 375 farmers sold their water to an electric utility for $79 million, and for oil shale development, Colorado farmers sold water for $2,300 an acre-foot.[11]

In *The Angry West*, Governor Lamm and Michael McCarthy maintained that farmers could not afford to pay for water without the subsidy:

> Westerners know, as nonwesterners do not, that drought tends to be cyclical, settling in perhaps twice a decade, then staying and searing and suffocating everything it touches for several seasons. Though westerners know their history, know the cycles, they remain at the mercy of drought. All they can do to survive is dam, impound, and protect every foot when times are good and hold it until times are bad. There is no fallback. And there are few alternatives.

In an open letter to Congress, Carter wrote, "I am aware of your concerns and I sympathize with them, but I cannot meet my commitment to balance the budget unless the Congress and I can cooperate in reducing unnecessary spending."[12]

In March 1977, the Senate approved a bill requiring the president to spend money for all but one of the nineteen projects. After public hearings that drew thousands of witnesses, the administration added more projects to be cut, but the House passed a bill funding all but one of Carter's deletions and stocking the dam builders with twelve new projects. In April the president revised his proposal: eighteen projects were to be dropped entirely, and another five were to be modified. Carter said, "In the arid West and across the entire nation, we must begin to recognize that water is not free—it is a precious resource. As with our energy problem, the cornerstone of future water policy should be wise management and conservation."[13]

A House amendment that supported Carter by killing all nineteen projects won 194 votes—enough to sustain a veto—but congressional leaders convinced Carter to go along with a compromise that cut only nine projects. So this battle between Carter and Congress appeared to be a draw. In August 1977 Carter signed an appropriations bill funding half of the hit list, approving Applegate Dam, the Atchafalaya channel, the Cache River channel, Columbia Dam in Tennessee, Hilldale Lake in Kansas, Richard B. Russell Dam in South Carolina, Tallahala Creek in Mississippi, and Bayou Bodcau in Louisiana. The Sierra Club's Brock Evans said that Carter's signing was not a "compromise" but a "betrayal."

Critical but optimistic, Brent Blackwelder said, "The Carter hit list generated lots of press. All the major papers did a series on water. CBS had TV programs. Even though there were a lot of media problems with the cuts being seen as a 'war on the West,' the issues of pork barrel finally reached the public." But battling symptoms was not enough for victory. The site-by-site attack was disappointing, and seeing futility in this approach, the Carter administration turned toward long-term reform.

REWRITING THE COOKBOOK

Carter next proposed to change the rationale that had justified bad projects. In June 1978 he announced a new water policy with four main objectives: to improve planning so that projects are economically and environmentally sound; to conserve water and reduce demand; to foster state planning and cooperation; and to increase attention to environmental quality.

Not surprisingly, projects had received straight A's when reviewed by the agencies that built them. The Carter policies therefore sent plans to the Water Resources Council for an independent review. The council would revise the principles and standards used in project justification and, by escaping the influence of the "iron triangle," would strike to the heart of the pork barrel process. For the first time, the government was to weigh environmental and economic objectives equally.

For every proposed dam or channel, the sponsoring agency was required to write a nonstructural plan. A limit was put on flood control benefits to undeveloped lands. States would pay 10 percent of hydroelectric and water supply costs and 5 percent for navigation, flood control, and "area redevelopment." Water conservation was required for sewage treatment grants, Housing and Urban Development programs, and new federal buildings. Reform of irrigation was weak but included technical assistance to farmers and water contracts with price revisions every five years instead of every forty. (Under the old contracts, irrigators never had to pay for the increasing costs of operations and maintenance during the forty-year period.) Fifty percent funding for state water management plans was proposed. New water projects were to provide in-stream flows for fish, wildlife, recreation, aesthetics, and water quality.

The policy reforms were mostly ineffective on projects already begun, leading one water lobbyist to say, "Even if you talk about no new authorizations, you've got fifty years of authorized projects out there waiting to be built. All this 'no new projects' stuff is as phony as a three-dollar bill. What the development agencies say is, 'call us in fifty years and then we'll apply the new policies.'" The reforms did not touch some projects in the thicket of controversy, but the new policies were a turnaround never before attempted, and in support, twenty-four conservation groups formed the Coalition for Water Project Review. "Profiles in Pork," weekly press releases sent out by coordinator Edward Osann of the National Wildlife Federation, alerted the press to upcoming votes. The effort paid off: Congress's press gallery was packed during important votes. Pork barrel was at least getting exposure.

The Carter reforms were the most progressive step ever taken toward water development reform; but would they last? Franklin Roosevelt's National Resources Planning Board, established in 1941 to review corps projects, disapproved only 76 of 426 requests, but Congress still authorized 62 of the rejected projects. Then the board was disbanded. The 1955 Hoover commission report was mostly ignored. The National Water Commission's 1973 report recommended dozens of changes and served as a springboard for groups like the Environmental Policy Center to push for reforms, but few resulted. Yet one indication that Carter's policies might endure came from two of the development agencies themselves: the corps and the Soil Conservation Service were each able to propose about twelve

projects under the new rules. The Bureau of Reclamation, however, justified only one project.

The new water policies were meant to redirect water development,
but the belief in the unlimited does not die easily. House majority leader
Jim Wright of Texas said, "If [Carter] wants to pick a fight, here's the place
to pick one."

FROM PORK BARREL TO POTHOLES

Reflecting on his 1977 compromise approving nine hit-list projects, Carter
said, "If I had it to do over again, I would have vetoed it." Another chance
came in 1978.

Water appropriations bills would have reinstated six of the nine projects dropped in the 1977 compromise, added 2,300 jobs for dam-building
agencies, and authorized fifty-three new construction starts. For one dam
failing to meet benefit–cost criteria, a bill simply declared, "Congress
hereby finds that the benefits . . . exceed the costs." Congress planned to
kill funding for the Water Resources Council, and it authorized three dozen
projects not even studied by the corps. For the Trinity River Canal in Texas
the appropriation bill recognized "national economic development benefits" as well as "net regional benefits," which New Mexico senator Pete
Domenici criticized as benefits "stolen from another area of the country."

The *Washington Post* reported, "With this largesse touching every state
and many congressional districts—in an election year when goodies for the
home folks count for something—little criticism is heard on Capitol Hill."[14]
Only two of forty-four House Public Works Committee members spoke
against the spending of $3.4 billion for water projects: David Bonoir of
Michigan and Robert Edgar of Pennsylvania. Howard Jarvis, who had promoted California's tax-cutting Proposition 13 in 1978, called the bill "the
big-tax, big-government, big-spending, big-waste bill of the year." On
October 7 Jarvis sponsored a full-page advertisement in the *Washington Post*:
"Congress: You must be kidding! Any politician who supports this bill now
must have his head in the sand." But it passed.

President Carter vetoed the bill on October 5, 1978, calling it "infla-
tionary . . . wasteful . . . and absolutely unacceptable." The veto held, with
190 House members supporting Carter, many of them freshmen who rode
to office on post-Watergate reform tickets.

Congressman Butler Derrick of South Carolina, who had unsuccessfully fought Russell Dam on the Savannah River, addressed a group of river

activists and said, "Five years ago you just didn't mess with anybody's water projects. That has changed. You're going to see projects looked at much more closely. That is the main thing that was accomplished with the veto."

Congress responded with an appropriation bill that deleted six of the nine projects that Carter objected to, cut eleven new projects, and dropped the 2,300 new jobs. Perhaps sensing that this was a reasonable compromise, Carter approved, but still to come was the water projects authorization bill—a separate measure—and with it a whirlwind of political maneuvering.

Just before dawn on one of the final days of the session, Senator Mike Gravel called up a bill to name a Shreveport, Louisiana, federal building after Congressman Joe Waggonner. Knowing that the water developers would try to slip their bill through, Brent Blackwelder and other conservationists had talked to Senators Proxmire, Leahy, and Abourezk, who agreed to watch for trouble, and now Abourezk asked Gravel, "Can we inquire what that thick stack of paper is?" It was a thirty-five-page amendment to the Shreveport bill authorizing new water projects costing $1 billion. That stopped Gravel, but in midafternoon, Pennsylvania congressman Allen Ertel talked to senators and had the Emergency Highway and Transportation Repair Act of 1978 released and passed by the Senate. The bill originally provided federal aid to patch potholes, but that language had been taken out and 158 water projects inserted under the pothole title. Wanting a levee for Harrisburg in his home district, Ertel asked the House Speaker to suspend rules and vote on the bill, but Congressman Robert Edgar objected. When pressed, Ertel admitted, "This is the pothole bill, but they took out the potholes and put in the water projects." Ertel pushed for a vote as time ran out, but an objection was heard regarding a quorum. Congressmen Edgar, Siberling, and others buttonholed colleagues and asked them to ignore the quorum call. Two hundred and sixty-five members did not answer, and the bill died.[15]

Beneath the parliamentary shenanigans, it was a historic moment. This was the first Congress in twenty years that did not pass a biennial authorization bill for water projects. Pork barrel had finally collapsed as environmental lobbyists, congressional reform, the Carter policies, and fiscal conservatism brought the process down. The irony most encouraging to environmentalists was that whereas the omnibus bill for dams failed, an omnibus bill for wild rivers and parks passed.

But the gains of 1978 were short-lived. In September 1979 Carter signed the $10.6-billion Energy and Water Development Act, authorizing nine projects outside the budget and without army corps review, stopping funds for the Water Resources Council, and budgeting Arcadia and McGee

Creek dams in Oklahoma with no water conservation planning. In its most celebrated abuse of the new water policies, the law waived the Endangered Species Act and "all other laws" for the completion of Tellico Dam. Majority leader Jim Wright had told the president that a veto "would just add fuel to the fire" and guarantee hostility from Congress. The Tellico approval brought river conservationists' greatest disappointment in Carter, but congressmen had attached Tellico riders to other bills, requiring vetos of forthcoming laws if Carter insisted on halting the dam.

Another disappointment was the Interior Department's approval of cheap irrigation contracts in Westlands, the Bureau of Reclamation's largest district in California. Cecil Andrus no longer prophesied the "end of the dam-building era" but said, "Water construction projects will continue in the West. We just want to make sure they are good, safe projects."

Presidential directives supported the wild and scenic rivers system in 1979, but Carter also approved record budgets for water development: a 29 percent increase for the Bureau of Reclamation in fiscal year 1980 and a 15 percent gain for the corps to a record budget of $3,060,400,000, though inflation eroded the amount to a real level that was lower than during some earlier years. Brent Blackwelder said, "We expected some massive cuts this year; instead we got increases. The problem with the president is that after every gain he retreats."

In October 1980, Carter approved $4 billion for water projects, including Yatesville and Orme dams. When funding was eliminated for Water Resources Council project reviews, the president said that he would work to reinstate the council's role the next year. One month later Ronald Reagan was elected.

REAGAN AND WATT

President Reagan won on a platform to cut government size, influence, and spending—promises not conducive to wasteful water projects. William Gianelli, director of the California Department of Water Resources when it developed ambitious plans to dam northern California rivers, was chosen as assistant secretary of the army, responsible for the corps. For secretary of the interior, Reagan named James Watt, president of the Mountain States Legal Foundation, representing corporations involved in resource development in the Rockies. Watt had said, "I fear that our states may be ravaged as a result of the actions of the environmentalists—the greatest threat to the ecology of the West." He asked if the environmentalists' real motive was "to weaken

America." To a *Wall Street Journal* reporter he explained, "My responsibility is to follow the Scriptures, which call upon us to occupy the land until Jesus returns."[16] Watt said that he was "bored" on the second day of a raft trip through the Grand Canyon.

Contradicting rhetoric to cut the budget, Watt declared of water development, "We are committed to new projects," and called for western governors to submit proposals. The wild and scenic rivers program was sliced to the bone, and rivers that would have been recommended even under Nixon or Ford were found "eligible but not suitable."

Allowing for inflation, water projects had faced a tightening economic noose since the mid-1970s. In 1982 Reagan's water development budget cut $230 million from the Carter proposal but was still the highest water development budget ever when other domestic programs were eliminated. The Bureau of Reclamation received about $1 billion—23 percent greater than the year before—a larger percentage increase than the much-debated growth in defense. After a $4-billion water development budget in 1983, the president's request for 1984 cut 7 percent.

James Watt used water projects—solidly backed in the West—to leverage his less popular development proposals. Ed Osann said, "Many in the West don't agree with what Watt's doing to expand mining, oil drilling, and gas exploration, but they can't press him too hard because he has to sign for the next water project." In his first year as secretary of the interior, Watt was repeatedly called to Congress and grilled about public lands giveaways, but after the secretary warned that sessions on the Hill were interfering with his approval of dams and canals, including the Central Arizona Project, congressmen backed off.

In 1983 a jobs bill to ease unemployment was passed, earmarking $545 million for water development. As unemployment reached 20 percent in Pittsburgh, Detroit, and even Oregon, one of the highest-funded job generators under the Bureau of Reclamation's allowance was for the Central Arizona Project, serving the suburbanization of Phoenix.

Under Watt, Robert Broadbent became commissioner of reclamation. He had practiced pharmacy in Boulder City, Nevada, for twenty-five years and served as a county commissioner. In a 1983 interview, the commissioner cited the Reclamation Reform Act as the focus of his work. The 1982 law requires water conservation planning, but the commissioner denied any new priority for the bureau's Irrigation Management Service, which advises farmers about how to save water. In 1980 the service consisted of only two full-time employees out of a 1,200-person bureau staff in California.

When asked if the era of water development was past, the commissioner said, "The budget is going up substantially. There are a lot of water resource problems that have to be answered and you can't answer them all with conservation. Five new starts are being considered right now." But the poor economy and Reagan's record federal deficit prevented authorization of costly dams and canals. To simply finish projects such as the bureau's Garrison Diversion and the corps's Tennessee–Tombigbee Waterway would dominate construction budgets for the rest of the century.

Reagan, a self-proclaimed "sagebrush rebel," was able to propose even more cost sharing than Carter had done, but without incurring the wrath of the western bloc. Reagan asked for user fees to recover all expenses for navigation, hydropower, and water supply. Thirty-five percent cost sharing was proposed for flood control and irrigation. As a result, new projects were stalled during the Reagan years with effectiveness equal to or greater than during Carter's term. Secretary of the Army William Gianelli, who supported cost sharing and also front-end funding of projects instead of yearly appropriations, sounded strangely like Cecil Andrus when he said, "Water project construction as we knew it in the past is not going to be that way in the future."[17] Interior Secretary Watt, however, did not support the cost-sharing formulas. Instead, he called for a "case-by-case" determination, with himself in charge.

Congress did not approve Reagan's user-fee proposal and planned to spend in the usual pork barrel fashion. The *Washington Post* reported in January 1982, "Throughout this painful budget-cutting process . . . more than 300 water projects emerged almost unscathed, including several that Reagan had targeted for extinction." Pushing for approval of Willow Creek Dam for flood control in Heppner, Oregon, population 1,500, Chairman Mark Hatfield of the Senate Appropriations Committee said, "I have to confess to you, that's just raw political power. . . . They'd petition to have me hanged at high noon if I didn't do anything about Willow Creek."[18] But in a precedent-setting case, Congress required 20 percent cost sharing for the Central Arizona Project's irrigation distribution system.

As chairman of the Water Resources Council, James Watt saw that all funding for the council was stopped. The principles and standards that had been so tediously developed for economic respectability were rescinded by Watt "to reduce the burden on agencies in complying with detailed and legally binding rules." The standards were replaced with unenforceable "guidelines" administered under Watt. Without the principles and standards, agencies were openly invited to tamper with project justifications. Nonstructural alternatives no longer needed to be considered. The environmental quality goal was dropped from its dual position with economic development.

Defending the principles and standards, a National Wildlife Federation spokesman said, "We don't recall this administration having come into office on a platform of making life easier for federal bureaucrats, particularly those like the federal dam builders with a penchant for spending money by the billions." About Watt's "guidelines" editors of the *Sacramento Bee* wrote, "If building inefficient water projects is not in the public's interest, then neither are these vague and incomplete project guidelines that make construction of inefficient projects more likely."

Commissioner Broadbent said that the Water Resources Council was

> just another layer of government that you didn't need. The new guidelines will allow us to consider a lot of things as justifications to build a project and to meet water quality standards. It will be easier to show a balanced justification. Personally, I feel the Water Resources Council was a bureaucratic nightmare. Government is tough enough already. Somewhere the buck stops and you have to make a decision, and the Water Resources Council was another review board that could never make up its mind on anything. The independent review is the Office of Management and Budget's job. The ultimate review agency is Congress.[19]

The council had represented the one serious effort to break control of water projects by the iron triangle of the construction agencies, Congress, and local promoters, and that effort was now abandoned. Watt's successor, William Clark, called for a repeal of some Reclamation Reform Act requirements regarding payments for irrigation water, and postponed consideration of increases in cost sharing.

Nevertheless—even though many of the Carter reforms failed and the Reagan administration rescinded environmental protection measures—the times had changed. Some new congressmen did not share the old boosterism for any dam on any river, and some were bright enough and determined enough to attack the politics that had needlessly destroyed so much.

CHANGING THE POLITICS

Bob Edgar gained an appreciation for rivers when he and his father hiked and fished, but growing up near Philadelphia he also saw what needed to be changed. "You could almost walk on the water, the pollution was so bad," he said in a 1983 interview. Edgar was ordained as a Methodist minister and served as Drexel University's chaplain. Then he decided to run for Congress. A Democrat had not been elected in his district since before the Civil War, but Republicans squabbled among themselves and Edgar won. At age thirty he went to Washington, in the Watergate reform class of 1974 that would change the pork barrel system. "My constituents did not elect me to come down here to continue business-as-usual supporting lopsided priorities," Edgar said, just hinting at what he would do.

Gaining a seat on the House Public Works Subcommittee on Water Resources, Edgar opposed wasteful water projects so efficiently that he was removed from the subcommittee by its leadership. He later reclaimed his seat.

Edgar stopped the "potholes repair" bill that meant $1 billion for water projects but nothing for potholes. He forced debate on another water development bill by threatening to call up 184 amendments, each exposing a congressman's pet boondoggle. About new authorizations Edgar said something basic to common sense but radical to pork barrel politics: "The criteria for all of these projects ought to be on their merit."

In June 1979 Edgar addressed Congress about a proposed dam: "The more I learn about the Stonewall Jackson project, the angrier I become. Angry at the Corps for abusing the system of benefit-cost analysis that is supposed to screen water projects. Angry at various bureaucracies for allowing the project to muddle along without serious review. And finally, angry at the Congress for its failure to stand up to the politics of pork." For this view he enjoys few favors from colleagues. Congressman Harley Staggers from West Virginia, where the proposed project was located, said, "What right has a minister from Philadelphia to question a project in my district?" After Edgar spoke on the floor of the House, Don Young from Alaska recommended a Pinocchio award for the member who sticks his nose the farthest into another member's affairs.

William Proxmire had been the leader in opposing pork barrel of all kinds, but Edgar could claim that role for water projects. Brent Blackwelder said, "He is one of the few people in Congress who seeks to ascertain the public interest. Then he pursues it. He saw public works as a disaster and he took it on, not to be dissuaded by the abuse heaped on him."

"I've attempted to bring attention to important problems by opposing all omnibus bills," Edgar said after having stopped three successive water project bills during a six-year period.

We need to rap the backs of the heads of Jamie Whitten and Tom Bevill and others. We're holding both good and bad projects hostage until we get a better water policy, one based on the environment, one that spends money wisely. In the past we've spent lots of money on new projects and some of them are very bad. We've built many projects without local investment. We don't rehabilitate and maintain older structures and waterways, and we ignore nonstructural alternatives. We need to correct problems of toxic wastes, declining aquifers, diversions of water, and projects creating unfair economic advantages to some people. How ridiculous it is to work three shifts a day on a bad project like the Tennessee–Tombighee Waterway that costs more than the money being spent on renewable energy. This adminis-tration [Reagan's] is not proenvironment. If we don't alter that, we could be in serious trouble as a society.

Edgar proposed a four-part reorientation of water development: "If we're going to build new projects, we need local cost sharing, nonstructural alternatives, a national policy recognizing the value of water and rivers, and assurance that environmental improvement will result. Until then, I'll be holding up new project starts."

In 1980 the lobbyists against destructive water projects included the American Tax Reduction Movement, the National Taxpayers Union, Common Cause, Americans for Democratic Action, and, an old ally, the League of Women Voters. Supported by this union of very liberal and very conservative causes, President Reagan in 1981 signed the first bill ever to deauthorize a group of water developments by cutting eight projects costing $2.5 billion, including Dickey–Lincoln dams in Maine, Meramec Park Dam in Missouri, Helm and Lincoln dams in Illinois, and Big Blue and Clifty Creek dams in Indiana. A bill to charge the taxpayer for Bureau of Recla-mation safety improvements was defeated in 1982 by environmentalists and taxpayer groups who argued that direct beneficiaries should pay their share of the safety costs. With new optimism, Brent Blackwelder said, "Our sys-tem of government allows people to influence the process. If people under-stand the process they can make a difference."

Another water lobbyist said, "It used to be that the appropriations members would gain fifty-five out of sixty votes in the committee and then go with that kind of strength to the floor and say, 'Come on, come on,' like Mohammed Ali, and everyone would be scared. Now we've broken the old system and made it okay to vote against pork." More than vote: in 1983 Congressman Silvio Conte, a Massachusetts Republican, wore a pig's mask in the House cloakroom and grunted on the floor of Congress to make his point.

Bob Teeters, chief of interagency coordination for the corps, said,

"The political support for development has diminished since the sixties. Now it's the exception—not the rule—when a congressman will go around wanting to spend lots of money." The corps itself had also changed, employing four hundred people to work on environmental issues.

A logjam of water projects piled up behind Edgar's political blockade. Corps division engineers had cleared 160 projects, and the chief of engineers had approved 60—all of them candidates for an omnibus bill. Yet Bob Teeters said, "The era of big water projects has come to an end. After the drought of 1977, there was no mass movement to build new dams the way there was after the eastern drought of the sixties. The best projects have been built, and the times have changed."

Bob Edgar said, "I'm an optimist. I think we can turn the pork barrel process around. There is more concern than there used to be. If a congressman supports projects that are wasteful now, he is criticized. I get strong endorsements from local newspapers, and help from the taxpayer groups." In 1982 Edgar won reelection by 11,000 votes (two years earlier his margin had been 1,200), despite the political pundits' predictions of defeat. "Congressmen who want new projects were beginning to ask, 'How can we accommodate the Bob Edgars of this world?' They want to come to some resolution so that we can get the Army Corps of Engineers back in business."

Edgar cautioned, "Pork barrel development could come back unless laws are improved so that our use of water and money is more resourceful. The army corps will be there, long into the future, nibbling at edges, anxious to get projects moving."

Edgar served as chairman of the 213-member Northeast–Midwest Congressional Coalition in the House, which reported that the South and West received 82 percent of the corps's dollars, compared to 17.9 percent in the Northeast and Midwest, where 45 percent of the people live. Edgar said,

> All of the Bureau of Reclamation dollars go to the West. The Central Arizona Project will spend $600 million on municipal and industrial water supply, while federal agencies are not allowed to help fund single-purpose water supply projects in the Northeast, where repairs are desperately needed. My goal is to see a higher priority on maintenance and rehabilitation. The bridges, sewers, and water systems—the basic building blocks that hold the country together—are old. If we don't renew them, society will be more and more distressed. We cannot continue with new megastructures without taking care of the old ones.

With the same concerns, Senators Daniel Patrick Moynihan of New York and Pete Domenici of New Mexico introduced a water resources policy and development bill calling for development funds on the basis of population and land area rather than on logrolling, which is now the case. Their bill requires 25 percent cost sharing by the states and puts water conservation "on an equal footing with structural, capital-intensive solutions."

In 1984 a bill was passed appropriating $3.8 billion to the corps and bureau, but no new construction starts were approved, and for the eighth year in a row no new corps projects were authorized.

Bob Edgar said, "We need to realize that water is a national treasure. It is the next big crisis after energy. We need new goals for water development, and an administration that implements water policy with protection and with love and care for the resource. We need to raise public awareness of water and our resources."

9

NEEDS AND ALTERNATIVES

R iver conservationists mobilized support for special places, they built powerful arguments based on science and economics, and they capitalized on other movements for political reform. But success would have ended if the real needs for water development could not have been met without more dams and canals. So after exposing faults in the procedures that were used to "justify" water projects, river protection groups built a case for meeting needs without the destruction and waste so prevalent in the past.

SUPPLY AND DEMAND

Before discussing the alternatives to big water projects, it is important to know how much water we really have, how much we use, and how much we will demand in the future. Only with this information can planners effectively prepare for water projects or for alternatives to the traditional solutions of dams and canals.

About 97 percent of the earth's water is in the oceans, 2.2 percent in the ice caps, and 0.3 percent too deep underground to pump out—leaving less than 0.5 percent available to people. Canada and Russia each has about 20 percent of the freshwater. The United States has 4 percent, with runoff highest in the Northwest and lowest in the Southwest and the Great Basin of Nevada and Utah.[1]

The United States Geological Survey (USGS) estimated that 450 billion gallons a day were withdrawn for all uses in 1980, with fresh surface water accounting for 65 percent, fresh groundwater for 20 percent, and saline water for 15 percent.[2] The East and the West withdrew roughly equal amounts, but 91 percent of the irrigation water was used in the West, where only 30 percent of the rain and snow fall, and the majority of water for homes, industry, and energy was used in the East. Per person, westerners used twice the water of easterners—three times, if water for hydroelectricity is counted.[3] Withdrawals peaked in 1980, then declined to about 400 billion gallons a day in 1985 and remained at roughly that level through 1995, according to U.S. Geological Survey web sites.

In 50,000 reservoirs of 50 acre-feet or more, 450 million acre-feet were stored (one acre-foot equals 325,851 gallons or 43,560 cubic feet). More than 1.8 million small reservoirs and ponds stored another 10 million acre-feet.

In medieval times, one person used an estimated 3 to 5 gallons of water per day (gpd); in the nineteenth century, 10 to 15 gpd. In 1980 the Water Resources Council (WRC) reported that in the United States an average of 118 gpd were used per person in homes and businesses—more than in any other nation. Withdrawals for all uses averaged 2,000 gpd per person, ranging from 19,000 in Idaho to 180 in Rhode Island. Californians withdrew twice the water of either of the next-largest users, Florida and Texas.[4] While the United States population increased 44 percent between 1950 and 1975, water use more than doubled. From 1975 to 1980, use climbed 8 percent, compared to 12 percent for the previous five years. The slower rate was credited to economic decline, droughts, restrictions on water use, and recycling.

Whereas most withdrawals are later returned (although sometimes unrecognizably altered) to a stream, consumptive use occurs when water is withdrawn and not returned, usually because of evaporation. About 100 billion gpd were consumed in 1980. In the East, 8 percent of freshwater withdrawals were consumed; in the West, 41 percent.[5]

Public water systems serving 81 percent of the people in seventeen thousand towns and cities used 8.5 percent of nationwide withdrawals and 6.9 percent of the water that was consumed, 66 percent coming from surface supplies (rivers and reservoirs). Manufacturing used 17 percent of the withdrawals and accounted for 7.7 percent of the consumption. Energy production took 26.3 percent of withdrawals and 1.3 percent of consumption, mostly for the cooling of power plants.[6]

For irrigation, 170 million acre-feet were withdrawn in 1980 to water fifty-eight million acres, an increase of 7 percent since 1975. Irrigation took 47 percent of withdrawals and 81 percent of consumption. Withdrawals were expected to decline slightly owing to overdraft in the Southwest as well as to improved efficiency; however, more than half of the irrigation water was consumed, and consumption was expected to increase. Sixty percent of the irrigation water came from surface supplies. California used 25 percent of all irrigation water—more than the next-highest irrigation users (Idaho and Colorado) combined.[7]

Hydropower plants withdrew by far the greatest amount of water, using 2.7 times the average annual runoff of the nation, but nearly all of this was quickly returned to streams after turning turbines. In 1980, hydroelectric capacity was up 17 percent from 1975,[8] accounting for 12 percent of America's electricity. By 2002 it dropped to 9.7 percent.

A person needs only five to six pints of water a day, but amounts used in agriculture and manufacturing are enormous. To produce one pound of beef can require 4,000 gallons of water. One pound of cotton requires 3,100 gallons, a pound of rice, 500. For a gallon of milk, 932 gallons of water are used; for an egg, 120 gallons.[9] About 40 percent of all water used in California is for livestock. This includes irrigated pasture, which in terms of total acreage uses more water than any other crop. Alfalfa ranks second, and cotton, third. Crops requiring the most water per acre are rice, using 8 acre-feet a year; pasture, using 5.2; alfalfa, using 4.9; and cotton, using 4. A medium-sized paper mill uses enough water for a city of a million, and a coal liquification plant producing fifty thousand barrels of oil a day would use the water of 100,000 people.[10] Aluminum production, which requires twelve times the energy needed for iron, is often dependent on hydroelectricity, one large plant using the energy of a 179,000-person city.

THE COMING YEARS

How much water do people need? Water Resources Council projections in 1980 called for withdrawals to decrease to 306.4 billion gpd by the year 2000, the cut being due to recycling and conservation, most importantly in manufacturing, expected to decrease from 60.9 billion gpd in 1975 to 29.1 billion gpd in 2000 because of recycling encouraged by water quality laws. But consumption for all water uses was expected to increase 27 percent by the year 2000.

In fact, water withdrawals did not decrease to the extent projected; in 1995, 402 billion gallons were withdrawn according to the Geological Survey. Consumption increased from 100 billion gallons per day in 1980 to 119 billion in 1990, the last date for which data was available at this writing.

With water efficiency measures becoming more feasible in the early 1980s, and a population that was expected to peak at 250 million by the year 2015, many people thought our needs for water would level off. But the hard-earned gains in efficiency were often canceled out by population increases. Instead of leveling-off when the baby boomers aged beyond their child-bearing years, the U.S. population grew from 203 million in 1970 to 293 million in 2003. Census Bureau mid-level projections then called for 404 million Americans by 2050, but current trends point to a population closer to half a billion. According to the Census Bureau, 80 percent of this growth will owe to immigration, which increased sharply in the 1990s. Reform of immigration laws is the only measure that will prevent skyrocketing growth from continuing indefinitely.

Some of the regions now growing new houses the fastest grew only sagebrush a few years ago. People move to the Southwest, where, insulated by sprinklers, they pretend that the desert does not exist. They bring their watered lawns and car washes, and they add swimming pools and air conditioners. The population of Phoenix increased 30 percent between 1970 and 1980; the Salt Lake City area, 37.2 percent; Albuquerque, 34.5 percent; and Austin, 36 percent. In the Denver area, one hundred immigrants arrived every day in the 1980s.[12] In the 1990s all these population rates exploded with increases. Utah, for example, grew by 29 percent in the 1990s alone.

Water deficits exist in 17 of 106 subregions, mainly in the Southwest and Midwest. Shortages are most acute in the Rio Grande and lower Colorado basins, where water is made scarce by agricultural control. Increased energy development in dry regions will aggravate shortages; in 1974 the Interior Department reported that energy development on the Rockies' west slope could require 25 percent of the upper Colorado River's flow. The Western States' Water Council estimated that new energy projects in eleven states would require 2.3 million acre-feet a year by 1990 (these great expectations for an energy boom have since faded). Boston, New York, Washington, and other cities will face rationing if a major drought occurs. In-stream flows for fish, wildlife, and recreation are inadequate throughout much of the West. Groundwater overdraft is severe on the plains from Nebraska to Texas, in central Arizona, and in the Central Valley of California. Although pollution makes surface water unusable, especially in the Northeast, Midwest, and Great Lake states, toxic and hazardous wastes that ruin groundwater may force a greater dependence on rivers.

Even though dams reduced floods in thousands of communities, support for flood control continued. Because of uncontrolled lowland development, flood losses tripled from $1.5 billion per year to more than $4 billion per year. In the 1975–2000 period, federal agencies spent \$140 billion preparing for and recovering from floods. In spite of the \$25 billion that the agencies had spent on dams and levees, flood damages for the 1994–1999 period alone topped \$40 billion, as detailed in American Rivers' 1999 report, *In Harm's Way: The Costs of Floodplain Development*.

With increasing attention to the long-neglected nonstructural solutions to flood problems, new flood control dams were not seriously considered in very many locations. Instead, hydroelectric generation became the big reason to build new dams in the 1980s and beyond.

The Federal Energy Regulatory Commission estimated that production of about 66,000 megawatts could be increased to 113,000.[13] Hydroelectric power in fact increased to 78,000 megawatts of installed capacity (not actual use) in 2002, without counting pumped storage projects, which added about 18,000 megawatts according to the Energy Information Administration's *Annual Energy Outlook*. The Federal Energy Regulatory Commission dropped its projections for new hydro development, but total electric demand was expected to grow by 1.9 percent per year between 2001 and 2025, according to the Energy Information Administration, and new proposals could still threaten some of the finest rivers.

The coming years could bring hundreds of new power dams and diversions from basins of plenty, such as the Susquehanna, Great Lakes, and Columbia, to thirsty cities and desert farms. The economic, social, and environmental costs could dwarf those of the past because the best sites are already developed. With a recurrence of the mid-1960s drought in the Northeast or the 1977 drought in the West, when twenty-nine states were eligible for disaster relief because there had been no rain, there may be renewed pressure to build dams and divert rivers. Farmers will fight for the status quo, which requires new projects so that irrigation in places such as southern California can remain "surplus" and available to large corporations at a fraction of the real cost. Indian tribes will claim water under the Winters Doctrine and use sources that other people planned to take. Energy developers will wield political power to get the water they want. Water developers compete among themselves, but on one point they have been united: they want more dams.

In the late 1960s the Susquehanna River Basin Study reported, "The abundant water in the Susquehanna Basin is being looked to by communities outside the drainage area as a supply source for the future." In the 1960s the California Water Plan called for dams on the Klamath, Trinity, Eel, and other northern rivers, and the Bureau of Reclamation's Pacific Southwest Water Plan recommended Grand Canyon dams, the connection of northern

California rivers to Lake Mead, and the study of diversions from the Northwest. The Colorado River was drained dry and ended as an intermittent stream in Mexico, yet more water was scheduled to be taken by Arizona and upper-basin states. The time of reckoning has been put off so far, but someday Colorado River allocations must be reduced, or more water will have to be taken from other basins through cloud seeding or diversions. In 1983—a flood year—Commissioner of Reclamation Robert Broadbent had no proposed solution to the overappropriation. Concerning a future crisis he said, "It's not going to happen for a number of years. The reservoirs are full. The wet cycle we're in now could last."[14]

The North American Water and Power Alliance (NAWAPA), a private group with headquarters in southern California, proposed dams in Alaska, Canada, and the Rockies, including a reservoir five hundred miles long and a colossal scheme with tunnels, canals, and lifts to shunt water to thirty-three states. Congressman Jim Wright wrote,

> This dream is, admittedly, both grandiose and visionary. However, the nation was built by visionaries. There have been some disturbing indications in recent years that we may have lost some of our capacity for dreaming and acting in those areas concerning our survival upon this earth. We must recapture that capability. . . . NAWAPA has an almost limitless potential if we possess the courage and the foresight to grasp it.[15]

Wright was Congress's majority leader in 1985.

Should we divert wild rivers for Sun Belt growth while ignoring other ways to avoid shortages? President Carter said, "We must face the prospect of changing our basic ways of living. This change will either be made on our own initiative in a planned and rational way, or forced on us with chaos and suffering by the inexorable laws of nature." To give up the search for new dams was once thought to mean locking up the desert cities, inflating food costs beyond family budgets, and surrendering to the next flood. President Reagan argued that cutting back on the use of water and energy lowers the standard of living, but others maintained that the standard of living would be lowered more if the Grand Canyon were dammed or the Columbia sucked south to Texas. How can needs be met without losing too much in the process of watering crops, turning turbines, or pushing barges?

THE OTHER FUTURE

In *Strategies of American Water Management*, Gilbert White pointed out that multiple use—embraced in river development since the 1930s—has not been accompanied by multiple means; instead of looking at different solutions to a water problem, the development agencies saw only more dams. Alternatives were ignored because contractors and engineers pushed for controversial construction, projects were proffered as panaceas in the wake of flood disasters, few precedents existed for alternatives, the large-dams-versus-small-dams argument preempted discussion of important issues, and, most important, no agency held the responsibility for addressing whole problems.[16] White and others argued that nonstructural solutions—ones not requiring a dam or a channel—may be cheaper, more effective, faster to build, reversible, and less destructive. Senate Document 97 of 1969 called for consideration of nonstructural alternatives, but it resulted in little action.

People turned to the technological fix to delay reform, but following recent droughts, boosters of development attracted fewer followers. Some talked of Auburn and Tocks Island dams, but many people were resigned to the fact that the big projects were too costly and that alternatives were within reach. In 1977 Amory Lovins wrote that "soft path technologies" for energy development are "not vague, mushy, speculative, or ephemeral, but rather flexible, resilient, sustainable, and benign," and public acceptance of this idea helped to prepare the way for alternatives in water development.

Growing evidence showed that most water needs could be met without costly and destructive new projects. Alternatives are available. Brent Blackwelder wrote, "The best way to dispel the suspicion that conservationists want to return the country to the Stone Age by opposing water resource development projects is to consider some of the superb alternatives we have proposed to traditional dam building, canal digging and stream channelization."

KEEPING DRY

Nonstructural supporters argued that we have done enough to keep floods away from people. People should also stay away from floods. House Document 89–465 of August 1966 stated, "Flood damages result from acts of men. Those who occupy the flood plain should be responsible for the results of their action." Locating new development above the floodplain is the key nonstructural solution. Through zoning, municipalities can minimize construction on lands expected to flood once every hundred years. Farms, yards, parks, and other kinds of open space can be encouraged.

The Tennessee Valley Authority helped local governments to manage floodplains, and by 1964, 38 of 150 communities had adopted land use regulations.[17] But such management was the exception, and few other communities restricted development. In 1966 President Johnson issued an executive order that the Army Corps of Engineers encourage proper land use on the floodplain. Seeking to reduce disaster relief, Congress passed the Federal Flood Insurance Program in 1968, offering subsidized flood insurance to residents in municipalities with floodplain regulations. Even with this incentive, however, few communities zoned land or required flood proofing of new buildings. During America's most damaging flood up to 1972, caused by Hurricane Agnes, only two residents in heavily hit Wilkes-Barre, Pennsylvania, were insured. Congress strengthened the program in 1973, denying federally guaranteed mortgages unless buildings are insured, thus requiring floodplain regulations for most real estate sales. Though the standards and enforcement were weak and do not eliminate riverfront construction, the program forced thousands of municipalities to regulate development. Nearly half of the money paid to flood victims is a subsidy, but program supporters argue that this is better than the giveaway of disaster relief. In several states, including Wisconsin, zoning is effective because mandatory state standards exist.

The government can buy the floodplain instead of buying upstream areas for reservoirs. Citizen or planning agencies proposed greenbelts for the Sangamon River in Illinois and the Current in Missouri. Along Tennessee's Duck River, acquisition of key parcels of the floodplain would be much cheaper than buying the reservoir area and building the dam. In opposing LaFarge Dam on the Kickapoo River, Senator Gaylord Nelson supported relocation and park development because the $50-million dam would protect property assessed at only $25 million. Some redevelopment programs have moved buildings to higher ground, as in Rapid City, South Dakota.

In a case in which the University of Washington's Office of Environmental Mediation brought opposing groups together to compromise, Washington's Middle Fork of the Snoqualmie was saved. Instead of damming some of the most spectacular river scenery in America, zoning was adopted, levees were proposed, and a North Fork dam was studied.

As an alternative to channelization of small streams, George Palmiter of Montpelier, Ohio, perfected techniques that use only chain saws and hand tools to make strategic changes that cause floodwaters to "clean out" the stream. At one-tenth the cost of bulldozer channelization, the Palmiter method was found to work better and require less maintenance,[18] all without environmental damage. Hired by local governments and landowners, Palmiter and his son exported their process throughout the Midwest.

In urban areas, local flooding has been reduced by means of porous pavement on parking lots, dry wells that absorb runoff, and ponds for storm water. Warning systems by county governments and evacuation plans by industries have cut losses.

Local governments often ignored nonstructural flood control because they would have to pay for it, whereas the army corps builds dams at no local expense. Then the Water Resources Development Act of 1974 authorized cost sharing for some nonstructural solutions and required federal agencies to consider these alternatives. On the South Fork of the Platte near Denver, the corps found that it would be cheaper to buy the floodplain than to channelize. A similar project at Indian Bend Wash in Arizona received a distinguished engineering award from the American Society of Civil Engineers. Along the Charles River above Boston, the corps bought wetlands to avoid the increased runoff from urbanization, and flood damage has been reduced by an estimated $17 million a year. But the Office of Management and Budget blocked most nonstructural programs, which in 1982 accounted for only $15 million in a $3.5-billion water development budget.

HARMLESS POWER

Energy became the issue of the 1970s, each source of power promising more trouble than the last. Faced with political barricades on Arabian oil, the Trans-Alaska Pipeline, Three Mile Island, strip mining and acid rain from coal, and oil shale devastation, hydropower looked harmless to many. Then studies by Amory Lovins and the Ford Foundation showed that rivers do not need to be dammed for electricity. In *Soft Energy Paths,* Lovins documented the potential for stretching existing supplies and for benign sources such as the sun and wind. A Ford Foundation study concluded that "it could well be technically and economically feasible to achieve stability in energy consumption while continuing economic growth." The Joint Economics Committee of Congress reported that energy conservation requires only one-fifth the costs of new generation. In 2001 the American Council for an Energy Efficient Economy estimated that the nation could save 60,000 megawatts in capacity if regulators adopted programs to improve air conditioning and lighting. This is twice the energy consumption of California.

To save energy means to save rivers from hydroelectric dams. In central Arizona, where Grand Canyon dams were proposed for hydropower, air conditioners accounted for up to one-third of energy consumed during hot months.[19] In the hydropower-dependent Northwest, a Skidmore, Owings, and Merrill study found that the average home could be made about 50 percent more efficient in electrical use.[20] The California Resources Agency found that the New Melones Dam would yield only one-sixteenth the amount of energy that would be saved if Californians properly inflated their tires, one-thirteenth the energy saved if they slowed down to 55 miles per hour, and one-eleventh the energy saved if they tuned their car engines.[21]

In the 1980s, people are verifying that we may be able to avoid all of the worst energy development options, including new dams. Americans reduced energy consumption by 2.2 percent in 1981.

Most new hydroelectric dams are for peaking power, generating electricity only a few hours a day. "Peaking demands are the easiest kind to alleviate," said Laura King, energy specialist for the Natural Resources Defense Council. Sacramento had intended to buy power from new dams proposed on the North Fork of the Stanislaus, but instead it launched a peak-load management program: on hot afternoons the power company transmits a signal to devices wired to air conditioners, shutting them down for ten minutes and, if done every hour, cutting demands by one-sixth. Additional savings can result through higher rates at peak hours, the rescheduling of industrial processes, and nighttime pumping of irrigation and city water supplies. Tests in three California cities indicated that management can reduce peak needs by 10 to 20 percent.

Hydroelectricity can be produced without destroying more streams. The Ohio River is continuously dammed for 981 miles. Hydraulically it is comparable to the Rhône of France, but hydroelectrically it is not; the Rhône generates 3,000 megawatts, the Ohio 180. Generators on this industrialized waterway would raise few objections.

Today only 3 percent of the major dams in the United States are used for hydropower. However, studies undertaken by the Army Corps of Engineers indicate that 5,162 existing small dams could yield 5,691 megawatts, equal to six nuclear power plants. Although even small generators at existing dams can dry up riverbeds if diversions are built, at many sites the impacts would be small. Municipal water lines and irrigation canals are a harmless source of power. In 1979, a 550-kilowatt generator was built on an irrigation canal in the San Joaquin Valley of California. The project's engineering firm estimated that 2,000 megawatts were available from similar sites in California.

MULTIPLE MEANS

Instead of new barge canals, Congressman Robert Edgar and others maintained that we should take better care of the locks and dams already built.

Whereas the Tennessee–Tombigbee Waterway will duplicate a route to the Gulf of Mexico, existing locks and dams on the Ohio, Monongahela, and Mississippi grow obsolete. The Environmental Policy Center called for rehabilitation of railroads, since the tracks already exist.

Recreation may be the easiest of all needs to meet without dams. Just use the rivers. River recreation boomed through the year 2000, yet the country had less than one hundred major protected national rivers, compared to fifty thousand large reservoirs. River parks were developed as alternatives to dams along the Delaware, Current, Buffalo, and Big South Fork of the Cumberland. In 1980 the WRC ranked the preservation of free-flowing streams as a high recreation priority in 73 of 106 subregions; protecting floodplains and wetlands was another priority—more flatwater was not even mentioned as a need.

Like dams, forests hold rainfall and release it slowly to streams, resulting in less flooding after heavy storms and in higher flows during droughts. Hydrologist Norman Curtis found that a forest of mature maple trees stored twelve inches of rain during a daylong storm, whereas open land held only three and one-half inches. Instead of dams, watershed management was New York's alternative in 1885 when the Adirondack Forest Preserve, including twenty thousand miles of streams, was created to preserve forests for protection of Hudson River supplies to the Erie Canal and New York City. The Weeks Act of 1911 called for federal acquisition of eastern national forests to protect navigable streams.[22]

Less irrigation may be needed if productive land could be saved in the rainy East, Midwest, and South, where three million acres of farms are urbanized each year. Different crops consuming less water can be grown in drylands. Grading equipment guided by lasers can level fields precisely to avoid excess flooding of low spots. Desalting plants using reverse osmosis to clean agricultural wastewater can make it usable again. The California Department of Water Resources estimated that treatment costs for reused water averaged $150 an acre-foot, compared to $175 to $245 for new dams.

STRETCHING WHAT WE HAVE

Conservation of water can save vast amounts and stretch supplies far into the future. In traditional western irrigation, conservation means controlling the flow of water; water is "conserved" if it is impounded. But to most people, conserving water means using less. Cutting demands in half can effectively double the supply of water.

Because agriculture uses 81 percent of water consumed, most conservation plans begin here. The Soil Conservation Service reported that farm irrigation efficiency is only 53 percent.[23] In 1976 the GAO found that half the irrigation water was wasted and that efficiency reached only 44 percent on farms supplied by the Bureau of Reclamation. The office reported, "Irrigation practices have not changed appreciably in the past three decades even though irrigation science and technology have made substantial advances." The California Department of Water Resources found a typical loss of 25 percent between reservoir and farm, and the USGS reported that unlined and uncovered canals lose 16 percent of their water.

Spray irrigation requires far less water than is used in the prevalent open ditch systems (sometimes one-sixth the amount), and drip irrigation, where hoses drip water slowly at the plants' roots, requires even less. Spray systems, however, need more energy for pumping, and many crops cannot be served by drip systems, which are expensive to install. Reducing the amount of water can sometimes increase crop yields: in Israel 9.5 tons of melons were grown with spray irrigation, 17 tons with drip systems.[24] The Bureau of Reclamation's Irrigation Management Service offered advice that increased crop yields 16 percent while cutting water use 15 percent. Other advantages of using less water are reduced fertilizer needs and fewer drainage problems. Funding for irrigation efficiency is less than 1 percent of the water resources money spent by the departments of interior and agriculture. In one year, the Irrigation Management Service helped farmers holding only 2 percent of California's irrigated lands.[25]

Some conservation measures will be adopted only after laws are reformed. Under the use-it-or-lose-it doctrine of the West, a farmer who curbs waste may forgo his right to the water in future years. But most reform will happen through simple economics. When the government stops subsidizing waste, farmers will respond. Higher prices for water will encourage conservation. Some figures indicate that increasing irrigation supplies through conservation will require one-tenth the cost of new dams.

Through a plan originally proposed by the Environmental Defense Fund, the Metropolitan Water District of Southern California may finance conservation facilities for the Imperial Irrigation District in exchange for the water that would be saved. This could yield about four hundred thousand acre-feet of Colorado River supplies—enough for two million people—for much less than new dams would cost.

Manufacturing and energy consume the second-largest volume of water. Now, because of the Clean Water Act, industries are recycling supplies. A Kaiser steel plant at Fontana, California, uses about 3 percent of the water that an average plant uses. Through recirculation, a steel plant in Maine cut use to one-tenth its earlier amount.[26]

The USGS estimated waste from public water systems at 20 percent. A RAND study stated that New York City could save 150 million gallons per day (gpd) if it only repaired leaks in water mains. In Boston, where only a third of the system's water reaches the taps, repairs in 260 miles of pipes reduced leakage to 2 percent.[27] By eliminating illegal fire hydrant use and cutting other waste, Philadelphia reduced peak demand by 200 million gpd.

In six large cities and many smaller ones, residential water is not metered, and flat-rate customers use up to two times the normal amount. A RAND study estimated that metering would save about 200 million gpd in New York. The Environmental Protection Agency estimated that metering saves 20 to 30 percent.

Most water suppliers encourage waste by charging less money per gallon from bulk users, but during a drought, officials in Marin County, California, changed their rate structure to reward conservation. After a reasonable monthly amount of water was used, the rate jumped from $1.22 to $10 per 100 cubic feet. With other methods, this reduced use by 75 percent. Montgomery County, Maryland, reduced withdrawals by charging large users more. Tucson, Arizona, cut use 30 percent through a 17 percent rate increase along with public education and forty thousand home kits for the retrofitting of plumbing fixtures.[28]

Reduced consumption also means sewage treatment savings. The New England Interstate Water Pollution Control Commission estimated that water conservation can cut sewer construction costs 5 percent or more and can add twenty years to the life of sewers and treatment plants.[29]

Although conservation can extend supplies in the Southwest, population growth will probably require that farmlands be retired so that the irrigation water can go to cities instead. Tucson has already bought farmers' water rights. Will this be enough, or will controls on migration someday be needed to limit population in arid lands? Arizona congressman John Rhodes said, "People from the congested East and elsewhere are attracted to Arizona. There is no way Arizona could keep them out, even if it wanted to. Americans have a right to live wherever they want."[30] Regulations will not stop people from moving, but the costs of water may. Elimination of subsidies would discourage new industry, energy development, and agriculture, leaving fewer reasons for people to move to the desert.

Even though it accounts for less than 10 percent of water withdrawals, home use of water is the only kind individuals can easily reduce. Forty-five percent of home water is for the toilet, 30 percent for baths and showers. In dry areas, outdoor watering takes 44 percent of domestic supplies.

The California Department of Water Resources found that saving water can lower home utility bills by $200 a year at 1980 prices, most of the savings resulting from reduced hot water. Shower fixtures that increase pressure can save 15 percent of water used; toilet dams that displace some of the water in the tank can save 20 percent. Water use can be cut by 55 percent in new houses and 43 percent in existing ones.[31]

Outdoors, careful sprinkling and less water consumptive plant species can lead to water savings of up to 60 percent. New plumbing fixtures costing only $12 per house can save 38 to 68 percent of domestic water. The benefits outweigh costs by at least 19–1—a claim that can be made for no dam. New technology can further increase savings. Dual water systems that separate and recirculate gray water, such as laundry waste, allow normal living on spartan supplies.

Evidence shows that people can save water and still live efficiently and comfortably. Brent Blackwelder said, "There are two aspects to conservation: efficiency and change in lifestyle. I believe in both, but efficiency alone can solve shortages for a long time. Europeans use much less water than we do, and no one accuses them of being backward or of having a Third World standard of living."

Bob Teeters of the Army Corps of Engineers said, "Water conservation is the significant reform that is persisting from the Carter administration." Being a management rather than a construction program, conservation costs less than new dams but creates more employment. The Department of Agriculture estimated that nearly eighty thousand jobs could be required to develop conservation potential in California alone.

Addiction to the obsolete will be abandoned slowly; as Mark Twain wrote, "Habit is habit, and not to be flung out of the window by any man, but coaxed downstairs one step at a time." But changes can be made; there is no need to rely on the dam-it-up approach that has dominated water development through most of our nation's history. Will the changes come soon enough? Even with the movement to save rivers, the national rivers system, the beginnings of political reform, and the knowledge of alternatives, many more rivers could be lost.

10

THE LAST WEALTH

To destroy a dam and turn a river free, a ceremony was held in northern Idaho in 1973. Governor Cecil Andrus detonated an explosion that fatally cracked the Washington Water Power Dam, and six miles of the Clearwater River ran free once more.[1] And on California's Mad River, Sweesey Dam, built in 1938, had been blasted away in 1970. Through the concrete ruins the river reclaims its channel, and Chinook salmon now spawn upstream from the dam's wreckage. All over the country small dams have given way to renewed flows of the rivers. In Minnesota alone, a thousand dams have been washed out or destroyed (fifteen hundred remain).[2]

In his pathbreaking book about the salmon, Anthony Netboy wrote, "If society in its wisdom some day decides that food and game fishes are more valuable to the nation than electricity (which can be generated elsewhere), some of the territory once inhabited by the salmon and steelhead will be returned to them."[3]

More dams will be destroyed, and long before they are gone, thousands will be useless or worse. In 1971 Gilbert White wrote, "Few who contemplate the bleak inaction of a railroad station which 50 years before was bustling with traffic . . . can escape at least a fleeting question as to whether the noble dams now being planned for 50 to 100 years ahead may not be similarly obsolete before those horizons are reached."[4]

Many dams are unsafe, such as the ones at Johnstown, Pennsylvania, and Buffalo Creek, West Virginia, that burst and killed thousands of people. Nationwide, 350 major dam failures have occurred, most of them at privately owned sites.[5] In Pennsylvania alone, 151 dams are unsafe, including yet another one near Johnstown.

To avoid disasters, money must be spent. Built in 1914, Coon Rapids

251

Dam on the Mississippi was sold to the Hennepin County Park Reserve District by the Northern States Power Company, which donated $800,000 for repairs, but the county's cost was $2.4 million. That is one small example. What will be the costs of safety below large dams?

In 1983 the Bureau of Reclamation reported that forty-four of its dams needed repairs. Water seeps in ominous dark patches through the concrete face of Shasta Dam—the 560-foot-high centerpiece of the Central Valley Project in California—and landslides plague the abutment of Trinity Dam. In a *Sacramento Bee* interview, the bureau's David Prosser said, "Until recently, we never had to deal with a question like how much longer could a dam safely stand before we had to do something to it. . . . We haven't thought things like a dam's life to be applicable."[6]

"We're trying to get away from the idea that old means unsafe," said Bob Teeters of the Army Corps of Engineers. "With proper maintenance, dams can be safe forever."[7]

Whether or not dams are maintained, every reservoir is filling with silt washed in by the river from up above. All of those flooded canyons and valleys, from John Muir's Hetch Hetchy to Mark Dubois's Stanislaus, are doomed to encasement in mud. At Lake Austin in Texas, silt decreased storage capacity by 96 percent in thirteen years. Mud in the corps's Fishtrap Dam in Kentucky was expected to reduce flood control capacity in ten years.[8] Little Pine Creek Dam in Pennsylvania was silt-filled in only thirty years. Government hydrologists say that Lake Powell will be full of silt in three hundred years or less, and many people think that this "gem of the Colorado" will be a brown quagmire in only a century. Federal reservoirs are designed with space for silt accumulation during the expected one-hundred-year life of the project, but what happens after that? "I don't think anybody has bothered to think about it," Bob Teeters said. "There are more pressing problems. Obsolescence of locks, for example, is a bigger concern."

In 1983 Stewart Udall said, "Glen Canyon is probably the most beautiful man-made lake in the world, but it's going to fill up with silt in a hundred years, and what is the judgment of posterity then? That's the real down side of the big dams—the rivers are not renewable." Flowing water is symbolic of renewable resources, but the damming of a river is the ultimate in the consumption of land.

Someday the reservoirs will be "dry" dams—mud flats with a river winding through, then spilling over the aged dam. And in time, the dams themselves will be worn by the river and washed away. As Henry David Thoreau wrote of a hydropower dam built in 1847, "Perchance after a thousand years . . . nature will have leveled the Billerica Dam, and the Lowell factories, and the Grass-ground [Concord] River will run clear again."

The blasting of the dam on Idaho's Clearwater River was a ceremony marking a new day for a revitalized river. And it may signify a coming age when people will recognize the uselessness of some dams and quicken the earth's process of destroying them.

For eighty years the attitude has been that we can bring in all the water we want simply by invoking enough technology and money. This belief had a religious fervor and approached the patriotic in moving people to act. That era is over, however, killed in part by costs but also accompanied by the undercurrent of a new religion that recognizes the importance of the natural world and of a new patriotism that sees the rivers as a part of America that is worth keeping.

Dams are with us for generations to come, but the National Water Commission reported in 1973 that the Bureau of Reclamation had nearly exhausted new justifiable projects. As deputy director of water resources for California, Jerry Meral wrote that the building of more dams is not attractive because the better sites are developed, in-stream needs are recognized, economic and environmental damage is too great, people want to keep water where it is instead of exporting it, and government funding will not keep up with costs. President Carter and Interior Secretary Andrus declared that the age of big dam building was over, and from the opposite political pole, President Reagan's commissioner of reclamation Robert Broadbent said, "I don't know that there are any major dams left except Auburn."

Bob Teeters of the army corps said, "It's my prediction that in five or ten years, water projects will be approved like parks used to be—one at a time. The irony is that now we have omnibus parks bills that designate many parks at once."

Unconvinced that the dam-building era is over, Utah governor Scott Matheson said in 1979, "By no means have we exhausted the need to develop water."[9] Just as the forties and fifties were the era for flood control dams, the eighties are the era for hydropower. And crises that arise overnight can jar resource policies from one extreme to another: Dickey–Lincoln dams on the St. John River in Maine had been nearly forgotten when the oil embargo of 1973 set the dam builders in motion. Politics in faraway Arabia almost resulted in the building of those two dams, and other crises could reactivate old threats on many rivers. When will the next push for dams be? Maybe when eastern cities that have not patched leaks face another drought, or when the Sun Belt civilization sprawls to its thirsty limits of growth. River conservationists may find that in stopping federal dams in the 1970s, they have simply opened the sites for corporate powers to preempt public water for single-purpose projects like hydropower and oil shale development. If lasting protection is not agreed on, old proposals could be reactivated. Look at the past: the corps called New Melones Dam "semi-deauthorized," then they built it. Is this the twilight to an era of bulldozing, or will the powerful interests that profit so greatly by controlling the flow of water simply wait for new opportunities?

Despite the uncertainties, Brent Blackwelder looks beyond the dam-and-canal-stopping work and sees new goals: groundwater management, water conservation, and, perhaps most important, preventing disastrous dams in other countries.

Much has been written about High Aswan Dam on Egypt's Nile. The dam created hydropower and irrigation benefits, but it also caused the loss of beneficial flooding and made farmers dependent on petroleum-based fertilizers. It caused erosion and salinization of the rich Nile Delta, the infection of millions of people with blood flukes that thrive because of the reservoir, the leaking of one-third of the water through the bedrock, and the devastation of Mediterranean fisheries.[10] Similar environmental, public health, and economic catastrophes plagued undeveloped countries around the globe. One hundred thousand people were forced from homes by a reservoir in the Ivory Coast.[11] Thirty major dams were under construction in India in 1980. One proposal in that country would relocate 1.4 million people. Tehri Dam, sixth largest in the world, was planned for a life of only forty years and may silt up more rapidly. On tributaries of the Amazon, Brazil planned a series of dams that would flood an area the size of Montana. In the Philippines, leaders of antidam forces were murdered, but the Chico Project was finally stopped.

Funding for dams in undeveloped countries came from the United States and U.S.-supported organizations such as the World Bank. The Army Corps of Engineers, Bureau of Reclamation, and American corporations boasted of their roles in exporting American dam-building technology.

Indians in Alberta fought hydroelectric projects on the Slave River. At the 1983 conference of the American Rivers Conservation Council, Chief Clifford Freeman said, "When they kill the environment, they will kill us, because we are a part of it. The dam is just for money. After these dams, there will be nothing left but suicides and alcohol problems. We can't allow a government that's supposed to be ours to do this. We will fight with our lives against this, because if we don't fight, we will be giving our lives anyway."

In Tasmania, the fight over Gordon-below-Franklin Dam became the largest conservation issue in Australian history: two thousand demonstrators who blocked bulldozers were arrested in 1983, and fifteen thousand people demonstrated in Melbourne. An election brought proriver leaders to office, halting the dam.[12]

In northern Norway, one hundred hydroelectric dams have been built, but a proposal on the Alta River—the last large undammed stream—was fought by the native Sami, or Laplanders. After many appeals that their land and culture be spared, one thousand people staged a sit-down, some chained to rocks in midwinter arctic conditions. After six weeks, a police force of six hundred removed the demonstrators. The dams are being built.

A Russian plan to divert the Yenisei and Ob rivers for irrigation would greatly reduce the freshwater entering the Arctic Ocean, possibly altering the ocean's salinity balance, the ice cap, and the world climate.[13]

Development proposals were rampant in many countries, but in the United States a new view emerged with regard to rivers and dams. We were learning how to use our rivers without consuming them—to meet needs while leaving rivers the way they are.

In 1982 Brent Blackwelder said, "If we don't have reforms and new policies on all aspects of water development, it will be like past years when we were playing defense all the time." It is those reforms that conservationists, a few congressmen such as Bob Edgar, and others worked for in that era of change.

Was it too much to ask, too much to work for, too much to expect, that the special rivers—the best natural places and homelands—could be saved so that people could be saved from the killing boredom, the stifling artificiality, the loneliness of life without wild creatures, the dread of a world so lopsidedly controlled by the institutions dedicated to making money? There was a new attitude about rivers, but to make the change permanent would require the energy of all those affected by the loss of special river places: park and wilderness enthusiasts, anglers, landowners, naturalists and ecologists, river runners, people who just like rivers, and those who found a metaphysical and spiritual power in the free-flowing water.

To save rivers demanded the enthusiasm of John Muir, the forethought of John Craighead, the prose of Wallace Stegner, the dedication of Mark Dubois, the calculations of Jerry Meral, the organization of Brent Blackwelder, the drive of David Brower, the public attention of William O. Douglas and Richard Chamberlain, the old political style of John Saylor, and the new style of Bob Edgar. No tactics were outdated, and none could be ignored. Personal explorations, conversations with friends, articles and press releases, river trips for politicians, letters to congressmen, lobbyists in Washington, coalitions of everyone affected by the changes, demonstrations, direct action, campaigning and voting—all were needed. All may be needed forever, because, even at our best, we save rivers only for a while. Then they need saving again.

River conservationists had grown into positions of influence, arguing that there are many kinds of values in the free-flowing rivers. By 1985 the opposition to dams and other destructive projects had matured through eighty years, involving many people, regions, and motives, all building toward greater awareness of rivers. The national and state wild and scenic rivers systems had been started. Water policy reforms had begun, and the politics of pork barrel were shaken. Yet the threats to rivers would increase again as resources became more scarce and as new pressures grew to squeeze the last wealth from the rivers that remained.

11

THE SECOND GENERATION OF RIVER CONSERVATION

The twenty-year period following the damming of the Stanislaus Canyon in California confirmed that the times had changed regarding American's attitudes about rivers. That spectacular stream in the Sierra Nevada foothills was the last to be lost to damming at the truly epic scale—a large dam, hundreds of feet high, damaging the river in profound ways, and attracting intense opposition.

The people working to protect the Stanislaus didn't know that the politics of water development were shifting so profoundly under their feet, but in 1982 Friends of the River stood at the brink of a new era. This was evident in a series of dam fights that followed. Conservation victories on five other nearby rivers immortalized the Sierra as the region where water development and river protection took their most critical turns since the beginning of the big-dam era in 1913 when O'Shaughnessy Dam in Yosemite National Park was authorized. The cycle of protection that was started with John Muir's passion to save Yosemite's Tuolumne River in Hetch Hetchy Valley was, in a grand sense, completed nearly a hundred years later.

Already in hot political debate while the Stanislaus was being flooded, a lower section of the nearby Tuolumne River was slated for dams and diversions for hydroelectric power. As we saw in Chapter 5, that stream was the follow-up engagement for Stanislaus activists who succeeded with federal wild and scenic river legislation for the Tuolumne in 1984, a stellar victory. Another dam proposal was stopped on the popular South Fork of the American River to the north.

The acid test, however, came on the Kings River, where the local

"Conservation District" proposed to build a 575-foot-high dam to grow surplus crops such as cotton. At stake was a magnificent foothills canyon, one of the finest trout fisheries in California, a popular whitewater run, and the river with the greatest undammed vertical drop in America: a 11,259-foot descent from alpine headwaters to Pine Flat Reservoir in the Sierra foothills.[1] Refining all the arguments about economics, recreation, biology, public lands, scarcity of resources, and economic alternatives, the Committee to Save the Kings River executed a campaign through grassroots support, media exposure, endorsements by influential supporters, and savvy lobbying. Upper reaches of the Kings were secured as a national wild and scenic river, while the threatened reach was congressionally designated as a "special management area" that blocked construction of the dam. In a record-breaking two-years' time, the Kings supporters went from a serious dam proposal to a nationally protected river. Indelibly marking the Kings as a sign of changing times, its campaign was carried out in Fresno—the heart of the industrial agricultural empire of America.

While Kings River activists turned the tide of development in their backyard, the Merced Canyon Committee waged a concurrent effort at the Merced River to the north, and Friends of the River worked to save the North Fork of the Kern to the south. Plans to build power and water supply dams were soundly defeated, ending 1987 with three magnificent additions to the national wild and scenic rivers system. No other single year saw the designation of rives that were so extraordinary and also highly threatened.

Further confirming the momentum of river conservation success, Two Forks Dam on the South Platte—part of a Denver Water Board scheme to pipe more runoff from the west side of the Rockies to the urbanizing east side—was administratively defeated in 1990 with a veto by the Environmental Protection Agency. And in Oregon, Elk Creek Dam—one-third completed by the Army Corps of Engineers—was finally halted when the state joined other anti-dam forces. Even the Corps ended up recommending restoration of this salmon-spawning tributary of the Rogue River (opposition by the local congressman blocked funding for the restoration). In West Virginia, a push to dam the exquisite Greenbrier River for flood control faded into the background as the Corps failed to justify expenses under new planning guidelines and the state failed to come up with its one-third cost share, all under the threat of protracted legal and political battles.

None of this is to say that dams were not built or that the threats went away. The Bureau of Reclamation constructed a new dam on the Provo River in the Wasatch Mountains of Utah, flooding a trout stream that might have been vigorously defended elsewhere. In spite of local opposition,

Warm Springs Dam was built by the Army Corps in 1983 for water supply on Dry Creek, a Russian River tributary north of San Francisco.[2] Not far upstream of the recently filled New Melones Reservoir, a local water district dammed the wild and remote valley of Highland Creek, a tributary to the North Fork of the Stanislaus where 9,700-year-old archaeological artifacts had been discovered.

Likewise in the East, wasteful and poorly justified projects had not entirely disappeared. In 1998, the Army Corps began construction on an eighty-six-foot-high dam flooding eight miles of the North Fork Hughes River in West Virginia, a stream with twenty-seven kinds of fish and a rich Appalachian forest that supported 110 migratory bird species. The specious reason for this dam was flatwater recreation, even though ten major reservoirs had already been built by the Corps in that small state and even though 58 percent of the alleged benefits consisted of activities that were done just as well or better without the dam—fishing and walking, for example.[3]

Clearly, the sacrifice of good rivers to dams of questionable value was not completely a thing of the past, yet these were all minor proposals compared to the grand schemes of the early- and mid-1900s, and these late-coming projects just barely slipped through the net of public opposition.

One classic megaproject remained on the books: Auburn Dam in California. Repeatedly beaten back by Friends of the River and local American River groups in the early 1980s, new permutations of the dam continued to cycle through the ambitions of local boosters and into the national political machinery. After repeated attempts to revive the behemoth from the dust of the 1975 earthquake described in Chapter 5, high water in 1986 led to Auburn's reincarnation as a flood control panacea. Working all the angles, sponsors even promoted an expandable dry-dam, initially to be filled only during floods. This, however, could easily have been upgraded to full-time storage at a higher level, so river conservationists continued to fight successfully against the expenditure of $700 million or even up to $2 billion depending on which option was picked. Dam opponents argued with ample evidence that far cheaper alternatives existed for flood control. With reinforcement of downstream levees in 2002, the justification for Auburn faded even further, but Congressman John Doolittle persisted in trying to authorize further study of America's most glaring artifact of pork barrel politics. The likelihood of construction was nil, but proactive campaigns to designate a national recreation area or wild and scenic river lacked the needed congressional support at the local level, so constant vigilance was the fate for those safeguarding a magnificent forty-eight-mile medley of wild canyons only an hour's drive from Sacramento.

No matter how bad a dam site it was, Auburn would likely have been built without opposition from river conservationists. Yet economics and hydrology were notably on their side here and elsewhere as the twentieth century rolled to a close. Quite simply, the good dam sites had already been built on long ago. A U.S. Geological Survey study found that the amount of water to be stored for each cubic foot of dam constructed fell from 10.4 acre-feet for dams before 1930 to 2.1 acre-feet for dams in the 1930s and 0.29 acre-feet for those built in the 1960s.[4] After that, the efficiencies dropped even further—only the dregs of damsites remained. Nonetheless, many of these economically unjustifiable dams were built in the 1970s, mere facades of a lingering misconception of progress. These included the pointless and damaging lower Snake River dams that drove the salmon toward extinction and dams in the upper Colorado basin that served to do little but evaporate water. In spite of bad economics, the dams were still being built through the 1970s. A powerful political movement was required to stop the momentum of further construction, and now, with the success on the Tuolumne, Kings, South Platte, and Greenbrier Rivers, that movement was fully engaged.

The change also indicated a deeper shift in American values and the collective public mood. The dam-building era reflected a belief in the control of nature and in heroic infrastructure as a symbol of human accomplishment. Following the Great Depression, the need for such icons was prevalent, and in the preparation and the aftermath of World War II, the linkage of construction with progress and security was profound.

As the generation doing this work reached the peak of its influential years, a new generation questioned the basic precepts of construction-as-progress. Life science and an awareness of ecology began to inform our decisions more. Fervor about cutting government costs gained ground and served to undermine the old concept of progress even from within the conservative bloc of voters. All these factors meant that America in general and water development in particular were ripe for change.

Although the big-dam proposals had mostly disappeared, hydropower developers proposed a plethora of small new projects in the late 1980s. These met a long list of tough questions from river groups at the local, state, and national levels. As a result, remarkably few among the hundreds of power-generating possibilities referred to in Chapter 9 were built. In the early 1990s, the incentives of the Public Utility Regulatory Policies Act expired, and along with them, most of the hydro plans were shuffled to the back burner, perhaps just awaiting the next energy crisis.

Even while river conservationists succeeded in blocking dam construction, especially at the most significant sites, the threat of new incursions grew ominously on the horizon. Chief among these, water supply dams could be resurrected at any time to serve a booming population all across America. Growth estimates in the 1980s had foreseen a leveling off of the population in the United States early in the twenty-first century, but those projections missed the mark by a mile owing to dramatic increases in immigration. While native-born Americans had a birth rate of two children per woman—which would have resulted in a stable population within a few decades—the new wave of immigration increased without foreseeable limits. Instead of leveling off at about 300 million people, the population soared toward a new "mid-level" estimate of 404 million by 2050. More alarming, actual growth in the early twenty-first century was occurring even faster than the Census Bureau's "high-level" estimate, which projected nearly half a billion people by mid-century.

All across the country, increased efficiency in the use of water and power could sometimes delay the day of reckoning and enable communities to survive without new dams for a while, but those efficiencies would ultimately reach limits if the population increase did not flatten out. If growth continued, new dams and diversions would be needed as certainly as any new resident flushes the toilet or waters the lawn.[5] Areas not directly affected by immigrant population growth were still affected by displacement as older, established populations in West Coast, southwestern, and eastern cities moved out to the suburbs, to rural areas, and to neighboring states, while their old communities filled with new arrivals from abroad. New demands for water in those outlying areas reached alarming proportions almost overnight.

Las Vegas, for example, grew by 1,000 new residents per week in the 1990s. To meet demand, the city proposed to dam the exquisite Virgin River near Zion National Park if the city didn't win the unlikely right to withdraw more water from the overused, heavily litigated Colorado River.[6] The Texas State Water Plan in 2002 called for new dams on the Guadalupe River—perhaps the finest natural river among few that remained in the state. It also suggested damming the Neches River, home to 300 species of birds and fifty species of mammals in the rich pinelands on the eastern side of the state. In 2002, a drought in the Southeast brought some of the driest conditions in a hundred years, severely stressing hundreds of municipal water supplies.[7] For the headwaters of the Tallapoosa River, Atlanta proposed dams that would flood important habitat and affect flows for many miles downstream. In Virginia, the city of Newport News hoped to dam the small Mattapaoni River, which formed one of the finer natural estuaries on the East Coast (the proposal was stopped in 2003).[8]

While booming growth fueled the demand side of water use projections, periodic and intensifying droughts accentuated the supply side of the problem. Western states saw a major drought in 2002, fueling fears of thirsty shortages. The Santa Clara Valley Water Authority south of San Francisco explored the possibility of damming streams in Henry Coe State Park—the second-largest state park in California—an incursion regarded as unthinkable before the latest population boom. The population in southern California alone was expected to grow by 43 percent, to 22.3 million people by 2020. To meet the new needs—in this case, 95 percent immigration-based—a new $8.5 billion state water plan proposed to dedicate $1.5 billion to new dams and water storage, $1.3 billion to river restoration, $1 billion to water quality, and $3 billion to improved efficiency. Many people feared that new storage would be the only part of the package to survive budget cuts; the state faced unprecedented shortfalls in the aftermath of the Enron energy debacle, which cost California's government billions of dollars in 2001 because it had to buy power on behalf of bankrupt utilities gouged by Enron's price fixing. Under the new water plan, the giant Shasta and Friant Dams would be enlarged, enforcement of the Endangered Species Act put on hold, and salmon runs further decimated.[9] Friends of the River fought off a bill that would authorize expansion of dams, but without that legislation the restoration projects languished as well.[10]

One only has to consider the Delaware River and the inducements to build Tocks Island Dam that followed the Philadelphia-area drought of the 1960s to realize that similar motivations could easily be reignited in the twenty-first century. Unless population growth is slowed, the intensifying droughts could trigger the beginning of a new era of dam building, this time focusing on smaller dams, usually on the tributaries of major streams, and closer to cities. The effects would still be profound on the rivers and on the health of whole watersheds.

Finally, this view of dam fighting at the turn of a new century would not be complete without considering the international front, where the momentum to build massive new dams continued almost unabated. Construction began on some truly colossal dams such as Three Gorges on the Yangtze River in China, which displaced millions of people in spite of worldwide opposition.[11] Hydropower dams such as those blocking the Bío Bío River of Chile were stacked up in waterways, even though they destroyed some of the most breathtaking wild rivers ever known. In the thirty-year period from 1970 to 2000, the number of large dams worldwide grew from 5,000 to 40,000. The rate then appeared to be slowing.

International Rivers Network (IRN), founded by Mark Dubois of the Stanislaus River and by hydrologist Philip Williams, brought attention to the need to protect rivers worldwide. Some reform efforts directed at groups such as the World Bank succeeded. The IRN sought to encourage grassroots organizing and to redirect international funding programs, but the losses still promised to increase in a world where developing nations strove to emulate the material standard of living found in the United States.[12]

In underdeveloped countries, dam construction threatened more rivers, but within America the demise of the big-dam era opened the way for a whole new generation of river conservation. With the threats of total destruction by large dams now diminished, river conservationists were able to turn their attention to a rash of other problems. These were more subtle than the utter destruction behind a dam but in many ways just as harmful to rivers.

In this increasingly complicated world, awareness of the rivers' values was enhanced by new knowledge about the importance that these watery paths offer to the greater systems of life.

ALL CREATURES IN THE ARK

A long tradition of protecting rivers for fish and wildlife dates back to initial efforts to establish wildlife refuges along the upper Mississippi River. But not until the 1970s was a focus on game species, such as trout in the upper Hudson and canvasback ducks on the Yukon at the Ramparts Dam site, broadened to include other creatures vital to the ecology of river systems. After 1973, endangered species rose to the top of this list, beginning with the snail darter in the Little Tennessee River at the Tellico Dam site (see Chapter 5). While public attention had gravitated to species such as the salmon in the Columbia River, less glamorous fish, such as the humpback chub and razorback sucker in the Colorado River basin, also began to receive attention.[13]

At the turn of the twenty-first century, interest further broadened to include the greater mix of life in the rivers and along their shores. What had originally seemed like an isolated need to protect habitat for an imperiled creature became recognized as a need for stewardship at a far greater scale.[14]

The skill of scientists in approaching the problems of rivers and in communicating with the public increased sharply with the popularization of ecology in the 1970s, and the weight of all this new science exerted an increasing effect on policy through the 1980s.

By the late 1990s, a series of scientific studies found that the ecological health of many rivers was abysmal. Surveys by zoologist Lawrence Master of the Nature Conservancy reported that 66 percent of the nation's freshwater mussels could face extinction, 50 percent of the crayfish species were in jeopardy, and 40 percent of the fishes and amphibians were at risk.[15] The survival of whole species was in doubt in 15 percent of the 2,100 separate watersheds in the United States. The American Fisheries Society reported that the rate of extinction for fish species doubled during the twentieth century. From 1979 to 1989 alone, the society added 139 species and subspecies to its list of rare fishes.[16] Not a single species on the list had recovered in that time. Biologist Anthony Ricciardi reported that freshwater animals were disappearing five times faster than terrestrial ones and three times faster than marine mammals. The projected future extinction rate for freshwater species was nearly 4 percent per decade—the same rate found in tropical rainforests, which had been considered one of the most threatened ecosystems on the planet.[17]

Overlooked because they are difficult to see, fishes throughout the United States and especially in the Southeast and Southwest had become endangered, quite simply, because their rivers had been damaged so badly.

While analysis of water quality for chemical contamination showed that 25 percent of American stream miles were substandard, fully 50 percent of the mileage was considered impaired when biological criteria were applied. This included consideration of the stream's ability to support the full range of native species, the health of the greater aquatic ecosystem, and the ability of the stream's life-giving systems—such as its food web—to maintain themselves.[18]

Searching for the most critical basins that supported imperiled populations, the Nature Conservancy found that eighty-seven of America's watersheds were each home to ten or more imperiled species. Most of these lay in the Southeast, and especially in the Tennessee, Ohio, Cumberland, and Mobile basins. To arrest species decline, the Conservancy launched a program focused on eight rivers: the Clinch of Virginia and Tennessee, Green of Kentucky, Cahaba of Alabama, Conasauga of Tennessee, Altamaha of Georgia, Kiamichi of Oklahoma, Guadalupe of Texas, and Verde of Arizona. Conservancy staff began by studying what was needed to maintain the endemic species in each stream. This typically involved restoring flows to a more natural regime and protecting riverfront land.[19] As river conservation evolved, more people began to understand the way rivers really worked and to realize the depth and breadth of problems that had been created.

In order to safeguard the full range of resident species and to restore rivers damaged by neglect and abuse, river enthusiasts after the demise of the big-dam era focused on three categories of better stewardship: the flow of water in the streams, the health of riparian habitat at the edge of the rivers, and the quality of the water. Public attention had certainly been given to these topics to some degree for decades, but now the full force of river conservation was free to concentrate on reforms. These three concerns became the cornerstones of the second generation of river conservation in America, propelling a maturing political movement rapidly into the twenty-first century.

RIVERS WITHOUT WATER

One might take for granted that water flows in rivers, but because of diversions for irrigation, for a growing population, and for hydroelectric power, many rivers are depleted of the flows needed for maintaining water quality and for a healthy system of life. In some cases, the streams are reduced to a minor trickle of runoff or to nothing.[20]

In addition to blatant dewatering, untold miles of rivers are affected badly by changes in the pattern of flows below dams or below diversions for people's use. For example, much of the life in rivers depends on nature's cycle of high water rushing seaward in the springtime. Salmon—to consider just one genus of fish—migrate upstream to spawn when the flows get high enough in the winter or spring. But below dams, the timing of flows has been upset; the high water of springtime is held back and released later. Low flows of summer are made even lower when water is diverted from the streams. As a result, a tumbling array of secondary problems arise. Cool water temperatures are critical to the life of fish and other creatures that have evolved under natural conditions for millennia, but depleted flows result in high summer temperatures that kill the fish.

Even more fundamentally, hydrologists led by pioneers such as Luna Leopold and biologists such as Lincoln Brower learned that the shape and form of the riverbed itself is governed by the rate and timing of the flows, and that this shape, or morphology, is critical to the ecology of the river. Floods, for example, scour out pools, which are used by many species and keep water chilled in their depths. Floods deposit gravel in other areas, creating riffles and rapids, which are needed to aerate the water and to expose gravel to a steady flow of oxygen contained in the water. When floods are eliminated, the pools gradually fill with silt, and the riffles erode, eliminating the "pool and riffle sequence" that is needed for a healthy aquatic eco-system. Instead, a "constant glide" results, with relatively steady current lacking the cool pools and oxygenating riffles.

Likewise, life along the river depends on the natural cycles of flow, not the least of which is flooding. Cottonwoods, for example, are keystone species—many other plants and animals depend on them. The seeds of the cottonwood need fresh silt or scoured areas to germinate, but when floods are contained by upstream dams, the trees begin to die out without replace-ment.

Lacking the diversity of habitat found in the flood-prone river, the diversity of life itself disappears, and with it, the ability of the ecosystem to maintain its essential processes and to be productive.[21]

Here's another phenomenon that people became more aware of when they looked at how rivers really operate: dams typically block the natural flow of silt by allowing it to settle out in the bottoms of reservoirs. While excessive silt from clear-cut forests, construction sites, and farmland is harm-ful to the river, a certain amount of silt occurs naturally and is important to the native life of the rivers. This silt is deposited on the insides of bends and on floodplains, creating productive riparian habitat. But the silt-free water that's released from a dam has extra erosive power. It proceeds to cut away the banks downstream but fails to rebuild sandbars as the inverse part of the process. The result is a "degrading" riverbed, which constantly erodes deeper, excavating valuable sand and gravel, exposing banks to cave-ins and mass-wasting, washing floodplain habitat downstream, and perhaps most important, hemorrhaging groundwater from the lowlands as the river slices deeper and deeper into its surrounding landscape. Once fruitful complexes of channels, sloughs, wetlands, floodplains, and gravelbars are replaced with biologically impoverished, downcut ditches.

When river conservationists turned their attention to these problems of adequate flow patterns in streams, one of their most effective methods of reform came from an unexpected source: hydroelectric dam relicensing.

Beginning with the Federal Power Act of 1920, as we saw in Chapter 4, dam owners were required to periodically justify their use and manage-ment of the water. Then the new Federal Power Act of 1986 obligated them to meet new environmental regulations signed into law after the original dams had been built. Reasoning that the power producers had benefited from the first forty or fifty years of their projects' operations, which had usually paid off the investments and earned handsome profits besides, the new law required attention to the dams' harmful effects. These included low flows in the rivers, dried-up channels where water is withdrawn, unnatural patterns of flow such as huge peaking releases followed by a trickle when the power companies were refilling their dams, and blocked passage for migrating fish.[22]

The Federal Energy Regulatory Commission oversaw about 2,000 dams in all, most of the licenses granted for a thirty- to fifty-year period.[23] From 1995 to 2010, more than 550 dams were scheduled to be relicensed. In 2003 alone, 105 licenses were pending.

Focusing on conservation and restoration through improved hydropower operations, the Hydropower Reform Coalition, chaired by American Rivers, grew to a hundred organizations lobbying for change, analyzing permit applications, and appealing decisions of the Federal Energy Regulatory Commission.[24] In dozens of cases, from the Saco River in Maine to the St. Louis in Minnesota and the Skagit in Washington, the relicensing procedures resulted in improved flows for fish, wildlife, riparian habitat, and river recreation.

Another approach to restoring flows in rivers involved fundamental questions of who owns or controls the water. Under long-established public law, river water is not private but rather public property, and states hold its ownership in trust. Regulatory agencies are responsible for administering the use of the water and for protecting streams from overuse. Under this authority, some states in the East have set limits for drawdowns. However, these required minimums are rarely adequate to truly nourish the life of the streams. Efforts to maintain even a depauperate flow are further compromised by a failure to consider the effects of groundwater withdrawals on rivers, lax or nonexistent enforcement, and unregulated use by some industries, many urban developments, and most farms.

Complicating the hydrologic mix, much water has been transferred from one basin to another, such as from the Shepaug to the Naugatuck in Connecticut, without concern for the health of the contributing stream. The Ipswich River in Massachusetts runs dry each year because towns outside the basin divert the flows and don't return them. Lengthy court cases have resulted about dozens of rivers. Because of these interbasin transfers, waterways as significant as the Sacramento and Eel in California and the Platte and Colorado throughout their multistate lengths have been abysmally degraded. On the scenic Farmington River in Massachusetts and the biologically rich Roanoke in Virginia, cities outside the river basins planned to divert substantial new flows. More and more across America, these kinds of water wars were replacing the dam fights of the past.

To serve a population that boomed from 2.9 million in 1990 to 4.1 million in 2000—and with no end of growth in sight—Atlanta aimed to tap its local Chattahoochee River to the legal limits of withdrawal and then to pursue other rivers. But Florida objected, owing to the draconian effects that the withdrawals would have on the productive estuary where the Chattahoochee ends up in Apalachicola Bay.[25] Such multistate conflicts over scarce resources were becoming increasingly common.

The problems of diversion were still seen most graphically in the West, where rivers as large as the Snake of southern Idaho—running with the volume of the entire Delaware River—was nearly dried up at one site because three huge irrigation canals bled from the river.[26] The Colorado River was nothing but mud, sand, and salty ooze before it reached its once-Edenic delta at the Gulf of California. The Rio Grande faced ecological collapse because 95 percent of its annual flow was sluiced away for crops and cities. Hundreds of streams in the West were reduced to dust or trickles below diversion sites, all in accordance with state laws stacked in favor of the water consumers.[27] In 1994, the Supreme Court recognized the relationships between water quality and quantity and ruled that the Clean Water Act can be used to address both, giving a boost to efforts aimed at keeping healthy flows in streams.

Outmoded western statutes, however, ordained that whoever used the water first had a right to continue the use, all based on historical circumstances a hundred years ago that made the development of irrigation in unsettled lands a priority. It didn't matter if the water was wasted, if the canals leaked half of their flow, if the crops were considered surplus, or if the diverters caused pollution. Until the late 1900s, in-stream flows to benefit the health of rivers were not regarded as a "beneficial" use at all, therefore they had no standing under western water laws. Anybody who saved water for the good of the stream simply enabled somebody else downstream to take that same water out for his own use.

This legal framework remained in place, but most states adopted at least token provisions for state-designated minimum flows. These did nothing to remedy excessive existing diversions and only meant that new requests to withdraw water would be denied if they depleted the stream beyond a specified amount. But at least the minimum instream flow requirements protected against yet more surface-water diversions that could otherwise desiccate the rivers even in times of higher runoff. One group involved in this issue, Idaho Rivers United, labored for years to establish a handful of minimum flow regulations, the process fraught with legal roadblocks, delays, and opportunity for vetoes by a farming-dominated state legislature. The Idaho conservationists' frustrating experience was typical throughout the West.[28]

To gain improved flows, a more productive approach surfaced, not unlike the strategies involved in relicensing hydroelectric projects: revising the management of federal dams—some of them massive storage dams. This arena was ripe for reform because most politicians at the federal level were not from the irrigation areas, and so they were more receptive to change. Plus, federal taxpayers funded the irrigation projects in the first place, so people all across the country could claim a valid stake in the management of the federal dams. And far more federal money than state money was available to study what was needed, to engineer the required changes, and to compensate those who would lose water, however unjustified its use.

Documenting this issue, *Dams and Rivers*, published by the U.S. Geological Survey, illustrated the downstream problems posed by large dams and identified some of the improvements that could be made by altering management of the federal facilities.[29]

A prime case here, the Central Valley Project Improvement Act of 1992 directed that some water be returned to the Trinity River of northern California—a once-outstanding salmon fishery that had lost up to 90 percent of its flow for the sake of agribusiness export and urbanization to the south. The new law required that 800,000 acre-feet of water from the twenty-dam complex called the Central Valley Project be dedicated to fish and wildlife, and it set a goal of doubling the anadromous fish runs from the Trinity and Sacramento River systems. Salmon, steelhead, delta smelt, and other species had been reduced to a ghost of their original numbers. However, implementation of the act proved to be difficult at best as agricultural interests sued and constantly appealed to prevent water from actually being used for environmental purposes. About the new law, the *San Francisco Chronicle* on October 31, 1992, quoted Jason Peltier of the Central Valley Project Water Association saying, "We'll do anything and everything to keep from being harmed. If that means obstructing implementation, so be it." Seeking to make implementation delays permanent, the Westlands Irrigation district sued the federal government to prevent restoration of flows to the Trinity River in a case still pending in 2003.

Searching for consensus, and finding some, a California program called Cal-Fed managed to make progress in this contentious battleground with programs and money aimed at water conservation, efficiency, and restoration as well as supply-side solutions that remained troublesome to river advocates.

In another interesting effort to reform the management of federal water projects, the operation of Glen Canyon Dam was revised to quell the severity of peaking power. Spiking releases had caused the river to surge from 15,000 cubic feet per second to 30,000 on a daily basis, up and down as the spigot was turned on and off. These extreme flow changes eroded beaches and damaged riparian habitat within Grand Canyon National Park.[30] In both the Columbia River, where the prized Pacific salmon runs were at risk, and the Colorado, where less charismatic species were no less threatened, major overhaul of federal dam management became the pivotal strategy for keeping imperiled species alive.

Also along this line, the Natural Resources Defense Council sued the federal Bureau of Reclamation to reclaim some remnant of California's San Joaquin River, 98 percent of which had been diverted for irrigation below Friant Dam near Fresno. Other efforts to reform the flows below federal dams were launched on the Green River in Utah, the Platte River in Nebraska, and the Snake in Idaho. In 1997, American Rivers launched a program to revise the Army Corps of Engineers' management of the heavily manipulated Missouri River in order to sustain unique fish and bird species and restore riparian corridors that could still be patched together along the route that Lewis and Clark had taken west.[31] In 2003, the group successfully sued the Army Corps to make adjustments to the system.

The key issue along all these rivers had evolved from one of building or not building new dams to reforming the way the existing dams were used. Seeking to institutionalize this shift, Interior Secretary Bruce Babbitt in 1993 committed to "transforming the Bureau of Reclamation from a civil works agency into a preeminent water management agency that is cost effective in serving its customers."[32] Changes, however, occurred on a piecemeal basis. While even the Federal Energy Regulatory Commission has to review the licenses and purposes of private hydroelectric dams periodically, the federal agencies are not required to review the management of their dams.

Still another approach for restoring the flows in rivers was undertaken by government as well as nonprofit groups. In some areas, city or regional agencies bought water rights from irrigators and redirected them to urban growth, thus avoiding further withdrawals from rivers.[33] In other cases, efficiency improvements on farms and ranches yielded water that was returned to rivers for instream use.[34]

For example, along the San Pedro River of Arizona, the Nature Conservancy bought ranchland including the rights to 3,500 acre-feet of water. The group planned to return 90 percent of this flow to the impoverished river and thus nourish its ailing cottonwood corridor, critical to wildlife of the region. In Idaho, the Shoshone and Bannock Tribes secured the rights to water that had been theirs before it was shunted away by white irrigators. The Indians planned to leave the water in the river to benefit wildlife and restore salmon, which needed higher flows farther down the river for their spawning runs.[35]

As promising as they were, these and other efforts represented just a drop in the bucket of restoration needs across the country. Along dozens of rivers, the cumulative effects of years of damaging withdrawals were still getting worse. At the Klamath River in northern California—once among the world's best steelhead streams—a massive fish kill occurred as a result of irrigators' upstream withdrawals. Water from a Bureau of Reclamation project had for years been diverted to irrigate pasture and crops in the upper Klamath Basin of Oregon, and for years, because of this and other problems, the downstream runs of salmon and steelhead had declined.[36] Other fish endemic to the upper river were endangered because of the low flows, and in the summer of 2001, the bureau was forced to reduce irrigation diversions in order to comply with the Endangered Species Act. In spite of $20 million in economic relief provided by Congress, irrigators responded with vitriolic protest, illegal opening of floodgates to their ditches, and personal appeals to the receptive administration of George W. Bush.

As a result, in 2002 the bureau and the U.S. Fish and Wildlife Service ignored the objections of agency biologists and reinstated full diversions to the farmers, dismissing the needs of commercial fishermen, downstream Indians, landowners in California, sport anglers, and river conservationists. Before the summer was over, 33,000 adult salmon had perished while trying to ascend the depleted Klamath to their ancestral spawning areas. The California Department of Fish and Game charged that high water temperatures stemming directly from low flows had allowed an epidemic of disease and the worst salmon kill ever in the West.[37] A suppressed report by the U.S. Geological Survey found that a restored level of fishing and tourism in the basin would exceed the economic value of the irrigated agriculture by a ratio of 8 to 1.[38] Furthermore, a study by the consulting firm ECONorthwest found that 63 percent of the water diverted from the Klamath for irrigation was inefficiently used owing to leaking ditches and other problems. Even so, the lopsided preference to the agricultural industry was sustained by the Bush administration, which continued the diversions in 2003. Conservation groups, downstream Indian tribes, and the state of California all took action to avert further losses, trying to buy land and water rights from upstream farmers who were willing to sell. Northern California congressman Mike Thompson introduced a bill to begin restoration, saying, "A poor water management policy has caused an environmental and economic catastrophe.''

THE LARGER CHANNEL OF LIFE

Biologists, hydrologists, and planners have long said that a river is more than water flowing in a channel. It includes the land along the river and the acreage that reaches back through valley-bottom lowlands to where the slope rises up above the influence of the river. This riverfront zone is called riparian land and includes the floodplain—the area likely to be covered when the water rises.

Riparian zones are the most important land for wildlife; some 70 percent of bird and mammal species are dependent on them in some areas for at least a part of their life cycle. This vegetated buffer is also critical to the stream itself, as trees or shrubs shade the water, stabilize the banks, and provide a nutrient base of leaves, insects, and other organic matter that falls into the current to become basic building blocks of freshwater ecosystems. The riparian zone includes much of our finest recreation land—waterfront in long pleasing strips of greenway within cities and also through the entire length of valleys.

In addition, riparian zones are vital to water quality—the riverbottom lowlands filter silt and purify runoff before it reaches the river. The volume of both groundwater and surface water also depend on the riparian area; here is where much of the runoff seeps into the water table to be stored and later released slowly in a way that benefits people and the entire ecosystem during droughts.

Floodplains accommodate the force of floods by allowing the water to spread out and slow down rather than rise higher and faster. This minimizes flood damage downstream. It also allows groundwater to recharge the subterranean reservoirs and provides habitat for hundreds of species along with spawning, rearing, and feeding areas for fish.

In short, riparian zones are among the most important of all lands for carrying out nature's basic functions on earth.[39] They are also among the most abused and threatened. By some estimates, 89 percent of the nation's riparian habitat has been lost or badly degraded.

For these reasons, the protection and restoration of riparian lands have become top priorities in the second generation of river conservation as people seek to protect whole river systems and not just the flowing water alone.

The most direct approach conservationists have taken is to simply buy the land and dedicate it to open space use. Public ownership can be justified here perhaps more than on any other type of property. Land trusts and conservancies across the United States have made acquisition of streamfronts a priority as they buy land or easements designed to prevent development. Their accomplishments are impressive, from the big scale of the Nature Conservancy, the Trust for Public Land, and the Conservation Fund, to the local efforts of several thousand groups such as the Southbury Land Trust in Connecticut, which in 2001 bought hundreds of acres of riverfront farmland and forest in the beautiful but developing valley of the Pomperaug River. Other successes in recent years included a plan to protect 100,000 acres of riparian land along Kentucky's Green River. This effort was enhanced by the federally funded Conservation Reserve Enhancement Program—a Clinton administration initiative that offered financial incentives for farmers to set aside ecologically valuable tracts. As of 2002, 2,000 acres along the Green River had been banked as open space in the initial part of this program.

In Alabama, the Nature Conservancy helped establish a new national wildlife refuge, protecting 3,500 acres along the biologically splendid Cahaba River in 2002. Nearby, in Mississippi, the final unprotected reach of the eighty-mile main stem of the Pascagoula River was acquired for open space.

In northern Maine and New Hampshire, the combined efforts of several conservancies and state programs protected tens of thousands of acres and hundreds of miles of river frontage by purchasing easements from industrial timber companies that were strapped for cash and beginning to liquidate cutover land for subdivisions.

States have also used land acquisition to protect riparian areas and water quality; Florida and California have extraordinarily successful programs. Using a tax on real estate transfers along with bond initiatives, Florida has bought hundreds of thousands of acres, focusing efforts on river frontage and wetlands including gems such as the Suwannee River through most of its 200-mile route to the Gulf of Mexico.[40] In California, voters over a twenty-year period passed a series of state bond initiatives totaling $21 billion for conservation purposes—much of it for land acquisition. One man—Jerry Meral of the California Planning and Conservation League—was the mastermind of many of these initiatives that secured key open space along rivers including the Sacramento, American, Merced, Eel, and Smith.

Specializing in riverfront land, the Western Rivers Conservancy, based in Portland, Oregon, bought critical frontage and then resold it to government agencies for management as protected open space. This small group safeguarded important reaches of the Snake River in Hells Canyon, Icicle Creek in the North Cascades of Washington, and the exquisite Chetco River canyon of the Siskiyou Mountains in southern Oregon.

Along the Hoh River of Washington, the group acquired large tracts from timber companies to begin restoration of one of the finest salmon rivers on the West Coast. Aiming to buy all the private property along the lower thirty miles of the river, the Western Rivers Conservancy sought to protect the entire watershed—from the summit of Mount Olympus to the ocean—as a safeguarded centerpiece of Olympic National Park. In this vision, the Hoh would become the best-protected river from source-to-ocean in America.

Another ambitious program of the Western Rivers Conservancy was to buy floodplains and restore them along the Willamette River. Flowing through the most heavily populated and farmed region of the state, the Willamette floods periodically with huge economic losses. According to hydrologic studies, restoration of 20,000 to 50,000 acres of floodplain could reduce flooding by 18 percent in downstream areas.[41] Using a similar approach with undisputed success, the Army Corps of Engineers had protected 8,500 acres of wetlands in the Charles River basin of Massachusetts at an acquisition cost of $10 million compared to $100 million that would have been needed for the same degree of flood protection by dams and levees. Acquisition along the Willamette proved to be difficult, but the Conservancy reclaimed much of the length of Oregon's Sandy River by buying land, retiring an old dam, and reinstating natural flows.

Related to these types of open-space ventures, a plethora of greenway corridors were enhanced for recreational use in towns and cities all across the United States in the 1980s and 1990s. While urban parks do not restore riverfronts as completely natural areas, they often prevent development and they can reclaim waterfronts from old industrial use. Most important, they introduce millions of Americans to the pleasures of experiencing a river firsthand. From Boise, Idaho, to Hartford, Connecticut; from the American River in Sacramento to the Chattahoochee in Atlanta, greenways have been at the core of many urban conservation efforts that recognize the intrinsic worth of rivers.[42]

Urban greenways have been at the popular fringe of efforts to protect riparian areas, but the role of local governments in floodplain management lay at the core. Floodplains are the most critical land for the biology and natural processes of the river and also the area incurring the greatest economic damage and human suffering during floods.

Concern about flood damage has typically focused on the 100-year floodplain—the riverbottom lands likely to be submerged at least once each hundred years. Some land, of course, floods almost every year, while other important floodplain land might flood only once every two hundred years. But the 100-year floodplain became a standard for defining flood-prone areas.

The courts have consistently backed open space zoning of these areas since the 1920s.[43] Even so, few municipal governments bothered to zone the floodplain until after the Hurricane Agnes Flood in the mid-Atlantic states in 1972—the most damaging flood in American history up to that time. In its wake, the federal flood insurance law was strengthened.

Most communities eventually enrolled in this program, which required municipalities to zone the floodplain to restrict new building and to require flood proofing of structures. Then landowners on the floodplain could buy federally subsidized flood insurance and secure federally insured mortgages, otherwise unavailable. In concept, the program provided an incentive to get communities to zone the riverfront for open space. In practice, loopholes prevented the zoning from being nearly as effective as it could be.[44] The program's most serious shortcoming was that it banned development only in the most hazardous zone where flood waters would be deepest and the current fastest. Beyond that, homes and other buildings were allowed provided they were "flood proofed"—built up on stilts or on fill so that the first-floor elevation was nominally above the 100-year flood level. Unfortunately, this policy caused even greater ecological damage to the floodplain because people then excavated large swaths of riparian habitat, disrupted the local flow, and piled up fill into large mounds to build their houses.

The program also had fiscal shortcomings, and in 1997 it ran at a $917 million deficit—essentially federally subsidized flood damage.[45] And, even with the insurance, disasters continued to be declared by presidents after every major flood; in the name of compassion for flood victims, the government still poured billions more dollars into development subsidies. Much of this federal aid was shortsightedly spent rebuilding in the same flood-prone places.

Even when local governments succeeded in adequately zoning the floodplain, they often failed in enforcement. In 1997, California incurred its most costly floods in history when 23,800 homes were destroyed and 120,000 people evacuated. Yet, at the same time, 58,000 new homes on floodplains were planned. Just weeks after the muddy waters receded, the city of Fresno approved eleven new houses along the San Joaquin River, and another developer proposed to build 360 flood-prone houses. In Sacramento, a developer persuaded the city council to let him "reclaim" the floodway by moving a levee closer to the river, thus aggravating dangers by giving the high water less room to spread out.[46] Not the least of problems, the nature of floods has been changed by building levees that constrict flows and force them higher, by urban development that paves-over land and prevents infiltration of rainwater, and by clear cutting and agricultural drainage that forces water off the land faster. As a result, 100-year floods are occurring with increasing frequency; one stretch of the Mississippi saw four 100-year floods in an eight-year period in the 1990s.

As a result of these weaknesses in the flood insurance program, people continued to build and rebuild on floodplains; indeed, 43 percent of the claims for damages under the insurance program were repeat claims from properties that were flooded again and again.[47] Relatively simple congressional reform could result in reduced flood damages, save public money, and protect open space in the flood zones—all goals sought by the original flood insurance legislation. But whenever reforms have been proposed, heavy lobbying by home building associations and chambers of commerce have killed the bills.[48]

In spite of $25 billion invested in federal attempts to control floods through dams and levee construction, annual damages from floods have only increased, tripling since 1951.[49] And beyond the costs of dams and levees, the federal government spent $5.6 billion per year on disaster relief during the twenty-five-year period from 1975 to 2000—most of it in response to flooding. Regardless of programs intended to prevent damage—in large measure a result of the false sense of security engendered by those programs—10 million homes remained in flood zones and more were being built there all the time.[50]

Following the record-breaking flood of 1993 along the Mississippi, Scott Faber of American Rivers directed a program of floodplain management reform. Also with leadership from the Association of State Floodplain Managers, a coalition lobbied heavily for improvements to the flood insurance program and they had some success. Important reforms allowed for relocation rather than rebuilding. Adding momentum to this initiative, a presidential committee chaired by General Gerald Galloway of the Army Corps of Engineers recommended a dramatic shift from structural to non-structural solutions such as relocation, to more effective controls on floodplain development, and to planning for flood hazards beyond the 100-year level—all echoing improvements advocated by Gilbert White thirty years before (see Chapter 7).

Reforms in the wake of the flood changed the flood insurance program a little, but changed the policies regarding the spending of public flood control funds more significantly. In perhaps the most important policy shift of its kind since widespread levee building was unleashed in the 1930s, Congress diverted money from levee reconstruction to open space protection and floodplain management. Instead of returning to flooded areas, people owning 8,000 homes and businesses—10 percent of those damaged in the Mississippi River flood—voluntarily chose to use disaster relief money to relocate. In addition, more than 50,000 acres were enrolled in federal easement programs to convert development or farmland to open space. The reform legislation also set aside $20 million annually from the proceeds of the federal flood insurance program specifically for relocation.[51]

In the wake of the 1997 California floods, Friends of the River likewise launched a program designed to improve state and local floodplain management policy. Both efforts were difficult to sustain because reform involves the nettlesome issue of land use on private property, and the ultimate resolution is often left to local government, readily influenced by developers. Support at the grassroots level was the essential remedy to this problem.

One might argue that riparian areas are just as important to the greater web of life as are wetlands—in fact they *are* wetlands. But river conservationists failed to garner the attention that wetlands did in the latter twentieth century, and they failed to create a scientific, public, or political movement to adequately protect riparian zones.

In spite of the difficulties, reforming the federal floodplain program, buying open space for the public along rivers, and supporting zoning at the local level had the potential to save taxpayers' money while protecting more streamfront than any other approach in the entire river conservation movement.

THE SCENT OF A RIVER

The salmon that emblematize healthy rivers fin their way upstream through a sense of smell. The particular chemistry of water differs depending on where it comes from, and the fish have an extraordinarily ability to single out the headwaters where their lives began. The acrid or rotten smells of pollution can overpower those subtle signals and interfere with the salmon's navigation to spawning grounds and with its goal of reproduction. And the odor of a river affects people's use of it as well. In the worst cases, the stench of a polluted stream can cause people to shun the water's edge and to abandon these lifelines of the continent to the status of liquid waste dumps.

Efforts to stop pollution of rivers reach back to the days when community leaders and citizens rallied to clean up messes left in the wake of early urbanization and industrialization in America. Though slow to recognize the problem, cities were forced to cope with pollution after catastrophes including the New York cholera outbreak of 1832. Some efforts were directed at river protection, such as demonstrations in Portland, Oregon, in 1938, when schoolchildren and the mayor carried signs saying, "The Youth of Portland Demand Clean Rivers."[52] But for the most part, early anti-pollution campaigns, including the Federal Water Pollution Control Act of 1948 and its many amendments, were rooted in concern for municipal water supplies and public health rather than for the rivers themselves.

In 1972—while dam fights were still being waged everywhere—the federal Clean Water Act brought a new focus on the importance of rivers. Streams everywhere were of paramount importance to secure safe drinking water, and this became the key argument to reverse the plague of pollution, but the law also established the goal of having clean rivers for other purposes. This landmark legislation called for all streams in the United States to meet swimming and fishing standards by 1985.[53]

With substantial and essential federal aid, local governments and industries took enormous strides as they faced new requirements to clean up their waste. Tax dollars were rationed out to towns and cities to help build necessary sewage plants. In the span of twenty years, thousands of communities upgraded or built their first treatment facilities, and many of the most polluted rivers were cleaned up. In New England, the Nashua, Merrimack, Concord, and Blackstone had run as lifeless sewers and outfalls of textile factories that dyed the streams a different color—red, green, orange—every day. In the 1970s and 1980s, those streams became clear again—pleasant amenities to the towns in which they flowed, even serving as renewed sources of drinking water in some cases. The Ohio River went from a polluted behemoth where even catfish and carp couldn't live to an odor-free (if not toxin-free) artery of the region, supporting pike and bass. The Willamette was transformed from a discharge pipe of Oregon's paper mills to an artery where salmon could again power their way up toward ancestral spawning beds.

But unfortunately, those gains, resulting largely from momentum of the 1970s, were far from complete.[54] At the turn of the new century, many rivers remained with illegal point sources of pollution coming from single pipes, such as the sewage plant at Westernport, Maryland, which dumped thick brown waste into the North Branch of the Potomac, and from single industries, such as the petrochemical plants lining the lower Mississippi for 150 relentless miles. Lacking enforcement of clean water laws, this grand culmination of America's greatest river became known as Cancer Alley.

But enough had been cleaned up that the reduction of point sources of pollution has been considered one of the great success stories in the environmental movement. An estimated 60 to 70 percent of the rivers were considered unsafe for swimming in 1972; because of the Clean Water Act, the percentage was cut to 39 by 2002.[55] Like the fight against unnecessary big dams, the cleanup of egregious water pollution marked a milestone in the environmental history of America.

To sustain these gains and to remedy the problems that remained became a new target of river conservationists as the big-dam era waned and attention turned to the second generation of problems that awaited. In 2000, the Environmental Protection Agency listed agriculture, hydrologic modifications, habitat degradation, urban runoff, forestry, and municipal sewage plants as the leading causes of pollution.[56] According to the EPA in 1994, sewage plants—for all the improvements—remained the second-most serious source of pollution, exceeded only by farm operations. Further, many of the problems that had been fixed by the Clean Water Act in the 1970s needed fixing again as equipment wore out, as facilities required upgrading, and—most important—as the population soared with many communities doubling or even tripling in size in the past few decades. The high cost of reinvestment may present an opportunity for "soft path" approaches—alternative means of cleaning waste and reducing stormwater problems by using natural filters such as floodplains, improving groundwater recharge, and cleaning waste through natural processes such as the filtration that wetlands afford.

Even where streams were cleaner than they had been, fish and shellfish often remained unsafe to eat because of persistent toxins residing in the silt. Posing even greater difficulties, every year thousands of new chemicals went untested for their effects on water. Because of exemptions for favored industries and small businesses, only about 340 of the mind-boggling 73,000 chemicals used in commerce were reported to federal regulating agencies.[57]

As a result, an epidemic of toxic wastes now replaces the stinking old sewage outfalls that motivated an earlier generation of pollution fighters. The outrage of Love Canal, which contaminated the homes of dozens of families with life-threatening fumes, brought the horrors of hazardous waste to the front page of American's newspapers in 1978. Whole fields full of drums of leaking toxic waste were discovered in Kentucky. Millions of gal-

lons of deadly wastes were being dumped through drain pipes linking a single gas station to the Susquehanna River in 1980.[58] In the Hudson—the
biological centerpiece of rivers in the Northeast—General Electric Corporation had released 1.3 million pounds of intensely toxic PCBs over a thirty-
year period up until 1977. The company resisted efforts to clean up the river
but in 2002 was finally ordered to dredge up some of the worst concentrations of toxins.[59] A train wreck spilled pesticides into the upper Sacramento
River in California and made a whole corridor of pristine river uninhabi-
table to fish and humans alike for weeks in 1991.

Showing clear evidence of the ripple effect that water pollution can
have, the rocket fuel perchlorate was found in nearly one-fifth of the lettuce
samples taken in a California survey in 2002. Some lettuce showed twenty
times the amount of toxin considered safe in drinking water. Known to
affect thyroid hormones and brain development, the chemical had not been
applied to the crops directly as a pesticide would be, but rather contaminated them through irrigation water; the entire river was polluted with it.
The likely source of this substance poisoning the food of millions of Americans was an upstream defense contractor or military base—facilities ironically proposed by the George W. Bush administration for exemption from
environmental laws under the auspices of "national security."[60]

The runaway use of agricultural pesticides contaminated fields, the
homes of farm workers, groundwater deposits, and rivers, especially in the
Midwest, South, and California. In spite of the awareness spawned by reve-
lations such as Rachel Carson's *Silent Spring*, the sales of pesticides doubled
from 1962 to 1992.[61] Nuclear waste has leaked into the Columbia River
from the Department of Energy's Hanford Nuclear Reservation in Washington, and radioactive contamination also threatens or infects the Snake
River of Idaho, the Savanna of Georgia and South Carolina, and the Rio
Puerco of New Mexico.[62]

Responding to public outrage over the worst pollutants—capable even
in minute doses of causing sickness, neurological damage, and death—
Congress passed the Superfund cleanup program in 1980, with large appropriations for the worst toxic dumps. Progress on this onerous cleanup task
has been painstakingly slow and expensive. Corruption involving favors to
industries plagued the effort during the Reagan administration when the
chief of the program was jailed. Crippling prospects further, the obligations
of private industry to clean up its own waste were reduced and slated for
elimination by the Republican Congress that took over in 1995. The corporations that had caused the toxic damage got off scot-free, and taxpayers
were left with the poisonous legacy and the bill.[63]

Meanwhile, the net of legitimate concern about toxic pollutants was growing wider. In *Our Stolen Future*, zoologist Theo Colborn revealed the potentially devastating effects of plastic residues as hormone disrupters that leak into our water supplies.[64] In *Living Downstream*, ecologist Sandra Steingraber pointed out shocking correlations between cancer and toxins in our drinking water.[65] Added to these concerns, the U.S. Geological Survey in 2000 found alarming concentrations of drug residues, cleansers, and personal-care products in treatment plant effluent and in streams. These chemicals are known to disrupt the hormones of wildlife and of people where water supplies are taken.[66]

Enormous tasks remain before society can finally come to grips with the problems of toxins in our water. Citizen groups formed where the problems became known, and national groups such as the Natural Resources Defense Council worked through the courts and Congress for tighter controls on chemical waste.

Plowing into the new era of river conservation at the turn of the twenty-first century, many groups recognized a fact that the Environmental Protection Agency had been stating for some time: 68 percent of our water pollution comes not from the point sources that had attracted so much attention in the past, but from polluted runoff emanating from large areas of land such as urban streets and farmed fields.[67] Agriculture was the largest single source by far, accounting for 48 percent of the total. Yet farmers enjoyed exemption from Clean Water Act requirements.

While most polluted runoff continued at record-breaking rates, some government programs helped farmers to curb the worst of the runoff coming from their land. For example, a state program in Wisconsin combined incentives for voluntary improvements with state requirements addressing agriculture.[68]

Feedlots were the worst agricultural problem, with tens of thousands of cattle crowded into concentrated pens, thousands of chickens jammed into single industrial barns, and 1,100 hogs crammed into one factory building, many of which might constitute a modern hog operation. Many single industrial animal operations polluted rivers with untreated waste equivalent to entire cities.[69] In the Southeast, pollution from flooded hog factories led to outbreaks of *Pfiesteria*, a one-celled dinoflagellate that caused massive fish kills and neurological damage to people—not from drinking the water but simply from breathing too much air near the water's edge.[70] Six thousand feedlots operated nationwide in 1997, but only one-fourth of them came under state purview for water quality. To improve this situation, the Clinton administration proposed feedlot regulations, but the Bush administration promptly curbed this effort in 2002 and a year later declared administrative changes in the Clean Water Act that exempted feedlots on small headwater streams—just the kind of place where pollution did the most damage.

Even below feedlots, river water often becomes drinking water, and the cumulative effects of pollution escaping the attention of Clean Water Act enforcers have very real health effects. In 1993, 400,000 people in Milwaukee became sick and a hundred died from drinking water contaminated with cryptosporidium, a parasite found in polluted water. According to the Center for Disease Control, 100,000 Americans each year drank water bearing known carcinogens and 900,000 became ill from their water supply. In 1995, more than 45 million Americans drank water contaminated with fecal matter, parasites, toxic chemicals, pesticides, disease-causing microbes, lead, or other pollutants at levels exceeding federal health standards.[71] Losing trust in the government systems intended to serve them, Americans in the 1990s spent $2 billion a year on bottled water and another $1 billion on water filters. Headwater reaches of some of our finest rivers are now threatened by withdrawals being made by the bottled water companies. The expensive, continuing, private investment in "pure" drinking water would not be necessary if pollution were stopped in our rivers and groundwater.

The Congressional Budget Office in 2002 estimated that up to $402 billion were needed over the next two decades to upgrade and repair public water systems—money that was not available because of political influence for other priorities.[72]

While the federal government did not take on the role of fixing drinking water problems, it did require the nation's 55,000 water companies and utilities to report on their water quality to 150 million consumers—perhaps the largest public notification program about water ever conducted.

Whether or not the consumers would do anything with the information was another question, however, surveys contracted by American Rivers found that by a wide margin people's greatest concern regarding rivers was the purity of their drinking water. This realization led river conservationists to work harder at explaining the connection between healthy streams and clean tap water to the public.[73] Former American Rivers director Kevin Coyle summarized, "Some people tend to trivialize what we are about, but what we are about is survival."

With 1987 amendments to the Clean Water Act, the federal approach went from outright grants to pay for sewage treatment plants in towns and cities across America to a revolving loan program. With it, the federal role, including requirements linking the grants to the National Environmental Policy Act, were weakened. States assumed more control, resulting in more of the money going to areas of potential growth. Many of the new sewage plants and lines thus accelerated suburban sprawl. Also in 1987, the federal law began to regulate the problems of stormwater runoff—rainfall that frequently overflowed sewers and resulted in uncontrollable pollution. For some years to come, cities across America would be grappling with the difficult challenge of separating stormwater from their sewage waste.

The original Clean Water Act also called for a policy of nondegradation of waters that are still exceptionally clean. With so much money and attention directed to cleaning up pollution problems after they surface, one might expect that precautions would be taken to avoid new pollution and to safeguard streams that had managed to stay clean so far. But that wasn't the case. State standards under the Clean Water Act typically allow a certain amount of pollution to occur under complex formulas involving "total maximum daily loads" of effluent. To effectively keep unspoiled streams pristine, a special designation was required, and the Clean Water Act called for this where water exceeded the standards for normal fishing and swimming.[74] But remarkably little has been done in this regard. "Outstanding" waters designation for streams as superlative as the headwater creeks of the Salmon River was resisted and stopped by the Idaho legislature. Although some states such as Pennsylvania tried to set up workable programs for nondegradation as early as the mid-1970s, inadequate measures were taken to assure that most of the cleanest streams will stay that way. The protection of outstanding waters remains one of the unrealized goals of the Clean Water Act.

River conservationists responded to seemingly intractable problems in the water quality arena with several approaches. Perhaps most important, they recognized that states had eagerly snatched up enforcement responsibilities under the federal Clean Water Act—the states wanted to call the shots on standards that were established and—even more important—on when the law was enforced and how. But then the states failed to do their job. Surveys by the National Wildlife Federation and River Network as well as the Environmental Protection Agency showed an appalling lack of enforcement.[75] Some states such as Texas, Idaho, and Michigan allowed industries the prerogative of voluntary compliance and self-monitoring. Furthermore, and in an outrage to democratic process, those industries could hide the results of their sampling from the public.[76]

To foster citizen action that pushes the states to do their job, River Network in 2000 launched a program of training local leaders about the Clean Water Act. Project director Gayle Killam aimed to place a vanguard of citizen activists in the field where they could leverage state agencies to require compliance with the law.[77]

River Network and other groups also conducted programs to train citizens in water monitoring so that they could take samples, analyze their streams, and determine what the problems were. Thus equipped, they could appeal for action by state enforcement agencies. Or they could sue the polluters themselves. Nationwide, the Waterkeepers Alliance promoted "riverkeeper" or "waterkeeper" organizations to take aggressive action documenting pollution and pressing for enforcement through legal action.[78]

Other groups concerned about water quality focused on watershed planning and restoration, discussed in the next chapter. Conscientious groups continued to bring lawsuits that required agencies and polluters to comply with clean water laws. The Pennsylvania Environmental Defense Foundation, for example, sued polluters and also brought agencies together to reclaim Babb Creek—a stream in the north-central highlands of the state that had been sterilized by acid mine drainage for many decades. In these ways and others, a broad base of citizen conservationists pushed for widespread cleanup of waters as the river conservation movement adapted to the complicated demands of a new century.

12

RIVERS IN THE
TWENTY-FIRST CENTURY

As awareness and interest in rivers grew, action spread from the isolated battles—one dam here, another one there—to the more diffuse work of protecting vital river functions in flow, habitat, and quality. The fiery intensity of the anti-dam groups faded along with some of the most urgent threats to rivers that had motivated so many, but a steadier involvement, spread over more rivers, now grew with people working for long-term stewardship of their streams. The greatest change in the river conservation movement through the 1980s and 1990s was that people organized around their whole river and not just around one specific threat to it.

AMERICAN RIVERS AND THE
ENDANGERED RIVERS LIST

Thirty years after its founding, American Rivers had grown from the small nerve center of lobbying in the nation's capital—just Bill Painter in 1973—to an organization with a staff of fifty, a board of thirty-three, and an impressive scientific and technical advisory committee drawn from the country's finest experts. The main office remained in Washington with ready access to the Capitol, but ten field offices had also been opened by 2000.

As the organization grew, its original purpose of adding rivers to the national wild and scenic rivers system and fighting dam proposals evolved with new and far-reaching goals. In 1992, the group aimed to enroll at least

2 percent of America's river miles in some form of secure protection, to restore degraded rivers and river systems, to conduct needed research, and to educate the public about threats and values. In keeping with a broadened view of river conservation, priorities embraced not only wild and scenic designation but also hydropower policy reform, floodplain management, endangered species, instream flow reservations, clean water protection, and urban rivers enhancement.[1] With a slightly different slant in 1997, the group set goals of protecting wild rivers, restoring hometown rivers, and repairing large rivers.[2] Among these goals in 2002, the group sought to shape the growing rivers movement into a powerful force for protection.

After realizing the tremendous media opportunity that had resulted from naming the Tuolumne as America's "most endangered river" in 1984, and after conferring this status to the Penobscot in 1985 and then to the Kings, where activists fully realized the impact of the designation as an anchor for publicity, the group began listing the ten most endangered rivers of America in 1986. Specific rivers were selected because of imminent and serious threats, but regional representation was also considered, and the group picked rivers where the additional attention could help to accomplish something. From a simple discussion among staff and with minor involvement by the board, the listing grew to a process reaching out to several thousand groups nationwide. Media coverage blossomed to include hundreds of newspapers, radio, and television, with two hundred stories running on the day of the list's release in 2003. Thanks largely to the endangered rivers list, this relatively small organization ranked fourth in media coverage among all environmental groups.

The prototype for the list could have been *Disasters in Water Development*, published by the Environmental Policy Center and American Rivers Conservation Council in 1973—an outraging list of wasteful dams and other federal projects that the group had targeted at the height of the dam-fighting era. Now as a media magnet each year, the most-endangered list soon went beyond the residual dam fights to include the broad sweep of issues from urban sprawl to toxic cleanup, hydroelectric relicensing, and runoff from feedlots. Throughout the years when a "most endangered" river was selected, six of them were threatened by new dams, ten suffered from flow patterns below federal dams, and three were imperiled by pollution from a mine (this was the same river, three years in a row—the Clark's Fork of the Yellowstone). Unlike the 1986 list, which was still entirely filled with dam threats, the 2002 list of eleven rivers included problems of flow regime below dams at two rivers, diversions at three rivers, pollution at two rivers, channelization and wetlands loss at two rivers, a new dam for water supply at one river, and logging with road construction at one. In 2003, half the rivers on the list were threatened by withdrawals owing to water shortages. The list reflected the pulse of the river conservation movement and could be seen as an indicator of the broadening priorities.

Former American Rivers president Kevin Coyle reflected, "Having lost the need for focus on emotionally charged damfights, the river conservation movement also lost the clearcut public message it had thrived on for many years." This message—that an irreplaceable and invaluable resource would be lost for no good reason and at horrible public cost in tax dollars as well as heritage values—was broadened through the 1980s and 1990s and the most endangered rivers list was an effective tool for doing this. The messages now focused on the need for stewardship, the responsibility of hydropower developers to fix some of the public damage they had caused while seeking private gain, and the economics of broad-based river conservation such as watershed reforms needed for the very existence of the salmon fishing industry.

While perception of the Army Corps of Engineers as a major threat to rivers faded along with the big dam fights, the 2002 endangered rivers list revealed that the corps had remained the chief problem to 60 percent of the rivers listed over the years. Though big proposed dams seldom appeared on the list, the corps' new schemes to channelize rivers, drain wetlands, alter flows, build levees, and, in some cases, construct new smaller dams routinely surfaced. Unfortunately the agency emerged from the 1970s era of reform with many of its old shortcomings intact. In 2000, the Army Inspector General found that the corps had deliberately manipulated data in an effort to justify a $1.2 billion expansion of locks on the upper Mississippi—an endless continuation of the fight over Lock and Dam 26 discussed in Chapter 7. With a report that could well have been written thirty years before, two panels of the National Academy of Sciences concluded that the corps still had an institutional bias for building large construction projects and that its planning process lacked environmental safeguards. In 2002, the academy called for an independent review process for corps proposals. Although the really large developments getting big headlines were not evident, the corps still had 1,400 projects to build, many of dubious value. Some congressional representatives happily subscribed to pork-barrel politics in the old style, but others pushed for an independent review of corps projects. Five bills were introduced to do this in 2002. None was passed, but neither was the biannual water resources development bill—a victim of its proponents' unwillingness to include reforms as part of the package.[3] As always, the condition of rivers was linked to the condition of politics.

THE FLOW OF PRESIDENTIAL INFLUENCE

The effect of alternating presidential administrations during the dam-building era had been profound, as we saw in the opening of Chapter 8. With the new generation of river concerns, the influence of the chief executive would—like the threats to rivers themselves—be less apparently dramatic but no less important to the long-term fate of waterways.

Jimmy Carter was the last president to deliberately take a high-profile role in policies and programs affecting rivers as he battled to cut construction of wasteful new dams and canals. He lost some important battles but succeeded in winning many and halted the momentum that had characterized pork-barrel water development since before the New Deal (see Chapter 8). Carter's involvement marked a profound turning point in the federal role regarding rivers.

Presidents Ronald Reagan and George H. W. Bush, on the other hand, sought to undercut protection programs or to simply neglect the fate of waterways. Though he allowed military spending and the national deficit to soar to unprecedented levels (until the George W. Bush administration), Reagan cut domestic spending and actually upgraded Carter's requirements for cost sharing of federal projects, nearly turning off the faucet of new starts. But the Reagan administration and that of George H. W. Bush both undermined other aspects of river conservation. They restricted funding to the Environmental Protection Agency, cut the ability of federal agencies to enforce regulations, unleashed widespread clearcutting on national forest land, perpetuated mining under the antiquated Mining Law of 1872, and thwarted any effort to reform subsidized grazing on public property throughout the West—all contributing to the long-term decline of rivers.[4]

Bill Clinton then presided over path-breaking reforms, with Vice President Al Gore leading the administration toward important decisions about the environment. The Northwest Forest Plan limited logging in many old-growth groves along salmon-spawning streams. Rivers within the enormous Tongass National Forest of Alaska were likewise protected from logging and siltation damage. Clinton's Forest Service Chief Mike Dombeck instituted history-making reform in 1999 by placing most roadless areas in national forests off limits to new road construction; in one action, he protected vast acreage and hundreds of streams from destructive logging. Dombeck's initiative ranked as one of the greatest single land and water protection measures ever established in America.

Daniel Beard, who had worked for years as Congressman George Miller's staff pushing legislative reforms to stop wasteful water projects, became

Clinton's commissioner of the Bureau of Reclamation in the early 1990s. Working under Interior Secretary Bruce Babbitt, Beard presided over the bureau's most resounding shift from dam builder to water manager.

In budget battles with the Republican Congress that was elected in 1994, Clinton held firm on spending for Environmental Protection Agency water programs (to disband federal enforcement was part of the "contract with America" that the Republican Congress embraced). Clinton stared down congressional leaders in a monumental budget standoff and kept most of the clean water money intact.

The administration also adopted a Clean Water Action Plan, which gave attention and funding to water quality with a priority unseen in many years.[5] Funding for acquisition and protection of riparian areas was passed in an effort to improve the quality of water flowing from farmland. This program targeted troublesome basins such as the Chesapeake Bay and its chief source, the Susquehanna River. Important funding was restored to the Land and Water Conservation Fund, which used revenues from offshore oil drilling to pay for open space acquisition. This program had been languishing under previous administrations that shunted the earmarked funds elsewhere.

But in spite of these efforts to grapple with pollution, the water quality of the nation's rivers began to decline—the most serious deterioration since the Clean Water Act had been passed. This reversal reflected a long-term trend in relative funding cuts and in compromised enforcement ever since the Reagan administration. The reversal was also the result of little-discussed population growth. Owing to eight-fold immigration increases compared to the 1924–1965 period, population soared with no let-up, even after the World War II baby boom had ended. Immigration, not counting an estimated 8 million illegal immigrants in the country, increased from 6 million in the 1970s, to 7 million in the 1980s, to 11 million in the 1990s. Birth rates among immigrants were far higher than among the native-born population—three children per family for Latinos versus 1.8 for non-Hispanic whites—causing the rate of population increase to accelerate even further.[6] The new population explosion exceeded all projections by wide margins. Water facilities in many parts of the country were overstrained by the new numbers and by unbridled consumption of water as long-term urban residents sold their houses to the new arrivals and moved out to distant suburbs and sprawling cities such as Phoenix, Orlando, Sacramento, and Austin. The hard-earned infrastructure improvements of the 1970s became inadequate and obsolete in hundreds of fast-growing communities, and with an increasing population of relatively poor immigrants, the older cities lacked the money to upgrade water facilities.

Reflecting the increased population and political pressures, the Environmental Protection Agency's ten-year assessment of water quality in 2000 showed either no improvement or deterioration.[7] In estuaries—the destination of virtually all rivers—conditions worsened in 13 percent of the locations between 1996 and 2000; from 1991 to 2001 the number of beach closings and pollution advisories grew six-fold.[8] The number of river miles placed under pollution warnings grew from 2 percent in 1993 to 14 percent in 2001.

As described in Chapter 11, a key problem in failing to meet the water quality challenge was lax enforcement by the states, nearly all of which had chosen to take over responsibilities for enforcing the Clean Water Act. During the Clinton administration, the Environmental Protection Agency was critical of the downward trend and made some effort at better enforcement, but was increasingly hamstrung by Congress after 1994.[9]

The Clinton administration also established a system of American Heritage Rivers. This designation required no congressional approval and carried no new requirements or regulations. With the goals of cultural and historic preservation, economic development, and natural resources conservation, the program sought to heighten awareness of selected rivers in populated regions and to encourage voluntary protection. An outpouring of support came from sponsors at 126 rivers. These were narrowed to fourteen that enjoyed broad-based backing and lacked opposition by local congressional representatives. Designations included the Blackstone and Woonasquatucket, which flowed in Massachusetts and Rhode Island; the Cuyahoga in Ohio; the Hanalei in Hawaii; the New in North Carolina, Virginia, and West Virginia; the St. Johns in Florida; the Susquehanna and Lackawanna in northern Pennsylvania; the Willamette in Oregon; the Detroit in Michigan; the Connecticut in Connecticut, Massachusetts, and New Hampshire; the Hudson in New York; the Rio Grande in New Mexico and Texas; and the Potomac in Virginia, Maryland, the District of Columbia, and West Virginia. Heritage status was intended to increase the chances of federal funding for programs and of coordinated attention by agencies that deal with rivers, but success depended mainly on the initiative and effectiveness of people within the local areas in launching their own efforts.

The relative calm that had surrounded presidential politics regarding rivers since the demise of the big-dam era abruptly ended when George W. Bush assumed the presidency in 2001. Soon after taking office, he pushed for oil drilling in the Arctic National Wildlife Refuge, which had the potential to harm dozens of pristine rivers including the Canning, one of the largest in the Arctic.

The Environmental Protection Agency had estimated that without increases in funding and enforcement, pollution loads from sewage by the year 2025 would be as bad as they were in 1968—the all-time worst. In spite of this, and affecting the fate of rivers everywhere, Bush further diminished enforcement for air and water pollution.[10] The EPA's ability to monitor and leverage states to do their job of enforcing clean water rules was cut, even though studies indicated that state enforcement was already a sham. Cases referred by the EPA for criminal prosecution decreased by 20 percent in Bush's first year in office. Industrial violators were paying 64 percent less in fines than they had during the Clinton administration.[11] Enforcement money was cut in 2003 despite the fact that nearly a third of the largest industries and municipal treatment plants were in serious violation of Clean Water Act requirements at least once in 2000 or 2001, according to EPA documents obtained under the Freedom of Information Act by the U.S. Public Interest Research Group. Based on an internal EPA assessment, the *New York Times* reported that only a small fraction of Clean Water Act violators faced enforcement attempts, and when formal actions were taken, fewer than half resulted in fines, and when fines were charged, they averaged less than $6,000.[12] Under the guise of the "war on terrorism," the agency reported that 40 percent of its pollution enforcement staff would be transferred to nonenforcement "security" tasks.[13]

Ever since the resounding congressional override of President Nixon's veto of the 1972 Clean Water Act, no president had been willing to blatantly undercut that popular legislation. But now the Bush administration moved to weaken some of the act's most important provisions. Bush and the Republican Congress in 2003 sought to exempt headwater streams—up to 60 percent of America's waterways—from Clean Water Act protections. The administration moved to minimize the federal role in protecting wetlands, to weaken requirements for sewage treatment, to make monitoring and compliance with water quality rules voluntary for industries, and to allow the dumping of solid wastes such as mining overburden directly into waterways.[14] This last provision was designed to permit mountaintop removal—the phenomenally destructive strip mining technique that decapitates entire mountaintops—up to 800 vertical feet—and dumps them over the side, hopelessly obliterating not only the life-filled streams of Appalachia but entire valleys such as Spruce Creek in the Coal River watershed of West Virginia.[15]

Regulation of feedlots had been started by the Clinton administration, but the Bush Environmental Protection Agency undercut the proposed rules by weakening groundwater controls, allowing states to exempt factory farms from the Clean Water Act, and allowing for voluntary compliance.[16]

The undermining of the clean water program extended to letting the computer system designed to track industrial polluters' permits fall into gross disrepair; tens of thousands of pollution sources failed to be listed in the database. Peter Gleick, director of a water research center called the Pacific Institute said, "The problem is more than just a failure to collect and manage information on polluters, or to enforce compliance with pollution permits that have been issued. It is a failure of the administration to stop the thousands of polluters without permits."[17]

When the courts wouldn't let Bush roll back the roadless area protections that Mike Dombeck had put in place for the national forests, the Republican Congress tried to pass riders as amendments to unrelated bills to undercut the Clinton-era policy. The Bush administration sought to reopen old-growth logging along salmon streams in the Northwest and Alaska under the guise of "forest health." It exempted oil and gas producers from stormwater pollution permits in 2003.

Though "states' rights" rather than "federal control" was the mantra of the conservative platform, a bill in the Republican Senate during this era sought to ban states from setting efficiency standards for appliances; the states' rights ideology proved to offer no contest for the power of vested interests in the industrial sector. Having great significance for rivers, the efficiency standards had been a cornerstone of successful efforts such as those of the Northwest Power Planning Council in reducing the rate of electric demand and thereby reducing the threats to dam more rivers for hydropower.

Bush rescinded a Clinton-era rule that had given the Department of the Interior the ability to deny mining permits on federal land. "Substantial irreparable harm" to the environment or to sacred Indian sites was no longer justification to deny a mining company virtually free access to mine public property any way they wanted.

Unlike James Watt in the Reagan administration, Bush avoided criticizing environmental goals directly but undermined them by masking issues under banners of better business, individual freedom, or national security and by routinely saying that he supported measures that he then promptly cut in the budget. Adding a whole new absurdity to the word "spin," Bush recognized the anniversary of the Clean Water Act by saying, "I encourage Americans to join me in renewing our commitment to protecting the environment and leaving our children and grandchildren with a legacy of clean water."[18] Likewise, Bush's "clear skies" proposal for air quality allowed three times the amount of mercury and 50 percent more sulfur to be released while doing nothing to reduce carbon dioxide—the main source of global warming. The weakened controls on smokestack emissions at power plants promised to increase the plague of acid rain that was causing brook trout streams in the East to become barren.[19]

With unprecedented hostility against the environment, the administration enacted 100 different measures to weaken environmental protection in its first two years in office.[20]

The reasons for Bush's actions were easily seen: development and mining interests benefiting from relaxed rules and weakened wetlands regulation contributed $18 million to the Bush–Cheney campaign and the Republican National Committee in the 2000 and 2002 election cycles.[21] Agribusiness gave another $19 million. The oil industry, in which Bush and Vice President Cheney had been chief executives, contributed additional money. While river conservation had always been a political issue, the raw power of campaign contributions had never so clearly determined the fate and final outcome of American waters and rivers everywhere.

In the midst of this assault, the *New York Times* conducted a poll and found that 62 percent of the citizens were worried about Bush administration environmental policies and thought that the federal government should be doing more to protect the environment. Only 7 percent said less should be done.

Against this shifting backdrop of presidential politics, the movement to conserve rivers responded with innovative approaches and traditional strategies.

STRUGGLING FOR VIABILITY: THE NATIONAL WILD AND SCENIC RIVERS SYSTEM

The nation's flagship program for protecting its most outstanding natural rivers reached its zenith during the Carter administration (see Chapter 6). As the fundamental reason for the founding of the American Rivers Conservation Council (later changed to American Rivers), the national wild and scenic rivers system was regarded as the primary way to prevent destructive dams, channelization, and other development that required federal money or permits.

After notable successes through 1980, the system ran onto a reef of political opposition beginning with the Reagan administration when Interior Secretary James Watt vetoed agency proposals and required that rivers not only be "eligible" for federal protection by nature of their quality but also "suitable," meaning politically acceptable without compromising development goals.

Shortchanging the wild and scenic rivers system occurred within a larger context of government and society beginning in the Reagan era. Public values were trivialized and openly attacked at the uppermost levels of American power, including the president himself, while personal property rights and privatism were glorified in the rhetoric of Republican politics and talk-show radio. In this way and others, the Reagan era induced widespread hostility to government in general and to federal involvement in particular. Attitudes that had earlier been regarded as blatantly selfish or isolationist were now popularized as profitable and as the triumph of individual liberty. Growing tired of the screeds heaped on them by antigovernment ideologues, dedicated public servants retired early. The so-called wise use movement became a highly organized effort to oppose public land protection and any kind of land use controls. With carefully crafted messages touting individual freedom and opposing big government, and with heavy funding from resource extraction industries, this effort accumulated force through the 1980s. Then it gained real national traction in the 1990s as politics shifted to the right.[22] As a result of these and other dynamics, new efforts to protect rivers in the wild and scenic rivers system became stalled and many were abandoned.[23]

However, the wild and scenic program described in Chapter 6 did not die. At least in a limited way, it was renewed again and again against great odds.

The resistance of the Republican administration and Senate was overcome in 1984 when key Republican Senators Pete Wilson of California and Mark Hatfield of Oregon supported wild and scenic designation of the Tuolumne River in California and the Illinois in Oregon.

In 1986, after years of debate and effort by Chris Brown, the leader of American Rivers, and others, the Cache la Poudre became the first stream to be nationally designated in Colorado, protecting a whitewater reach threatened by a dam. Also that year, legislation designating the Columbia Gorge as a national scenic area included parts of the White Salmon and Klickitat Rivers in Washington as wild and scenic. Short sections of Black Creek in Mississippi and Saline Bayou in Louisiana became the first southern blackwater streams in the system, and designation saved a short section of the Horsepasture River in North Carolina from a hydroelectric diversion.

In 1987, Friends of the River and local groups succeeded in gaining protection for three of the most remarkable rivers ever to be added to the system: the Kings, Merced, and Kern, covered in Chapter 11. Each had been explicitly endangered by a dam proposal, proving that the wild and scenic designation was still an effective tool to counter threats.

With support from the powerful Republican Senator Mark Hatfield in 1988, an omnibus bill designated sections of forty-four rivers plus nine tributaries in Oregon—most of them on federal land managed by the Forest Service or Bureau of Land Management.

To cope with the political difficulties of the "wise use" movement, a strategy emphasizing local citizen involvement in wild and scenic rivers was pioneered by National Park Service planners Phil Huffman, Drew Parkin, and Jamie Fosburgh in New England. Painstaking care was taken to inform local residents about river protection proposals and to thoroughly air the concerns that anyone brought to the table. This approach was used effectively on the Farmington River in Connecticut, where core groups of local citizens wanted river protection and were willing to engage in the lengthy public process to gain local government and citizen support. Similar approaches were then used on other northeastern rivers. New England, with conservative political roots but an ethic of public responsibility as well, became a new center of river conservation activity.

Here and elsewhere, additional rivers were added to the wild and scenic system—streams as small as the Middle Fork Vermilion in Illinois, as wild as the Clark's Fork of the Yellowstone in Wyoming, and as unlikely as the Niobrara in Nebraska—a ranch-banked lifeline of the Great Plains. The Allegheny had been supported by Pennsylvania Congressman John Saylor at the outset of the original wild and scenic legislation but had been repeatedly passed over. Finally gaining support from the local congressman, it was designated in 1992. Also in Pennsylvania, the Clarion had been too polluted when it was first studied for the system in the 1970s, but after cleanup of pulp mill waste in Johnsonburg and abatement of mine acid, it was designated, canceling the threat of St. Petersburg Dam.

Following the Oregon model of naming a whole group of public-land rivers at once, eight streams, mainly in national forests, were designated in Arkansas in 1992. Another twenty-two national forest rivers, including branches and tributaries, were protected that year in Michigan. At a slower pace through the following ten years from 1992 through 2002, nineteen new rivers were designated and additions were made to four others. Six of these followed the Farmington model of intensive public involvement before designation and became known collectively as the Partnership Wild and Scenic Rivers.

The management of designated national wild and scenic rivers varied widely throughout the thirty-five-year history of the system. Many of the most popular western rivers were well managed by federal agency professionals seeking to do the best job possible. Other rivers were all but ignored. The magnificent system of national rivers in northern California, officially under state management, were said to be "self-administering" by state officials. The rivers were essentially cared for by federal land managers—many of the streams flowed within national forests. In the Southeast, the New became the first river added to American Rivers' Most Endangered Rivers list *after* designation as a national wild and scenic river. Rampant real estate development had followed in the aftermath of the Blue Ridge hydropower dam controversy covered in Chapter 5. One of the jewels of the Northeast, the Allagash was treated shoddily by the state of Maine, which allowed a dam to be rebuilt, roads to be expanded, and clearcuts to encroach on the river corridor.[24]

Perhaps just as important as the rivers that were actually designated, many of the best streams on federal land benefited from an enormously prescient action dating to the Carter administration. A Nationwide Rivers Inventory had been started then and was finally completed in 1982, with updates in 1993 and 1996.[25] In all, National Park Service planners found that 69,000 miles in 2,600 river segments still flowed with superlative qualities that made them potentially eligible for national wild and scenic protection. An executive order by President Carter had directed federal agencies to manage these and other qualifying rivers as if they were protected in the wild and scenic system. This shield against damage was to remain in place unless the agencies drew up plans that assigned other uses to the rivers. The directive was only administrative—subject to varying execution and to weakening with presidential politics—but it remained an effective tool, giving many miles of streams a meaningful if not permanent degree of protection.[26] In all, some 1,000 river segments covering 10,000 miles were affected in this long-term holding pattern that benefited the rivers.

In the late 1990s, the National Park Service's John Haubert, who had been involved with the national wild and scenic rivers program almost since its inception, summed up what it took to designate a new national wild and scenic river: the public must be aware of a real threat such as a proposed dam or diversion; grassroots support needed to be strong; and the local congressional representative had to be supportive.

Some rivers made it through the increasingly difficult maze of political resistance but, ironically, the end of the big-dam era also meant that incentives for a proactive stand to save rivers receded as well. Without the threat of damming, the urgency seemed to be gone, and people had less interest in federal designation aimed at protecting the status quo of rural character or wildness. River conservationists still argued that, right then—when the push for development was weak—was the opportune time to assure long-term protection of a river by gaining wild and scenic designation. But the general public remained unimpressed by the need to plan ahead or to take distant threats seriously. In general, when we quit building big wasteful dams we also quit enlisting the federal government to save rivers from additional dams in the future.

While resistance from landowners had increased and the perception of need had been dampened, river conservation leaders themselves recognized the limitations of the wild and scenic act and began to pursue a broader agenda of protecting rivers all over the United States. After all, most of the country's streams flowed through private land, and the act was relatively ineffective in dealing with problems there. The wild and scenic act's focus on "outstandingly remarkable" rivers left many worthy waterways out—places that River Network founder Phil Wallin fondly called the "outstandingly common" rivers in America. As a practical and legal matter, the act focused on single reaches of river at a time and on narrow corridors along those rivers. However, ecological thought and a growing awareness of watershed-wide issues increasingly pointed toward solving problems at a much grander geographic level.

Wild and scenic status normally required an act of Congress, and two acts of Congress if the stream was first named a "study" river. Even in good times, all of that political capital couldn't possibly be arranged for all the rivers deserving attention, so people seeking to make a difference began to look harder at other options. None of the above shortcomings obviated the need or the benefit of enrolling rivers in the wild and scenic system, but they all led conservation groups to work with other strategies.[27]

Less ambitious types of designations began to be considered. American Rivers proposed a national river registry in 1992 to encourage protection of rivers flowing through private land while avoiding regulatory issues. The Pacific Rivers Council in 1993 recommended a national watershed registry to promote stewardship at the watershed level. The American Heritage Rivers Initiative was conceived in the same broadening spirit but focused on hometown rivers where many people lived, and the program sought to improve riverfront communities. Among all the proposals, this was the one that gained administrative backing during the Clinton years. But facing increasing difficulty in the federal political arena, and realizing that the existing tools for river conservation were underused, legislation for new approaches was not pursued.

In the 1990s, the growth of the national wild and scenic rivers system slowed considerably, but it remained a viable program. Out in front of the rest of the country, Friends of the River in 2002 helped Senator Barbara Boxer draft a bill to designate twenty-two California rivers in the wild and scenic system along with dozens of new wilderness areas. In 2003, it appeared that actual designation might be accomplished by smaller, more localized bills where political support was the greatest.

While devoting most of its energy to other aspects of conservation such as the management of dams on the Missouri and Columbia Rivers, dam removal, restoration of salmon habitat, improved water quality from feedlots and polluted runoff, and increased stewardship of urban rivers, American Rivers still maintained a wild and scenic rivers program. The group continued to lobby to designate streams where political support could be found and, increasingly, to defend designated rivers from political attacks.

WHOLE WATERSHEDS

Although the protection of premier sections of streams through the national wild and scenic rivers system received less attention, involvement soared in the broadest possible approach—the care of whole watersheds.

A watershed is all the land that drains into a particular stream. It's the same as a river basin, but the word usually refers to a smaller stream.

The movement to address whole watersheds grew out of the awareness that, as John Muir said 100 years ago, everything is connected: "Whenever we try to pick out anything by itself, we find it hitched to everything else in the universe." Facing the challenges of the second generation of river conservation—problems of flow, riparian habitat, and water quality—it didn't take people long to realize that they had to address activities that occurred far from the rivers themselves. Flows, for example, are depleted not only by direct diversions from dams upstream but also by suburbanization, which paves over large acreages and causes water to run off too fast, thereby leaving little to soak into the ground for a slow release that extends into the dry season. Logging in the headwaters likewise affects the flow in the river many miles away because it hastens flood runoff, leaves less water for dry seasons, raises water temperatures by allowing more sunlight to hit the ground, and increases the flow of silt even far below the clearcuts.[28] Riparian habitat is destroyed by development that might be linked to the extension of a road or a sewer line coming from the next community or the next county. With the awareness that polluted runoff accounted for 68 percent of the total water pollution, activists realized that the silt and pesticides coming from farms accounted for the worst contamination. The farms might lie at the riverbank or they might lie at the top of the mountain.

Awareness of these connections led conservationists to larger and larger circles of influence around their rivers, and eventually they realized that entire watersheds needed attention. Protecting one segment of a river was an effort doomed to at least some degree of failure because of effects from far away, whether they were altered flows, encroaching development, soil disturbance, or acid rain that often began miles away from even the most distant watershed boundary. In this case, even the *wind*shed affected the health of the river.

There was nothing really novel about the watershed approach. The idea went back to John Wesley Powell, the intrepid explorer of the Colorado River in the mid-1800s and an advocate of basinwide planning in the West.[29] Progressive thinking before and during the New Deal, spurred by luminaries such as Benton MacKay and Arthur E. Morgan, also emphasized the importance of watershed-based planning.[30] The Soil Conservation Service and its related Soil and Water Conservation Districts promoted watershed associations in the 1950s, 1960s, and 1970s. But interest in watershed work faded as many of those groups lacked the initiative to go beyond a set of traditional tasks aimed at fighting erosion on farms and at building conventional alliances to clean up water supplies. Separating themselves further from the growing movement to save rivers, the old-style watershed associations often operated in lockstep with the Soil Conservation Service of the Department of Agriculture, even to the point of rubber stamping the agency's wetlands drainage projects and promoting small dam construction under a USDA program called Resource Conservation and Development.

In the 1980s, and with a growing force in the 1990s, river conservationists again recognized the connections between their streams and the greater watershed with all its related issues of land use. It became popular, once again, to be involved at the watershed level.

As President of American Rivers in 1992, Kevin Coyle encouraged the watershed approach, aligning the future of river saving with the "emerging watershed strategy." Without abandoning efforts to protect specific sections of rivers, he articulated the importance of looking beyond: "Ideally, the way to conserve river systems is to improve land use planning within entire basins to reduce pollution run-off, stream encroachments, and dewatering."[31] Ten years later, Coyle reflected on the shift that had occurred: "I can't think of a natural resource agency at the federal or state level that doesn't now focus on watersheds as a core concept in matters of pollution, flow, or natural resources management." He also noted that most average citizens still didn't even know what a watershed was.

With an eye on this problem, and with its mission of helping local and statewide river groups organize and be effective, River Network embraced the watershed strategy with the goal of supporting a watershed council in each of the nation's 2,100 watersheds by the year 2020.[32] Likewise, the Pacific Rivers Council outlined an elaborate strategy for river conservation through a watershed approach. With a solid scientific background, the group called for preservation of unspoiled river refuges, protection of head-water regions because they nourish the rest of the river, and restoration of linkages between refuges.[33] In 1991, the Environmental Protection Agency endorsed watershed-based work.[34] An EPA conference on watersheds drew 2,000 people in 1996. When the Clinton administration drafted its *Clean Water Action Plan*—the most explicit document to direct federal clean water programs—it called the watershed approach the "key to the future."

Consider the Hudson as an example of the need to look beyond the edge of the river. Faced with a deteriorating water supply system and threats to water quality, New York planned to spend $8 billion on new filtration to counteract the effects of sprawl and pollution in the watersheds that the city tapped. Instead, the Hudson Riverkeeper proposed a program to buy the most critical land and protect other tracts in ways that would maintain good water quality, all at far less cost. After a contentious political struggle, the city adopted the watershed strategy.[35] Dozens of other examples show variety in dealing with the challenge of broadening concern to the whole watershed.[36]

Many of the new groups that were organized in this era took the form of watershed councils, best examined in context of the broader organization of modern river conservation activities.

ORGANIZING FOR RIVERS

As the nation's principal lobbying group for river protection, American Rivers in the 1980s expanded its role far beyond the national wild and scenic rivers system. After serving as the third director and leading the group in significant strides, Chris Brown stepped down in 1987 and later took over leadership of the National Park Service's Rivers, Trails, and Conservation Assistance Program, which advised local governments and river conservation groups all across the country. This effective service grew from a staff of eighteen in Washington and Philadelphia—where it had been started by the Park Service's Glenn Eugster—to ninety-five staff nationwide in 2003.

Kent Olson led American Rivers on an expansion that the board of directors called its "great leap" forward. More fundraising brought in more money enabling the staff to expand from five in 1987 to twenty in 1990. Membership doubled to 13,000. Articulate, determined, and savvy in the ways of organization building, Olson increased the group's profile as "the nation's principal river conservation organization." In 1990, Kevin Coyle became director. Seizing one of the great opportunities of his time, he took initiative in the wake of the 1993 Mississippi floods to show Americans that poor floodplain management—not flooding—was the core problem. He effectively carried the American Rivers message to the major media, appearing on *Larry King Live* and other programs. The organization led efforts to establish better federal policies and laws about floodplain reloca-tion, insurance, and disaster relief. Also in this era, Tom Cassidy of Ameri-can Rivers helped save the extraordinary Tatshenshini and Alsek Rivers in British Columbia and Alaska from the fate of a copper mine that would have opened up the continent's greatest wilderness and exposed its rivers to almost certain catastrophe from acid mine drainage.

Taking the American Rivers leadership role in 1995, Rebecca Wodder launched the group on another great leap, increasing the staff to fifty—good news for rivers but still a tiny effort compared to a group like the Nature Conservancy, which employed 3,200 people. But making every person count, American Rivers doubled its membership to 30,000 and pushed for far-reaching programs focusing on the Missouri and Snake Rivers, dam operation and removal, water scarcity, hydropower dam relicensing, reforming the Army Corps of Engineers, floodplain management, urban river enhancement, wild river protection, and political battles to retain the progressive gains of the past thirty years amid the hostile Congress that had started in 1995 and the hostile presidential administration that took over in 2001.

Meanwhile, Phil Wallin, who got his start in river conservation by working with Mark Dubois on the Stanislaus River in California, had led an effort to stop a dam from ruining New Mexico's elegant Rio Chama and to protect a section of that stream as a national wild and scenic river. In the process of organizing his own grassroots campaign, he realized that other groups all over the country needed help in getting organized. And beyond that, he saw clearly that the national debates could no longer be based on wasteful federal dams and the most spectacular wild rivers. Rather, local concerns and local politics were becoming the passwords in river conservation.

Wallin moved to Portland, Oregon, and started River Network in 1987 with the goal of filling this gap in the greater river conservation movement. In a creative means of funding the effort, Wallin used skills he had learned while working for the Trust for Public Land and made real estate deals, buying riverfront properties at below market value and then reselling them to government agencies that would manage the land as open space.

Sending field staff out to help people all across the country, and also supporting local groups by telephone, Internet, newsletters, funding alerts, and self-help books, River Network grew to a staff of twenty-five in 2003. When it was founded, a handful of statewide river conservation groups existed in places such as California, Ohio, and Idaho. With encouragement by River Network through the next decade, the number of statewide groups increased to thirty-three. Many of the larger groups encouraged smaller ones to form. In the late 1980s, several hundred river and watershed groups had been active; by 1999 there were 3,000.[37] In 2001, people formed twenty-five new groups in Wisconsin alone.

But in the national arena, the political likelihood of new programs addressing the problems of rivers had become slim. Furthermore, the tools already in place were underused in every river basin in the nation. Stepping into this breach, River Network strove to help people work with the legal tools they already had and to organize for a lasting presence in their watersheds. River Network trainers taught people how to plan, raise funds, manage staff, speak to the media, and assemble the nuts and bolts of successful river protection campaigns.

Don Elder, a trumpet player in the Birmingham Symphony who had started Alabama's Cahaba River Society, was hired as the River Network program director and inspired workers and conservation leaders all over the country to become involved and to succeed at increasingly challenging work. Along with other staff, Pat Munoz, who had started working with American Rivers in the mid-1970s and had become one of the most experienced river conservation professionals, trained activists in fund raising and organizing. In 2003, Elder became the director of River Network after Phil Wallin had formed a separate land-buying organization called the Western Rivers Conservancy and after Ken Margolis, who had served as director for five intervening years, stepped down.

Striving to help as many of the local and statewide groups as possible, River Network staged a national River Rally in 1999. For the first time since the damfighters conferences of the 1970s and early 1980s—milestone events in river conservation history—the rally presented an opportunity for groups from all over the country to come together and learn from each other. In short order, the River Network rally became the central annual event in the greater river conservation movement. In 2003, 450 people attended, dwarfing the river conferences of the earlier era.

As the roles of these groups unfolded, American Rivers served as the Washington connection in river conservation, lobbying Congress and the administration, pioneering on policy matters, drafting new proposals, gaining political currency, and garnering support for national programs. It also reached out through its regional offices to target specific conservation opportunities such as the campaign to restore the Missouri River. Meanwhile, River Network promoted, trained, and supported the grass roots in local, regional, and statewide organizations all over the country, expanding the base of the river conservation movement.

The fastest growing arm of river conservation in 2003 was the Waterkeeper movement. Beginning with Robert Boyle and later led by John Cronin and Robert F. Kennedy, Jr., the Hudson Riverkeeper set a style of aggressive citizen and legal action to clean up pollution. Taking flight, the effort inspired others to launch their own riverkeeper or waterkeeper programs. On the Chattahoochee River of Georgia, Sally Bethea led a hard-hitting campaign to clean up the river that sustains Atlanta at its core. By 2003, more than a hundred waterkeeper organizations had formed across the country, efforts often directed by a charismatic activist willing to find the pollution and battle the perpetrator through the media, the bureaucracy, and the courts. As Kevin Coyle said, "The Waterkeepers symbolize the idea that the only truly protected river is one guarded by a vigilant local group of dedicated people."

Working nationwide, Clean Water Action focused on water quality and the political integrity of the Clean Water Act and garnered 700,000 members by direct canvassing and other means. The Izaak Walton League continued to represent anglers and other freshwater enthusiasts. Trout Unlimited grew in stature as an angler's group driven by professional science and a fierce determination to protect freshwater and the habitat of wild trout. The Natural Resources Defense Council worked on enforcement of the Clean Water Act and helped to sponsor the Clean Water Network, which promoted important reforms.

Among the largest conservation groups, the National Wildlife Federation, with 4 million members and supporters in affiliated groups, maintained a water and rivers program led by David Conrad, who had begun his career working for Howard Brown at American Rivers in the 1970s. With 1.2

million members, the World Wildlife Fund sometimes touched on river issues. The Sierra Club, with 550,000 members, had led some of the classic early battles for river protection in the Grand Canyon, Hells Canyon, and other places but later focused more on broader issues of the conservation agenda (see Chapter 6). Among the large environmental groups, work on rivers occurred mainly when it overlapped with other more dominant agendas.

The Nature Conservancy had for years saved specific and localized riverfronts and other kinds of land by buying property or easements outright and by maintaining preserves. Then, in 1999, the group launched a Freshwater Initiative designed to protect and restore the most important streams for biological diversity. This pathbreaking effort, founded and led by hydrologist Brian Richter, focused on restoring flows to depleted streams such as the San Pedro in Arizona, and safeguarding the rich array of threatened aquatic species in southern Appalachian rivers (see Chapter 11).[38]

Much of the older drive for rivers—founded in crucibles of crisis and evident in the anti-dam groups such as Friends of the River in California and the New England Rivers Center—was replaced in the late 1990s with a new interest in watershed councils. Rather than pursue the advocacy-based models of the past, whereby people banded together for political pressure in well-defined, high-pitched battles to save their streams, the new groups sought to include representatives from all different points of view, each member a "stakeholder." Many of these councils were run by consensus, thus the players had to avoid issues they could not agree on and instead had to work where they found at least nominal common ground.

Some organizations pursued this model because they realistically knew that the cooperation of all the interest groups was essential for success. As director of the Rivers Council of Washington, Joy Huber promoted councils as a new form of democracy in America, bringing people together for shared decision making. "When people come together," she said, "they find they have common goals and a shared, undeniable dependency on water and soil."[39] Other citizens formed watershed councils to avoid the gridlock that comes with lawsuits or the risk that comes with political campaigns—winner take all. In the Yakima River basin of Washington, irrigation groups controlling most but not all of the local politics wanted to dam and divert more water, but they had been fought to a standstill. Because they had nowhere else to go, they enlisted in the watershed council approach, reasoning that, by sitting down and talking, they could work their way toward a solution and get at least part of what they wanted.[40] The important fact here is that the water developers had first been fought to a standstill. To make a watershed council work, river advocates needed to be strong enough at the outset to bring the other side to the bargaining table.

The new brand of watershed groups broadened the base of interest in the future of rivers and often made it possible to work through difficult community dilemmas about the fate of important places. In some cases, the councils filled a void because the older-style advocacy groups simply didn't exist. In a more practical vein, foundations, the Environmental Protection Agency, and state governments all favored funding watershed councils over activists whose clear goal was to save their river from development. Agency staff and the politicians who authorized the money could regard the stakeholder groups as more inclusive. And without doubt, the councils raised less trouble for bureaucrats, politicians, and the typical power structure of local communities than did the older-style advocacy groups.

Although watershed councils had undeniable potential for addressing the more widespread and complex problems facing rivers, they also had potential drawbacks. Once engaged in a consensus process, the energy of citizens can be exhausted by meetings alone, leaving the higher goals of saving a river to suffer whatever fate might bring after an elaborate process enduring for months or years. In stakeholder councils where competing demands had to be met, people's passion for protecting their stream could easily be eroded by time, compromise, and endless process that often denied any clear success for the river itself.

Invariably, groups that stepped back and recognized that a wide range of concerns affected their river then had to refocus again just to avoid paralysis and to actually do something. For example, in realizing that suburban sprawl is the root cause of riparian habitat loss, watershed groups then had to resolve to get local governments to zone the floodplain—a traditional goal that river conservationists might have pursued without any pretext of considering the whole watershed or without ever attempting to involve a broad council of members.

More troublesome for river advocates, the business, industry, and agricultural members of watershed councils had the financial ability to meet endlessly, to send multiple representatives and thereby pack meetings, to hire outside legal and scientific help, and to otherwise dominate the process. All these factors could put conservation representatives on the defensive. Negotiation could simply become a pretext for delay, and delay a pretext for not doing anything. For example, the Alabama Rivers Alliance tried for years to get the local utility company to clean up its power plants through a consensus approach. Eventually, the Alliance gave up and went to court. They had wasted their time, and as Wendy Wilson of River Network said of this situation, "Four years in a 'trust me,' adaptive-management, continu-ous-process-loop frays the soul." At its worst, activists called this process "talk-and-pollute," explaining, "We talk and they pollute."

Perhaps most troubling, the new organizations had the capability of displacing the old activist groups. Some critics maintained that stakeholder groups actually drove out activism.[41] Because the councils include all interest groups, with close ties to both business and government, they can make the advocacy-based representatives appear to be unreasonable.

A particularly troublesome topic within the stakeholder groups were negotiations about compliance with laws. Activists believed that there should be no compromise about following existing environmental statutes; violations were not a topic for discussion but rather for enforcement. Yet discussion is what the council-type groups were set up to do, and it was only natural that such groups—when they included violators of the law—would instinctively begin talking not about full compliance but about which provi-sions of the law should be enforced and when, if ever.

Finally, watershed-based work often lacked the gut-level passion that the older river-saving efforts used to have. One can become emotionally motivated to save a river because rivers are special places. You can go there, see the light on the water, watch the fish spawning in the riffles, feel the shade of rustling cottonwoods on a hot summer day, float weightlessly in the current, listen to the whitewater, jump in, and swim. Watersheds, on the other hand, are comparatively abstract. They're everywhere, and one might as well try to relate personally or emotionally to a county, township, or state. It's possible, but it doesn't happen as much. Without a strong spark of connection, people's interest in watershed management was not as likely to endure as would their attachment to saving the river that they had come to know and love. In reflecting on the shift to watershed councils in his state, Doug Finlayson, Chairman of the Washington Rivers Council, saw the benefits but also said, "Something has gone out of the old movement—rivers."

Chris Brown eloquently promoted a watershed approach to river problems, but wrote that he did not come easily to that view. "Watersheds do not 'sing.' They have none of the place-specific poetry, legend and beauty that have inspired generations of Americans to become activists for saving rivers. I worry that the watershed approach, with its expectations of consensus-based decision making, will compromise the advocacy that is the irreplaceable engine of conservation progress." But he also added, "My desire to see a *logical* conservation approach coupled with the fact that numerous river and watershed advocacy groups are undertaking and participating in watershed approaches in thoughtful, energetic, and effective ways, has converted me to watershed thinking.[42]

And as Don Elder reported, "Many of the consensus groups are achieving big breakthroughs, accomplishing great things for rivers that advocacy efforts, alone, probably would never have done." His comments were borne out by success on the Pomperaug River in Connecticut, the Big Thompson in Colorado, the Henrys Fork in Idaho, and dozens of other rivers.

In summary, no single approach worked best everywhere. Stakeholder-type councils to resolve differences and advocacy groups to save rivers from explicit threats each filled important niches and needs. Don Elder added, "Through watershed councils, the notion of stewardship is spreading even in horrible political times. But we also need to remember that without the legal drivers such as Clean Water Act enforcement, a lot of people would never come to the table."

With multiple approaches, river conservation moved ahead, 100 years after John Muir had begun his battle to save Hetch Hetchy Valley and the Tuolumne River in Yosemite National Park. Both approaches became important in the recipe for river conservation in the new century.

While consensus building became a key objective of many groups, the political front could not be ignored. Seeing the need to unite many different river groups in an effective voice for legislative action, Ann Mills, conservation director of American Rivers in 2002, announced her group's desire to establish a "river agenda." American Rivers established a steering committee of national, state, and local groups that took the lead in developing a list of goals, beginning with defense of the Clean Water Act from the Bush administration's many-pronged attack. Under formulation in 2003, the agenda offered the potential for a new level of cooperation as myriad river groups pulled together for the common good of waters everywhere. This effort aimed for a new level of participation in order to influence public policy about rivers that were ever more endangered during combative political times.

FULL CYCLE—THE PROMISE
OF DAM REMOVAL

The Clearwater River dam that Governor Cecil Andrus blasted away, described at the beginning of Chapter 10, signaled an upcoming change in our society's outlook on rivers. In that chapter—the closing of the first edition of this book when it was initially published in 1986—I discussed the day when dams would be eliminated at a meaningful scale. At the beginning of the twenty-first century, that day has come.

As the Turner Foundation stated in 2000, removing dams quickly went "from the laughable to the visionary to the pragmatic." Leading the nation-wide effort for dam removal, American Rivers was careful to note that this was not any sort of radical movement. Ann Mills noted that far fewer than 1 percent of the dams in the country were under any consideration for removal, and that many rivers could be restored without losing significant benefits that worthwhile dams provided. "By continuing the trend to selec-tively remove those dams that don't make sense—those dams where costs outweigh benefits, that pose a public safety hazard, or both—we can begin to restore the ecological, safety, and economic benefits associated with free-flowing rivers."[43]

In the 1990s, dam removal became one of the highlights of the river conservation movement. Conservationists sought to eliminate barriers to fish and other aquatic life and to restore the rapids, riffles, temperature, habi-tat, and health of downstream flows.

Many of the dams had become unsafe. In its report card on America's infrastructure, the American Society of Civil Engineers in 2001 gave dams, as a collective group of public facilities, a grade of D. The Association of State Dam Safety Officials estimated that the average life expectancy of a dam, without major reconstruction, was only fifty years. More than one-fourth of the 75,000 dams taller than six feet were older than twenty-five years.

Other dams were removed for economic reasons. Many dams had been used long ago to produce mechanical water power but had no modern purpose. Under the Army Corps of Engineers' inventory of large dams, for example, only 3 percent produced hydroelectric power. Only 10 percent provided for water supplies, and 14 percent for irrigation (the most com-mon use was recreation—31 percent).[44] In Wisconsin, repair of outmoded small dams typically cost two to five times more than removal. One dam on the Deerskin River would have required $400,000 to repair but only $15,000 to remove.

One of the higher profile cases involved Edwards Dam on the Kenne-bec River in Maine. The dam had been built in 1837 and eliminated seven-teen miles of habitat for Atlantic salmon and nine other species of anadromous fish in return for a pittance of electricity. A settlement among the state and federal agencies, river groups, and the dam owner led to the dam's removal, and this was the first major dam that the Federal Energy

Regulatory Commission ruled should be eliminated. Interior Secretary Bruce Babbitt presided over the media-packed demolition in 1999.

Babbitt also championed the cause of dam removal elsewhere. "Not so long ago, Interior Secretaries were dedicating new dams," he wrote. "Today, I am swinging ceremonial sledgehammers as we join with local governments, power companies, water providers and citizens to bring down old, environmentally destructive dams."[45] Babbitt's awakening did not, however, prevent him from giving the go-ahead to the Animas–La Plata project in Colorado, infamous as the last of the Bureau of Reclamation's old-style pork barrel schemes for damming and diverting without adequate justification.[46]

Dam removal was not new. Since 1912, 465 dams have been deliberately removed in the United States. Thousands of others—mostly small—have washed out naturally during floods. In just one tropical storm in Georgia, for example, 100 dams failed in 1994.

However, the goal of river restoration brought about a whole new scale of removal activities. In the 1980s, ninety-two dams were taken out and in the 1990s, 177 were eliminated. Massachusetts became the first state to adopt a systematic approach to dam removal when Natural Resources Commissioner Bob Durand launched a River Restore Program in 1999. In 2003, the one-hundredth dam was removed since the Edwards Dam demolition.

In Wisconsin, Sarah Johnson formed the Wisconsin Rivers Alliance with a primary goal to eliminate small, unused, ecologically damaging, unsafe dams plugging dozens of rivers. On the Baraboo River, the removal of four dams brought back 115 miles of free-flowing river—the entire main stem.

Wisconsin led the nation with seventy-three recent removals as of 1999. California had forty-seven, Ohio thirty-nine, Pennsylvania thirty-eight, and Tennessee twenty-five. The dams averaged 21 feet in height, but four had risen 120 feet or higher. The tallest—Occidental Chem Pond Dam D on the Duck River in Tennessee—was 160 feet.

Restoring anadromous or sea-running fish was one of the more ambitious and popular goals of dam removal. On the Conestoga River in Pennsylvania, officials eliminated seven dams between 1996 and 1999, improving conditions considerably in a stream heavily degraded by agriculture and damming. The intent was to reintroduce sea-going shad, historically plentiful in the river and once important for sport, commerce, and food. The Pennsylvania Fish and Boat Commission led the effort with an expenditure of only $218,500, and the Environmental Protection Agency matched that amount through its Chesapeake Bay program. Eight more Conestoga dams were scheduled to come out.

On the Naugatuck River in Connecticut, three dams were removed in order to return Atlantic salmon to an industrial river that had been one of the most degraded in America. With ambitious restoration goals, local officials planned to remove other dams, build fish passage facilities where dams could not be taken out, and upgrade six sewage treatment plants. Nine towns along the river launched greenway plans to enhance river recreation.

One of the greatest possibilities for restoration in the Pacific Northwest involved plans to eliminate two large dams on the Elwha River of the Olympic Peninsula in Washington and bring back one of the finest salmon runs the world had ever known. By 1999, all parties had agreed to remove the dams, but the needed federal money was not authorized because Republican Senator Slade Gorton refused to grant approval without a serious weakening of the Federal Power Act as it applied to new hydroelectric plans. But Gorton was voted out of office in 2000, and the dams are scheduled for removal in 2007.

On the Rogue in Oregon, the elimination of Savage Rapids Dam would allow salmon to return to an important section of that great Pacific Coast river. The dam was once used for irrigation but it had fallen into disrepair and for years provided nothing but a flatwater pool for people who had built homes along the riverbanks. Removal would be far less expensive than upgrading the dam for salmon passage, now required by law. Pressured by economics as well as state and federal mandates, board members of the local irrigation district repeatedly voted to get rid of their dam, only to be recalled by prodam voters and replaced by members who again resisted federal and state rules regarding fish passage. Owing to economics and legal requirements, the dam was likely to be removed eventually.

The most visionary of all the feasible proposals for dam removal was to bring back the once plentiful but now imperiled runs of salmon and steelhead to the Columbia River basin and in particular to its largest tributary, the Snake River.

In the 1960s and 1970s, four new dams on the lower Snake River began to push a viable population of fish toward extinction. Before those final few dams in the Columbia–Snake system went up, commercial fishermen in Oregon and Washington still had jobs. Idaho still had a sport season on salmon—a huge economic event.

The dams that were built back-to-back on the lower 140 miles of the Snake provided only 5 percent of the Northwest's electricity, an amount that could easily be replaced by efficiency improvements according to the

Northwest Power Planning Council and studies by the Northwest Energy Coalition.[47] The primary purpose in the tenuous justification for the dams—originally opposed even by the Army Corps of Engineers because they were uneconomic—was to make Lewiston, Idaho, a seaport, accessible to barges 465 miles from the ocean. The primary commodity on these barges was wheat bound for Asia. By building the Snake River dams, the Northwest unwittingly traded its own abundance of food, in the form of high-value and increasingly rare wild salmon, for a completely subsidized system for barging wheat on its way to foreign markets. The grain was in such chronic surplus that other farmers, over a period of years, were being paid hundreds of millions of dollars not to grow it. The fish were in such chronic scarcity that they were listed as endangered species.

The proposal to dismantle the four lower Snake River dams would still allow barges to go to nearby Pasco, Washington; only 11 percent of the commodities shipped on the Columbia system came from above Pasco anyway. Truck and rail could easily fill the transportation gap, as they always had done before 1976.[48]

Though dam removal would eliminate a relatively small amount of barging, it would have an overall positive economic effect, according to a RAND study in 2002 that found significantly more jobs would result if the dams were removed than if they remained in place. The net economic effect on the region would be positive, even without considering many of the benefits of a restored river.[49] Considering a wide spectrum of public costs and benefits, conservative economic projections found that taxpayers would save $183 million a year by laying the four dams to rest.[50]

The most reputable groups of scientists studying the issue, including the Independent Scientific Group of the Northwest Power Planning Council, indicated that dam removal was the best possibility for saving the fish. Many biologists believed that bypassing the dams was the *only* possibility for saving the salmon from extinction.[51]

Conservationists, scientists, fishermen, and the Indian tribes all argued that this living emblem of the Pacific Northwest—once the source of 25,000 commercial fishing jobs—could be reinstated to provide a fishery worth $250 to $500 million a year.[52] Even in its crippled state, a short salmon fishing season on hatchery fish in 2001 injected $90 million into local communities in Idaho alone, according to the Idaho Fish and Wildlife Foundation.

Meanwhile, efforts to maintain salmon with the dams intact cost the federal government alone more than $500 million a year in the Columbia basin, according to the Northwest Power Planning Council—money spent on hatcheries, habitat reclamation, dam modification, and lost hydroelectric power, all foregone in an effort largely aimed at counteracting the deadly effects of the dams.

The Army Corps alone spent more than $100 million a year on its own approach to the problem: it tried to barge the young fish downstream to get them past the hazards of the dams.[53] But after undergoing this treatment for thirty years, the wild salmon were nearly extinct.

By dismantling the dams and restoring the runs of fish, treaties with the Indians could be honored and an entire ecosystem put on the path of recovery. Truly a keystone species, the salmon were eaten or used by 137 different creatures, and the health of entire riparian corridors throughout the Northwest had been dependent on these anadromous fish as they spawned, died, and were eaten by other wildlife—the salmon-based nutrients redistributed along all the streams that the fish could reach.

Opponents to dam removal—the heavily subsidized barging, aluminum, agriculture, and hydroelectric industries—pinned their arguments on two points. They maintained that scientists could not assure that the salmon would recover and they argued that problems other than the dams were to blame for the salmon's demise. But the scientific groups put good odds on the fishes' recovery, and while habitat, hatcheries, and commercial fishing all presented problems to the salmon, it was widely believed that the largest share of human-caused losses—perhaps 90 percent—owed to the dams.[54]

Salmon populations were up in 2002 and 2003, though most of the spawners were hatchery rather than wild or naturally occurring fish. Many biologists credited the increased runs to temporarily favorable ocean conditions—a cycle that ebbs and flows, the low points leaving salmon increasingly vulnerable to the hazards of the dams. Irrespective of such cycles, fisheries biologists hired by Trout Unlimited predicted that wild spring chinook salmon—the mainstay of the Columbia runs—could be nearly extinct by 2016 unless major changes were made.

The political battle to save the salmon from extinction was one of truly epic proportions in the history of river conservation in America. Never before had a species of such symbolic and economic importance been so threatened with irrevocable extinction by dams and river destruction. Never before had so much been at risk economically. Yet the federal government continued to rely on only minor changes in dam operations, and few politicians risked the ire of the big subsidized industries that benefited from the dams.

Supporters of dam removal got a boost in May 2003 when U.S. District Judge James Redden ruled that the federal government's plan for salmon recovery, which scarcely considered dam removal as an option, was inadequate and had to be rewritten.

The Save Our Wild Salmon Coalition and the thirty groups it represented scrambled to work on many fronts to gain support for dam removal. In 2003, congressional representatives acting on behalf of the fishermen and others introduced the Salmon Planning Act, which called for a National Academy of Sciences analysis of the federal programs affecting Columbia salmon, a General Accounting Office study of removing the four lower Snake River dams, and authorization for the Army Corps of Engineers to remove the dams if recommended. Though eighty-four cosponsors quickly signed on to the bill, it had a long way to go.

Led by Pat Ford of the Save Our Wild Salmon Coalition, the river conservationists battled on persistently, hoping that the political times would change, hoping that the influence of the subsidized industries benefiting from the dams could be beaten in the arena of public opinion, hoping that the salmon would hold out long enough to allow people to give them back some small part of the great river system that they needed.

SOURCES AND DESTINATIONS

By the late 1990s, the original, straightforward goal of saving rivers from dams had grown to the more complicated aim of protecting streams from a multitude of threats affecting waters everywhere, all the time. A movement that had matured over several decades was now pointed in new and promising directions.

Throughout the changes, river conservation became more professional, and, as people worked full time, they became more capable in many ways. When river conservationists received paychecks for their work, they were more able to sustain the long commitments necessary to cope with persistent problems. And they did this with increasing support.

Year after year, public approval seemed to be growing for river protection. Polls by many different sponsors showed that Americans endorsed environmental programs. In 1995, 73 percent of the people polled considered themselves environmentalists, with support crossing all socioeconomic lines.[55] The pollsters concluded, "Americans share a common set of environmental beliefs and values. . . . There is a single cultural consensus." Marked disagreements were "only among our most extreme groups." A 2000 Roper poll for the National Environmental Education and Training Foundation found that 60 percent of Americans believed that economic and environmental health go hand in hand. But if they had to choose between the two, 70 percent said they would support the environment over the economy. A 1994 poll contracted by American Rivers showed that 94 percent of the people were "very concerned" about the quality of America's fresh water supply. Ninety-five percent thought that leaving our children with a safe water supply should be a national priority.[56] A *National Geographic* poll in 2000 found that 98 percent of the people said conserving rivers was an important environmental priority, and 65 percent said they were interested in getting personally involved in conserving and protecting rivers.[57]

Reflecting those trends, the number of groups and individuals active in river or watershed protection increased sharply, and many of those people were willing to become politically involved. For example, the Save Our Wild Salmon Coalition generated an astounding 250,000 comments about salmon recovery when the federal government was developing its Snake River salmon recovery plan.

Even though there was no recognized disagreement among Americans that their water and natural resources should in principle be protected, the field of river conservation remained a battleground as property rights groups fought land use regulations, as rural communities in the West resisted reforms on federal land, and as the influence of big money in politics led more elected officials to support the destruction of rivers in stealth. Much as Tellico Dam in Chapter 5 was approved through an amendment that never saw the light of day, Congress passed laws allowing "salvage" logging of healthy forests without citizen appeals, exempted useless pet projects from environmental reviews, and cut funding for enforcement of water quality laws—laws that they would never have had a chance of repealing in a public debate.

While the awareness of rivers as centers of biological wonder had increased markedly in the 1990s and the conditions of our waterways shocked people who cared about the greater systems of life, the importance of rivers as public water supplies concerned the average American more, so water quality became important in expanding the support to save rivers.[58] As people saw more effects of pollution—as they watched the news about *Pfiesteria* and toxic spills—the chances of their becoming river advocates increased. Clean water seemed deeply ingrained as a fundamental American right, and reclaiming lost ground in the fight against pollution would remain at the forefront of river conservation efforts. But it wasn't the only concern as the new century unfolded and river conservationists looked toward the future.

Among all programs discussed in these last two chapters about the modern era, improvements in floodplain protection offered perhaps the most protection to rivers at the least total cost. For example, although years of effort might go into a single dam removal to benefit a river for several miles, an effective county floodplain ordinance could protect an entire complex of river corridors from damaging new development that would otherwise run rampant. And unlike some other approaches that depended on state or federal support, or on new laws, or on ample funding, zoning of the floodplain could be done for a modest cost by local people anywhere. Eighteen thousand communities were already enrolled in the flood insurance program in 2000; new efforts to make floodplain protection more effective could build on that commitment rather than starting from scratch. With tight budget constraints, citizens were increasingly outraged at inequitable subsidies, and the flood insurance program begged for reforms to save taxpayers money while improving the way riverfronts were tended. In addition, acquisition by land trusts—an increasingly popular strategy—was a tailor-made tool for floodplains and riparian zones. In the new era of budgetary limits and increased responsibility at the local level, floodplain protection offered tremendous possibilities for river advocates.

In a poll of river conservation leaders in 2003, the two issues rating the most concern were sustaining adequate flows in streams and the effects of growth and sprawling development. "This appears to be *the* issue of the twenty-first century," said Margaret Bowman of American Rivers, which conducted the poll. Her view was reflected in that of Lt. General Robert B. Flowers, the Chief of the Army Corps of Engineers, who said, "Fresh water in this century will be as important as oil in the twentieth century." Groups working on the problems of water quantity and adequate flows in rivers pursued the reforms discussed in Chapter 11. Where water supplies were threatened, groups including American Rivers typically tried to address urban sprawl and to increase the efficiency of water use (see Chapter 9).

Protecting drinking water, managing floodplains, and sustaining healthy flows in streams were three of the directions that river conservation was headed in the new century. But above all, the fate of rivers everywhere hinged on population pressure. With a relatively stable population, the hard-earned gains of conservation could endure. But where population grows without limits—which includes most of the United States—the gains of yesterday will simply be eaten up by the human needs of tomorrow.

According to the Census Bureau's mid-level projections, America's population is slated to double to 571 million in the twenty-first century. California is scheduled to double in only thirty-seven years. But actual growth, according to the 2000 census, is already running ahead of the bureau's *high-level* projection. According to the Census Bureau, immigration (along with the children of the new immigrants) accounts for 80 percent of that growth. If the growth rate doesn't change, the population of the United States will explode to 1.2 billion people by 2100.[59]

Against those kinds of pressures for more water, more energy, more living space, more dams—more everything—the fate of natural rivers will be bleak if not hopeless in all but the most exceptional cases where rivers are protected in national parks or as national wild and scenic rivers. And even some of those would be sacrificed if the population curve is not adjusted downward. Any agenda for the future of rivers thus depends on coming to grips with unchecked population growth. Yet river conservation organizations and Americans in general remain reluctant to address this critical issue.

The record of history and the data of polls have shown that the public's commitment to protect rivers tends to be based on the importance of pure drinking water, outrage at unfair and damaging subsidies, and the loss of economic resources such as the salmon. But these concerns are not necessarily what motivated hundreds of thousands of people who became involved in saving their streams over the course of the years covered in this book.

Behind all the explanations drawing on economics and science, beyond all the justifications regarding public needs and tax dollars, what has moved river conservationists since John Muir has been a deep and abiding love of rivers—a personal commitment to the beauty of the river's flow and to all the wonder that surrounds it.

WHERE THE RIVER MEETS THE SEA

In the prologue to this book, I imagined a river that began high on the land. The stream grew, accumulating water as it flowed, and a great river resulted.

The story of people's involvement in protecting our rivers grew in a similar way, picking up new reasons to care for these places, new approaches to protecting them, and new experiences as the years passed, one decade merging into the next, then one century into another.

In the end, the river meets the sea, and if we could journey downstream far enough, we would see our stream there in all its garnered glory and all its accumulated distress. In those final bends nearing the ocean, we would see the results of everything we had done to the river and everything we had done to its watershed—to all the land that timelessly feeds rainfall and snowmelt into the flow.

This story about people's involvement with rivers—from headwaters to sea, from 1900 to 2004—is important for the simple reason that the rivers are important. But the story tells far more than the fate of separate waterways. In that final mile approaching sea level, each river indicates how well we have done in our stewardship of the earth. In the end, the rivers, and how we care for them, show much about what we do and about who we are.

SOURCES

Much of the information in *Endangered Rivers and the Conservation Movement* was taken from printed sources. Many sources are identified within the text itself and are not repeated here. In the source notes I have mainly cited sources that are readily available. Dozens of government documents were also used, including reports by the Army Corps of Engineers printed each year for every state, project reports by the corps, state and annual reports by the Bureau of Reclamation, many brochures by the federal dam-building agencies, environmental impact statements, testimony from hearings, wild and scenic river studies, and General Accounting Office reports. Most of these are not cited in the notes but can be found in large libraries or through the public information staffs of the agencies.

Following numbered notes to the chapters, other sources relevant to topics treated in a given chapter are listed.

Hundreds of magazines, bulletins, and newsletters were also consulted. Dealing specifically with water and the environment are *American Forests* by the American Forestry Association, *American Rivers* by the American Rivers Conservation Council, *Audubon* by the National Audubon Society, *Headwaters* by Friends of the River, *National Parks* by the National Parks and Conservation Association, *National Wildlife* by the National Wildlife Federation, *Not Man Apart* by Friends of the Earth, *Outdoor America* by the Izaak Walton League, *Sierra* by the Sierra Club, *Trout* by Trout Unlimited, *Trends* by the National Park Service, *Water Spectrum* by the Army Corps of Engineers, and *Wilderness* by the Wilderness Society. Some of these are available in large libraries; old issues of some publications may be found only at the organizations' headquarters. Other magazines included *Atlantic, Canoe, Collier's, Conservationist, Forbes, GEO, Harper's, National Geographic, Newsweek,*

Outdoor Life, Plateau, Sports Afield, Time, U.S. News and World Report, and *Western Wildlands.* Major newspapers consulted include the *New York Times, Washington Post, Los Angeles Times,* and *Sacramento Bee.* The files of the American Rivers Conservation Council and the Environmental Policy Center were especially helpful. Files of the Army Corps of Engineers and National Park Service were also used.

I also drew heavily from more than a hundred interviews and from visits to most of the rivers in the book. Interviews are listed after other sources.

CHAPTER 2: A DELICATE BALANCE

1. Marie Morisawa, *Streams: Their Dynamics and Morphology* (New York: McGraw-Hill, 1968).

2. William H. Amos, *The Infinite River* (New York: Ballantine, 1970).

3. H. B. N. Hynes, *The Ecology of Running Waters* (Toronto: University of Toronto Press, 1970).

4. Charles M. Clusen, ed., *Engineering a Victory for Our Environment* (San Francisco: Sierra Club, 1973).

5. Oral Bullard, *Crisis on the Columbia* (Portland, Oreg.: Touchstone Press, 1968).

6. Army Corps of Engineers, *The Corps Cares About Fish* (Seattle: The Corps, North Pacific Division, 1982). Brochure.

7. Anthony Netboy, *The Salmon: Their Fight for Survival* (Boston: Houghton Mifflin, 1974).

8. Bruce Brown, *Mountain in the Clouds* (New York: Simon & Schuster, 1982).

9. Paul Bodin, *Are California's North Coast Rivers Really "Wasting Away to Sea"?* (Arcata, Calif.: Northcoast Environmental Center, 1982). Booklet.

10. Tim Palmer, *Youghiogheny: Appalachian River* (Pittsburgh, Pa.: University of Pittsburgh Press, 1984).

11. Department of the Interior, Bureau of Outdoor Recreation, *Outdoor Recreation: A Legacy for America* (Washington, D.C.: The Department, 1973).

Other Sources

Collins, Robert O., and Nash, Roderick. *The Big Drops.* San Francisco: Sierra Club Books, 1978.

Dunne, Thomas, and Leopold, Luna B. *Water in Environmental Planning.* San Francisco: W. H. Freeman, 1978.

Editors of Outdoor World. *Rivers of North America.* Waukesha, Wis.: Outdoor World, 1973.

Helfman, Elizabeth. *Rivers and Watersheds in America's Future.* New York: David McKay, 1965.

Hoyt, W. G., and Langhein, Walter B. *Floods.* Princeton: Princeton University Press, 1955.

Moyle, Peter B. *Fish: An Enthusiast's Guide.* Berkeley: University of California Press, 1993.

Russell, Richard J. *River Plains and Sea Coasts.* Berkeley and Los Angeles: University of California Press, 1967.

Thomas, Bill. *American Rivers: A Natural History.* New York: Norton, 1978.

U.S. Forest Service, North Central Experiment Station. *Proceedings: River Recreation Management and Research Symposium.* St. Paul, Minn.: The Service, 1977.

Waters, Thomas F. *Wildstream: A Natural History of a Free Flowing River.* St. Paul, Minn.: Riparian Press, 2000.

White, Gilbert, ed. *Environmental Effects of Complex River Development.* Boulder, Colo.: Westview Press, 1977.

CHAPTER 3: CHANGING THE FLOW OF WATER

1. Gilbert White, *Strategies of American Water Management* (Ann Arbor: University of Michigan Press, 1971), 1.

2. Michael Robinson, *Water for the West* (Chicago: Public Works Historical Society, 1979), 2.

3. Albert N. Williams, *Water and Power* (New York: Duell, Sloan & Pearce, 1951), 10.

4. Norman Smith, *A History of Dams* (London: Peter Davies, 1971) 146.

5. Ibid., 145.

6. John M. Kauffmann, *Flow East* (New York: McGraw-Hill, 1973).

7. Anthony Netboy, *The Salmon: Their Fight for Survival* (Boston: Houghton Mifflin, 1974), 182.

8. Paul Shepard, *Man in the Landscape* (New York: Knopf, 1967), 141.

9. Daniel Boorstin, *The Americans: The Democratic Experience* (New York: Random House, 1973).

10. Ibid.

11. Barry Allen and Mina Hamilton Haefele, *In Defense of Rivers* (Delaware Valley Conservation Association, 1976), 115. Available from the American Rivers Conservation Council.

12. Western Writers of America, *Water Trails West* (New York: Avon, 1978).

13. Henry Nash Smith, *Virgin Land* (New York: Vintage Books, 1950), 181.

14. Pacific Northwest River Basins Commission, *Roll on Columbia* (Vancouver, Wash.: The Commission, about 1980). Brochure.

15. John Boslough, "Rationing a River," *Science* 81 (June 1981): 26.

16. Robinson, *Water for the West*.

17. Smith, *Virgin Land*, 209.

18. Robinson, *Water for the West*, 12.

19. Wallace Stegner and Page Stegner, *American Places* (New York: Greenwich House, 1983), 14.

20. Fred Powledge, *Water* (New York: Farrar, Straus & Giroux, 1982), 279.

21. Charles R. Goldman and James McEvoy III, *Environmental Quality and Water Development* (San Francisco: W. H. Freeman, 1973), 43.

22. Robinson, *Water for the West*, 9.

23. W. Turrentine Jackson and Stephen D. Mikesell, *The Stanislaus River Drainage Basin and the New Melones Dam* (Davis, Calif.: California Water Resources Center, University of California, June 1979).

24. Raymond F. Dasmann, *The Destruction of California* (New York: Collier Books, 1966).

25. Army Corps of Engineers, *Historical Highlights of the Army Corps of Engineers* (Washington, D.C.: The Corps, 1973). Brochure.

26. Army Corps of Engineers, *The Headwaters District*, by Leland Johnson (Pittsburgh, Pa.: The Corps, about 1979).

27. Beatrice Hort Holmes, *History of Federal Water Resources Programs and Policies, 1961–70* (Washington, D.C.: U.S. Department of Agriculture, 1979), 6.

28. Arthur Morgan, *Dams and Other Disasters* (Boston: Porter Sargent, 1971), 311.

29. Army Corps of Engineers, Youghiogheny River files, Army Corps of Engineers office, Pittsburgh, Pa.

30. Robert H. Haveman, *Water Resources Investment and the Public Interest* (Nashville, Tenn.: Vanderbilt University Press, 1965).

31. Thomas Y. Canby, "Water: Our Most Precious Resource," *National Geographic*, August 1980, and American Rivers, *In Harm's Way: The Costs of Floodplain Development* (Washington, D.C.: American Rivers, 1999).

32. Bureau of Reclamation, *Hydropower* (Washington, D.C.: The Bureau, about 1980). Brochure.

33. Smith, *A History of Dams*, 59.

34. *Scholastic*, March 25, 1940.

35. Natural Resources Defense Council, newsletter, January 1978.

36. Federal Energy Regulatory Commission, *Water Power* (Washington, D.C.: The Commission, about 1980). Brochure.

37. "Water for Peace," *Department of State Bulletin*, September 26, 1966, 456–57.

38. Roy Gordon, "Engineering for the People: 200 Years of Army Public Works," *Military Engineer*, May/June 1976, 180–85.

39. Bureau of Reclamation, *Reclamation* (Washington, D.C.: The Bureau, 1975). Brochure.

40. Ibid.

41. Robinson, *Water for the West*.

42. William E. Warne, *The Bureau of Reclamation* (New York: Praeger, 1973).

43. Boslough, "Rationing A River," 26.

44. White, *Strategies of American Water Management*.

45. Peter Wiley and Robert Gottlieb, *Empires in the Sun* (New York: Avon, 1982), 88.

46. Holmes, *History of Federal Water Resources*, 53.

47. Kathleen K. Wiegner, "The Water Crisis: It's Almost Here," *Forbes*, August 20, 1979.

48. Bureau of Reclamation, *Reclamation*.

49. David F. Salisbury, "Water Fights: The West Goes to Court," *Christian Science Monitor*, March 1, 1979, 12–13.

50. Department of the Interior, Office of Audit and Investigation, *Review of the Central Valley Project, Bureau of Reclamation* (Washington, D.C.: The Department, January 1978).

51. Department of the Interior, press release, October 9, 1981.

52. Bureau of Reclamation, *Reclamation*.

53. Department of the Interior, Geological Survey, *Estimated Use of Water in the United States in 1980* (Alexandria, Va.: The Survey, 1983).

54. Frank Graham, Jr., *Man's Dominion: The Story of Conservation in America* (New York: M. Evans, 1971), 245.

55. Frank E. Smith, *The Politics of Conservation* (New York: Pantheon, 1966), 206.

56. Elmo Richardson, *Dams, Parks and Politics* (Lexington: University Press of Kentucky, 1973), 14.

57. Fred Powledge, "Can TVA Change Its Spots?" *Audubon*, March 1983, 61–75.

58. Powledge, *Water*, 84.

59. Luna B. Leopold and Thomas Maddock, *The Flood Control Controversy* (New York: Ronald Press, 1954), 88.

60. Thomas Y. Canby, "Water: Our Most Precious Resource," *National Geographic*, August 1980.

61. "The Browning of America," *Newsweek*, February 23, 1981, 26.

62. Larry Kohl, "Quebec's Northern Dynamo," *National Geographic*, March 1982.

63. Robinson, *Water for the West*, 83.

64. Arthur Maass, *Muddy Waters: The Army Engineers and the Nation's Rivers* (Cambridge: Harvard University Press, 1951), 214.

65. White, *Strategies of American Water Management*.

66. Samuel Hays, *Conservation and the Gospel of Efficiency* (New York: Atheneum, 1959), 114.

67. Holmes, *History of Federal Water Resources*, 62.

68. Goldman and McEvoy, *Environmental Quality and Water Development*, 56.

69. Richard D. Lamm and Michael McCarthy, *The Angry West* (Boston: Houghton Mifflin, 1982), 168.

70. "By a Damsite," *Time*, June 19, 1944, 79–30.

71. Canby, "Water."

72. Army Corps of Engineers, *National Waterways Study* (Washington, D.C.: The Corps, July 1981).

73. Ted Simon, *The River Stops Here* (New York: Random House, 1994).

Other Sources

Chandler, William U. *The Myth of TVA*. Cambridge, Mass.: Ballinger, 1984.

Cullen, Allan H. *Rivers in Harness: The Story of Dams*. Philadelphia: Chilton Books, 1962.

Davis, Kenneth S. *River on the Rampage*. New York: Doubleday, 1953.

Degan, James P. "The Desert Shall Rejoice and Be Made to Blossom as the Rose." *The Living Wilderness*, Summer 1982.

Fradkin, Philip L. *A River No More*. New York: Knopf, 1981.

Hart, Henry C. *The Dark Missouri*. Madison: University of Wisconsin Press, 1957.

Kahrl, William L., ed. *California Water Atlas*. Los Altos, Calif.: William Kaufmann (dist.); Sacramento: Governor's Office of Planning and Research, 1979.

Martin, Russell. *A Story that Stands Like a Dam: Glen Canyon and the Struggle for the Soul of the West*. New York: Henry Holt, 1989.

Owen, Marguerite. *The Tennessee Valley Authority*. New York: Praeger, 1973.

Stegner, Wallace. *Beyond the Hundredth Meridian*. Boston: Houghton Mifflin, 1953.

CHAPTER 4: THE BEGINNINGS OF RIVER PROTECTION

1. Charles R. Goldman and James McEvoy III, *Environmental Quality and Water Development* (San Francisco: W. H. Freeman, 1973), 81.

2. James Mitchell Clarke, *The Life and Adventures of John Muir* (San Francisco: Sierra Club Books, 1979), 306.

3. Ibid., 304.

4. Frank Graham, Jr., *Man's Dominion: The Story of Conservation in America* (New York: M. Evans, 1971), 166.

5. Goldman and McEvoy, *Environmental Quality and Water Development*, 53.

6. Samuel Hays, interview with author, April 1979.

7. Frederick Haynes Newell, *Water Resources: Present and Future Uses* (New Haven: Yale University Press, 1920), 148.

8. Goldman and McEvoy, *Environmental Quality and Water Development*, 80.

9. Judson King, *The Conservation Fight: From Theodore Roosevelt to the Tennessee Valley Authority* (Washington, D.C.: Public Affairs Press, 1959), 17.

10. Ibid., 19.

11. Ibid, 14.

12. Department of the Interior, *Outdoor Recreation Action*, Spring 1977.

13. National Parks Association, newsletter, September 30, 1920.

14. Ibid., October 1923.

15. Edward James, ed., *Dictionary of American Biography* (New York: Scribner, 1973).

16. National Parks Association, newsletter, June 1, 1920.

17. Ibid., December 1921.

18. "The Browning of America," *Newsweek*, February 23, 1981, 26.

19. George Laycock, *The Diligent Destroyers* (Garden City, N.Y.: Doubleday, 1970), 33.

20. Bruce Brown, *Mountain in the Clouds* (New York: Simon & Schuster, 1982), 95.

21. Army Corps of Engineers, *The U.S. Army Corps of Engineers and the Environmental Community: A History to 1969*, by Michael Robinson (Washington, D.C.: The Corps, 1982). Draft.

22. Ibid.

23. Marguerite Owen, *The Tennessee Valley Authority* (New York: Praeger, 1973), 91.

24. W. V. Howard, *Authority in TVA Land* (Kansas City, Mo.: Frank Glenn, 1948), 94.

25. Elmer T. Peterson, *Big-Dam Foolishness* (New York: Devin-Adair, 1954), 103.

26. Goldman and McEvoy, *Environmental Quality and Water Development*, 55.

27. Peterson, *Big-Dam Foolishness*, 62.

28. Paul Friggins, "The Battle of the Blue," *Farm Journal*, April 1953, 51.

29. Henry C. Hart, *The Dark Missouri* (Madison: University of Wisconsin Press, 1957), 147.

30. Martin Heuvelmans, *The River Killers* (Harrisburg, Pa.: Stackpole Books, 1974).

31. E. T. Scoyen, "Kilowatts in the Wilderness," *Sierra Club Bulletin* 37 (1952): 75–84.

32. Elmo Richardson, *Dams, Parks and Politics* (Lexington: University Press of Kentucky, 1973), 9.

33. National Parks Association, *National Parks*, October 1948.

34. Ibid.

35. *The Living Wilderness*, Summer 1948.

36. Richardson, *Dams, Parks and Politics*, 119.

37. Ibid, 123.

38. Ted Schad, interview with author, April 1983.

39. Richardson, *Dams, Parks and Politics*, 123.

40. Ibid, 66.

41. Frank Graham, Jr., "Dave Brower: Last of the Optimists?" *Audubon*, November 1982.

42. Peter Wiley and Robert Gottlieb, *Empires in the Sun* (New York: Avon, 1982), 288.

43. Paul Brooks, *Speaking for Nature* (San Francisco: Sierra Club Books, 1980), 250.

44. Bernard DeVoto, "Shall We Let Them Ruin Our National Parks?" *Saturday Evening Post*, July 22, 1950, 44.

45. Ibid., "The Easy Chair," *Harper's,* March 1954, 10–11; September 1954, 10–11; May 1955, 9.

46. "Are You for or Against the Echo Park Dam?" *Collier's*, February 1955.

47. Richardson, *Dams, Parks and Politics*, 139.

48. Wiley and Gottlieb, *Empires in the Sun*, 43.

49. Raymond Moley, "Pork, Unlimited," *Newsweek*, May 9, 1955, 108.

50. Brooks, *Speaking for Nature*, 250.

51. Roderick Nash, *Wilderness and the American Mind* (New Haven: Yale University Press, 1967), 213.

52. Richardson, *Dams, Parks and Politics*, 68.

53. Nash, *Wilderness and the American Mind*, 215.

54. Philip L. Fradkin, *A River No More* (New York: Knopf, 1981), 193.

55. *Congressional Record*, 84th Cong. 1st sess., vol. 101 (April 19, 1955), 4657.

56. John McPhee, *Encounters with the Archdruid* (New York: Farrar, Straus & Giroux, 1971), 165.

57. Brown, *Mountain in the Clouds*, 97.

58. A. Dan Tarlock, "Preservation of Scenic Rivers," *Kentucky Law Journal*, 1967, 762.

59. Alvin M. Josephy, Jr., "Cornplanter, Can You Swim?" *American Heritage*, December 1968, 4–9.

60. Arthur E. Morgan, *Dams and Other Disasters* (Boston: Porter Sargent, 1971), 321.

61. Ibid., 48.

62. John M. Kauffmann, *Flow East* (New York: McGraw-Hill, 1973).

63. Eliot Porter, *The Place No One Knew* (San Francisco: Sierra Club Books, 1963), 34.

64. *Congressional Record*, 85th Cong. 2d sess., February 29, 1956, 3619–21.

65. Francois Leydet, *Time and the River Flowing* (San Francisco: Sierra Club, 1964), 127.

66. Martin Litton, interview with author, April 1983.

67. Richard Leonard, interview with author, August 1984.

68. Verne Huser, "Rainbow in the Rock," *American Forests*, February 1974, 42.

69. Fradkin, *A River No More*, 197.

70. Leydet, *Time and the River Flowing*, 112.

71. Department of the Interior, Geological Survey, *Water Yield and Reservoir Storage in the United States*, Circular 409, by Walter B. Langbein (Washington, D.C.: The Department, 1959).

72. Leydet, *Time and the River Flowing*, 129.

73. Editorial, *Sierra Club Bulletin*, March 1965.

74. Leydet, *Time and the River Flowing*, 112.

75. Stewart Udall, interview with author, April 1983.

76. William K. Wyant, *Westward in Eden* (Berkeley and Los Angeles: University of California Press, 1982), 347.

77. Laycock, *The Diligent Destroyers*, 63.

78. Paul Brooks, *The Pursuit of Wilderness* (Boston: Houghton Mifilin, 1971), 82.

79. S. H. Spurr, "Rampart Dam: A Costly Gamble," *Audubon*, May/June 1966, 173.

80. *Pine Bluff Commercial*, February 13, 1972.

81. *Ozark Society Journal*, Autumn 1982.

Other Sources

Everhart, William C. *The National Park Service*. New York: Praeger, 1972.

Frank, Bernard, and Netboy, Anthony. *Water, Land, and People*. New York: Knopf, 1950.

Harvey, Mark W. T. *A Symbol of Wilderness: Echo Park and the American Conservation Movement*. Seattle: University of Washington Press, 1994.

Krutch, Joseph Wood. "Dam the Grand Canyon?" *Audubon*, September 1966.

League of Women Voters. *The Big Water Fight*. Brattleboro, Vt.: Stephen Green Press, 1966.

Moreell, Ben. *Our Nation's Water Resources: Policies and Politics*. Chicago: University of Chicago Law School, 1956.

Seaborg, Eric. "The Battle for Hetch Hetchy." *Sierra*, Nov./Dec. 1981, 61–65.

(This and *Wilderness and the American Mind* by Roderick Nash are excellent sources regarding Hetch Hetchy.)

Stegner, Wallace, ed. *This Is Dinosaur: Echo Park Country and Its Magic Rivers*. New York: Knopf, 1955.

Udall, Stewart. *The Quiet Crisis*. New York: Avon, 1963.

"The Upper Hudson: Time for Decision." *Conservationist*, December 1968, 2–5.

Worster, Donald. *Rivers of Empire: Water, Aridity, and the Growth of the American West*. New York: Pantheon, 1985.

Interviews

Harold Alexander, Arkansas Fish and Game Department
Frank Bell, canoeist, North Carolina
Bill Chandler, Environmental Policy Institute
Arthur Davis, Bureau of the Budget
Samuel Hays, professor of history, University of Pittsburgh
Richard Leonard, Sierra Club
Martin Litton, river outfitter
Jerry Meral, deputy director, California Department of Water Resources
Ted Schad, Bureau of Reclamation and other agencies
Elsie Spurgeon, resident, Confluence, Pa.
Claude Terry, river outfitter
Stewart Udall, secretary of the interior
John Varley, Fish and Wildlife Service, Yellowstone National Park
Edgar Wayburn, Sierra Club

CHAPTER 5: THE MOVEMENT TO SAVE RIVERS

1. Army Corps of Engineers, *The U.S. Army Corps of Engineers and the Environmental Community, 1969–1980*, by Jeffrey Stine (Washington, D.C.: The Corps, 1982). Draft.

2. "A Lawyer Answers the Technocrats," *Trial*, August/September 1969, 14.

3. Don G. Cullimore, "The Cassatot River . . . Another Legal Milestone," *American Forests*, May 1971, 8.

4. Beatrice Hort Holmes, *History of Federal Water Resources Programs and Policies, 1961–70* (Washington, D.C.: U.S. Department of Agriculture, 1979), 114.

5. "The Cross-Florida Boondoggle," *Enfo: A Publication of the Florida Conservation Foundation*, June 1974.

6. Bob Teeters, interview with author, March 1983.

7. Eugene H. Methvin, "The Fight to Save the Flint," *Reader's Digest*, August 1974.

8. Governor Jimmy Carter, *Statement on Spewrell Bluff Dam* (Atlanta: The Governor's Office, October 1, 1973).

9. Bruce Hannon and Julie Cannon, "The Corps Out-Engineered," *Sierra Club Bulletin*, August 1969.

10. Army Corps of Engineers, *The Corps and the Environmental Community*.

11. Chuck Hoffman, interview with author, March 1983.

12. "The GAO Released Its Long-awaited Report on the Proposed Red River Dam," *National Parks*, November 1975, 25.

13. "Fish v. Dams," *Time*, February 17, 1958, 88–89.

14. Brock Evans, "Success at Hells Canyon," *Sierra*, April 1976.

15. Brock Evans, interview with author, April 1983.

16. Verne Huser, "Will Hells Canyon Be Sold Down the River?" *American Forests*, June 1972, 12.

17. Evans, "Success at Hells Canyon."

18. Michael McCloskey, interview with author, March 1981.

19. Thomas Schoenbaum, *The New River Controversy* (Winston–Salem, N.C.: J. F. Blair), 1979.

20. Holmes, *History of Federal Water Resources*, 66.

21. Will Morgan, *The Effect of Federal Water Projects on Cultural Resources* (Washington, D.C.: Environmental Policy Institute, September 1977).

22. Harold A. Feiveson, Frank W. Sinden, and Robert H. Socolow, eds., *Boundaries of Analysis: An Inquiry into the Tocks Island Dam Controversy* (Cambridge, Mass.: Ballinger, 1976).

23. Pete duPont, "The Tocks Island Dam Fight," *Sierra*, July 1972, 13.

24. Peter Wiley and Robert Gottlieb, *Empires in the Sun* (New York: Avon, 1982), 179.

25. "The Indian Water Wars," *Newsweek*, June 13, 1983, 80–82.

26. House Committee on Government Operations, *Teton Dam Disaster: H.R. 94-1 167*, 94th Cong., 2d sess., September 23, 1976.

27. Thomas Dunne and Luna B. Leopold, *Water in Environmental Planning* (San Francisco: W. H. Freeman, 1978), 410.

28. "Auburn Dam: Earthquake Hazards Imperil $1-Billion Project," *Science*, August 1977.

29. Tim Palmer, "The Auburn Dam Debate," *Sacramento*, April 1981, 46–53.

30. Michael Catino, interview with author, January 1981.

31. Robert Broadbent, interview with author, March 1983.

32. William O. Douglas, *A Wilderness Bill of Rights* (Boston: Little, Brown, 1965).

33. Elizabeth Kaplan, "Carter Signs Tellico Dam Bill: Snail Darter to Join Dinosaurs," *Not Man Apart*, November 1979.

34. National Indian Youth Council, "Tellico Dam," *Before Columbus*, December 1, 1979.

35. Peter Matthiessen, "My Turn," *Newsweek*, December 17, 1979.

36. "Troubled Waters," *Country Journal*, April 1978, 88.

37. Robert Cahn, "The Triumph of Wrong," *Audubon*, November 1979, 12.

38. Zygmunt Plater, interview with author, April 1983.

39. Stewart Udall, interview with author, March 1983.

40. Richard Saltonstall, "The Case for a Wild River," *Country Journal*, July 1975.

41. Joel Garreau, *The Nine Nations of North America* (New York: Avon, 1982), 22.

42. Tim Palmer, *Stanislaus: The Struggle for a River* (Berkeley and Los Angeles: University of California Press, 1982).

43. Craig Wright, "The Tuolumne River: A Question of Balance," *Headwaters*, September 1983. Friends of the River newsletter.

44. *Los Angeles Times*, December 14, 1982.

45. Anne W. Simon, *The Thin Edge* (New York: Avon, 1978), 160.

Other Sources

Brooks, Paul. *The Pursuit of Wilderness*. Boston: Houghton Mifflin, 1971.

"Decision on the Snake." *Time*, April 1, 1966, 79–80.

Drew, Elizabeth. "Dam Outrage: The Story of the Army Engineers." *Atlantic*, April 1970, 51–62.

Environmental Policy Center. *Disasters in Water Development*. Washington, D.C.: The Center, 1976.

"The Gillham Dam Project on the Cassatot River Is Back on the Tracks." *Audubon*, July 1972, 100.

Laycock, George. *The Diligent Destroyers*. Garden City, N.Y.: Doubleday, 1970.

Mager, Russ. "Wilderness and the Living Middle Snake." *The Living Wilderness*, Autumn 1969.

Miller, James Nathan. "Bitter Battle of the Waterways." *Reader's Digest*, September 1977, 83.

Norton, Boyd. *Snake Wilderness*. San Francisco: Sierra Club Books, 1972.

Rubin, Hal. "The Political Aftershocks of Carter's Auburn Dam Decision." *California Journal*, May 1977.

"Too Many Dam Failures." *Literary Digest*, July 9, 1921.

Trueblood, Ted. "Must the Salmon River Die?" *Field and Stream*, October 1960, 10.

U.S. Council on Environmental Quality. *The Delaware River Basin*. Washington, D.C.: The Council, 1975.

Interviews

Barry Allen, Coalition to Save the Delaware
John Amodio, Tuolumne River Preservation Trust
Betty Andrews, Friends of the River
Tom Arnold, New England Rivers Center
Brent Blackwelder, Environmental Policy Institute
Robert Broadbent, commissioner of reclamation, Sacramento, Calif.
Howard Brown, American Rivers Conservation Council
Marjorie Carr, Florida Defenders of the Environment
Michael Catino, Bureau of Reclamation, Sacramento, Calif.
Kevin Clark, Bureau of Land Management, Folsom, Calif.
David Conrad, Friends of the Earth
Mark Dubois, Friends of the River
Brock Evans, National Audubon Society
Alexander Gaguine, Friends of the River
Tom Graff, Environmental Defense Fund
Chuck Hoffman, River Conservation Fund
Huey Johnson, secretary, the Resources Agency, Calif.
Dick Linford, river outfitter
Martin Litton, river outfitter
Billy Martin, Bureau of Reclamation, Sacramento, Calif.
Michael McCloskey, Sierra Club
Jerry Meral, California Department of Water Resources
Bill Painter, American Rivers Conservation Council
Guy Phillips, California Assembly Office of Research
Zygmunt Plater, lawyer, Boston, Mass.
Mike Quick, National Park Service, Delaware Water Gap
Bob Teeters, Army Corps of Engineers
Greg Thomas, Natural Resources Defense Council

CHAPTER 6: NATIONAL RIVERS

1. John Craighead, interview with author, February 1983.
2. Ibid. "Wild River," *Montana Wildlife*, June 1957.
3. Ibid. "Wild Rivers," *Naturalist*, Autumn 1965.
4. Paul Bruce Dowling, interview with author, February 1983.
5. Senate Subcommittee on Public Lands, Committee on Interior and Insular Affairs, *The Ozark Rivers Hearings*, 88th Cong., 1st sess. April 8 and 9, May 13, 1963.
6. Ted Swem, interview with author, March 1983.
7. Department of the Interior, *National Wild and Scenic Rivers Study Team to the Secre-*

taries of the Interior and Agriculture, by Stanford Young (Washington, D.C.: The Department, 1964). Draft.

8. Senate Select Committee on National Water Resources, *Senate Report 29*, 87th Cong. 1st sess. 1961.

9. Arthur Davis, interview with author, February 1983.

10. Outdoor Recreation Resources Review Commission, *Outdoor Recreation for America* (Washington, D.C.: The Commission, January 1962).

11. Stewart Udall, interview with author, March 1983.

12. Senate Committee on Interior and Insular Affairs, *Report 792*, 89th Cong. 1st sess., September 28, 1965.

13. House Committee on Interior and Insular Affairs, *Report 1623*, 90th Cong. 2d sess., July 3, 1968.

14. Congress, *Wild and Scenic Rivers Act As Amended Through P.L. 95–625*, Washington, D.C., November 10, 1978.

15. Michael McCloskey, interview with author, March 1983.

16. Comptroller General, Federal Protection and Preservation of Wild and Scenic Rivers Is Slow and Costly (Washington, D.C.: General Accounting Office, May 22, 1978).

17. John Viehman, "Advocate for the Rivers: A Conversation with Howard Brown," *Canoe*, June 1981, 20.

18. Department of the Interior, National Park Service, *Nationwide Rivers Inventory* (Washington, D.C.: The Park Service, 1979).

19. Tim Palmer, "The North Coast National Rivers," *American Forests*, August 1981, 30.

20. Christopher N. Brown, "River Conservation in the 1980s," *Western Wildlands*, Summer 1983, 26.

21. Department of the Interior, National Park Service, "Stream Protection in the United States," by Stanford Young (Seattle: The Park Service, April 1982). Unpublished report.

22. River Conservation Fund, *America's Rivers: An Assessment of State River Conservation Programs*, by Robert C. Hoffman and Keith Fletcher (Washington, D.C.: The Fund, 1984).

23. David Sumner, "Rivers Running Free," *Sierra*, September 1981, 41.

24. Tim Palmer, "A Time For Rivers," *Wilderness*, September 1984.

Other Sources

A Citizen's Guide to River Conservation. Washington, D.C.: The Conservation Foundation, 1984.

Palmer, Tim. *The Wild and Scenic Rivers of America*. Washington, D.C.: Island Press, 1993.

The River Conservation Fund. *Flowing Free*. Washington, D.C.: The Fund, 1977.

U.S. Department of the Interior. *National Wild and Scenic Rivers System: Guidelines for*

Eligibility, Classification, and Management of River Areas. Washington, D.C.: The Department, revised September 1980.

U.S. Department of the Interior. Bureau of Outdoor Recreation. "Wild and Scenic Rivers." *Outdoor Recreation Action,* Spring 1977. Utter, Jack G., and Schultz, John D., eds. *A Handbook on the Wild and Scenic Rivers Act.* Missoula: University of Montana School of Forestry, 1976.

Interviews

Maurice Arnold, Bureau of Outdoor Recreation
Brent Blackwelder, American Rivers Conservation Council
Cliff Blake, National Forest Service
Stewart Brandborg, the Wilderness Society
Christopher Brown, American Rivers Conservation Council
Howard Brown, American Rivers Conservation Council
Al Buck, Bureau of Outdoor Recreation
Don Christensen, Bureau of Outdoor Recreation
Bern Collins, National Park Service
John Craighead, wildlife biologist, Missoula, Mont.
Dale Crane, staff, House Interior and Insular Affairs Committee
Arthur Davis, Outdoor Recreation Resources Review Commission
Paul Bruce Dowling, the America the Beautiful Fund
Bob Eastman, National Park Service
Glenn Eugster, National Park Service
Brock Evans, Sierra Club and National Audubon Society
Roger Fickes, Pennsylvania Department of Environmental Resources
Dave Foreman, Earth First
Mike Fremont, Rivers Unlimited, Ohio
Maurice Goddard, Pennsylvania Department of Environmental Resources
John Haubert, National Park Service
Chuck Hoffman, the River Conservation Fund
Jim Huddleston, Bureau of Outdoor Recreation
John Kauffmann, National Park Service
Loren Kreck, Columbia Falls, Mont.
Tom Lennon, National Forest Service
Deen Lundeen, National Forest Service
Michael McCloskey, Sierra Club
Bob McCullough, Trout Unlimited
Jerry Meral, Planning and Conservation League, Calif.
Pat Munoz, American Rivers Conservation Council
Gaylord Nelson, Senate and the Wilderness Society
Bill Painter, American Rivers Conservation Council
Pat Porchot, Bureau of Outdoor Recreation

Bob Potter, Oregon State Scenic Rivers Program
John Saylor, House of Representatives
Ted Schad, staff, Select Senate Committee on National Water Resources
Larry Stevens, Outdoor Recreation Resources Review Commission
Ted Swem, National Park Service
Stewart Udall, secretary of the interior
Grant Werschkull, Smith River Alliance
Stanford Young, National Park Service

CHAPTER 7: POLITICS AND PROBLEMS OF WATER DEVELOPMENT

1. Daniel Patrick Moynihan, press release, March 5, 1981.

2. Elizabeth Drew, "Dam Outrage: The Story of the Army Engineers," *Atlantic*, April 1970, 51–62.

3. Gilbert White, *Strategies of American Water Management* (Ann Arbor: University of Michigan Press, 1971), 25.

4. Jim Wright, *The Coming Water Famine* (New York: Coward-McCann, 1966).

5. William Ashworth, *Under the Influence* (New York: Hawthorn/Dutton, 1981), 84.

6. Library of Congress, Congressional Research Service, *United States Army Corps of Engineers Background Paper* (Washington, D.C.: The Service, January 8, 1974).

7. George L.aycock, *The Diligent Destroyers* (Garden City, N.Y.: Doubleday, 1970), 123.

8. Comptroller General, *Improvements Needed in Making Benefit-Cost Analysis for Federal Water Resource Projects* (Washington, D.C.: General Accounting Office, September 7, 1973).

9. Ibid., *Changes in Federal Water Projects Repayment Policies Can Reduce Federal Costs* (Washington, D.C.: General Accounting Office, September 7, 1981).

10. Bruce Hannon and Roger Bezdek, "Few Jobs Created by Dams," *Engineering Issues, Journal of Professional Activities*, September 1973, 521–31.

11. Library of Congress, *Army Corps of Engineers Background Paper*.

12. Comptroller General, *Congressional Guidance Needed on Federal Cost Share of Water Resources Projects When Project Benefits Are Not Widespread* (Washington, D.C.: General Accounting Office, November 13, 1980).

13. White, *Strategies of American Water Management*, 50.

14. A. Marsh, "Daniel Boone's Wilderness May Be Tamed by a Lake," *Smithsonian*, September 1975, 56–62.

15. Council on Environmental Quality, *Loss of Agricultural Land*, by Roger Blobaum, for the Citizens Advisory Committee (Washington, D.C.: The Council, 1974).

16. C. B. Belt, Jr., "The 1973 Flood and Man's Constriction of the Mississippi River," *Science*, August 1975.

17. Thomas Y. Canby, "Water: Our Most Precious Resource," *National Geographic*, August 1980.

18. Laurence Pringle, *Wild River* (Philadelphia: Lippincott, 1975).

19. National Water Commission, *Water Policies for the Future* (Port Washington, N.Y.: Water Information Center, 1973).

20. Tim Palmer, "What Price 'Free' Energy?" *Sierra*, July 1983.

21. Phillip Johnson, "Will Small Dams Create Big Problems?" *National Wildlife*, October 1981, 18.

22. Bureau of Reclamation, *Hydropower* (Washington, D.C.: The Bureau, about 1980). Brochure.

23. Lee Lane, "Waterway User Charges," *Sierra Club Bulletin*, May 1977.

24. Gene Marine, *America the Raped* (New York: Avon, 1969).

25. James Nathan Miller, "Big Dam Decision at Alton," *Reader's Digest*, February 1976.

26. Ibid.

27. Environmental Policy Center, *Benefit Claims of the Water Development Agencies* (Washington, D.C.: The Center, June 1976). Booklet.

28. Department of Transportation, *Inland Waterways Users Taxes and Charges* (Washington, D.C.: The Department, February 1982).

29. Environmental Policy Center, *Disasters in Water Development* (Washington, D.C.: The Center, 1976).

30. James Nathan Miller, "Trickery on the Tenn-Tom," *Reader's Digest*, September 1978.

31. "The Engineering of Deceit," *New York Times*, December 14, 1978.

32. Paul Gibson, "Boondoggle," *Forbes*, March 1, 1976.

33. Lane, "Waterway User Charges."

34. Comptroller General, *Federal Charges for Irrigation Projects Reviewed Do Not Cover Costs* (Washington, D.C.: General Accounting Office, March 13, 1981).

35. George Laycock, "Dam the Big Hole," *Field and Stream*, May 1967, 12.

36. Robert Broadbent, interview with author, March 1983.

37. Richard D. Lamm and Michael McCarthy, *The Angry West* (Boston: Houghton Mifflin, 1982), 195.

38. John Johnson, "Big Farms Harvest U.S. Crop Payments," *Sacramento Bee*, November 3, 1983, A24.

39. Richard L. Berkman and W. Kip Viscusi, *Damming the West* (New York: Grossman, 1973).

40. Henry Nash Smith, *Virgin Land* (New York: Vintage Books, 1950), 299.

41. "The East–West Water Conflict," *American City*, August 1966, 37.

42. Fred Powledge, *Water* (New York: Farrar, Straus & Giroux, 1982), 193.

43. Gaylord Nelson, interview with author, March 1983.

44. Peter Wiley and Robert Gottlieb, *Empires in the Sun* (New York: Avon, 1982), 61.

45. Smith, *Virgin Land*, 144.

46. Michael Robinson, *Water for the West* (Chicago: Public Works Historical Society, 1979), 100.

47. Ibid., 44.

48. Powledge, *Water*, 113.

49. "A Bumper Crop of Subsidies," *Newsweek*, July 25, 1983, 60.

50. "The Browning of America," *Newsweek*, February 23, 1981, 26.

51. Department of Agriculture, Soil Conservation Service, *America's Soil and Water: Conditions and Trends* (Washington, D.C.: The Service, 1980).

52. John Graves, *The Water Hustlers* (San Francisco: Sierra Club, 1971).

53. William Wyant, *Westward in Eden* (Berkeley and Los Angeles: University of California Press, 1982), 345.

54. Rice Odell, *Environmental Awakening* (Cambridge, Mass.: Ballinger, 1980), 76.

55. Paul Shepard, *Man in the Landscape* (New York: Knopf, 1967), 149.

56. "The Indian Water Wars," *Newsweek*, June 13, 1983, 80–82.

57. Water Resources Council, *The Nation's Water Resources* (Washington, D.C.: The Council, 1978).

58. Jon R. Luoma, "Water: Grass-roots Opposition Stymies Garrison Diversion," *Audubon*, March 1982, 114.

59. John Boslough, "Rationing a River," *Science* 81, June 1981.

60. Hank Fisher, "Montana's Yellowstone River: Who Gets the Water?" *Sierra*, July 1978.

61. Robert Herbst, interview with author, March 1979.

62. Brad Knickerbocker, "Salt Where Crops Should Be," *Christian Science Monitor*, June 21, 1979, 12–13.

63. Odell, *Environmental Awakening*, 81.

64. Water Resources Information Center, *Water Atlas of the U.S.* (Port Washington, N.Y.: The Center, 1973), plate 81.

65. Rice Odell, "Silt, Cracks, Floods, and Other Dam Foolishness," *Audubon*, September 1975.

66. Guy P. Gibson, "Cracking the German Dams," *Atlantic*, December 1943, 45–50.

Other Sources

Ashworth, William. *Nor Any Drop to Drink*. New York: Summit Books, 1982.

Cronin, John, and Kennedy, Robert F., Jr. *The Riverkeepers: Two Activists Fight to Reclaim Our Environment as a Basic Human Right*. New York: Scribner, 1997.

Eckstein, Otto. *Water-Resource Development: The Economics of Project Evaluation*. Cambridge: Harvard University Press, 1965.

Ferejohn, John A. *Pork Barrel Politics*. Stanford, Calif.: Stanford University Press, 1974.

Gernerd, Kurt A. "Protection of Instream Flows." *Water Spectrum*, Spring 1982.

"The Homestead Act Hits Home." *Time*, October 17, 1977, 20.

Johnson, Rich. *The Central Arizona Project*. Tucson: University of Arizona Press, 1977.

McCaull, Julian. "Dams of Pork." *Environment*, January 1975.

Miller, James Nathan. "Needed: A Bill of Rights for Our Rivers." *Reader's Digest*, July 1971.

Mishan, E. J. *Cost–Benefit Analysis*. New York: Praeger, 1976.

Moss, Frank E. *The Water Crisis*. New York: Praeger, 1967.

Schwinden, Ted. "Water of the Yellowstone." *Montana Outdoors*, May 1978.

Sheridan, David. "The Overwatered West: Overdrawn at the Well." *Environment*, March 1981.

Turner, Frederick. "Sumerian Implications." *Wilderness*, Summer 1982.

Interviews

Brent Blackwelder, Environmental Policy Center
Robert Broadbent, commissioner of reclamation
Christopher Brown, American Rivers Conservation Council
James Cook, Bureau of Reclamation, Sacramento, Calif.
Ronald Corso, Federal Energy Regulatory Commission
Arthur Davis, Bureau of the Budget
Quenton Edson, Federal Energy Regulatory Commission
Robert Herbst, assistant secretary of the interior
Gaylord Nelson, Senate
Edward Osann, National Wildlife Federation
James Posewitz, Montana Fish and Game Department
Ronald Robie, California State Water Resources Control Board
Richard Roos-Collins, Friends of the River
Russell Shay, Sierra Club
Jeffrey Stine, historian under contract with the Army Corps of Engineers, Washington, D.C.
Don Sundeen, Fish and Wildlife Service, Portland, Oreg.
David Weiman, lobbyist, Washington, D.C.
Frank Welsch, Phoenix, Ariz.
Stanford Young, National Park Service

CHAPTER 8: A NEW ERA

1. Western Writers of America, *Water Trails West* (New York: Avon, 1978), x.

2. U.S. Army Corps of Engineers, *The Headwaters District*, by Leland Johnson (Pittsburgh, Pa.: The Corps, about 1979), 77.

3. George Laycock, *The Diligent Destroyers* (Garden City, N.Y.: Doubleday, 1970), 200.

4. Elmo Richardson, *Dams, Parks and Politics* (Lexington: University Press of Kentucky, 1973).

5. Beatrice Hort Holmes, *History of Federal Water Resources Programs and Policies, 1961–70* (Washington, D.C.: U.S. Department of Agriculture, 1979), 142.

6. Peter Wiley and Robert Gottlieb, *Empires in the Sun* (New York: Avon, 1982), 52.

7. The Conservation Foundation, newsletter, December 1976.

8. Arthur Magida, "Renovating the Bureaucracy," *Environmental Action*, October 1977, 3.

9. Philip L. Fradkin, *A River No More* (New York: Knopf, 1981), 9.

10. Richard Lamm and Michael McCarthy, *The Angry West* (Boston: Houghton Mifflin, 1982), 188.

11. Ibid., 37.

12. William Ashworth, *Under the Influence* (New York: Hawthorn/Dutton, 1981), 165.

13. Fradkin, *A River No More*, 11.

14. Ward Sinclair, *Washington Post*, August 29, 1978.

15. *Washington Post*, October 23, 1978.

16. Fred Powledge, *Water* (New York: Farrar, Straus & Giroux, 1982), 248.

17. John Johnson, *Sacramento Bee*, July 13, 1983, A28.

18. *Washington Post*, January 25, 1982.

19. Robert Broadbent, interview with author, March 1983.

Other Sources

Hubbard, Henry. "Carter Versus Congress: Another Showdown Over Water." *National Wildlife*, April 1979.

Interviews

Brent Blackwelder, Environmental Policy Institute
Robert Broadbent, commissioner of reclamation
Robert Edgar, House of Representatives
Guy Martin, assistant secretary of the interior
Edward Osann, National Wildlife Federation
Ted Schad, Bureau of the Budget
Bob Teeters, Army Corps of Engineers

CHAPTER 9: NEEDS AND ALTERNATIVES

1. Department of Agriculture, Soil Conservation Service, *America's Soil and Water: Conditions and Trends* (Washington, D.C.: The Service, 1980).

2. Water Resources Council, *The Nation's Water Resources, 1975–2000*, vol. 1, *Summary* (Washington, D.C.: The Council, 1979).

3. Fred Powledge, *Water* (New York: Farrar, Straus & Giroux, 1982), 37.

4. Department of the Interior, Geological Survey, *Estimated Use of Water in the United States in 1980*, Circular 1001 (Alexandria, Va.: The Survey, 1983).

5. Ibid.

6. Water Resources Council, *The Nation's Water Resources.*

7. Department of the Interior, Geological Survey, *Estimated Use of Water in the United States.*

8. Ibid.

9. "The Browning of America," *Newsweek*, February 23, 1981, 26.

10. Ibid.

11. Natural Resources Defense Council, newsletter, January 1978.

12. John Naisbitt, *Megatrends* (New York: Warner Books, 1984).

13. Water Resources Council, *The Nation's Water Resources.*

14. Robert Broadbent, interview with author, March 1983.

15. Jim Wright, *The Coming Water Famine* (New York: Coward-McCann, 1966).

16. Gilbert White, *Strategies of American Water Management* (Ann Arbor: University of Michigan Press, 1971), 46.

17. Beatrice Hort Holmes, *History of Federal Water Resources Programs and Policies, 1961–70* (Washington, D.C.: U.S. Department of Agriculture, 1979), 27.

18. "Muddy Water," *Wall Street Journal*, September 13, 1982.

19. Philip L. Fradkin, *A River No More* (New York: Knopf, 1981), 201.

20. Natural Resources Defense Council, newsletter, January 1978.

21. Tim Palmer, *Stanislaus: The Struggle for a River* (Berkeley and Los Angeles: University of California Press, 1982).

22. Robert Rienow and Leona Train Rienow, *Moment in the Sun* (New York: Ballantine, 1967), 76.

23. Department of Agriculture, Soil Conservation Service, *America's Soil and Water.*

24. "The Browning of America," 26.

25. Tim Palmer, *Stanislaus*, 155.

26. Environmental Policy Institute, *Survey of Water Conservation Programs in the Fifty States*, by Brent Blackwelder and Peter Carlson (Washington, D.C.: The Institute, 1982).

27. Ibid.

28. Ibid.

29. Ibid.

30. Rice Odell, *Environmental Awakening* (Cambridge, Mass.: Ballinger, 1980), 86.

31. Environmental Policy Institute, Survey of Water Conservation Programs in the Fifty States.

Other Sources

California. Department of Water Resources. *Water Conservation in California*. Bulletin 198. Sacramento: The Department, 1976.

Gibbons, John, and Chandler, William. *Energy: The Conservation Revolution*. New York: Plenum Press, 1981.

Jones, Andrew, and Dyer, Jim. "The Water Efficiency Revolution." *River Voices*, Spring 1993.

Lovins, Amory. *Soft Energy Paths: Toward A Durable Peace*. San Francisco: Friends of the Earth, 1977.

McGhee, Ronnie, Reardon, Mary, and Shulman, Arleen, eds. *Readings in Water Conservation*. Washington, D.C.: National Association of Counties Research, about 1976.

U.S. Environmental Protection Agency. *Clean Water Through Conservation*. Washington, D.C.: The Agency, April 1995.

U.S. Environmental Protection Agency. Office of Water Program Operations. *Proceedings, National Conference on Water Conservation and Municipal Wastewater Flow Reduction*. Washington, D.C.: The Agency, August 1979.

U.S. Water Resources Council. *Floodplain Management Guidelines*. Washington, D.C.: The Council, February 10, 1978.

"Watering a Continent." *Newsweek*, February 22, 1965, 53.

Interviews

Brent Blackwelder, Environmental Policy Institute
Robert Broadbent, commissioner of reclamation
Verne Huser, Office of Environmental Mediation, University of Washington
Laura King, Natural Resources Defense Council
Jonas Minton, California Department of Water Resources
George Palmiter, Channelization Consultant, Montpelier, Ohio
Bob Teeters, Army Corps of Engineers

CHAPTER 10: THE LAST WEALTH

1. Charles M. Clusen, ed., *Engineering a Victory for Our Environment* (San Francisco: Sierra Club, 1973), 5.

2. Thomas F. Waters, *Streams and Rivers of Minnesota* (Minneapolis: University of Minnesota Press, 1977), 329.

3. Anthony Netboy, *The Salmon: Their Fight for Survival* (Boston: Houghton Mifflin, 1974), 310.

4. Gilbert White, *Strategies of American Water Management* (Ann Arbor: University of Michigan Press, 1971), 84.

5. Rice Odell, "Silt, Cracks, Floods, and Other Dam Foolishness," *Audubon*, September 1975.

6. Jeff Raimundo, "Dam-Safety Bill Faces Key Test Despite U.S. Public Inattention," *Sacramento Bee*, September 18, 1983, A4.

7. Bob Teeters, interview with author, March 1983.

8. Odell, "Silt, Cracks, Floods, and Other Dam Foolishness."

9. Kathleen K. Wiegner, "The Water Crisis: It's Almost Here," *Forbes*, August 20, 1979.

10. Claire Sterling, "Super Dams: The Perils of Progress," *Reader's Digest*, July 1972.

11. Ibid.

12. William Steffen, "Furor over the Franklin," *Sierra*, September 1984, 45–49.

13. Fred Powledge, *Water* (New York: Farrar, Straus & Giroux, 1984), 276.

Interviews

Brent Blackwelder, Environmental Policy Institute
Robert Broadbent, commissioner of reclamation
Clifford Freeman, Chief, Driftpile, Alberta, Canada
Bob Teeters, Army Corps of Engineers
Stewart Udall, secretary of the interior
Philip Williams, hydrologist, San Francisco, Calif.

CHAPTER 11: THE SECOND GENERATION OF RIVER CONSERVATION

1. Tim Palmer, *The Kings River* (Fresno, Calif.: The Committee to Save the Kings River, 1987), available from Friends of the River, Sacramento.

2. L. Martin Griffin, *Saving the Marin-Sonoma Coast* (Healdsburg, Calif.: Sweetwater Press, 1998), 190.

3. Ted Williams, "Who Can Save a Wetland?" *Audubon,* September 1999, 66.

4. Robert S. Devine, "The Trouble with Dams," *The Atlantic Monthly,* August 1995.

5. Lindsey Grant, *Juggernaut: Growth on a Finite Planet* (Santa Ana, Calif.: Seven Locks Press, 1996).

6. Timothy Egan, "Las Vegas Stakes Claim in 90's Water War," *New York Times,* April 10, 1994, 18.

7. American Rivers et al., *Paving Our Way to Water Shortages: How Sprawl Aggravates the Effects of Drought* (Washington, D.C.: American Rivers, 2002), 4.

8. American Rivers, *America's Most Endangered Rivers of 1998* (Washington, D.C.: American Rivers, 1998), 38.

9. Paul Koberstein, "Draining California Dry," *Cascadia Times,* July/August 2000, 7–9.

10. Steve Evans, "FOR's River Conservation Achievements of 2002," *Headwaters,* Winter 2003, 8.

11. Patrick McCully, *Silenced Rivers: The Ecology and Politics of Large Dams* (London: Zed Books, 2001).

12. World Commission on Dams, *Dams and Dam Development* (London: Earthscan, 2000).

13. Mary Christina Wood, "Reclaiming the Natural Rivers: The Endangered Species Act as Applied to Endangered River Ecosystems," *Arizona Law Review* 40 (1998): 197.

14. National Research Council, *Restoration of Aquatic Ecosystems* (Washington, D.C.: National Academy Press, 1991).

15. Lawrence L. Master, Stephanie R. Flack, and Bruce A. Stein, eds., *Rivers of Life* (Arlington, Va.: The Nature Conservancy, 1998).

16. Melvin L. Warren and Brooks M. Burr, "Status of Freshwater Fishes in the United States: Overview of Imperiled Fauna," *Fisheries,* January 1994, 6–19.

17. Anthony Ricciardi, "Endangered Freshwater Species," *American Rivers,* newsletter, Spring 2000.

18. James R. Karr and Ellen W. Chu, *Restoring Life in Running Waters* (Washington, D.C.: Island Press, 1999).

19. The Nature Conservancy, *Rivers of Life.*

20. David M. Gillilan and Thomas C. Brown, *Instream Flow Protection* (Washington, D.C.: Island Press, 1997).

21. Colbert E. Cushing and J. David Allan, *Streams: Their Ecology and Life* (San Diego: Academic Press, 2001).

22. John D. Echeverria, Pope Barrow, and Richard Roos-Collins, *Rivers at Risk* (Washington, D.C.: Island Press, 1989).

23. National Park Service Rivers, Trails and Conservation Assistance Program, *River Renewal* (Washington, D.C.: The Service, May 1996), 3.

24. American Rivers, "Celebrating 30 Years of Protecting and Restoring America's Rivers," *American Rivers,* newsletter, Winter 2003, 6.

25. Douglas Jehl, "Atlanta's Growing Thirst Creates Water War," *New York Times,* May 24, 2002.

26. Tim Palmer, *The Snake River: Window to the West* (Washington, D.C.: Island Press, 1991).

27. High Country News, *Western Water Law Made Simple* (Washington, D.C.: Island Press, 1987).

28. Sarah F. Bates, David H. Getches, Lawrence J. MacDonnell, and Charles F. Wilkinson, *Searching out the Headwaters: Change and Rediscovery in Western Water Policy* (Washington, D.C.: Island Press, 1993).

29. Michael Collier, Robert H. Webb, and John C. Schmidt, *Dams and Rivers* (Tucson, Ariz.: United States Geological Survey, Circular 1126, 1996).

30. Committee to Review the Glen Canyon Environmental Studies, *River and Dam Management* (Washington, D.C.: National Academy Press, 1987).

31. American Rivers, *North America's Most Endangered and Threatened Rivers of 1997* (Washington, D.C.: American Rivers, 1997), 3.

32. Daniel P. Beard, *Blueprint for Reform: The Commissioner's Plan for Reinventing Reclamation* (Washington, D.C.: The Bureau, 1993).

33. Western Network, *Water in the West: Western Water Flows to Cities* (Washington, D.C.: Island Press, 1985).

34. University of Colorado School of Law, Natural Resources Law Center, *Restoring the Waters* (Boulder, Colo.: The Center, 1997).

35. Palmer, *The Snake River.*

36. American Rivers, *America's Most Endangered Rivers of 2002* (Washington, D.C.: American Rivers, 2002), 18.

37. "A Killing in the Klamath," *Cascadia Times,* Fall 2002, 3.

38. Joshua Zaffos, "Klamath Water Worth More in River," *High Country News,* December 9, 2002, 5.

39. Tim Palmer, *Lifelines: The Case for River Conservation* (Washington, D.C.: Island Press, 1994); also B. L. Swift, "Status of Riparian Ecosystems in the United States," *Water Resources Bulletin* 20, no. 2 (April 1984); Constance Elizabeth Hunt, *Down by the River* (Washington, D.C.: Island Press, 1988); and Pacific Rivers Council, "Putting Our Work in Perspective," *Freeflow,* December 2002, 1.

40. Tim Palmer, *America by Rivers* (Washington, D.C.: Island Press, 1996), 106.

41. River Network, *An Evaluation of Flood Management Benefits through Floodplain Restoration on the Willamette River,* by Philip Williams and Associates (Portland, Oreg.: River Network, 1996).

42. National Park Service, Rivers and Trails Conservation Assistance Program, *Economic Impacts of Protecting Rivers, Trails, and Greenway Corridors* (Washington D.C., 1990); also The Conservation Fund, *Greenways* (Washington, D.C.: Island Press, 1993).

43. Rutherford H. Platt, *Land Use and Society* (Washington, D.C.: Island Press, 1996).

44. Jon Kusler and Larry Larson, "Beyond the Ark," *Environment,* June 1993.

45. Tom Knudson and Nancy Vogel, "The Gathering Storm," special insert, *Sacramento Bee,* November 23–27, 1997.

46. American Rivers, *North America's Most Endangered and Threatened Rivers of 1997.*

47. Timothy Beatley, David J. Brower, and Anna K. Schwab, *An Introduction to Coastal Zone Management* (Washington, D.C.: Island Press, 1994).

48. David R. Godschalk et al., *Natural Hazard Mitigation* (Washington, D.C.: Island Press, 1999), and Rutherford H. Platt, *Disasters and Democracy* (Washington, D.C.: Island Press, 1999).

49. Interagency Floodplain Management Review Committee, *Sharing the Challenge: Floodplain Management into the 21st Century,* or *"The Galloway Report"* (Washington, D.C.: U.S. Government Printing Office, June 1994).

50. American Rivers, *In Harm's Way: The Costs of Floodplain Development* (Washington, D.C.: American Rivers, 1999), 10–11.

51. Scott Faber, "Flood Policy and Management," *River Voices,* published by River Network, Summer 1997, 1.

52. Brent Walth, *Fire at Eden's Gate* (Portland: Oregon Historical Society Press, 1998), 139.

53. Robert W. Adler, Jessica C. Landman, and Diane M. Cameron, *The Clean Water Act 20 Years Later* (Washington, D.C.: Island Press, 1993).

54. Richard A Smith, Richard B. Alexander, and M. Gordon Wolman, "Water-quality Trends in the Nation's Rivers," *Science* 235 (March 27, 1987).

55. Nancy Stoner, *Clean Water at Risk* (New York: Natural Resources Defense Council, 2002), 3.

56. U.S. Environmental Protection Agency, *National Water Quality Inventory, 2000 Report* (Washington, D.C.: EPA Office of Water, 2002), 14.

57. Environmental Working Group, *Dishonorable Discharge* (Washington, D.C.: The Group, October 1996).

58. Jack Brubaker, *Down the Susquehanna to the Chesapeake* (University Park: The Pennsylvania State University Press, 2002), 60.

59. American Rivers, *America's Most Endangered Rivers of 2001* (Washington, D.C.: American Rivers, 2001), 34.

60. Miguel Bustillo, *LA Times–Washington Post* Service, "Tests Find Toxic Fuel Ingredient in Lettuce," *The Oregonian*, April 28, 2003, A9.

61. J. Curtis and T. Profeta, eds., *After Silent Spring* (New York: Natural Resources Defense Council, 1993).

62. Tim Palmer, *Lifelines*.

63. Lolly Merrell, "Life in the Wasteland," *High Country News,* December 9, 2002, 9.

64. Theo Colborn, Diane Dumanoski, and John Peterson Myers, *Our Stolen Future* (New York: Dutton, 1996).

65. Sandra Steingraber, *Living Downstream* (New York: Vintage, 1997).

66. U.S. Geological Survey, *Pharmaceuticals, Hormones, and Other Organic Wastewater Contaminants in U.S. Streams, 1999–2000: A National Reconnaissance* (Iowa City: The Survey, 2002).

67. Environmental Protection Agency, *National Water Quality Inventory: 2000.*

68. Ed Odgers, "Wisconsin's 'Bad Actors' Program: Controlling Agricultural Runoff," *River Voices,* published by River Network, September 1992.

69. Ted Williams, "Assembly Line Swine," *Audubon,* March–April 1998.

70. Rodney Barker, *And the Waters Turned to Blood* (New York: Simon & Schuster, 1997).

71. Natural Resources Defense Council, *Just Add Water* (New York: The Council, 1996).

72. U.S. Congressional Budget Office, *Future Investment in Drinking Water and Wastewater Infrastructure* (Washington, D.C.: The Office, May 2002).

73. Don Elder and Rita Haberman, "Playing the Drinking Water Card," *River Voices,* published by River Network, Fall 1996, 1.

74. Don Elder, Gayle Killam, and Paul Koberstein, *The Clean Water Act: An Owner's Manual* (Portland, Oreg.: River Network, 1999).

75. National Wildlife Federation, *Pollution Paralysis: State Inaction Puts Waters at Risk* (Vienna, Va.: The Federation, 1998), and John H. Cushman, Jr., "States Neglecting Pollution Rules, White House Says," *New York Times*, December 15, 1996.

76. Jenny Coyle, "Right-to-Know-Nothing Laws Boon to Polluters," *Planet,* published by the Sierra Club, November 1997.

77. Don Elder, Gayle Killam, and Paul Koberstein, *The Clean Water Act: An Owners Manual* (Portland, Oreg.: River Network, 1999).

78. John Cronin and Robert F. Kennedy, Jr., *The Riverkeepers* (New York: Scribner, 1997).

CHAPTER 12: RIVERS IN THE TWENTY-FIRST CENTURY

1. American Rivers, *The River Protection Imperative: A Five-year Strategic Plan— 1992–96* (Washington, D.C.: American Rivers, 1991), unpublished paper.

2. American Rivers, *Shaping Solutions for a New Century* (Washington, D.C.: American Rivers, 1997).

3. American Rivers, *America's Most Endangered Rivers of 2002* (Washington, D.C.: American Rivers, 2002).

4. Tim Palmer, *The Heart of America* (Washington, D.C.: Island Press, 1999).

5. U.S. Environmental Protection Agency and U.S. Department of Agriculture, *Clean Water Action Plan: Restoring and Protecting America's Waters* (Washington, D.C.: The Agency, 1998).

6. "Half a Billion Americans?" *The Economist*, August 22, 2002.

7. U.S. Environmental Protection Agency, *National Water Quality Inventory, 2000 Report* (Washington D.C.: The Agency, 2002).

8. Nancy Stoner, *Clean Water at Risk* (New York: Natural Resources Defense Council, 2002), 5.

9. John H. Cushman, Jr., "States Neglecting Pollution Rules, White House Says," *New York Times*, December 15, 1996.

10. Dashka Slater, "The Big Book of Bush," *Sierra*, September/October 2002.

11. Lolly Merrell, "Life in the Wasteland," *High Country News*, December 9, 2002, 8.

12. Reuters News Service, "EPA finds few punished for water pollution, says report," www.enn.com/news/2003-06-10/s.

13. Brian Stempeck, "Agency's criminal enforcement decreases in Bush's first year," *Greenwire*, January 11, 2002, www.eenews.net.

14. Stoner, *Clean Water at Risk*, 7.

15. Penny Loeb, "Shear Madness," *U.S. News and World Report*, special report, October 13, 1997, 3.

16. Paul Koberstein, "The Bush Legacy: Year One," *Cascadia Times*, Spring 2002, 5.

17. Katharine Q. Seelye, "U.S. Report Faults Efforts to Track Water Pollution," *New York Times*, May 27, 2003.

18. Ted Williams, "Upstream and Out of Mind," *Fly Rod and Reel*, April/May 2003.

19. Scott Weidensaul, *Mountains of the Heart* (Golden, Colo.: Fulcrum, 1994), 74.

20. Rob Perks et al., *Rewriting the Rules: The Bush Administration's Assault on the Environment* (New York: Natural Resources Defense Council, 2003).

21. Stoner, *Clean Water at Risk*, 13.

22. John Echeverria and Raymond Booth Eby, eds., *Let the People Judge: Wise Use and the Private Property Rights Movement* (Washington, D.C.: Island Press, 1995).

23. Tim Palmer, *The Wild and Scenic Rivers of America* (Washington, D.C.: Island Press, 1993).

24. Maine Public Employees for Environmental Responsibility, *Losing Paradise: The Allagash Wilderness Waterway under Attack* (Washington, D.C.: The Public Employees, 2002); also Kent Olson, *River of Broken Promises* (Bar Harbor, Me.: Allagash Partners, 2001).

25. National Park Service, *The Nationwide Rivers Inventory* (Washington, D.C.: The Service, 1982).

26. John Haubert, *A Third Decade of River Protection* (Washington, D.C.: National Park Service, 1998), unpublished paper.

27. American Rivers, *Private Lands River Protection Program* (Washington, D.C.: American Rivers, 1992), 5, unpublished paper.

28. Mitch Lansky, *Beyond the Beauty Strip* (Gardiner, Me.: Tilbury House, 1992); also Elliott A. Norse, *Ancient Forests of the Pacific Northwest* (Washington, D.C.: Island Press, 1990).

29. Wallace Stegner, *Beyond the Hundredth Meridian: John Wesley Powell and the Second Opening of the West* (Lincoln: University of Nebraska Press, 1982).

30. Benton MacKaye, *The New Exploration: A Philosophy of Regional Planning* (New York: Harcourt Brace, 1928), 36.

31. Kevin Coyle, "The Future of River-Saving—the Emerging Watershed Strategy," *American Rivers*, Fall 1992.

32. River Network, *Watershed 2000* (Portland, Oreg.: River Network, 1995).

33. Bob Doppelt et al., *Entering the Watershed* (Washington, D.C.: Island Press, 1993), xxxiii.

34. U.S. Environmental Protection Agency, *Watershed Events: The Watershed Protection Approach: An Overview* (Washington, D.C.: EPA Office of Wetlands, Oceans, and Watersheds, 1991).

35. John Cronin and Robert F. Kennedy, Jr., *The Riverkeepers* (New York: Scribner, 1997), 208, 225.

36. River Network, *River Voices,* Portland, Oreg., entire issues, Summer 1994, Fall 1995, Winter 1997.

37. River Network, *1998–1999 River and Watershed Conservation Directory* (Portland, Oreg.: River Network, 1999).

38. The Nature Conservancy, *Freshwater Initiative* (Arlington, Va.: The Conservancy, 1999).

39. Tim Palmer, *The Heart of America* (Washington D.C.: Island Press, 1999), 190.

40. Tim Palmer, *The Columbia* (Seattle: The Mountaineers Books, 1997), 111.

41. Jim Britell, *Partnerships, Roundtables and "Quincy-type" Groups Are Bad Ideas that Cannot Resolve Environmental Conflicts,* 1997, unpublished paper, www.britell.com (accessed October 28, 2003).

42. Christopher N. Brown, "The Watershed Approach," *River Voices*, published by River Network, Winter 1997, 6.

43. American Rivers, Friends of the Earth, and Trout Unlimited, *Dam Removal Success Stories* (Washington, D.C.: American Rivers, 1999), xvii.

44. American Rivers, Friends of the Earth, and Trout Unlimited, ix.

45. Bruce Babbitt, "Streams of Consciousness," *River* magazine, October 1998, 38.

46. Tim Palmer, *Lifelines: The Case for River Conservation* (Washington, D.C.: Island Press, 1994), 132–36.

47. Northwest Energy Coalition and Natural Resources Defense Council, *Going with the Flow: Replacing Energy from Four Snake River Dams* (Seattle: The Coalition, 2000).

48. Save Our Wild Salmon Coalition, *Wild Salmon Forever* (Seattle: The Coalition, 1994).

49. RAND Publications, *Generating Electric Power in the Pacific Northwest* (Washington, D.C.: Rand, 2002).

50. Susan Whaley and Rocky Barker, "Breaching Saves Money," *Idaho Statesman,* September 22, 1997.

51. Richard N. Williams et al., *Return to the River* (Portland, Oreg.: The Independent Scientific Group for the Northwest Power Planning Council, 1996). Also, Idaho Department of Fish and Game, *Idaho's Anadromous Fish Stocks: Their Status and Recovery Options* (Boise, Idaho: The Department, 1998), and Columbia River Inter-Tribal Fish Commission, *Wy-kan-ush-mi Wa-kish-wit: Spirit of the Salmon* (Portland, Oreg.: The Commission, 1995).

52. Institute for Fisheries Resources, *The Cost of Doing Nothing: The Economic Burden of Salmon Declines in the Columbia River Basin* (Eugene, Oreg.: 1996).

53. Lisa Mighetto and Wesley J. Ebel, *Saving the Salmon: A History of the U.S. Army Corps of Engineers; Efforts to Protect Anadromous Fish on the Columbia and Snake Rivers* (Portland, Oreg.: U.S. Army Corps of Engineers, 1994).

54. Tim Palmer, *The Columbia: Sustaining a Modern Resource* (Seattle: The Mountaineers, 1997).

55. Willett Kempton, James S. Boster, and Jennifer A. Hartley, *Environmental Values in American Culture* (Cambridge, Mass.: MIT Press, 1995), 94.

56. American Rivers, *A Study of the Public's Awareness and Attitudes towards Environmental Issues Related to America's Rivers* (Washington, D.C.: American Rivers, 1994).

57. Penn, Schoen & Berland Associates, Inc., *Summary of Findings: National Geographic Society's River Poll* (Washington, D.C.: P, S & B, 2001), unpublished paper.

58. Don Elder and Rita Haberman, "Playing the Drinking Water Card," *River Voices,* by River Network, Fall 1996, 1.

59. Lindsey Grant, "Diverging Demography, Converging Destinies," *NPG Forum,* by Negative Population Growth, January 2003.

ORGANIZATIONS INVOLVED IN RIVER PROTECTION

The following is a selected list. Several thousand river and watershed groups are organized in the United States at the national, state, and local levels. River Network is the best source for current names and addresses.

River Network
P.O. Box 8787
Portland, OR 97207
800-423-6747
www.rivernetwork.org

American Rivers
1025 Vermont Ave. NW, Suite 720
Washington, D.C. 20005
800-296-6900
www.americanrivers.org

Clean Water Action
4455 Connecticut Ave. NW, A 300
Washington, D.C. 20008
202-895-0420
www.cleanwateraction.org

Trout Unlimited
1500 Wilson Blvd. # 310
Arlington, VA 22209
800-834-2419
www.tu.org

American Canoe Association
7432 Alban Station Blvd. Suite B-226
Springfield, VA 22150
703-451-0141
www.aca-paddler.org

American Fisheries Society
5410 Grosvenor Lane, Suite 110
Bethesda, MD 20814
301-897-8616
www.fisheries.org

American Whitewater Affiliation
1424 Fenwick Lane
Silver Spring, MD 20910
866-262-8429
www.americanwhitewater.org

Izaak Walton League of America
707 Conservation Lane
Gaithersburg, MD 20878
800-453-5463
www.iwla.org

The Nature Conservancy
4245 North Fairfax Drive, Suite 100
Arlington, VA 22203
800-628-6860
http://nature.org

Friends of the River
915 20th Street
Sacramento, CA 95814
916-442-3155
www.friendsoftheriver.org

National Park Service
Rivers and Trails Assistance Program
1849 C St. NW
Washington, D.C. 20240
202-354-6900
www.nps.gov.rtca

INDEX

development of, 18–19, 26–27; Hells
Canyon and, 107–10; justification for,
192–95; permits for, 4, 55; plans for,
44, 177; private development of, 38–
39, 60; projections for, 241, 246; relicensing of, 266–67; revival of, 260; St.
John River and, 125–27; subsidies for,
188, 190; Tuolumne River and, 131–
32. *See also names of individual dams*
hydrology, 6. *See also* rivers
Hydropower Reform Coalition, 267

Ickes, Harold, 40, 65, 85
Idaho Power Company, 69
Idaho Rivers United, 268
Illinois River Canal, 17, 196
Illinois River, OR, 177, 294
immigration, 262, 289
Indians, 11, 15–16, 78–79, 115, 254, 292;
Cherokee, 120–24; Cree, 39; Iroquois,
76; Navajo, 74; Nez Perce, 193; Seneca, 76–78; Shoshone, 271; Washoe,
208; water rights and, 32; Yavapai,
114–15, 207; Yuki, 175; Yukon River
and, 90
Inland Waterways Commission, 41, 55
instream flows, 208–12, 265–72, 315
interest rates for water projects, 189–90
International Rivers Network, 263
Ipswich River, 267
iron triangle, 185–86
irrigation, 2, 13, 203–5, 316; acreage and
amount of, 1, 34, 238–39; alternatives
to, 247–48; Bureau of Reclamation
and, 33; displacement by, 201–3; early
development of, 16, 19–20, 28–29;
groundwater and, 205–8; justification
for, 198–202; subsidies for, 185, 188,
199–205; waste and, 3, 248, 271. *See
also* Bureau of Reclamation
Izaak Walton League, 60–61, 64, 303, 349

Jacks Fork River, 10, 157, 163
Jackson Lake Reservoir, 57

Jackson, President Andrew, 217
Jackson River, 117
James Bay Project, 39
James River, MO, 55
Jarvis, Howard, 226
Jefferson, President Thomas, 203, 217
John Day Dam, 26, 88
Johnson, Harold, 118
Johnson, President Lyndon, 42, 79, 87,
100, 135, 163, 166–67, 220, 244
Johnson, Robert Underwood, 50–52
Johnson, Sarah, 309
Jones, Barton, 77
Jones–Esch Act, 56
Jordahl, Bud, 157
Jordan, Len, 166
Juniata River, 17

Kauffmann, John, 66, 157
Kaweah River, 58
Keating Dam, 135
Kennebec River, 16, 308–9
Kennedy, President John F., 85, 100, 135,
160, 162, 167, 183, 219–220
Kennedy, Robert F., Jr., 303
Kentucky Rivers Coalition, 106
Kent, William, 51
Kern River, 258
Kesterson National Wildlife Refuge, 213
Kiamichi River, 264
Kickapoo River, 38, 113, 244
Killam, Gayle, 283–84
King, Laura, 246
Kings River, 40, 58, 64–65, 257–58, 286
Kinzua Dam, 69, 76–79
Kissimmee River, 192
Klamath River, 175, 177, 271–72
Kleppe, Thomas, 111
Klickitat River, 294
Knopf, Alfred, 72
Koch, Ed, 202
Kootenai River, 88, 115
Kostmayer, Peter, 113
Krug, J. A., 78

tion, 113; funds needed for, 282;
groundwater and, 207–8; runoff as,
279–83; salinity, 212–13; sewage, 8,
137, 279; silt, 8, 37; toxins, 8, 279–81;
water conservation and, 248–50
Pomerance, Rafe, 169
Pomperaug River, 273, 307
Popple River, 177
population projections, 189, 240, 261,
268, 289, 315
pork barrel, defined, 183
Porter, Eliot, 79, 81
Posewitz, Jim, 211
Potomac River, 64, 79, 165, 279, 290
Powell, John Wesley, 20–21, 83, 299
presidential administrations, 217–18,
288–93
Progressive Movement, 54, 56
Prosser, David, 252
Prostka, Harold, 116
Provo River, 258
Proxmire, Senator William, 183, 188,
209, 232
Public Utility Regulatory Policies Act, 4,
39, 193, 260
Pyramid Lake, 208
Pytlak, Shirley, 116

Quakers, 76–77

Rainbow Bridge, 82–83
Rainy River, 55
Raker, John, 51
Rampart Dam, 45, 89–92, 212
RAND, 311
Rankin Rapids Dam, 125, 161
Rapid River, ID, 109, 171
Rappahannock River, 93, 168
RARE II, 181
Reagan administration, 10, 34, 41, 129,
174–76, 191, 209, 228–33, 280, 288,
293–94
Reclamation Act of 1902, 198

Reclamation Reform Act, 200, 205, 231
recreation, 119; alternatives to dams, 247;
amounts of, 10; justification of dams
and, 188–89, 259; whitewater, 10,
127, 172
recycling of water, 248–49
Redden, James, 312
Red River Dam, 105–6
Red River, NM, 167
Red River of the North, 209
Reed, Nathaniel, 196
Reed, Senator James, 52
Reisner, Marc, 17
Republican National Committee, 293
restoration, 102, 266–84
Rhodes, John, 249
Ricciardi, Anthony, 264
Richey, Charles, 196
Richter, Brian, 304
Rio Chama, 301
Rio Grande, 24, 29, 167, 173, 181, 268,
290
Rio Puerco, 280
riparian issues, 5–7, 212, 266, 272–77.
See also floods; instream flows; wildlife
Ritter, Willis, 83
River Agenda, 307
River Network, 283–84, 297, 301–2,
349; River Rally and, 302–3
rivers: attitudes about, 135–37, 285,
313–16; biological importance of,
263–65; history of, 11; literature and,
11; miles of, 5; natural functions of,
5–10, 265–66, 272. *See also names of
individual rivers*
Rivers and Harbors Act of 1970, 101
Rivlin, Alice, 201
Roanoke River, 267
Roaring River, CA, 58
Roaring River, KY, 65
Robinson, Michael C., 68, 104–5
Rodman Dam, 100
Rogue River, 42, 61, 88, 159, 167, 177,
188, 258, 310

ABOUT THE AUTHOR

Tim Palmer has been involved in river protection since 1970 as a writer, photographer, planner, conservationist, speaker, and consultant to citizen organizations. He has written fifteen books about rivers, conservation, and the American landscape.

His book *The Columbia* won the National Outdoor Book Award in 1998. *The Heart of America: Our Landscape, Our Future* won the Independent Publishers Book Award in 2000. *Yosemite: The Promise of Wildness* received the Director's Award from the National Park Service, and his 2002 book, *Pacific High: Adventures in the Coast Ranges from Baja to Alaska*, was a finalist for the Ben Franklin Book Award. His books about river conservation have been used widely in college and university classrooms.

He received the Lifetime Achievement Award from American Rivers in 1988 for his writing work. In 2000, Perception, Inc. honored him as the River Conservationist of the Year, and in 2002, California's Friends of the River gave him its highest honor, the Peter Behr Award. *Paddler* magazine named him one of the ten greatest river conservationists in the United States, and in 2000 the editors of that publication included him as one of the "hundred paddlers of the century."

He has canoed or rafted on more than three hundred different rivers in the United States and Canada, and his collection of river photographs is one of the most complete in existence. He frequently speaks and gives slide shows at colleges, universities, conservation events, and conferences nation-wide. He can be reached at tim@timpalmer.org.